AMERICAN RELIGIOUS CREEDS

VOLUME III

J. GORDON MELTON, EDITOR

Triumph™ Books
New York, New York

TRIUMPH BOOKS EDITION 1991
An Imprint of Gleneida Publishing Group, Inc.

This edition published by special arrangement with
Gale Research Inc.

Library of Congress Cataloging-in-Publication Data

Encyclopedia of American religions, religious creeds.
    American religious creeds : an essential compendium of more than
450 statements of belief and doctrine / J. Gordon Melton, editor.
    p.   cm.
    Reprint. Originally published: The Encyclopedia of American
religions, religious creeds. Detroit, Mich. : Gale Research Co.,
1988.
    Includes indexes.
    ISBN 0-8007-3014-3 (v. 1). — ISBN 0-8007-3015-1 (v. 2). — ISBN
0-8007-3016-X (v. 3)
    1. Creeds—Encyclopedias. 2. United States—Religion—1960—
Encyclopedias. I. Melton, J. Gordon. II. Title.
BL427.E52   1991
291.2′0973—dc20   90-47872
                                            CIP

Acknowledgments

Grateful acknowledgment is due to the
following publishers for use of their material.

"Account of Our Religion, Doctrine and Faith [Hutterite Brethren]." Reprinted from *Baptist Confessions of Faith*, edited by William L. Lumpkin, copyright © 1959 by Judson Press.

"Affirmations for Humanistic Jews [Sherwin T. Wine, Society for Humanistic Judaism]." Reprinted from *Judaism Beyond God: A Radical New Way to Be Jewish* by Sherwin T. Wine (copyright © 1985 by Sherwin T. Wine; reprinted by permission of the Society for Humanistic Judaism, 28611 W. Twelve Mile Rd., Farmington Hills, Mich. 48334), Society for Humanistic Judaism, 1985, p. 244.

Confessions [of the General Church of the New Jerusalem]. Reprinted from *Liturgy and Hymnal for the Use of the General Church of the New Jerusalem* (copyright 1916, 1921, 1939, and 1966 by the General Church of the New Jerusalem; reprinted by permission of the publisher), General Church of the New Jerusalem, 1966, pp. 217–20.

Creed of the Church of Scientology © 1954 L. Ron Hubbard. All Rights Reserved. Grateful acknowledgment is made to L. Ron Hubbard Library for permission to reprint a selection from the copyrighted works of L. Ron Hubbard.

"Dogma" and "Doctrine [Church of Seven Arrows]." Reprinted from *Shaman's Notes 2: Structure of Complete Belief-Systems* (copyright 1985 by Church of Seven Arrows; reprinted by permission of the publisher), Church of Seven Arrows, 1985, pp. 14–26.

"I Believe [Rabbi Joseph H. Gelberman, Little Synagogue]." Reprinted from *To Be . . . Fully Alive: A Collection of Essays for Life Enhancement on the Spiritual and Psychological Potential of Man* by Dr. Joseph H. Gelberman (copyright © 1983 by Dr. Joseph H. Gelberman; reprinted by permission of the publisher), Coleman Graphics, 1983, pp. xxiii-xxv.

"Our Message [Family of Love (Children of God)]." Reprinted from *The Basic Mo Letters* by Moses David (© Children of God, 1976), Children of God, 1976, pp. 27–31.

"Principles of Miracles." Reprinted from *A Course in Miracles* (copyright © 1975 by the Foundation for Inner Peace; reprinted by permission of the publisher), Foundation for Inner Peace, 1975, pp. 1–4.

"Statement of Principles" and "Affirmations of the Ethical Movement [American Ethical Union]." Reprinted from *Ethical Perspectives: Statements of the Ethical Culture Movement* (© 1972 New York Society for Ethical Culture; reprinted by permission of the publisher), New York Society for Ethical Culture, 1972.

"The Theological Declaration of Barmen." Reprinted from *The Church's Confession Under Hitler* by Arthur C. Cochrane, Westminster Press, 1962, pp. 237–42.

Contents

AMERICAN RELIGIOUS CREEDS—VOLUME III

Contents

Contents

Contents

Introduction

Just as *The Encyclopedia of American Religions* provided the first comprehensive study of religious and spiritual groups in the United States since the U.S. Census Bureau's last edition of *Religious Bodies* (1936), *American Religious Creeds* represents the first comprehensive compilation of the creeds, confessions, and statements of belief of America's religious groups in over a century. *American Religious Creeds* presents more than 450 creedal texts, covering not only Christian churches, but also the hundreds of Jewish, Islamic, Buddhist, Hindu, and other traditions possessing a following in the United States and Canada. In addition, historical notes and comments are provided to help researchers, librarians, students, and other information seekers understand the context in which creeds were written, revised, or discarded.

Authentic Text Used for All Creeds

The texts of the religious creeds presented in this volume are in their authentic form, although obvious typographical errors have been corrected. The authentic wording, grammar, and punctuation of each statement remains intact. In some cases, a creed's format was altered slightly for stylistic consistency and clarity. No attempt was made to introduce foreign material or explanatory notes into the body of the creed's text. Where alternate readings of a statement's text have been available, the editor chose an English language text currently in use by the church. Further, no attempt has been made to provide theological exposition, detailed textual analysis, or variant readings of a text, except in those few cases in which contemporary Christian churches disagree over the exact wording of the older creeds.

Types of Creeds and Statements Covered

Creeds are formal statements of belief to which members of a church are expected to give their intellectual assent. The writing of religious creeds is primarily an activity of Christian churches. At the same time, some other churches publish less rigid statements of belief reflecting a consensus of church teachings, while recognizing some variance of belief among members (and even leaders). A number of religious groups publish statements with an understanding that such beliefs are entirely secondary in the life of the group; emphasis is placed more upon piety, religious experience, liturgy, behavior (ethics), or membership in an ethnic group. On the other hand, some churches are strictly anti-creedal. Nevertheless, even the most anti-creedal and experience-oriented groups usually have a small body of assumed intellectual content (a system of beliefs that can be put into words) and, on occasion, official group statements are written for members' use. Such statements are considered to fall within the scope of this work.

Each creedal statement presented in this volume is acknowledged by at least one existing church or religious group described in the second edition of *The Encyclopedia of American Religions* (or its supplement). While the latter contains 1,550 entries, this work contains over 450. This difference is due to several factors. First, many creedal statements serve a variety of individual churches. For example, the Nicene Creed is the basic statement of faith for all Eastern Orthodox groups; divisions in this tradition have been based on nondoctrinal issues such as ethnicity, language, and political allegiances. Second, some groups simply have no summary statement of belief. The Plymouth Brethen groups, for example, are noncreedal, and many Hindu and Buddhist groups are centered more on experience than doctrine. Finally, some groups' statements are not listed because the editor, after repeated attempts, could not locate those creeds.

Contemporary Focus

Unlike previous collections, *American Religious Creeds* seeks to maintain a contemporary focus by presenting primarily creeds currently acknowledged by those religious groups operating in the United States and Canada. This volume makes no attempt to gather creedal statements from the various religious traditions, especially the older Christian families and, therefore, it is not intended to replace previously published works on Christian creeds, such as Philip Schaff's 1877 compilation, *The Creeds of Christendom* (Harper & Brothers, 1877); *Creeds of the Churches* (John H. Leith, editor; Doubleday, 1963); Arthur C. Cochrane's *Reformed Confessions of the 16th Century* (Westminster, 1966); Williston Walker's *Creeds and Platforms of Congregationalism* (Pilgrim, 1969); and William L. Lumpkin's *Baptist Confessions of Faith* (Judson, 1959).

Religious statements for *American Religious Creeds* were compiled from a variety of sources located in the files of the Institute for the Study of American Religion, including sources gathered over the years directly from the religious groups. Other material was obtained through mailings during the compilation of material for production of the most recent edition of *The Encyclopedia of American Religions*.

Contents and Arrangement

American Religious Creeds comprises 23 chapters organized into three volumes. The first chapter covers the four ancient Christian creeds (acknowledged and used by a majority of existing Christian groups and not associated with one in particular). The remaining chapters cover the statements of the individual churches, religious bodies, and spiritual groups that constitute the major religious families operating in the United States and Canada. Material within each chapter is arranged alphabetically by name of religious group or church, not by name of creed. Some material has been rearranged to highlight those creeds and confessions serving an entire religious family or group of churches. In addition, statements that partially define religious families or subfamilies are placed at the beginning of the appropriate chapter or subchapter. (See the detailed contents pages preceding this Introduction for an overview of the arrangement of each of the chapters in this volume.)

Creeds presented in *American Religious Creeds* contain the following elements:

Creed Title. The actual or descriptive title, followed by the name of the primary group related to the statement. (Where no formal title was given, a descriptive title was assigned.) Names of primary religious groups not contained in the creed's formal title are added parenthetically. (Other religious groups that acknowledge the particular statement are mentioned in the notes following the text.)

Text of Religious Creed. The full text of the creed in its authentic form.

Notes. These appear in italic type following the text of individual creeds. When applicable, these remarks provide data about the origin of the creed, call attention to particular ideas and emphases covered (or, in some cases, omitted) by the text, discuss variant readings of the text as used by different churches, and point out relationships to other religious statements. Also mentioned here are other religious groups that acknowledge the particular creed.

Name and Keyword Index Provided

To facilitate access to the material, *American Religious Creeds* contains a Creed/Organization Name and Keyword Index. This index lists, in a single alphabetic sequence, full titles of all the creeds presented in the volume as well as the names of all the religious traditions and individual churches mentioned in the text and notes. In addition, creed title and church name citations also appear in the index rotated by key word in title/name. Creed names appear in italic type to distinguish them from religious organizations. Citations refer users to the volume and page where the indexed creed or religious group appears.

Institute for the Study of American Religion

The Institute for the Study of American Religion was founded in 1969 for the purpose of researching and disseminating information about the numerous religious groups in the United States. More recently, the Institute's scope has been expanded to include religious groups in Canada, making it the only research facility of its kind to cover so broad a range of activity. After being located for many years in Evanston, Illinois, the Institute moved to Santa Barbara, California, in 1985. At that time, its collection of more than 25,000 books and its extensive files were donated to the Special Collections department of the library of the University of California—Santa Barbara.

Suggestions Are Welcome

Users of this volume with inquiries, additional information, corrections of inadvertent errors, or other suggestions for improvements are invited to write the Institute in care of its director. The Institute is particularly interested in obtaining copies of statements missing from this volume for inclusion in future editions.

Dr. J. Gordon Melton
Institute for the Study of American Religion
Box 90709
Santa Barbara, CA 93190-0709

AMERICAN RELIGIOUS CREEDS

VOLUME III

Chapter 1

Liberal Family

Liberal

PRINCIPLES [DEISTICAL SOCIETY OF NEW YORK (1790s)]

Proposals for forming a society for the promotion of moral science and the religion of nature—having in view the destruction of superstition and fanaticism—tending to the development of the principles of a genuine natural morality—the practice of a pure and uncorrupted virtue—the cultivation of science and philosophy—the resurrection of reason, and the renovation of the intelligent world.

At a time when the political despotism of the earth is disappearing, and man is about to reclaim and enjoy the liberties of which for ages he has been deprived, it would be unpardonable to neglect the important concerns of intellectual and moral nature. The slavery of the mind has been the most destructive of all slavery; and the baneful effects of a dark and gloomy superstition have suppressed all the dignified efforts of the human understanding, and essentially circumscribed the sphere of intellectual energy. It is only by returning to the laws of nature, which man has so frequently abandoned, that happiness is to be acquired. And, although the efforts of a few individuals will be inadequate to the sudden establishment of moral and mental felicity; yet, they may lay the foundation on which a superstructure may be reared incalculably valuable to the welfare of future generations. To contribute to the accomplishment of an object so important, the members of this association do approve of the following fundamental principles:—

1. That the universe proclaims the existence of one supreme Deity, worthy the adoration of intelligent beings.

2. That man is possessed of moral and intellectual faculties sufficient for the improvement of his nature, and the acquisition of happiness.

3. That the religion of nature is the only universal religion; that it grows out of the moral relations of intelligent beings, and that it stands connected with the progressive improvement and common welfare of the human race.

4. That it is essential to the true interest of man, that he love truth and practise virtue.

5. That vice is every where ruinous and destructive to the happiness of the individual and of society.

6. That a benevolent disposition, and beneficent actions, are fundamental duties of rational beings.

7. That a religion mingled with persecution and malice cannot be of divine origin.

8. That education and science are essential to the happiness of man.

9. That civil and religious liberty is equally essential to his true interests.

10. That there can be no human authority to which man ought to be amenable for his religious opinions.

11. That science and truth, virtue and happiness, are the great objects to which the activity and energy of the human faculties ought to be directed.

Every member admitted into this association shall deem it his duty, by every suitable method in his power, to promote the cause of nature and moral truth, in opposition to all schemes of superstition and fanaticism, claiming divine origin.

Notes: *Among the first of the radical religious groups of the United States, the Deistical Society of New York was founded by Elihu Palmer. The society espoused the religion of nature, which contrasted sharply with orthodox Christianity. It affirmed one God, adherence to the laws of nature, and the necessity of virtue and benevolence. Persecution in the name of religion was decried.*

* * *

STATEMENTS BY AMERICAN ATHEISTS, INC.

DEFINITIONS

1. Atheism is the life philosophy (Weltanschauung) of persons who are free from theism. It is predicated on the ancient Greek philosophy of Materialism.

1

2. American Atheism may be defined as the mental attitude which unreservedly accepts the supremacy of reason and aims at establishing a system of philosophy and ethics verifiable by experience, independent of all arbitrary assumptions of authority or creeds.

3. The Materialist philosophy declares that the cosmos is devoid of immanent conscious purpose; that it is governed by its own inherent, immutable and impersonal law; that there is no supernatural interference in human life; that man—finding his resources within himself—can and must create his own destiny; and that his potential for good and higher development is for all practical purposes unlimited.

ATHEISM TEACHES THAT:

There is no heavenly father. Man must protect the orphans and foundlings, or they will not be protected.

There is no god to answer prayer. Man must hear and help man.

There is no hell. We have no vindictive god or devil to fear or imitate.

There is no atonement or salvation by faith. We must face the consequence of our acts.

There is no beneficent or malevolent intent in nature. Life is a struggle against preventable and unpreventable evils. The cooperation of man is the only hope of the world.

There is no chance after death to "do our bit." We must do it now or never.

There is no divine guardian of truth, goodness, beauty and liberty. These are attributes of man. Man must defend them or they will perish from the earth.

Notes: *Among the most militant of atheist organizations is American Atheists, Inc., founded by Madelyn Murray O'Hair. Reproduced here are three basic definitions used by the organization as well as a brief statement on what Atheism teaches. Despite the popular claim that atheism is a positive world view in which God plays no role, these statements seem overwhelmingly to be denials of Christian and/or theistic positions.*

*   *   *

STATEMENT OF PRINCIPLES AND AFFIRMATIONS OF THE ETHICAL MOVEMENT (AMERICAN ETHICAL UNION)

STATEMENT OF PRINCIPLES

(1) We believe that morality is independent of theology. We hold that the moral law is imposed upon us by our own rational nature and that its authority is absolute. We maintain that the moral life should be brought to the foreground in religion.

(2) We affirm the need of a new statement of the ethical code of mankind. The formulations of duty which were given by the greatest religious teachers of the past are not sufficient for the changed conditions of modern society. We believe that moral problems have arisen in this industrial, democratic, scientific age, which require new and larger formulations of duty. Hence a new interest in ethical problems and a profounder study and discussion of them are demanded.

(3) We regard it our duty as a Society for Ethical Culture, to engage in works of philanthropy on as large a scale as our means will allow. The ultimate purpose of such philanthrophy should be the advancement of morality. When we contemplate the low moral condition of society and its indifference to moral aims, we feel called upon to do what we can to raise our fellow men to a higher plane of life and to awaken within them a deeper moral purpose.

(4) We hold that the task of self-reform should go hand in hand with efforts to reform society. The mere fact of membership in an Ethical Society must be regarded as a tacit avowal of the desire to lead a wholly upright life and to aid in developing a higher type of manhood and womanhood than has been known in the past.

(5) We believe that organization is indispensable to carrying out the aims of ethical culture and that this organization should be republican rather than monarchical. While we recognize the need of a public lecturer for the Society, we believe that the work of ethical culture in its broadest sense—the study, discussion, and the application of its principles, should be carried on as far as possible by the members themselves.

(6) We agree that the greatest stress should be laid on the moral instruction of the young, to the end that in the pure hearts of children may be sown the seeds of a higher moral order, that early in life they may be impressed with the work and dignity of human existence, and that the work of social and individual perfection may be carried on with larger and nobler results from generation to generation.

AFFIRMATIONS OF THE ETHICAL MOVEMENT

CENTRALITY OF ETHICS

We believe that ethical aspirations should be central in religion and in life, and that ethical conduct need not be dependent on theological belief. For too long men have been divided by their creeds. We do not ask that men put aside their religious beliefs, but rather that they recognize that no one world-view has a monopoly of wisdom or virtue. We ask that men reach across the theological lines which have divided them and seek unity in their common ethical concerns.

ETHICS AND MORALITY

We hold that the morality of an action is not determined by its conformity to any rigid moral code, but by the application of certain general ethical principles to the particular circumstances surrounding the action. Among these general principles are the following:

We affirm the dignity and worth of all human beings, however different their abilities or backgrounds. We do not consider a person's worth to be dependent on his usefulness or his conduct towards others, though we are by no means indifferent to his conduct. We hold that it is the task of ethics to encourage him to base his conduct on a respect for the worth of others.

Recognizing the principle of reciprocity in human relations we affirm that any action which brings out the distinctive worth in others brings out the distinctive worth in one's self. By the same token any action which demeans others demeans one's self.

Increasing one's capacity for bringing out the distinctive worth in others and one's self is what we mean by ethical growth. This process begins in the family and extends into friendships and civic endeavor, culminating in a sense of loyalty and relatedness to the total community of man. Through such relationships we believe a person can find his greatest personal fulfillment and meaning in life.

RELIGION

We are a movement committed to man's quest for values worthy of his supreme allegiance. Many of our members identify this quest as religious. Others designate it as philosophical.

We see the various conceptions of "God," "Divine Revelation," and "Immortality" as expressions of man's attempt to find meaning in the universe and guidance in life. We are profoundly sympathetic with this endeavor, and we believe that a study of traditional doctrine can often yield valuable ethical insight. Hence, we acknowledge the traditional religions as being among the sources of our own ethical and religious concerns.

At the same time, the traditional theological conceptions contain much that is inadequate and misleading, and we deny any moral responsibility to adhere to doctrines if reason and experience belie them. Moreover, though many believers have found great inspiration in such doctrines, the acceptance of dogmatic assumptions is tantamount, in our view, to accepting restraints on man's ethical and religious development. This we find objectionable, for we see the essence of religion in a commitment to growth: growth in passion for truth, growth in appreciation of beauty, and growth in dedication to good.

Truth, beauty, and good are in themselves abstractions, which must continually be made real in the lives and efforts of human beings. For us religion is essentially an ethical process, not an act of subscribing to beliefs. We believe that the religious is to be the most fully realized within the ethical life, rather than beyond it.

HUMANISM

Our Humanism is a faith that there is in human beings something worthy of ethical or religious commitment: a capacity for growth and creativity, for sensitivity and responsiveness to other people, and for being responsibility-carrying members of a human community. We think this capacity can best be cultivated if we assume it to be present in people even when not immediately manifest. Our humanist faith as Ethical Culturists can be justified only by the quality of human relationships resulting from the attempt to live by it.

This faith is grounded in a respect for the human accomplishments of the past. We find inspiration for this faith in the humanist tradition of the past—in the humanism of ancient Greece, in the humanism of the Renaissance, in the scientific, philosophical and religious humanisms of later centuries.

Our humanism is a commitment to humanity-as-a-whole and to the humanity in those we meet; and it is also a commitment to a vision of humanity as it yet may be and to the responsibility for helping achieve this vision. This commitment gains strength in the knowledge that humanity has the capacity for surviving the individual and carrying on the values for which he lived.

MAN AND NATURE

Unlike many traditional religions ethical culture does not regard man as the being for whom the world was created. We maintain not that man is the objective center of nature, but rather that he should be treated as central in any attempt to find human meaning in nature.

We do not share the confidence of some that man can formulate doctrines which give a final and over-all explanation of the universe in which we find ourselves.

Though some things which were once in the realm of mystery have already been explained, and others will yet be successfully probed, we see no reason for believing that man will ever completely penetrate the unknown. Our confidence in man's abilities is mingled with a sense of humility in the face of a vast universe beyond man's experience.

SCIENCE

We look upon scientific method as man's greatest ally in his attempt to discover truths about the universe. Many of us see Ethical Culture as an attempt to apply the insights of science to religion and human relations. While we do not expect the exactitude of the physical sciences, we hold that some sort of empirical verification is required for religious and ethical hypotheses. This does not rule out certain kinds of intuition, which can be useful even in science.

Our commitment is to the scientific spirit—not to any particular school of opinion or conceptual scheme, but rather to the methods of free and honest inquiry.

We are keenly aware that science has not always been used for the good of man. When, in the name of science, human beings are treated merely as statistics and human values are trampled upon, science is misused. Science is made for man, not man for science. It is the task of ethics to determine the human use of scientifically acquired knowledge.

DEMOCRACY

We believe in the democratic process—not alone in government, but also in the family and in all other day-to-day interpersonal relations, for it is only through participation in decisions affecting their lives that people will develop their own inner resources.

Democracy means that people have the right to determine their own destiny and that decisions should be made in such a way that people will grow through the process, not

**STATEMENT OF PRINCIPLES AND AFFIRMATIONS OF
THE ETHICAL MOVEMENT (AMERICAN ETHICAL
UNION) (continued)**

become more dependent. It requires the formulation of social policy through free and open dialogue and the removal of barriers between races, classes, and religions. It entails the widespread development of critical intelligence and creative ability, not the concentration of these qualities in any elite group.

Democracy is a process of growth, and a concern for growth is central to our ethic.

SOCIAL RESPONSIBILITY

We hold that ethics involves a responsibility to the society in which we live, including a responsibility for the conditions which prevail within that society. Though we do not agree on any one concept of the ideal society, we do agree that societies are subject to judgment by certain ethical standards, such as those expressed in the Universal Declaration of Human Rights. We have an ethical responsibility to study the social issues of our time and lend our support to efforts to secure for all people the political, economic, social and cultural rights to which they are entitled.

WORLD COMMUNITY

Social responsibility and the possibilities for friendship and cooperation do not end at national borders. A humanist ethic demands a concern for the well-being of all peoples. Hence, we accept the responsibility for fostering loyalty to the emerging world community and to seeking practical expressions of this loyalty.

Man stands today on the threshold of nuclear destruction and also on the threshold of a new era in which science can provide for the material needs of all people and maintain the proper balance between human population and natural resources. Which threshold is crossed will probably depend upon whether man succeeds in broadening group loyalty to embrace the community of man.

ETHICAL UNIVERSALISM

We believe there is a universality to our ethical message and that where men are divided in their creeds they may yet unite in certain fundamental ethical concerns. At the same time we recognize that for many human beings an ethical faith without a theology may be inadequate. We claim universalism for our ethical message, not for our Movement. We would in fact question the desirability of all men belonging to the same religious movement, for we believe that religious freedom can best be fostered by the cooperative co-existence of numerous religious traditions, each respecting the right of the individual to choose the tradition most meaningful to him.

FREEDOM OF BELIEF

Because we cherish the freedom of the individual to work out his own answers to the great questions of life, we reject any creedal or dogmatic statement of our beliefs. A scientific and democratic ethic demands full intellectual freedom as an essential condition for the advancement of truth.

Notes: *The Statement of Principles was originally adopted by the American Ethical Union in the 1870s and reflects the Union's early concern for ethics and social reform. The Affirmations of the Ethical Movement, circulated by the Union almost a century later, reflects the Union's broadening concerns during the twentieth century. The statement was written by a special commission of the Fraternity of Leaders of the Union. Central to the Union's position is the autonomy of ethical concerns from religious or world view decisions, though the Union is decidedly Humanist in outlook.*

*   *   *

HUMANIST MANIFESTO I (AMERICAN HUMANIST ASSOCIATION)

The time has come for widespread recognition of the radical changes in religious beliefs throughout the modern world. The time is past for mere revision of traditional attitudes. Science and economic change have disrupted the old beliefs. Religions the world over are under the necessity of coming to terms with new conditions created by a vastly increased knowledge and experience. In every field of human activity, the vital movement is now in the direction of a candid and explicit humanism. In order that religious humanism may be better understood we, the undersigned, desire to make certain affirmations which we believe the facts of our contemporary life demonstrate.

There is great danger of a final, and we believe fatal, identification of the word *religion* with doctrines and methods which have lost their significance and which are powerless to solve the problem of human living in the Twentieth Century. Religions have always been means for realizing the highest values of life. Their end has been accomplished through the interpretation of the total environing situation (theology or world view), the sense of values resulting therefrom (goal or ideal), and the technique (cult) established for realizing the satisfactory life. A change in any of these factors results in alteration of the outward forms of religion. This fact explains the changefulness of religions through the centuries. But through all changes religion itself remains constant in its quest for abiding values, an inseparable feature of human life.

Today man's larger understanding of the universe, his scientific achievements, and his deeper appreciation of brotherhood, have created a situation which requires a new statement of the means and purposes of religion. Such a vital, fearless, and frank religion capable of furnishing adequate social goals and personal satisfactions may appear to many people as a complete break with the past. While this age does owe a vast debt to traditional religions, it is none the less obvious that any religion that can hope to be a synthesizing and dynamic force for today must be shaped for the needs of this age. To establish such a religion is a major necessity of the present. It is a responsibility which rests upon this generation. We therefore affirm the following.

FIRST: Religious humanists regard the universe as self-existing and not created.

SECOND: Humanism believes that man is a part of nature and that he has emerged as the result of a continuous process.

THIRD: Holding an organic view of life, humanists find that the traditional dualism of mind and body must be rejected.

FOURTH: Humanism recognizes that man's religious culture and civilization, as clearly depicted by anthropology and history, are the product of a gradual development due to his interaction with his natural environment and with his social heritage. The individual born into a particular culture is largely molded to that culture.

FIFTH: Humanism asserts that the nature of the universe depicted by modern science makes unacceptable any supernatural or cosmic guarantees of human values. Obviously humanism does not deny the possibility of realities as yet undiscovered, but it does insist that the way to determine the existence and value of any and all realities is by means of intelligent inquiry and by the assessment of their relation to human needs. Religion must formulate its hopes and plans in the light of the scientific spirit and method.

SIXTH: We are convinced that the time has passed for theism, deism, modernism, and the several varieties of "new thought."

SEVENTH: Religion consists of those actions, purposes, and experiences which are humanly significant. Nothing human is alien to the religious. It includes labor, art, science, philosophy, love, friendship, recreation—all that is in its degree expressive of intelligently satisfying human living. The distinction between the sacred and the secular can no longer be maintained.

EIGHTH: Religious humanism considers the complete realization of human personality to be the end of man's life and seeks its development and fulfillment in the here and now. This is the explanation of the humanist's social passion.

NINTH: In place of the old attitudes involved in worship and prayer the humanist finds his religious emotions expressed in a heightened sense of personal life and in a cooperative effort to promote social well-being.

TENTH: It follows that there will be no uniquely religious emotions and attitudes of the kind hitherto associated with belief in the supernatural.

ELEVENTH: Man will learn to face the crises of life in terms of his knowledge of their naturalness and probability. Reasonable and manly attitudes will be fostered by education and supported by custom. We assume that humanism will take the path of social and mental hygiene and discourage sentimental and unreal hopes and wishful thinking.

TWELFTH: Believing that religion must work increasingly for joy in living, religious humanists aim to foster the creative in man and to encourage achievements that add to the satisfactions of life.

THIRTEENTH: Religious humanism maintains that all associations and institutions exist for the fulfillment of human life. The intelligent evaluation, transformation, control, and direction of such associations and institutions with a view to the enhancement of human life is the purpose and program of humanism. Certainly religious institutions, their ritualistic forms, ecclesiastical methods, and communal activities must be reconstituted as rapidly as experience allows, in order to function effectively in the modern world.

FOURTEENTH: The humanists are firmly convinced that existing acquisitive and profit-motivated society has shown itself to be inadequate and that a radical change in methods, controls, and motives must be instituted. A socialized and cooperative economic order must be established to the end that the equitable distribution of the means of life be possible. The goal of humanism is a free and universal society in which people voluntarily and intelligently cooperate for the common good. Humanists demand a shared life in a shared world.

FIFTEENTH AND LAST: We assert that humanism will: (a) affirm life rather than deny it; (b) seek to elicit the possibilities of life, not flee from it; and (c) endeavor to establish the conditions of a satisfactory life for all, not merely for the few. By this positive morale and intention humanism will be guided, and from this perspective and alignment the techniques and efforts of humanism will flow.

So stand the theses of religious humanism. Though we consider the religious forms and ideas of our fathers no longer adequate, the quest for the good life is still the central task for mankind. Man is at last becoming aware that he alone is responsible for the realization of the world of his dreams, that he has within himself the power for its achievement. He must set intelligence and will to the task.

J.A.C. Fagginer Auer
E. Burdette Backus
Harry Elmer Barnes
L.M. Birkhead
Raymond B. Bragg
Edwin Arthur Burtt
Ernest Caldecott
A.J. Carlson
John Dewey
Albert C. Dieffenbach
John H. Dietrich
Bernard Fantus
William Floyd
F.H. Hankins
A. Eustace Haydon
Llewellyn Jones
Robert Morss Lovett
Harold P. Marley
R. Lester Mondale
Charles Francis Potter
John Herman Randall, Jr.
Curtis W. Reese
Oliver L. Reiser
Roy Wood Sellars
Clinton Lee Scott
Maynard Shipley
W. Frank Swift
V.T. Thayer
Eldred C. Vanderlaan

HUMANIST MANIFESTO I (AMERICAN HUMANIST
ASSOCIATION) (continued)

Joseph Walker
Jacob J. Weinstein
Frank S. C. Wicks
David Rhys Williams
Edwin H. Wilson

Notes: *One of two statements generally accepted as reflective of the Humanist position, the original Humanist Manifesto was issued in 1933 and signed by a number of prominent early Humanist thinkers. True to the Humanist perspective, the statement not only clarifies a position on cosmological (or theological) issues, but makes pronouncements on a variety of social (i.e., human) problems. The position on a collective society has separated Humanists from others who share their cosmological views (see item 14).*

* * *

HUMANIST MANIFESTO II (AMERICAN HUMANIST ASSOCIATION)

PREFACE

It is forty years since *Humanist Manifesto I* (1933) appeared. Events since then make that earlier statement seem far too optimistic. Nazism has shown the depths of brutality of which humanity is capable. Other totalitarian regimes have suppressed human rights without ending poverty. Science has sometimes brought evil as well as good. Recent decades have shown that inhuman wars can be made in the name of peace. The beginnings of police states, even in democratic societies, widespread government espionage, and other abuses of power by military, political, and industrial elites, and the continuance of unyielding racism, all present a different and difficult social outlook. In various societies, the demands of women and minority groups for equal rights effectively challenge our generation.

As we approach the twenty-first century, however, an affirmative and hopeful vision is needed. Faith, commensurate with advancing knowledge, is also necessary. In the choice between despair and hope, humanists respond in this *Humanist Manifesto II* with a positive declaration for times of uncertainty.

As in 1933, humanists still believe that traditional theism, especially faith in the prayer-hearing God, assumed to love and care for persons, to hear and understand their prayers, and to be able to do something about them, is an unproved and outmoded faith. Salvationism, based on mere affirmation, still appears as harmful, diverting people with false hopes of heaven hereafter. Reasonable minds look to other means for survival.

Those who sign *Humanist Manifesto II* disclaim that they are setting forth a binding credo; their individual views would be stated in widely varying ways. The statement is, however, reaching for vision in a time that needs direction. It is social analysis in an effort at consensus. New statements should be developed to supersede this, but for today it is our conviction that humanism offers an alternative that can serve present-day needs and guide humankind toward the future.

Paul Kurtz
Edwin H. Wilson

The next century can be and should be the humanistic century. Dramatic scientific, technological, and ever-accelerating social and political changes crowd our awareness. We have virtually conquered the planet, explored the moon, overcome the natural limits of travel and communication; we stand at the dawn of a new age, ready to move farther into space and perhaps inhabit other planets. Using technology wisely, we can control our environment, conquer poverty, markedly reduce disease, extend our life-span, significantly modify our behavior, alter the course of human evolution and cultural development, unlock vast new powers, and provide humankind with unparalleled opportunity for achieving an abundant and meaningful life.

The future is, however, filled with dangers. In learning to apply the scientific method to nature and human life, we have opened the door to ecological damage, overpopulation, dehumanizing institutions, totalitarian repression, and nuclear and biochemical disaster. Faced with apocalyptic prophesies and doomsday scenarios, many flee in despair from reason and embrace irrational cults and theologies of withdrawal and retreat.

Traditional moral codes and newer irrational cults both fail to meet the pressing needs of today and tomorrow. False "theologies of hope" and messianic ideologies, substituting new dogmas for old, cannot cope with existing world realities. They separate rather than unite peoples.

Humanity, to survive, requires bold and daring measures. We need to extend the uses of scientific method, not renounce them, to fuse reason with compassion in order to build constructive social and moral values. Confronted by many possible futures, we must decide which to pursue. The ultimate goal should be the fulfillment of the potential for growth in each human personality—not for the favored few, but for all of humankind. Only a shared world and global measures will suffice.

A humanist outlook will tap the creativity of each human being and provide the vision and courage for us to work together. This outlook emphasizes the role human beings can play in their own spheres of action. The decades ahead call for dedicated, clear-minded men and women able to marshal the will, intelligence, and cooperative skills for shaping a desirable future. Humanism can provide the purpose and inspiration that so many seek; it can give personal meaning and significance to human life.

Many kinds of humanism exist in the contemporary world. The varieties and emphases of naturalistic humanism include "scientific," "ethical," "democratic," "religious," and "Marxist" humanism. Free thought, atheism, agnosticism, skepticism, deism, rationalism, ethical culture, and liberal religion all claim to be heir to the humanist tradition. Humanism traces its roots from ancient China, classical Greece and Rome, through the Renaissance and the Enlightenment, to the scientific revolution of the modern world. But views that merely reject theism are not equivalent to humanism. They lack commitment to the positive belief in the possibilities of human progress and to the values central to it. Many within religious groups, believing in the future of humanism, now claim humanist credentials. Humanism is an ethical process through which we all can move, above and beyond the divisive particulars, heroic personalities, dogmatic creeds, and ritual customs of past religions or their mere negation.

We affirm a set of common principles that can serve as a basis for united action—positive principles relevant to the present human condition. They are a design for a secular society on a planetary scale.

For these reasons, we submit this new *Humanist Manifesto* for the future of humankind; for us, it is a vision of hope, a direction for satisfying survival.

RELIGION

FIRST: In the best sense, religion may inspire dedication to the highest ethical ideals. The cultivation of moral devotion and creative imagination is an expression of genuine "spiritual" experience and aspiration.

We believe, however, that traditional dogmatic or authoritarian religions that place revelation, God, ritual, or creed above human needs and experience do a disservice to the human species. Any account of nature should pass the tests of scientific evidence; in our judgment, the dogmas and myths of traditional religions do not do so. Even at this late date in human history, certain elementary facts based upon the critical use of scientific reason have to be restated. We find insufficient evidence for belief in the existence of a supernatural; it is either meaningless or irrelevant to the question of the survival and fulfillment of the human race. As nontheists, we begin with humans not God, nature not deity. Nature may indeed be broader and deeper than we now know; any new discoveries, however, will but enlarge our knowledge of the natural.

Some humanists believe we should reinterpret traditional religions and reinvest them with meanings appropriate to the current situation. Such redefinitions, however, often perpetuate old dependencies and escapisms; they easily become obscurantist, impeding the free use of the intellect. We need, instead, radically new human purposes and goals.

We appreciate the need to preserve the best ethical teachings in the religious traditions of humankind, many of which we share in common. But we reject those features of traditional religious morality that deny humans a full appreciation of their own potentialities and responsibilities. Traditional religions often offer solace to humans, but, as often, they inhibit humans from helping themselves or experiencing their full potentialities. Such institutions, creeds, and rituals often impede the will to serve others. Too often traditional faiths encourage dependence rather than independence, obedience rather than affirmation, fear rather than courage. More recently they have generated concerned social action, with many signs of relevance appearing in the wake of the "God Is Dead" theologies. But we can discover no divine purpose or providence for the human species. While there is much that we do not know, humans are responsible for what we are or will become. No deity will save us; we must save ourselves.

SECOND: Promises of immortal salvation or fear of eternal damnation are both illusory and harmful. They distract humans from present concerns, from self-actualization, and from rectifying social injustices. Modern science discredits such historic concepts as the "ghost in the machine" and the "separable soul." Rather, science affirms that the human species is an emergence from natural evolutionary forces. As far as we know, the total personality is a function of the biological organism transacting in a social and cultural context. There is no credible evidence that life survives the death of the body. We continue to exist in our progeny and in the way that our lives have influenced others in our culture.

Traditional religions are surely not the only obstacles to human progress. Other ideologies also impede human advance. Some forms of political doctrine, for instance, function religiously, reflecting the worst features of orthodoxy and authoritarianism, especially when they sacrifice individuals on the altar of Utopian promises. Purely economic and political viewpoints, whether capitalist or communist, often function as religious and ideological dogma. Although humans undoubtedly need economic and political goals, they also need creative values by which to live.

ETHICS

THIRD: We affirm that moral values derive their source from human experience. Ethics is *autonomous* and *situational*, needing no theological or ideological sanction. Ethics stems from human need and interest. To deny this distorts the whole basis of life. Human life has meaning because we create and develop our futures. Happiness and the creative realization of human needs and desires, individually and in shared enjoyment, are continuous themes of humanism. We strive for the good life, here and now. The goal is to pursue life's enrichment despite debasing forces of vulgarization, commercialization, bureaucratization, and dehumanization.

FOURTH: *Reason* and *intelligence* are the most effective instruments that humankind possesses. There is no substitute: neither faith nor passion suffices in itself. The controlled use of scientific methods, which have transformed the natural and social sciences since the Renaissance, must be extended further in the solution of human problems. But reason must be tempered by humility, since no group has a monopoly of wisdom or virtue. Nor is there any guarantee that all problems can be solved or all questions answered. Yet critical intelligence, infused by a sense of human caring, is the best method that humanity has for resolving problems. Reason should be balanced with compassion and empathy and the whole person fulfilled. Thus, we are not advocating the use of scientific intelligence independent of or in opposition to emotion, for we believe in the cultivation of feeling and love. As science pushes back the boundary of the known, one's sense of wonder is continually renewed, and art, poetry, and music find their places, along with religion and ethics.

THE INDIVIDUAL

FIFTH: *The preciousness and dignity of the individual person* is a central humanist value. Individuals should be encouraged to realize their own creative talents and desires. We reject all religious, ideological, or moral codes that denigrate the individual, suppress freedom, dull intellect, dehumanize personality. We believe in maximum individual autonomy consonant with social responsibility. Although science can account for the causes of behavior, the possibilities of individual *freedom of choice* exist in human life and should be increased.

SIXTH: In the area of sexuality, we believe that intolerant attitudes, often cultivated by orthodox religions and puritanical cultures, unduly repress sexual conduct. The right to birth control, abortion, and divorce should be recognized. While we do not approve of exploitive, denigrating forms of sexual expression, neither do we wish to prohibit, by law or social sanction, sexual behavior between consenting adults. The many varieties of sexual exploration should not in themselves be considered "evil." Without countenancing mindless permissiveness or unbridled promiscuity, a civilized society should be a *tolerant* one. Short of harming others or compelling them to do likewise, individuals should be permitted to express their sexual proclivities and pursue their life-styles as they desire. We wish to cultivate the development of a responsible attitude toward sexuality, in which humans are not exploited as sexual objects, and in which intimacy, sensitivity, respect, and honesty in interpersonal relations are encouraged. Moral education for children and adults is an important way of developing awareness and sexual maturity.

DEMOCRATIC SOCIETY

SEVENTH: To enhance freedom and dignity the individual must experience a full range of *civil liberties* in all societies. This includes freedom of speech and the press, political democracy, the legal right of opposition to governmental policies, fair judicial process, religious liberty, freedom of association, and artistic, scientific, and cultural freedom. It also includes a recognition of an individual's right to die with dignity, euthanasia, and the right to suicide. We oppose the increasing invasion of privacy, by whatever means, in both totalitarian and democratic societies. We would safeguard, extend, and implement the principles of human freedom evolved from the *Magna Carta* to the *Bill of Rights*, the *Rights of Man*, and the *Universal Declaration of Human Rights*.

EIGHTH: We are committed to an open and democratic society. We must extend *participatory democracy* in its true sense to the economy, the school, the family, the workplace, and voluntary associations. Decision-making must be decentralized to include widespread involvement of people at all levels—social, political, and economic. All persons should have a voice in developing the values and goals that determine their lives. Institutions should be responsive to expressed desires and needs. The conditions of work, education, devotion, and play should be humanized. Alienating forces should be modified or eradicated and bureaucratic structures should be held to a minimum. People are more important than decalogues, rules, proscriptions, or regulations.

NINTH: *The separation of church and state and the separation of ideology and state are imperatives*. The state should encourage maximum freedom for different moral, political, religious, and social values in society. It should not favor any particular religious bodies through the use of public monies, nor espouse a single ideology and function thereby as an instrument of propaganda or oppression, particularly against dissenters.

TENTH: Humane societies should evaluate economic systems not by rhetoric or ideology, but by whether or not they *increase economic well-being* for all individuals and groups, minimize poverty and hardship, increase the sum of human satisfaction, and enhance the quality of life. Hence the door is open to alternative economic systems. We need to democratize the economy and judge it by its responsiveness to human needs, testing results in terms of the common good.

ELEVENTH: *The principle of moral equality* must be furthered through elimination of all discrimination based upon race, religion, sex, age, or national origin. This means equality of opportunity and recognition of talent and merit. Individuals should be encouraged to contribute to their own betterment. If unable, then society should provide means to satisfy their basic economic, health, and cultural needs, including, wherever resources make possible, a minimum guaranteed annual income. We are concerned for the welfare of the aged, the infirm, the disadvantaged, and also for the outcasts—the mentally retarded, abandoned or abused children, the handicapped, prisoners, and addicts—for all who are neglected or ignored by society. Practicing humanists should make it their vocation to humanize personal relations.

We believe in the *right to universal education*. Everyone has a right to the cultural opportunity to fulfill his or her unique capacities and talents. The schools should foster satisfying and productive living. They should be open at all levels to any and all; the achievement of excellence should be encouraged. Innovative and experimental forms of education are to be welcomed. The energy and idealism of the young deserve to be appreciated and channeled to constructive purposes.

We deplore racial, religious, ethnic, or class antagonisms. Although we believe in cultural diversity and encourage racial and ethnic pride, we reject separations which promote alienation and set people and groups against each other; we envision an *integrated* community where people have a maximum opportunity for free and voluntary association.

We are *critical of sexism or sexual chauvinism*—male or female. We believe in equal rights for both women and men to fulfill their unique careers and potentialities as they see fit, free of invidious discrimination.

WORLD COMMUNITY

TWELFTH: We deplore the division of humankind on nationalistic grounds. We have reached a turning point in human history where the best option is to *transcend the limits of national sovereignty* and to move toward the building of a world community in which all sectors of the human family can participate. Thus we look to the development of a system of world law and a world order based upon transnational federal government. This would appreciate cultural pluralism and diversity. It would not exclude pride in national origins and accomplishments nor the handling of regional problems on a regional basis. Human progress, however, can no longer be achieved by focusing on one section of the world, Western or Eastern, developed or underdeveloped. For the first time in human history, no part of humankind can be isolated from any other. Each person's future is in some way linked to all. We thus reaffirm a commitment to the building of world community, at the same time recognizing that this commits us to some hard choices.

THIRTEENTH: This world community must *renounce the resort to violence and force* as a method of solving international disputes. We believe in the peaceful adjudication of differences by international courts and by the development of the arts of negotiation and compromise. War is obsolete. So is the use of nuclear, biological, and chemical weapons. It is a planetary imperative to reduce the level of military expenditures and turn these savings to peaceful and people-oriented uses.

FOURTEENTH: The world community must engage in *cooperative planning* concerning the use of rapidly depleting resources. The planet earth must be considered a single ecosystem. Ecological damage, resource depletion, and excessive population growth must be checked by international concord. The cultivation and conservation of nature is a moral value; we should perceive ourselves as integral to the sources of our being in nature. We must free our world from needless pollution and waste, responsibly guarding and creating wealth, both natural and human. Exploitation of natural resources, uncurbed by social conscience, must end.

FIFTEENTH: The problems of *economic growth and development* can no longer be resolved by one nation alone; they are worldwide in scope. It is the moral obligation of the developed nations to provide—through an international authority that safeguards human rights—massive technical, agricultural, medical, and economic assistance, including birth control techniques, to the developing portions of the globe. World poverty must cease. Hence extreme disproportions in wealth, income, and economic growth should be reduced on a worldwide basis.

SIXTEENTH: *Technology is a vital key* to human progress and development. We deplore any neo-romantic efforts to condemn indiscriminately all technology and science or to counsel retreat from its further extension and use for the good of humankind. We would resist any moves to censor basic scientific research on moral, political, or social grounds. Technology must, however, be carefully judged by the consequences of its use; harmful and destructive changes should be avoided. We are particularly disturbed when technology and bureaucracy control, manipulate, or modify human beings without their consent. Technological feasibility does not imply social or cultural desirability.

SEVENTEENTH: We must expand communication and transportation across frontiers. Travel restrictions must cease. The world must be open to diverse political, ideological, and moral viewpoints and evolve a worldwide system of television and radio for information and education. We thus call for full international cooperation in culture, science, the arts, and technology *across ideological borders*. We must learn to live openly together or we shall perish together.

HUMANITY AS A WHOLE

IN CLOSING: The world cannot wait for a reconciliation of competing political or economic systems to solve its problems. These are the times for men and women of good will to further the building of a peaceful and prosperous world. We urge that parochial loyalties and inflexible moral and religious ideologies be transcended. We urge recognition of the common humanity of all people. We further urge the use of reason and compassion to produce the kind of world we want—a world in which peace, prosperity, freedom, and happiness are widely shared. Let us not abandon that vision in despair or cowardice. We are responsible for what we are or will be. Let us work together for a humane world by means commensurate with humane ends. Destructive ideological differences among communism, capitalism, socialism, conservatism, liberalism, and radicalism should be overcome. Let us call for an end to terror and hatred. We will survive and prosper only in a world of shared humane values. We can initiate new directions for humankind; ancient rivalries can be superseded by broad-based cooperative efforts. The commitment to tolerance, understanding, and peaceful negotiation does not necessitate acquiescence to the status quo nor the damming up of dynamic and revolutionary forces. The true revolution is occurring and can continue in countless non-violent adjustments. But this entails the willingness to step forward onto new and expanding plateaus. At the present juncture of history, commitment to all humankind is the highest commitment of which we are capable; it transcends the narrow allegiances of church, state, party, class, or race in moving toward a wider vision of human potentiality. What more daring a goal for humankind than for each person to become, in ideal as well as practice, a citizen of a world community. It is a classical vision; we can now give it new vitality. Humanism thus interpreted is a moral force that has time on its side. We believe that humankind has the potential intelligence, good will, and cooperative skill to implement this commitment in the decades ahead.

We, the undersigned, while not necessarily endorsing every detail of the above, pledge our general support to *Humanist Manifesto II* for the future of humankind. These affirmations are not a final credo or dogma but an expression of a living and growing faith. We invite others in all lands to join us in further developing and working for these goals.

Lionel Abel, *Prof. of English, State Univ. of New York at Buffalo*

Khoren Arisian, *Board of Leaders, NY Soc. for Ethical Culture*

Isaac Asimov, *author*

George Axtelle, *Prof. Emeritus, Southern Illinois Univ.*

Archie J. Bahm, *Prof. of Philosophy Emeritus, Univ. of N.M.*

Paul H. Beattie, *Pres., Fellowship of Religious Humanists*

HUMANIST MANIFESTO II (AMERICAN HUMANIST ASSOCIATION) (continued)

Keith Beggs, *Exec. Dir., American Humanist Association*

Malcolm Bissell, *Prof. Emeritus, Univ. of Southern California*

H.J. Blackham, *Chm., Social Morality Council, Great Britain*

Brand Blanshard, *Prof. Emeritus, Yale University*

Paul Blanshard, *author*

Joseph L. Blau, *Prof. of Religion, Columbia University*

Sir Hermann Bondi, *Prof. of Math., King's Coll., Univ. of London*

Howard Box, *Leader, Brooklyn Society for Ethical Culture*

Raymond B. Bragg, *Minister Emer., Unitarian Ch., Kansas City*

Theodore Brameld, *Visiting Prof., C.U.N.Y.*

Lester R. Brown, *Senior Fellow, Overseas Development Council*

Bette Chambers, *Pres., American Humanist Association*

John Ciardi, *poet*

Francis Crick, *M.D., Great Britain*

Arthur Danto, *Prof. of Philosophy, Columbia University*

Lucien de Coninck, *Prof., University of Gand, Belgium*

Miriam Allen deFord, *author*

Edd Doerr, *Americans United for Separation of Church and State*

Peter Draper, *M.D., Guy's Hospital Medical School, London*

Paul Edwards, *Prof. of Philosophy, Brooklyn College*

Albert Ellis, *Exec. Dir., Inst. Adv. Study Rational Psychotherapy*

Edward L. Ericson, *Board of Leaders, NY Soc. for Ethical Culture*

H.J. Eysenck, *Prof. of Psychology, Univ. of London*

Roy P. Fairfield, *Coordinator, Union Graduate School*

Herbert Feigl, *Prof. Emeritus, Univ. of Minnesota*

Raymond Firth, *Prof. Emeritus of Anthropology, Univ. of London*

Antony Flew, *Prof. of Philosophy, The Univ., Reading, England*

Kenneth Furness, *Exec. Secy., British Humanist Association*

Erwin Gaede, *Minister, Unitarian Church, Ann Arbor, Mich.*

Richard S. Gilbert, *Minister, First Unitarian Ch., Rochester, N.Y.*

Charles Wesley Grady, *Minister, Unit. Univ. Ch., Arlington, Ma.*

Maxine Green, *Prof., Teachers College, Columbia University*

Thomas C. Greening, *Editor*, Journal of Humanistic Psychology

Alan F. Guttmacher, *Pres., Planned Parenthood Fed. of America*

J. Harold Hadley, *Min., Unit. Univ. Ch., Pt. Washington, N.Y.*

Hector Hawton, *Editor*, Question, *Great Britain*

A. Eustace Haydon, *Prof. Emeritus of History of Religions*

James Hemming, *Psychologist, Great Britain*

Palmer A. Hilty, *Adm. Secy., Fellowship of Religious Humanists*

Hudson Hoagland, *Pres. Emeritus, Worcester Fdn. for Exper. Bio.*

Robert S. Hoagland, *Editor*, Religious Humanism

Sidney Hook, *Prof. Emeritus of Philosophy, New York University*

James F. Hornback, *Leader, Ethical Society of St. Louis*

James M. Hutchinson, *Minister Emer., First Unit. Ch., Cincinnati*

Mordecai M. Kaplan, *Rabbi, Fndr. of Jewish Reconstr. Movement*

John C. Kidneigh, *Prof. of Social Work., Univ. of Minnesota*

Lester A. Kirkendall, *Prof. Emeritus, Oregon State Univ.*

Margaret Knight, *Univ. of Aberdeen, Scotland*

Jean Kotkin, *Exec. Secy., American Ethical Union*

Richard Kostelanetz, *poet*

Paul Kurtz, *Editor*, The Humanist

Lawrence Lader, *Chm., Natl. Assn. for Repeal of Abortion Laws*

Edward Lamb, *Pres., Lamb Communications, Inc.*

Corliss Lamont, *Chm., Natl. Emergency Civil Liberties Comm.*

Chauncey D. Leake, *Prof., Univ. of California, San Francisco*

Alfred McC. Lee, *Prof. Emeritus, Soc.-Anthropology, C.U.N.Y.*

Elizabeth Briant Lee, *author*

Christopher Macy, *Dir., Rationalist Press Assn., Great Britain*

Clorinda Margolis, *Jefferson Comm. Mental Health Cen., Phila.*

Joseph Margolis, *Prof. of Philosophy, Temple Univ.*

Harold P. Marley, *Ret. Unitarian Minister*

Floyd W. Matson, *Prof. of American Studies, Univ. of Hawaii*

Lester Mondale, *former Pres., Fellowship of Religious Humanists*

Lloyd Morain, *Pres., Illinois Gas Company*

Mary Morain, *Editorial Bd., Intl. Soc. for General Semantics*

Charles Morris, *Prof. Emeritus, Univ. of Florida*

Henry Morgentaler, *M.D., Past Pres., Humanist Assn. of Canada*

Mary Mothersill, *Prof. of Philosophy, Barnard College*

Jerome Nathanson, *Chm. Bd. of Leaders, NY Soc. Ethical Culture*

Billy Joe Nichols, *Minister, Richardson Unitarian Church, Texas*

Kai Nielsen, *Prof. of Philosophy, Univ. of Calgary, Canada*

P. H. Nowell-Smith, *Prof. of Philosophy, York Univ., Canada*

Chaim Perelman, *Prof. of Philosophy, Univ. of Brussels, Belgium*

James W. Prescott, *Natl. Inst. of Child Health and Human Dev.*

Harold J. Quigley, *Leader, Ethical Humanist Society of Chicago*

Howard Radest, *Prof. of Philosophy, Ramapo College*

John Herman Randall, Jr., *Prof. Emeritus, Columbia Univ.*

Oliver L. Reiser, *Prof. Emeritus, Univ. of Pittsburgh*

Robert G. Risk, *Pres., Leadville Corp.*

Lord Ritchie-Calder, *formerly Univ. of Edinburgh, Scotland*

B. T. Rocca, Jr., *Consultant, Intl. Trade and Commodities*

Andre D. Sakharov, *Academy of Sciences, Moscow, U.S.S.R.*

Sidney H. Scheuer, *Chm., Natl. Comm. for an Effective Congress*

Herbert W. Schneider, *Prof. Emeritus, Claremont Grad. School*

Clinton Lee Scott, *Universalist Minister, St. Petersburgh, Fla.*

Roy Wood Sellars, *Prof. Emeritus, Univ. of Michigan*

A. B. Shah, *Pres., Indian Secular Society*

B. F. Skinner, *Prof. of Psychology, Harvard Univ.*

Kenneth J. Smith, *Leader, Philadelphia Ethical Society*

Matthew Ies Spetter, *Chm., Dept. Ethics, Ethical Culture Schools*

Mark Starr, *Chm., Esperanto Info. Center*

Svetozar Stojanovic, *Prof. of Philosophy, Univ. Belgrade, Yugoslavia*

Harold Taylor, *Project Director, World University Student Project*

V.T. Thayer, *author*

Herbert A. Tonne, *Ed. Board,* Journal of Business Education

Jack Tourin, *Pres., American Ethical Union*

E.C. Vanderlaan, *lecturer*

J.P. van Praag, *Chm., Intl. Humanist and Ethical Union, Utrecht*

Maurice B. Visscher, *M.D. Prof. Emeritus, Univ. of Minnesota*

Goodwin Watson, *Assn. Coordinator, Union Graduate School*

Gerald Wendt, *author*

Henry N. Weiman, *Prof. Emeritus, Univ. of Chicago*

Sherwin Wine, *Rabbi, Soc. for Humanistic Judaism*

Edwin H. Wilson, *Ex. Dir. Emeritus, American Humanist Assn.*

Bertram D. Wolfe, *Hoover Institution*

Alexander S. Yesenin-Volpin, *mathematician*

Marvin Zimmerman, *Prof. of Philosophy, State Univ. NY at Bflo.*

ADDITIONAL SIGNERS

Gina Allen, *author*

John C. Anderson, *Humanist Counselor*

Peter O. Anderson, *Assistant Professor, Ohio State University*

William F. Anderson, *Humanist Counselor*

John Anton, *Professor, Emory University*

Sir Alfred Ayer, *Professor, Oxford, Great Britain*

Celia Baker

Ernest Baker, *Associate Professor, University of the Pacific*

Marjorie S. Baker, *Ph.D., Pres., Humanist Community of San Francisco*

Henry S. Basayne, *Assoc. Exec. Off., Assn. for Humanistic Psych.*

Walter Behrendt, *Vice Pres., European Parliament, W. Germany*

Mildred H. Blum, *Secy., American Ethical Union*

W. Bonness, *Pres., Bund Freirelgioser Gemeinden, West Germany*

Robert O. Boothe, *Prof. Emer. Cal. Polytechnic*

Clement A. Bosch

Madeline L. Bosch

Bruni Boyd, *Vice Pres., American Ethical Union*

J. Lloyd Brereton, *ed.,* Humanist in Canada

Nancy Brewer, *Humanist Counselor*

D. Bronder, *Bund Freirelgioser Gemeinden, West Germany*

Charles Brownfield, *Asst. Prof., Queensborough Community College, CUNY*

Costantia Brownfield, *R.N.*

Margaret Brown, *Assoc. Prof., Oneonta State Univ. College*

Beulah L. Bullard, *Humanist Counselor*

Joseph Chuman, *Leader, Ethical Soc. of Essex Co.*

Gordon Clanton, *Asst. Prof., Trenton State College*

Daniel S. Collins, *Leader, Unitarian Fellowship of Jonesboro, Ark.*

Wm. Creque, *Pres., Fellowship of Humanity, Oakland, Ca.*

M. Benjamin Dell, *Dir., Amer. Humanist Assn.*

James Durant IV, *Prof., Polk Comm. College, Winter Haven, Fla*

Gerald A. Ehrenreich, *Assoc. Prof., Univ. of Kansas School of Medicine*

Marie Erdmann, *Teacher, Campbell Elementary School*

Robert L. Erdmann, *Ph.D., IBM*

Hans S. Falck, *Disting, Professor, Menninger Foundation*

James Farmer, *Director, Public Policy Training Institute*

Ed Farrar

Joe Felmet, *Humanist Counselor*

Thomas Ferrick, *Leader, Ethical Society of Boston*

Norman Fleishman, *Exec. Vice Pres., Planned Parenthood World Population, Los Angeles*

Joseph Fletcher, *Visiting Prof., Sch. of Medicine, Univ. of Virginia*

Douglas Frazier, *Leader, American Ethical Union*

Betty Friedan, *Founder, N.O.W.*

Harry M. Geduld, *Professor, Indiana University*

Roland Gibson, *President, Art Foundation of Potsdam, N.Y.*

Aron S. Gilmartin, *Minister, Mt. Diablo Unitarian Church, Walnut Creek, Ca.*

Annabelle Glasser, *Director, American Ethical Union*

Rebecca Goldblum, *Director, American Ethical Union*

Louis R. Gomberg, *Humanist Counselor*

Harold N. Gordon, *Vice President, American Ethical Union*

Sol Gordon, *Professor, Syracuse University*

Theresa Gould, *American Ethical Union*

Gregory O. Grant, *Captain, USAF*

Ronald Green, *Asst. Professor, New York University*

LeRue Grim, *Secretary, American Humanist Association*

S. Spencer Grin, *Publisher,* Saturday Review/World

Josephine R. Gurbarg, *Secy., Humanist Society of Greater Philadelphia*

Samuel J. Gurbarg

Lewis M. Gubrud, *Executive Director, Mediator Fellowship, Providence, R.I.*

Frank A. Hall, *Minister, Murray Univ. Church, Attleboro, Mass.*

Harold Hansen, *President, Space Coast Chapter, AHA*

Abul Hasanat, *Secretary, Bangladesh Humanist Society*

HUMANIST MANIFESTO II (AMERICAN HUMANIST ASSOCIATION) (continued)

Ethelbert Haskins, *Director, American Humanist Association*

Lester H. Hayes, *Public Relations Director, American Income Life Insurance Company*

Donald E. Henshaw, *Humanist Counselor*

Alex Hershaft, *Principal Scientist, Booz Allen Applied Research*

Ronald E. Hestand, *author and columnist*

Irving Louis Horowitz, *editor*, Society

Warren S. Hoskins, *Humanist Counselor*

Mark W. Huber, *Director, American Ethical Union*

Harold J. Hutchison, *Humanist Counselor*

Sir Julian Huxley, *former head, UNESCO, Great Britain*

Arthur M. Jackson, *Exec. Dir., Humanist Community of San Jose; Treasurer, American Humanist Association*

Linda R. Jackson, *Director, American Humanist Association*

Steven Jacobs, *former President, American Ethical Union*

Thomas B. Johnson, Jr., *consulting psychologist*

Robert Edward Jones, *Exec. Dir., Joint Washington Office for Social Concern*

Marion Kahn, *Pres., Humanist Society of Metropolitan New York*

Alec E. Kelley, *Professor, University of Arizona*

Marvin Kohl, *Professor, SUNY at Fredonia*

Frederick C. Kramer, *Humanist Counselor*

Eugene Kreves, *Minister, DuPage Unit. Church, Naperville, Ill.*

Pierre Lamarque, *France*

Helen B. Lamb, *economist*

Jerome D. Lang, *Pres., Humanist Assoc. of Greater Miami, Fla.*

Harvey Lebrun, *Chairman, Chapter Assembly, AHA*

Helen Leibson, *President, Philadelphia Ethical Society*

John F. MacEnulty, Jr., *Pres., Humanist Soc. of Jacksonville, Fla.*

James T. McCollum, *Humanist Counselor*

Vashti McCollum, *former President of AHA*

Russell L. McKnight, *Pres., Humanist Association of Los Angeles*

Ludlow P. Mahan, Jr., *Pres., Humanist Chapter of Rhode Island*

Andrew Malleson, *M.D., psychiatrist*

Clem Martin, *M.D.*

James R. Martin, *Humanist Counselor*

Stanley E. Mayabb, *Co-Fndr.: Humanist Group of Vacaville and Men's Colony, San Luis Obispo*

Zhores Medvedev, *scientist, U.S.S.R.*

Abelardo Mena, *M.D., senior psychiatrist, V.A. Hospital, Miami, Fla.*

Jacques Monod, *Institut Pasteur, France*

Herbert J. Muller, *Professor, University of Indiana*

Robert J. Myler, *Title Officer, Title Insurance & Trust Company*

Gunnar Myrdal, *Professor, University of Stockholm, Sweden*

H. Kyle Nagel, *Minister, Unit. Univ. Church of Kinston, N.C.*

Dorothy N. Naiman, *Professor Emerita, Lehman College, CUNY*

Muriel Neufeld, *Executive Committee, American Ethical Union*

Walter B. Neumann, *Treasurer, American Ethical Union*

G.D. Parikh, *Indian Radical Humanist Association, India*

Eleanor Wright Pelrine, *author, Canada*

Bernard Porter, *President, Toronto Humanist Association*

William Earl Proctor, Jr., *President, Philadelphia area, AHA*

Gonzalo Quiogue, *Vice Pres., Humanist Assn. of the Philippines*

James A. Rafferty, *Lecturer, USIU School of Human Behavior*

Anthony F. Rand, *President, Humanist Society of Greater Detroit*

A. Philip Randolph, *President, A. Philip Randolph Institute*

Ruth Dickinson Reams, *President, Humanist Association National Capital Area*

Jean-Francois Revel, *journalist, France*

Bernard L. Riback, *Humanist Counselor*

B. T. Rocca, Sr., *President, United Secularists of America*

M. L. Rosenthal, *Professor, New York University*

Jack C. Rubenstein, *Executive Committee, AEU*

Joseph R. Sanders, *Professor, University of West Florida*

William Schulz, *Ph.D. cand., Meadville/Lombard, Univ. of Chicago*

Walter G. Schwartz, *Dir., Humanist Comm. of San Francisco*

John W. Sears, *clinical psychologist*

Naomi Shaw, *Pres., National Women's Conference, AEU*

R. L. Shuford, III, *Instructor, Charlotte Country Day School*

Sidney Siller, *Chm. Comm. for Fair Divorce and Alimony Laws*

Joell Silverman, *Chm., Religious Education Committee, AEU*

Warren A. Smith, *Pres., Variety Sound Corp.*

A. Solomon, *coordinator, Indian Secular Society*

Robert Sone

Robert M. Stein, *Co-Chairman, Public Affairs Committee, AEU*

Stuart Stein, *Director, American Ethical Union*

Arnold E. Sylvester

Emerson Symonds, *Director, Sensory Awareness Center*

Carolyn Symonds, *marriage counselor*

Ward Tabler, *Visiting Professor, Starr King School*

Barbara M. Tabler

V. M. Tarkunde, *Pres., All Indian Radical Humanist Assn., India*

Erwin Theobold, *Instructor, Pasadena City College*

Ernest N. Ukpaby, *Dean, University of Nigeria*

Renate Vambery, *Ethical Soc. of St. Louis, President, AHA St. Louis Chapter*

Nick D. Vasileff, *St. Louis Ethical Society*

Robert J. Wellman, *Humanist Chaplain, C.W. Post Center, Long Island University*

May H. Weis, *UN Representative for IHEU*

Paul D. Weston, *Leader, Ethical Culture Society of Bergen County*

Georgia H. Wilson, *retired, Political Sc. Dept., Brooklyn College*
H. Van Rensselaer Wilson, *Prof., Emer., Brooklyn College*
James E. Woodrow, *Exec. Dir., Asgard Enterprises, Inc.*

Notes: *This second Humanist Manifesto was issued in 1973, forty years after the first, with the intention of updating the original on a number of points, and venturing observations on a broader range of issues. In light of events taking place since the first statement appeared (World War II, the Holocaust), its tone was thought to be overly optimistic. Widely circulated prior to its formal publication, the Humanist Manifesto II appeared with the signatures of a number of prominent academics. In the years since its publication, many more prominent individuals, primarily from the United States and England, have also signed it.*

The Humanist Manifesto II was also an attempt to expand upon the agreement of the Amsterdam Declaration, the somewhat hastily written statement of the International and Ethical Union issued in 1952.

*   *   *

AMSTERDAM DECLARATION [INTERNATIONAL HUMANIST AND ETHICAL UNION (AMERICAN HUMANIST ASSOCIATION AND THE AMERICAN ETHICAL UNION)]

This congress is a response to the widespread demand for an alternative to the religions which claim to be based on revelation on the one hand and totalitarian systems on the other. The alternative offered as a third way out of the present crisis of civilization is Humanism, which is not a sect, but the outcome of a long tradition that has inspired many of the world's thinkers and creative artists, and given rise to science. Ethical Humanism unites all those who cannot any longer believe the various creeds and are willing to base their convictions on respect for man as a spiritual and moral being. The fundamentals of modern ethical Humanism are as follows:

1. *It is democratic.* It aims at the fullest possible development of every human being. It holds that this is a matter of right. The democratic principle can be applied to all human relationships and is not restricted to methods of government.

2. *It seeks to use science creatively, not destructively.* It advocates a worldwide application of scientific method to problems of human welfare. Humanists believe that the tremendous problems with which mankind is faced in this age of transition can be solved. Science gives the means but science itself does not propose ends.

3. *Humanism is ethical.* It affirms the dignity of man and the right of the individual to the greatest possible freedom of development compatible with the rights of others. There is a danger that in seeking to utilise scientific knowledge in a complex society individual freedom may be threatened by the very impersonal machine that has been created to save it. Ethical Humanism, therefore, rejects totalitarian attempts to perfect the machine in order to obtain immediate gains at the cost of human values.

4. *It insists that personal liberty is an end that must be combined with social responsibility* in order that it shall not be sacrificed to the improvement of material conditions. Without intellectual liberty, fundamental research, on which progress must in the long run depend, would not be possible. Humanism ventures to build a world on the free person responsible to society. On behalf of individual freedom humanism is undogmatic, imposing no creed upon its adherents. It is thus committed to education free from indoctrination.

5. *It is a way of life,* aiming at the maximum possible fulfillment, through the cultivation of ethical and creative living. It can be a way of life for everyone everywhere if the individual is capable of the response required by the changing social order. The primary task of humanism to-day is to make men aware in the simplest terms of what it can mean to them and what it commits them to. By utilizing in this context, and for purposes of peace, the new power which science has given us, humanists have confidence that the present crisis can be surmounted. Liberated from fear the energies of man will be available for a self-realisation to which it is impossible to foresee the limit.

Ethical Humanism is thus a faith that answers the challenge of our times. We call upon men who share this conviction to associate themselves with us.

Notes: *Both the American Humanist Association and the American Ethical Union participated in the formation of the International Humanist and Ethical Union, which brought together like minded individuals and organizations from a number of countries in Europe and North America. At the original meeting in the Netherlands in 1952, a declaration was drafted. The statement reflected the broad concensus, but, proving unsatisfactory to many, later spurred the production of the Humanist Manifesto II.*

*   *   *

THE SIXTEEN COMMANDMENTS (CHURCH OF THE CREATOR)

Basic to our Religion. To emphasize that the Sixteen Commandments as set forth in NATURE'S ETERNAL RELIGION are still and forever the Basic Commandments of CREATIVITY we spell them out again in this, the White Man's Bible. Since I have already expanded on the commandments in NATURE'S ETERNAL RELIGION, I will not repeat it here, and let the record stand.

1. It is the avowed duty and holy responsibility of each generation to assure and secure for all time the existence of the White Race upon the face of this planet.

2. Be fruitful and multiply. Do your part in helping to populate the world with your own kind. It is our sacred goal to populate the lands of this earth with White people exclusively.

THE SIXTEEN COMMANDMENTS (CHURCH OF THE CREATOR) (continued)

3. Remember that the inferior colored races are our deadly enemies, and the most dangerous of all is the Jewish race. It is our immediate objective to relentlessly expand the White Race, and keep shrinking our enemies.

4. The guiding principle of all your actions shall ·be: What is best for the White Race?

5. You shall keep your race pure. Pollution of the White Race is a heinous crime against Nature and against your own race.

6. Your first loyalty belongs to the White Race.

7. Show preferential treatment in business dealings with members of your own race. Phase out all dealings with Jews as soon as possible. Do not employ niggers or other coloreds. Have social contacts only with members of your own racial family.

8. Destroy and banish all Jewish thought and influence from society. Work hard to bring about a White world as soon as possible.

9. Work and creativity are our genius. We regard work as a noble pursuit and our willingness to work a blessing to our race.

10. Decide in early youth that during your lifetime you will make at least one major lasting contribution to the White Race.

11. Uphold the honor of your race at all times.

12. It is our duty and our privilege to further Nature's plan by striving towards the advancement and improvement of our future generations.

13. You shall honor, protect and venerate the sanctity of the family unit, and hold it sacred. It is the present link in the long golden chain of our White Race.

14. Throughout your life you shall faithfully uphold our pivotal creed of Blood, Soil and Honor. Practice it diligently, for it is the heart of our faith.

15. As a proud member of the White Race, think and act positively, Be courageous, confident and aggressive. Utilize constructively your creative ability.

16. We, the Racial Comrades of the White Race, are determined to regain complete and unconditional control of our own destiny.

Notes: *The Church of the Creator has issued a number of statements as manifestos, but these sixteen guiding commandments are the most authoritative document accepted by church members. The commandments delineate quite clearly the church's racial attitudes and the actions appropriate for anyone who accepts them.*

THE HUMANITARIAN CREED (CHURCH OF THE HUMANITARIAN GOD)

I am alive today to help in some way a fellow man. May my daily service to humanity be a credit for this proving ground that is Earth.

Let no man, or no country, or any allegiance deter me from observing the natural law of sustaining life.

I pledge myself to rebuke injustice openly and to aid my fellow man as best I can.

May I injure or kill no other human, except in a moral case of self-defense. I pledge never to serve in the armed forces of any nation at a time when that nation is engaged in immoral combat.

Above all, may I forever seek and accept truth, and the reason for my being.

Notes: *This creed defines humanitarianism as taught by the Church of the Humanitarian God.*

* * *

THE CREED (CONFRATERNITY OF DEISTS)

I BELIEVE in ONE GOD—THE SUPREME INTELLIGENCE.

I BELIEVE that constructive exercise of human intelligence contributes to the glorification of THE SUPREME.

I BELIEVE that ALL man-written scriptures are literary works, having no value as religious, historical or chronological records.

I BELIEVE that the church of the Deist should constitute the FREE UNIVERSITY, disseminating SCIENTIFIC knowledge and nurturing the arts.

I BELIEVE that it is my social duty to work mutually for the Spiritual and Temporal elevation of the people.

Notes: *Deism, as promulgated by the confraternity, is the religion of the free and carries few of the connotations of classical Deism. The creed allows a wide variation of opinion on even the most basic issues.*

* * *

SOME BASIC STATEMENTS ASSUMED BY THE SOCIETY OF EVANGELICAL AGNOSTICS

One should approach all questions and issues with an open mind.

One should consider it to be immoral to advocate conclusions without adequate or satisfactory evidence.

One should accept not knowing as a fundamental reality in one's life

Notes: *The three statements around which the society is organized constitute a definition of agnosticism.*

WHAT DO UNITARIANS BELIEVE?
[UNITARIAN-UNIVERSALIST ASSOCIATION (AMERICAN UNITARIAN ASSOCIATION)]

For the purpose of rendering, if I may, some little assistance to the large number of persons all about us, who are asking the above question, as well as with the hope, possibly, of stirring up others still, who have not yet done so, to inquire, I have prepared the following brief summary of information regarding the principles and positions of Unitarians.

FREEDOM OF INQUIRY IN RELIGION. We believe that the same God who is the author of religion is also the author of reason; that there is no other way in which truth can possibly be separated from error in religion except by investigation and the use of reason; and therefore, that it is of the highest importance that there should be everywhere the freest and fullest inquiry with reference to religious things,—in this inquiry every man being permitted to stand upon his own feet, and to judge for himself, subject to no dictation or pressure from councils, synods, conferences, presbyteries, creeds, catechisms, fathers of the church, doctors of the church, or preachers.

NO CREED. We have no creed, that is, no authoritative statement of beliefs which persons are required to subscribe to; first, because we believe to the fullest extent in liberty of thought, and would do nothing to check it; secondly, because, in the very nature of the case, it is impossible for any two persons to see all truth exactly alike, and therefore a creed made by one man for another must be more or less inadequate if not false; thirdly, because if we had a creed fitted to our wants to-day, we should either have to stop growing in knowledge and insight or else get a new one to-morrow; fourthly, because neither Jesus nor the Apostles taught any, nor did the early church possess any; fifthly, because history gives unmistakable proof that creeds and authoritative statements of doctrine have always tended to tear the Christian Church to pieces, to multiply sects, to suggest and foster persecutions, and to hinder progress.

SOMETHING BETTER. But while we have no creed or fixed statements of doctrine which we prescribe as a condition of Christian fellowship, we *do* have a *great, central principle*, and a *few great, simple, central faiths*. Our central principle is this: the necessary harmony of true religion with reason, or the supreme authority of reason and moral consciousness in the search after religious truth. From this fundamental principle, everywhere held to among us, has resulted as essential agreement as to the general, fundamental faiths upon which our movement builds—an agreement probably quite as great as can be found in churches which have authoritative creeds.

GOD. We believe God to be one, not three or more; an intelligent First Cause, not an ultimate blind force; beyond our utmost thought powerful, wise, holy, just, good, not malignant, or indifferent, or in any way imperfect: the embodiment of all, and more than all, that we can possibly mean by that name which Jesus taught us to call him, "our Father," and hence one who can never cease to love and care for all his children, in this world or any other.

INSPIRATION. We believe that inspiration is not something which can be locked up in writing, or confined to any age or people; but that now, to-day, and here with us, just as truly as 2,000 or 8,000 years ago and in Palestine, the Infinite Spirit of Wisdom, Truth, Beauty and Love, waits to come with its inspiration into every receptive mind.

REVELATION. We believe that revelation is progressive, not stationary; that it is of all times, countries and races, not of the remote past or of a single people only; that it comes through many channels, including nature, history and the mind of man, not through any single channel alone, or in any miraculous way; that, so far from revelation being confined to one book, all moral and spiritual truth known to man belongs to it; that as a race we are now standing only in the morning dawn of revelation, not in its evening twilight.

THE BIBLE. We believe that the Bible is the greatest, the most influential, the most important, the noblest depository of this revelation that has come down to us from the past, and is therefore to be prized by us as the most precious and sacred of books; though not as the only sacred book of the world, nor by any means an infallible book.

JESUS. Accepting the Bible teaching that all men are "sons of God," we yet believe that Jesus, by reason of the exceptional purity and perfectness of his character, was pre-eminently what the New Testament in a number of places calls him, *the* son of God. We believe him to have been divine, but not Deity,—as we believe that humanity, in the degree of its perfection, is everywhere divine. We teach tender love and earnest reverence toward him, but we do not worship him, because, among other reasons, he himself, both by word and example, taught us to worship only God—his Father and ours.

COMING TO JESUS. While we believe that no words in our day are more often used among certain large classes of religious people, in a sense which has in it *no sense*, but is mere sentimentalism and cant, we at the same time most sincerely believe in a real coming to Jesus:—that is, a coming (through study and reflection and effort) to a constantly more and more perfect conformity to his pure and exalted spirit and life.

BELIEVING IN JESUS. Believing in Jesus we do not understand to consist in believing any speculative theological doctrines *about* him,—as his incarnation, his deity, his atonement, his relation to a trinity. True believing in Jesus we understand to consist in believing in *him*,—in what he was and did, in the kind of life he lived and character he exhibited; in such love to God and man, such devotion to truth and duty, such beautiful self-sacrifice, such patience and gentleness, such bravery and fidelity as he everywhere taught and exemplified.

FOLLOWING CHRIST. We believe that the truest following of Christ is to go about doing good.

CONVERSION. The word "convert" means "to turn," or "to turn about." Inasmuch, therefore as all men, being imperfect, are liable to commit errors, and fall to walking in ways that are not right, we believe that all men have need to be converted, not once but again and again.

WHAT DO UNITARIANS BELIEVE? [UNITARIAN-UNIVERSALIST ASSOCIATION (AMERICAN UNITARIAN ASSOCIATION)] (continued)

THE NEW BIRTH. We believe that to be born again, and to continue to be born again, into new and perpetually new, into finer and higher and forevermore finer and higher spiritual life, is what Jesus taught to be the law of our being, and the design of the Creator for all men.

SALVATION. We believe in salvation by character, not salvation by purchase or transfer; and that Jesus saves men solely by helping them to become better, not by vicariously atoning for their sins.

The whole idea, in all its forms, that God, before he can or will pardon men's sins, must have some third party to make him willing, or some sort of "plan" or "scheme," whereby he becomes able to pardon, we utterly reject. We believe that God's paternity is real, and not a mere pretense of paternity, and therefore that the moment any human child of his manifests sincere penitence and seeks forgiveness of his sin, God freely and joyfully forgives—without any thought, ever, of requiring first the suffering of an innocent person in the place of the guilty. In our reading of the Parable of the Prodigal Son—that part of the teaching of Jesus in which he illustrates most fully God's dealing with his erring children—we find the father represented as running to meet the penitent son "while he was yet a great way off": and we do not find even a hint that the elder brother, who had not sinned, was required first to make an "atonement" for the younger, or to "intercede" for him, or to "satisfy justice," or to "propitiate" the father, or do anything in any way to promote the father's willingness or ability to forgive.

THE GUILT OF THE RACE FOR ADAM'S TRANSGRESSION. We believe that nobody can be guilty for anybody's sin but his own.

GOOD AND EVIL. We believe that the world is not fallen, but incomplete: and that, in the nature of things, evil is transient and good eternal.

HUMAN NATURE. We believe that human nature is imperfect but not inherently bad; that it has been wisely appointed to man to rise by slow degrees and long and even painful effort out of low conditions into conditions even higher and better, and not that we are the degenerate descendants of pure and perfect ancestors in some remote past. We believe that the race as a whole occupies a higher plane to-day than ever before, and that this progress of the past gives us ground for faith in a greatly increased progress in the future.

RETRIBUTION. We believe that no wrong-doing will go unpunished, and no right-doing unrewarded; that all punishment for sin is natural, not arbitrary, reformatory in its aim, not vindictive, and therefore cannot, in the nature of things, be everlasting.

HEAVEN AND HELL. The doctrine of an eternal hell we unqualifiedly reject, as the foulest imputation upon the character of God possible to be conceived, and as something which would render happiness in heaven itself impossible, since no beings whose hearts were not stone, could be happy anywhere knowing that half the human family, including many of their own loved ones, were in torments. Instead of such a dark and God-dishonoring doctrine, we believe that the future existence will be one ruled by Eternal Justice and Love, that he whom in this world we call "our Father," will be no less a Father to all his human children in the world to come, and that that world will be so planned as not only to bring eternal good to all who have done well here, but also to offer eternal hope to such as have done ill here.

FAITH AND WORKS. We believe in faith:—faith in God, faith in man, faith in truth, faith in duty; and that all these faiths are "saving faiths." We believe in works:—that the more good works a man does, so that his motives be good, the better pleasing to heaven is his life; and that no salvation of any worth ever comes to any human being except through faithful and earnest work.

WORSHIP, LOVE AND SERVICE OF GOD. We believe that man is as much made to worship as to think; but that perfect worship of God includes reverence for everything high and pure in humanity; that perfect love of God includes love to all God's children; that he best serves God who is most useful, and who obeys best every law of his being—physical, intellectual, moral, spiritual.

CHURCH MEMBERSHIP. We believe that the true basis of church membership and all Christian fellowship is not an intellectual belief of formulated creeds or articles of faith, but a sincere desire to unite for a common purpose of Christian worship, moral culture and human helpfulness.

SCIENCE AND RELIGION. We believe that science and religion, having the same author, can never, by any possibility be antagonistic; but that true religion is scientific and true science is religious. We cheerfully acknowledge that science has already been of incalculable service to religion, in helping to rid it of many degrading and hurtful superstitions and errors; and we bid all scientific investigators a most sincere god-speed in any and every investigation which can throw light upon any of the great religious questions of the time.

FELLOWSHIP OF RELIGIONS. While we believe that Christianity is the highest and best religion of the world, we believe also that the other great religions of mankind have in them much that is true and of God; and that God, instead of having arbitrarily chosen out one single people and made it the sole channel of his communication with the race, leaving the rest in midnight darkness, "has not left himself without witness" among any people, and that "in every nation he that feareth God and worketh righteousness (according to the best light he has) is accepted with God."

THE ABOVE. The above, while not a creed, or authoritative statement, or one binding upon any but the writer, is yet believed to be in essential harmony with what is commonly held and taught as fundamental among Unitarians: as it is also believed to be in essential harmony with reason, science, the best scholarship and thought of the age, and the teachings of Jesus.

SOME LEADING POINTS OF UNITARIAN BELIEF, WITH SCRIPTURE REFERENCES

1. One God, and only one, the Father, a Spirit, the only proper object of worship: in contradistinction from a trinity, and worship of Jesus or of the Virgin Mary. Matt. vi. 9; Mark xii. 29; Jno. iv. 24; xvii. 3; xx. 17; Eph. iv. 6; 1 Tim. ii. 5.

2. Jesus not God the Son, but the son of God his sonship consisting in moral god-likeness, many others besides him being called in Scripture "sons of God"); not Deity but divine (all humanity being the "offspring of God," and therefore, in the degree of its perfection, divine). Matt. xvi. 16; Acts ix. 20; Acts xvii. 29; 1 Jno. iii. 1,2; Hosea i. 10; Matt. v. 9; Gen. i. 37; James iii. 9.

3. Human nature not inherently evil (or, as the creeds of at least two of our great Christian denominations say, "dead in sin, wholly defiled in all the faculties and parts of soul and body, and therefore bound over to the wrath of God"), but, created "in the image of God," and even in its lowest estate containing much that is beautiful, noble and well-pleasing to God. Gen. i. 26,27; Rom. ii. 14,15; Mark x. 14, 15; Luke vii. 1-9 and 36-48.

4. God's love universal and everlasting, extending as much to the next world as to this; all punishment remedial and disciplinary; all men finally to be saved. Is. xlix. 15; Jer. xxxi. 3; Ps. cxxxvi. 1; Matt. xviii. 14; Col. i. 20; Heb. xii. 5-10: 1 Cor. xv. 22-28; Luke xv. 20-24.

5. The Bible the most important and sacred of books, but not to be accepted as infallible, because in some of its parts opposed to the teachings of science, the best conscience and reason of our time and the teachings of Jesus. Matt. v. 33-44. Compare Matt. v. 44 with Ps. cix., with Deut. xix. 13-21, with Josh. xi. 6-23, and with 1 Sam. xv. 2-11. Joshua x. 12-13; Jonah i. 17, and ii. 10.

6. Conscience sacred: inquiry to be full and free. Luke xii. 54-57; Rom. xiv. 1-5; 1 Cor. x. 15; 1 Thess. v. 21.

7. Man's whole duty included in love to God and love to man. Mark xii. 29-33; Rom. xiii. 8-10.

Notes: *Unitarians have been reluctant to issue any official "creeds" or "affirmations of belief." However, individuals have periodically attempted such statements. This treatise written by prominent Unitarian minister Jabez T. Sutherland was issued by the American Unitarian Association in 1906 and frequently reprinted throughout the first half of the twentieth century (prior to the Unitarian-Universalist merger).*

THE WINCHESTER PROFESSION, THE ESSENTIAL PRINCIPLES OF THE UNIVERSALIST FAITH, AND THE BOND OF FELLOWSHIP AND STATEMENT OF FAITH [UNITARIAN-UNIVERSALIST ASSOCIATION (UNIVERSALIST CHURCH IN AMERICA)]

THE WINCHESTER PROFESSION

Article I. We believe that the Holy Scriptures of the Old and New Testament contain a revelation of the character of God, and of the duty, interest and final destination of mankind.

Article II. We believe that there is one God, whose nature is Love, revealed in one Lord Jesus Christ, by one Holy Spirit of Grace, who will finally restore the whole family of mankind to holiness and happiness.

Article III. We believe that holiness and true happiness are inseparably connected, and that believers ought to be careful to maintain order and practice good works; for these things are good and profitable unto men.

THE ESSENTIAL PRINCIPLES OF THE UNIVERSALIST FAITH

The Universal Fatherhood of God.

The Spiritual Authority and Leadership of His Son, Jesus Christ.

The trustworthiness of the Bible as containing a revelation from God.

The certainty of just retribution for sin.

The final harmony of all souls with God.

BOND OF FELLOWSHIP AND STATEMENT OF FAITH

The bond of fellowship in this church shall be a common purpose to do the will of God as Jesus revealed it and to co-operate in establishing the Kingdom for which he lived and died.
To that end we avow our faith in
God as Eternal and All-conquering Love,
The spiritual leadership of Jesus,
The supreme worth of every human personality,
The authority of truth known or to be known,
And in the power of men of good will and sacrificial spirit to overcome all evil and progressively to establish the Kingdom of God.

Notes: *On at least three occasions the Universalist Church in America (prior to its merger into the Unitarian-Universalist Association) passed statements representative of its positions on those issues most important in the formation of the church. The Winchester Profession was adopted in 1803 with a "liberty clause," making explicit the understanding that it was not binding upon any member or congregation. In 1870 it was adopted by the church's general convention without the liberty clause. The Principles statement replaced the Profession in 1899, with the liberty clause added. The Bond of Fellowship was adopted in 1935.*

STATEMENT OF BELIEFS AND DOCTRINES (UNITED LIBERTARIAN FELLOWSHIP)

STATEMENT OF BELIEFS

God is the supreme universal reality; all that has ever existed or will ever exist; the fundamental force of the universe.

Human beings have the capacity to think and act. It is our rational functioning mind which differentiates us from the rest of existence.

It is our duty to use our minds and bodies to search for the truth, as we are capable of understanding it, and to act in accordance with that truth.

All individuals are capable of influencing their own destinies, and must accept the accompanying responsibility for their own actions and their consequences. We are each responsible for governing our own affairs and being the guardian of our own physical and spiritual well being.

The basic principle of human conduct derived from the religious principles of the Fellowship is that no one may initiate the use of force or fraud on another. Every individual must grant to others the freedom of body and spirit which is required for the development and manifestation of their religious nature.

DOCTRINES

The worldly manifestation of the beliefs of the Fellowship is a doctrine of maximum individual freedom and autonomy, consistent with the right of each person of life, liberty, and the fruits of their labor. Each member of the Fellowship is bound by the beliefs to refrain from, and refuse to contribute to, any aggressive action which forcibly deprives another of their property or their right to pursue life in their own chosen manner.

In particular, a member of the Fellowship may not:

force others to use their money, lives, or property, in ways inconsistent with their own beliefs;

accept money or property obtained by wrongfully taking it from others;

accept money from public insurance against physical harm, property damage, death, disability, old age, retirement, or medical care;

prevent or punish others who ingest substances into their own bodies for religious, medical, or any other purpose;

prevent or punish others who engage in private voluntary actions together for commercial, intellectual, spiritual, or any other reason.

Notes: *This statement describes a method of approaching religious truth and the religious life much more than it asserts a set of mutually held beliefs.*

STATEMENT OF THE UNITED SECULARISTS OF AMERICA

OUR POLICY

We uphold the right of every person to freedom of thought, of inquiry, and of expression, and we oppose every form of tyranny over the mind of man.

We look to advancing science rather than to religious tradition in formulating our concepts of man and the universe.

We are committed to the intellectual, ethical, and cultural growth of all peoples and their advancement toward a more rational, humane and civilized world order.

Politically, our organization is non-partisan, and it stands for the full Constitutional and civil rights of all citizens.

WE ADVOCATE

Complete separation of church and state.

Taxation of all church property.

The exclusion of all religious indoctrination from the public schools.

No public tax funds to be used for any kind of aid to any private or church-connected institution.

More adequate government support of public education, recreational facilities, and cultural opportunities for all the people.

Effective enforcement of the Constitutional rights, privileges, and obligations of all citizens.

Notes: *This brief statement appeared in each issue of the United Secularists' magazine,* Progressive World.

*   *   *

Mail Order Churches

WE BELIEVE (MISSIONARIES OF THE NEW TRUTH)

We believe in man as a seeker of Truth, an inquirer, thirsting to know himself, his fellows in life and the Universe about him.

We believe that the nobility of man lies in the *seeking* of these Truths. If a man is to live a meaningful, happy life, he must seek the Truth.

We believe that there are many areas in life within which a man should seek the Truth, spiritual, emotional, political and many others.

We believe that our members should actively seek these Truths by all just means available to us.

We believe that certain Truths will differ for each man as each man is different. Subjective Truths of a man's spiritual and emotional life must relate to his uniqueness of structure, experience, capabilities and environment. For this reason we place no restrictions on a man's search for Truth except that he follow his best convictions with honesty and integrity. We thus exhort all our members to seek the Truth by all just means, in any place and in any way that they see fit.

We believe that since we accept all devout seekers of Truth, we should welcome all believers in established faiths as well as those who have not yet embraced any form of religion. Many men have found a wealth of meaningful Truth in the Bible. We recognize the great wisdom of the Bible but recognize that wisdom may also derive from many other sources.

We pledge to ourselves and to all mankind that we will honor, respect and love all men as fellow seekers of Truth. We pledge to keep our faith as free as possible from encumbering dogma and stultifying moral and social strictures.

Finally, we pledge to actively propagate our faith and to follow and promote those Truths revealed to us in our holy search.

Notes: *The Missionaries of the New Truth is now defunct, its leaders having sought Truth in psychedelic drugs until arrested and convicted.*

* * *

THIS IS MY CREED (OMNIUNE CHURCH)

Believe what ye will, so long as ye do good to thy fellow man: For verily, he that doeth Godly deeds is a Godly man: And he that hath loving-kindness in his heart hath God in his soul.

Notes: *The Omniune Church, like other churches organized basically to grant ministerial licenses, has followed the tendency to make broad, vague affirmations which allow the widest possible potential membership.*

Chapter 2
Latter-Day Saints Family

Utah Mormons

BASIC BELIEFS (AARONIC ORDER)

1. We believe in the triune godhead of the Bible, namely—God, the Father; Jesus Christ, the Son; and the Holy Spirit.

2. We worship Jesus Christ as the literal Son of God. He is also the Jehovah of the Old Testament, the Saviour and Redeemer of this world, and the only name under heaven whereby man must be saved.

3. We believe that men generally are in a fallen state and thereby estranged from God, and will remain so unless they repent and become obedient to His commandments.

4. We believe that salvation is available to all men if they (1) exercise faith in the Lord, Jesus Christ, and accept His atoning sacrifice, (2) sincerely repent of their sins, (3) undergo baptism by immersion for the remission of sins, and (4) receive the Holy Spirit.

5. We believe that full acceptance of the Gospel of Christ must lead to discipleship, which requires literal consecration of all things to Him. No one can serve in a leadership capacity, nor can any man officiate in the Priesthood in the True Church of God, unless he first qualifies as a disciple.

6. We accept the Bible as the Word of God and the ultimate basis of our doctrine. We also believe that God has revealed and does yet reveal many other truths to men in the flesh.

7. We believe in the literal restoration of lineal Israel in these last days as spoken in the Bible, which restoration has already begun with the re-establishment through the angel Elias of the House of Levi and Aaron.

8. We believe that God ordained the Levites and Aaronites to be priests and teachers for Israel for all time. The present-day Aaronic Order is the continuation and promised restoration of that original priesthood body.

9. We believe that Christian communal living is essential to the purification and restoration of the Levites, and that it is part of the divine plan to separate us from the world to become a peculiar people for the Lord.

10. We honor the seventh day of the week as the Sabbath of the Lord.

11. We believe in the literal second coming of the Lord, Jesus Christ, and that His return is imminent.

Notes: *The Aaronic Order is a sabbatarian communal group.*

*   *   *

THE ARTICLES OF FAITH (CHURCH OF JESUS CHRIST OF LATTER-DAY SAINTS)

1. We believe in God, the Eternal Father, and in His Son, Jesus Christ, and in the Holy Ghost.

2. We believe that men will be punished for their own sins, and not for Adam's transgression.

3. We believe that through the Atonement of Christ, all mankind may be saved, by obedience to the laws and ordinances of the Gospel.

4. We believe that the first principles and ordinances of the Gospel are: first, Faith in the Lord Jesus Christ; second, Repentance; third, Baptism by immersion for the remission of sins; fourth, Laying on of hands for the gift of the Holy Ghost.

5. We believe that a man must be called of God, by prophecy, and by the laying on of hands, by those who are in authority to preach the Gospel and administer in the ordinances thereof.

6. We believe in the same organization that existed in the Primitive Church, viz., apostles, prophets, pastors, teachers, evangelists, etc.

7. We believe in the gift of tongues, prophecy, revelation, visions, healing, interpretation of tongues, etc.

8. We believe the Bible to be the word of God as far as it is translated correctly; we also believe the Book of Mormon to be the word of God.

THE ARTICLES OF FAITH (CHURCH OF JESUS CHRIST OF LATTER-DAY SAINTS) (continued)

9. We believe all that God has revealed, all that He does now reveal, and we believe that He will yet reveal many great and important things pertaining to the Kingdom of God.

10. We believe in the literal gathering of Israel and in the restoration of the Ten Tribes; that Zion will be built upon this [the American] continent; that Christ will reign personally upon the earth; and, that the earth will be renewed and receive its paradisiacal glory.

11. We claim the privilege of worshiping Almighty God according to the dictates of our own conscience, and allow all men the same privilege, let them worship how, where, or what they may.

12. We believe in being subject to kings, presidents, rulers, and magistrates, in obeying, honoring, and sustaining the law.

13. We believe in being honest, true, chaste, benevolent, virtuous, and in doing good to all men; indeed, we may say that we follow the admonition of Paul—We believe all things, we hope all things, we have endured many things, and hope to be able to endure all things. If there is anything virtuous, lovely, or of good report or praiseworthy, we seek after these things.—*Joseph Smith.*

Notes: *The Latter-Day Saints, especially the older groups, retained enough Protestantism (from which most of the early members came) to put together statements of faith in a similar fashion, usually following a similar format. While appearing to affirm the traditional Christian doctrine of the Trinity as spelled out in the Nicene Creed (i.e., one God manifest in three persons: Father, Son, and Holy Ghost), the Latter-Day Saints statements actually affirm the three persons of the Godhead as three separate deities, not one.*

Joseph Smith, Jr., the prophet and founder of the Church of Jesus Christ of Latter-Day Saints, wrote the articles of faith prior to his death in the 1840s. In its first generations, the church was a charismatic body in which the manifestation of the gifts of the spirit were evident (item 7). Mormons believe that Christ, by His atonement, established a situation by which individuals could be saved if they followed the church's laws and ordinances (i.e., if they have faith, repent their sins, are properly baptized, and have a minister of the church lay hands upon them). The emphasis upon immersion is similar to that of the Baptist church.

* * *

DECLARATION OF ESSENTIAL BELIEFS (ZION'S ORDER OF THE SONS OF LEVI)

I believe in being just, fair and charitable towards all men, and claim the right to be treated likewise. Matthew 5:1 through 18; 1st Cor. 13; Romans 14 and first three verses of chapter 15 are the basis for such beliefs and essential to promotion and maintenance of this united order work.

I believe in kindness and pure holy love towards all humanity regardless of nationality, race, color, or politics, and liberty to all according to their obedience to eternal laws and tenable laws of our land.

I believe in equal rights to all humanity according to their abilities and adaptabilities, efficiency and cooperation with the management, and necessary tenacious qualities that must be in whatever business or other any seeks employment, and that all adults should have a right to vote except they that are mentally deranged, incompetent, or criminals, or aliens.

I believe in looking for the good in all persons. Good thoughts make good, joyous feelings. We all have evil as well as good in our makeup, or at least what some thinks of as evil. The proclaimed Savior of perfection was found fault with so much that they crucified him. Thinking of evil in others makes us feel evil or bad, thus let us look for, and think good.

I believe if we claim freedom in a nation for ourselves, to keep that freedom we must zealously allow and maintain and foster just as much freedom for every other human dwelling in that nation, else we lose our freedom.

I believe in accepting truth no matter where it is found and rejecting error likewise. Though rejecting such errors, I do not condemn the maker of such, but seek a way if possible to help that one in an orderly and unoffensive way to see their error and correct such to their joy.

I believe in eternal and divine Creators and worship them. I feel that all peoples that believe in such are worshipping the same creators, whether they call them by the same names as I do or not. And also that all will be rewarded for the good they do regardless of what religion they claim or do not claim, and that we must all suffer for evils or broken laws according to our understanding or lack thereof. Thus degrees of glory. (Ref. 1st Cor. 15:40-42; and Mark 4:20)

I believe that Christ Jesus will return, at which time the willful wicked shall be destroyed for a period of time until they learn their lesson and return or are resurrected to a repentant life in a degree of glory.

I believe the Savior shall also at His return redeem the righteous and they shall dwell with Him a thousand years in progressive joy and the devil and his chief followers shall be bound for a thousand years. During that time all of the inventions of marvel will be put to good usage of purity and holiness: television and radio programs then will be all good.

I believe in the ultimate end of the thousand years reign of the Savior that the leader of evils shall be loosed again for a short time, and great multitudes of followers will make their great stand against the righteous and their defeat shall be such that nearly all will return to the Lord and reject the great deceivers. And only a terrible end shall be for the devil and they with beastly natures and false prophets. (Ref. Rev. 7:9)

I believe all methods of doctoring and healing arts hold a worthy place, and what is good and an aid for one is not so for another. And that all should be used judiciously without prejudice. My choice is Physical Culture methods.

I believe from years of experience in dealing with uncounted thousands seeking help physically, mentally, and spiritually that happiness, success, and joy only can be obtained by a balancing of the three above mentioned, plus a balanced education, free from racial, religious, cultural, color, nationality, tribal, personal, continental, or family bias or prejudice whether one is religious or not so. Yet moral decency must prevail always with an inner responsibility of fairness felt towards all our fellow men. This takes faith coupled with works of love. (Ref. Ephes. 2:5 thru 10.)

I believe last but not least in the redemptive powers of Jesus Christ through the Law of Grace, and that Faith, Repentance, Baptism by immersion for the remission of sins, and the laying on of hands of the gift of the Holy Ghost was essential for me because of my convictions.

Notes: *This statement was composed by founder Marl V. Kilgore.*

*   *   *

Polygamy-Practicing Mormons

ARTICLES OF FAITH (CHRIST'S CHURCH)

1. We believe in God the Eternal Father—as Michael-Adam-God, the Creator; and in His Son, Jesus Christ, the Savior of the World; and in the Holy Ghost, Joseph Smith, Jr., the Witness and Testator and third member of the Godhead that rules the Earth!

2. We believe the first principles and ordinances of the Gospel of Jesus Christ, are:

   (1) Faith in the Lord Jesus Christ, His saving blood, that He atoned for our sins if we accept Him and keep His commandments.

   (2) That in order to receive effective Baptism and the other ordinances and blessings of the Gospel, all men and women must and shall offer the sacrifice of a broken heart (repentance) and a contrite (teachable) spirit.

   (3) Every candidate for receiving the Holy Ghost must be baptised, by immersion in water, by one having authority of Jesus Christ, who himself holds the Priesthood of the Living God and who personally has the Holy Ghost!

   (4) The laying on of hands of those who have the Holy Priesthood and the Holy Ghost, for the conferring of the Holy Ghost.

3. We believe that no one shall be confirmed, or accepted as a member of Christ's Church, until they have shown by a righteous walk of life, and have been voted upon by the members of the body of the Church. They are then to be confirmed a member of the Church by the laying on of hands.

4. We believe that men will be punished for their own sins and not for Adam's transgression.

5. We believe that through the Atonement of Christ all mankind may be saved by obedience to the laws and ordinances of the Gospel.

6. We believe that a man must be called of God, by prophecy, and by the laying on of hands by those who are in authority to preach the Gospel and administer in the ordinances thereof.

7. We believe in the Gifts of the Spirit, namely, the gift of tongues, prophecy, revelation, visions, healings, interpretations of tongues, etc.

8. We believe the Holy Bible to be the word of God as far as it is translated correctly, we also believe the Book of Mormon, the Doctrine and Covenants and the Pearl of Great Price to be the word of the Lord.

9. We believe all that God has revealed, all that He does now reveal, and we believe He will yet reveal many great and important things pertaining to the Kingdom of God!

10. We believe in the literal gathering of Israel and in the restoration of the Ten Tribes; that Zion will be built upon this the American continent; that Christ will reign personally upon the earth; and that the earth will be renewed and receive its paradisiacal glory.

11. We claim the privilege of worshipping the Almighty God according to the dictates of our own conscience and allow all men the same privilege, let them worship how, when, or what they may.

12. We believe in being subject to Almighty God and those kings, presidents, rulers and magistrates who honor and sustain the divine laws of God.

13. We believe in being honest, true, chaste, benevolent, virtuous, and in doing good to all men; indeed we may say that we follow the admonition of Paul—we believe all things, we have endured many things, and hope to be able to endure all things. If there is anything virtuous, lovely, or of good report or praiseworthy, we seek after these things. (*The Branch Magazine*, Volume 1, Number 3, Provo, Utah: Christ's Church, 1979, pp. 2-3)

Notes: *Christ's Church follows the Mormon Fundamentalist position concerning the practice of polygamy, but its statement of faith deals with the more basic beliefs concerning God, the gospel ordinances, atonement, the gifts of the Spirit, and progressive revelation.*

*   *   *

ALEXANDER'S CREED (CHURCH OF JESUS CHRIST IN SOLEMN ASSEMBLY)

We believe in POSTERITY: that the glory of God is intelligence and that intelligence is the right use of knowledge.

We believe in REALITY: that all truth is self-evident and can be and should be demonstrated by those who profess a love for the truth.

We believe in FREEDOM: that all men should worship diety according to the dictates of their own consciences.

We believe in RESPONSIBILITY: that the supreme law makes all men free and that everyone is therefore responsible for his own acts.

ALEXANDER'S CREED (CHURCH OF JESUS CHRIST IN SOLEMN ASSEMBLY) (continued)

We believe in JUSTICE: that all men are at all times immediately surrounded by the best opportunity to win the greatest exaltation they are capable of.

We believe in GRACE: that the law of God is written in the hearts and minds of those elected to the redemption of Israel.

We believe in PATRIARCHAL GOVERNMENT: that the brotherhood of man does not and cannot exist independent of the Fatherhood.

Notes: *Polygamy-practicing groups dissent from the Church of Jesus Christ of Latter-Day Saints primarily by their adherence to the practice of polygamy, rather than in any matter of belief. Thus many of the groups would accept the articles of that church, believing that they had not departed from the faith and practice of the church from the time of its founding. They have no need to write an additional statement of faith.*

The brief statement of the Church of Jesus Christ in Solemn Assembly does little to illuminate the beliefs of this church without some detailed knowledge of the church's doctrine otherwise.

*   *   *

ARTICLES OF FAITH (CHURCH OF THE FIRST BORN)

1. We believe in Michael, the Eternal Father, and in His Son, Jesus Christ, and in Joseph Smith, the Witness and Testator.

2. We believe that men will be punished for their own sins, and not for Adam's transgression; for He partook of mortality, that He might bring forth mortal bodies for His spiritual offspring.

3. We believe that through the Atonement of Christ, all mankind may be saved, by obedience to the laws and ordinances of the Gospel of the First-born.

4. We believe that the first principles and ordinances of the Gospel are; first, Faith in Michael the Archangel, and in His Son Jesus Christ, and in Joseph the Testator; second, Repentance; third, Baptism by immersion for the remission of sins; fourth, Laying on of hands for the gift of the Holy Ghost.

5. We believe that man must be called of God, by prophecy, and by the laying on of hands, by those who are in authority to preach the gospel and administer in the ordinances thereof.

6. We believe in the same organization that Adam first established-upon this earth, viz: the Right of the First-born, Patriarchs, Prophets, Priests, etc; and that the Church of Jesus Christ is an appendage thereto, that the Gentiles might be heirs of salvation.

7. We believe in the Holy Spirit of Promise, the gift of tongues, prophecy, revelation, visions, healing, interpretation of tongues etc.

8. We believe the Bible to be the word of God as far as it is translated correctly; We also believe that the Fullness of the Everlasting Gospel was restored by the Prophet Joseph Smith, and that any departure therefrom is apostasy.

9. We believe all that God has revealed, all that He does now reveal, and we believe that He will yet reveal many great and important things pertaining to the Church and Kingdom of the First-born.

10. We believe that the literal descendants of Israel are legal heirs of the Church and Kingdom of the First-born; and that the Patriarchal Reign shall be re-established upon this continent, as in Adam's day.

11. We claim the privilege of worshiping Almighty God according to the dictates of our own conscience, and allow all men the same privilege, let them worship how, where, or what they may.

12. We believe in being subject to kings, presidents, rulers, and magistrates, in obeying, honoring, and sustaining the law - as declared in the 98th sec. of the Doctrine and Covenants.

13. We believe that this is the dispensation of the Fullness of Times, when all things shall be revealed, and that men are required to obey all the laws and ordinances; we also believe that the Lord will send One Mighty and Strong, to set in order the House of God.

Notes: *These articles are based directly upon those of the Church of Jesus Christ of Latter-Day Saints. The statement differs primarily in the identification of the angel Michael with God the Father (item 1) and in its focus on the prophesied "One Mighty and Strong" (item 13).*

*   *   *

S.A.I. BELIEFS (SONS AHMAN ISRAEL)

1. We believe in an all-powerful, all-loving Heavenly Father and Heavenly Mother, in their son Jesus Christ, in their Holy Spirit pervading all things, in innumerable choirs of archangels, angels, ministers of flame, just men made perfect, etc.

2. We believe we are the literal offspring of these parents, that we have come down to this earth to experience the mystery of mortality preparatory to becoming one with the Messiah, thru whom we have hope of eventual maturity into his very image, becoming Heavenly Progenitors ourselves in the eternities.

3. We believe man has been created to experience joy, not only in this life, but in the life to come; and that thru observance of celestial law upon which all blessings are predicated, man may indeed come to experience perpetual peace and never ending happiness.

4. We believe most of mankind to be in a state of darkness and division from divinity, slaves to their lower passions, tossed to and fro by their love of materialism and by conspiring and self seeking men;

and that only thru gaining a true knowledge of the plan and pattern of the Gospel and by applying such, can man place himself in a position to be purified thru the grace of Jesus Christ.

5. We believe that redemption from this fall can come only thru surrendering our lives to Yeheshuah the Christ, and thru developing a close and intimate relationship to Him thru His Holy Ordinances, and only in this manner is it possible to be quickened by His Spirit and thus become heir to all things.

6. We believe that a religion that does not require the sacrifice of all things never has power sufficient to produce the faith necessary unto life and salvation; and that the mocking finger of the Spiritual Sluggard will ever be pointed at those embarking on the sublime Spiritual quest toward perfection.

7. We believe it possible to learn the dynamics of the creation of worlds even in this life, and that a fully restored priesthood program must include instruction in developing the seeds of Godliness latent within, and in the various methods of controlling the elements and situations in which we dwell.

8. We believe that eternal happiness and everlasting life is obtainable only inasmuch as we take upon ourselves the nature and name of the Messiah, and in enduring to the end of our trial by faith; and that despite the depth of depravity to which we have lowered ourselves, the everenduring mercy of God is ever ready to restore us to his Holy presence.

9. We believe this miraculous cleansing from all sin by the Messiah is effected thru his infinite mercy which can only be received in its fulness thru the temple ordinances and ritualistic ceremonies, without which we have little if any hope of salvation, for in their mystery is hidden the mystery which is Christ who is our only sure road to eternal felicity, peace, and purity.

10. We believe these Holy Ordinances can and will cause tremendous transformation and change within those that receive such in a proper manner and by qualified servants of God, and that it is the Spiritual Counterpart and not the physical rite that effects this metamorphosis.

11. We believe the Law of Moses is dead in Christ, nevertheless we feel that much which is considered such, including many of the more ancient and patriarchal portions and many of the feasts and Holy Days, are yet applicable and advantageous for the Spiritual growth of modern man; and that from the ashes of the Old Law shall arise Phoenix like, a new covenant wherein Israel may be renewed in their relationship to God.

12. We believe that aspiring men, seeking self-honor and glory, have ever been the plague of religious leadership; and that self-righteous gossip and condemnation of others has ever been the folly of their followers; and only thru total tolerance concerning the weakness of others, and thru the ascension of humble and unassuming men to positions of influence, may Zion be rebuilt and the Kingdom of God restored.

13. We believe in the perfect equality of the sexes, that the ultimate destiny of righteous women is to follow in the footsteps of their heavenly mother on high, becoming Queens and Goddesses in the eternities above. To do this we feel it imperative that women share with men the burden of priesthood on earth, that they might reign with them in heaven.

14. We believe that an actual transformation into a new creature in Christ must occur for man to inherit perfect peace, and that the temple ceremonies known to most are insufficient and devoid of the necessary power needed to effect this metamorphosis, and are but an introduction and preparation for deeper and more holy endowments reserved for the more valiant and elect.

15. We believe pearls of great truth can be gleaned from even the most unlikely sources, that some have fallen into the defiling hands of the adversary and are reclaimable; and that there is truth in all religions and that they exist in the will of God for the benefit of all incapable of accepting the fulness of God's higher law.

16. We believe that continual angelic visitations, revelations, and visions must and will prevail in the lives of all that magnify their priesthood properly, and that an increased influx of the Holy Spirit is a direct result of daily inflaming oneself with love for both God and man.

17. We believe it man's prerogative to live only a few of the laws of God, following leaders that encourage such; but feel it more pleasing in the eyes of God to break away from such stagnation, seeking whole heartedly avenues where one may more quickly progress on the road to godhood.

18. We believe in a secret oral tradition of the gospel as revealed by Moses to seventy select elders on Mount Sinai, and perpetuated thru an ancient institution known as the school of the prophets; being a tradition taught by Elijah, Essenes, Jesus, Valentinus, Joseph Smith, etc. and presently preserved in such ancient texts as the Sephir Yetzira, Sephir Zohar, Pistis Sophia, etc.

19. We believe in what is scriptually known as the times of Jacob's trouble, a time of nuclear holocaust survivable thru construction of underground communities of refuge made impregnable to the destroyer; and that thru such communities the elect will preserve all that is virtuous, lovely, and true in anticipation of a dawning of a new age of peace and light after man has learned not to wage war anymore.

20. We believe in the literal gathering of Israel, that the times of the gentiles has come to an end, that the earth and man will be renewed after the tribulation to come; that we can recreate The Garden of Eden once again thru equal sharing of possessions, by purging our minds and bodies of all corruption, and

by learning to live in harmony with natural law and with one another.

21. We believe that thru observance of celestial law, and thru applying principles of perfection, fallen man is redeemed from his alienation from God and brought back into the presence of the Elohiem; that the shekinah glory will return once again to Israel, and a fulness of God's Holy Spirit be enjoyed by all the faithful.

22. We believe that those that endure to the end and who rise up above all things thru their perseverance and fortitude, and who have perfected themselves thru charity, devotion, and ordinance work, will return home into the presence of God and the Lamb, being crowned with eternal glory and celestial splendor, seeing as they are seen, and knowing as they are known, being heir to all the grandeur of godliness.

Notes: *This esoteric organization (see items 14, 16, and 18) departs at numerous points from traditional Mormon belief and practice.*

* * *

Missouri Mormons

ARTICLES OF FAITH [CHURCH OF CHRIST (TEMPLE LOT)]

1. We believe in God the Eternal Father, who only is Supreme; Creator of the universe; Ruler and Judge of all; unchangeable and without respect of persons.

2. We believe in Jesus Christ, the Only Begotten Son of God, the manifestation of God in flesh, who lived, suffered, and died for all mankind; whom we own as our only Leader, Witness and Commander.

3. We believe in the Holy Ghost, the Spirit of Truth, the Comforter, which searcheth the deep things of God, brings to our minds things which are past, reveals things to come, and is the medium by which we receive the revelation of Jesus Christ.

4. We believe that men will be punished for their own sins and not for Adam's transgression, and that as a consequence of the atonement of Christ "all little children are alive in Christ, and also all they that are without the law. For the power of redemption cometh on all they that have no law; wherefore, he that is not condemned, or he that is under no condemnation, can not repent; and unto such, baptism availeth nothing." (Moroni 8:25, 26)

5. We believe that through the atonement of Christ all men may be saved by obedience to the laws and ordinances of the Gospel; viz.: Faith in God and in the Lord Jesus Christ; Repentance and Baptism by immersion for the remission of sins; Laying on of Hands for: (a) Ordination; (b) Blessing of Children; (c) Confirmation and the Gift of the Holy Ghost; (d) Healing of the Sick.

6. We believe in the literal second coming and millennial reign of Jesus Christ; in the resurrection of the Dead, and in Eternal Judgment; that men will be rewarded or punished according to the good or evil they may have done.

7. We believe in the powers and gifts of the everlasting Gospel; viz.: The word of wisdom; the word of knowledge; the gift of faith; the gift of healing; working of miracles; prophecy; discerning of spirits; divers kinds of tongues; interpretation of tongues.

8. We believe the fruits of the spirit to be love, joy, peace, long suffering, gentleness, goodness, faith, meekness and temperance.

9. We believe that in the Bible is contained the word of God, that the Book of Mormon is an added witness for Christ, and that these contain the "fullness of the gospel."

10. We believe in the principle of continuous revelation; that the canon of scripture is not full, that God inspires men in every age and among all people, and that He speaks when, where, and through whom He may choose.

11. We believe that where there are six or more regularly baptized members, one of whom is an elder, there the Church exists with full power of church extension when acting in harmony with the law of God.

12. We believe that a man must be called of God by revelation, and ordained by those having authority, to enable him to preach the gospel and administer the ordinances thereof.

13. We believe in the same church organization as existed in the time of Christ and His Apostles. The highest office in the church is that of an apostle, of whom there are twelve, who constitute special witnesses for Jesus Christ. They have the missionary supervision and the general watchcare of all of the churches.

14. The primary function of the general church, of which each local church is a component part, is missionary and the building up and extension of the Kingdom of God in all the world.

15. We believe that local churches should govern their own affairs, and that general church officials should not dominate or interfere therewith. On invitation such general officers may, with propriety, give counsel and assistance. Local congregations are subject to the Articles of Faith and Practice and must be governed thereby.

16. We believe the Church of Christ comprehends the true brotherhood of man where each esteems his brother as himself and wherein the divine command to "love your neighbor as yourself" is demonstrated by the prevalence of social equality.

17. We believe that all men are stewards under God and answerable to Him not only for the distribution of accumulated wealth, but for the manner in which such wealth is secured. The primary purpose of stewardship is not the increase of church revenue or

the mere contribution of money by those who have to those who have not, but to bring men to a realization of the common fatherhood of God, and the universal brotherhood of man in all the affairs and expressions of life, and to maintain such social adjustment that each may enjoy the bounty and gifts of God, and be free to exercise his talents and ability to enrich the life of all.

18. We believe that men should labor for their own support and that of their dependents. Ministers of the gospel are not absolved from this responsibility, but when chosen or appointed by the church to devote their entire time to missionary work, their families are to be provided for out of the general church funds. The admonition of Christ that the ministry should not provide purse or scrip for their journey, but go trusting in God and the people is applicable.

19. We believe that the temporal affairs of the general church are to be administered by the general bishopric under the direction of the general conferences of the church and under the supervision of the Council of Twelve. The temporal affairs of the local churches shall be administered by local bishops under the supervision and direction of the local congregations.

20. We believe that marriage is ordained of God, and that the law of God provides for but one companion in wedlock for either man or woman. In case of a breach of this covenant by adultery, the innocent one may remarry.

21. We are opposed to war. Men are not justified in taking up arms against their fellows except as a last resort in defense of their lives and to preserve their liberty.

22. We believe in the literal gathering of Israel, and in the restoration of the ten lost tribes.

23. We believe a temple will be built in this generation, in Independence, Missouri, wherein Christ will reveal himself and endow his servants whom he chooses with power to preach the gospel in all the world to every kindred, tongue, and people, that the promise of God to Israel may be fulfilled.

24. We believe that a New Jerusalem shall be built upon this land "unto the remnant of the seed of Joseph." (Ether 6:6-8; III Nephi 10:1-4), "which city shall be built, beginning at the Temple Lot." (Doc. and Cov. 83:1)

25. We believe that ministry and membership should abstain from the use of tobacco, intoxicating liquors and narcotics, and should not affiliate with any society which administers oaths or covenants in conflict with the law of God, or which interferes with their duties as freemen and citizens.

Notes: *The Latter-Day Saints groups remaining in the midwest after the death of Joseph Smith, Jr., never accepted polygamy or many other doctrines that became prominent during the period under Brigham Young's leadership. The*

Missouri Mormons have tended to follow a montheism, believing that Jesus Christ was not God, but God's Son.

Compare the articles of the Church of Christ (Temple Lot) with those of the Church of Jesus Christ of Latter-Day Saints. There is no assertion of three deities. The number of ordinances (item 5) has increased. Pacifism is advocated. Tobacco, alcohol and drugs are opposed. Most distinctively, the church owns property in Independence, Missouri, which it believes will be the site of a future kingdom of God (item 24). These identical articles are followed by the Church of Christ with the Elijah Messenger, formed by former members of the Church of Christ (Temple Lot).

* * *

FAITH AND DOCTRINE (CHURCH OF JESUS CHRIST RESTORED)

"We believe in God, the Creator of all things, our Father, who is unchangeable, from everlasting to everlasting, without beginning of days or end of years, the source of all righteous inspiration, whose capacity for love and wrath are beyond man's ability to know or find out. We believe He has given His Son the task of judging each man according to the works and faith they have practiced while on this earth. Therefore, there is no condemnation for the man who lives and dies ignorant of God's laws. Men choosing to ignore God's laws, however, live under the threat of condemnation from day to day and their just judgment is sure, except they repent and live according to all the principles of the gospel of Christ.

"We believe that just as God spoke to man in days past, so he speaks today. We expect it. We experience it. We are grateful because it delivers man's mind from unstability, confusion and anxiety.

"We believe that Jesus of Nazareth was and is the Only Begotten Son of God; that with God He presided in the beginning over the creation of all things and that it was by Jesus Christ that God created all things that are.

"We believe God directs, comforts, teaches, chastizes and/or reproves men by the ministry of His Holy Spirit, either directly or through divinely called ministers.

"We believe that as man 'feels after God' by diligent study and constant prayer, he is practicing faith and that by willfully enduring and gradually overcoming all things, under the protection and guidance of divinely called ministers, his faith will become knowledge.

"We believe that Jesus built His own church for the purpose of making men perfect in this life. Anything less than this, is not of Jesus Christ. The church that preaches the fullness of His gospel, accordingly promises the perfection of the soul in this life on condition of total obedience to godly principles.

"We believe repentance from doing sin and living an unproductive life (dead works), is essential for any man, woman or youth who by reason of intelligence (knowing right from wrong) are accountable before God and therefore as often as may be necessary, must conscientiously practice sincere repentance.

"Baptism by immersion in water, as performed by the Son of God in the river Jordan by an authoritative minister of God, for the remission of sins, is absolutely necessary to man's salvation. Without it there is no membership in the church and kingdom of Christ.

"We believe the Eucharist or Sacrament of the Lord's Supper, properly observed by authoritative ministers of God, provides for those who are members of Jesus' church and them alone, the opportunity to consider the blessed sacrifice of the Lamb, Jesus, to give thanks for that atonement His death made possible, and to confess to God publicly or privately the sins that separate man from his Maker and the Holy Ghost.

"The physical body and the spirit (or intelligence) in every man born into this world constitutes the soul of man and because God so loved the world (the souls of men), He allowed His Only Begotten Son to come in the meridian of time, to offer the only acceptable sacrifice for the sins of the world—His death on a cross and by so doing He gave His Father (and our Father) an acceptable offering and a complete and effectual reconciliation and mediation for mankind. Men may lay claim to this atonement only in the church that bears His name and teaches all He taught.

"We believe the fullness of the doctrine of Christ Jesus, is the only way by which man may be saved, and that giving support to any church which does not preach the fullness of the doctrine of Jesus is supporting that which may be well-intentioned perhaps but nevertheless, a counterfeit and therefore, her promises are vain.

"Man is required (if he desires the salvation of his soul) to live by every word that proceedeth forth out of the mouth of God. We believe those words as they are found recorded in the Inspired Correction of the Scriptures (Bible)—even though all biblical references in this tract are to the King James Version—plus the Book of Mormon, the Doctrine and Covenants, and the latest revelations (called Supplements), received by our present prophet, Elder Stanley King and sanctioned by the saints.

"We believe that just as the original Church of Christ as organized by Jesus himself, apostacized, so also the Reorganized Church of Jesus Christ of Latter Day Saints—lawful successor to the church restored by Joseph Smith, Jr. in 1830—has also apostacized administratively. There are many good honorable people within that denomination as there are in many other denominations of the world today but this fact does not negate the evidences of her unfortunate apostacy.

"We believe Joseph Smith, Jr. was and is the great Prophet of this last dispensation and that as a man he may possibly have erred from time to time but as God's servant, ordained from before the foundation of the world, to speak forth His Word, He did not err.

"We believe Sanctification must be attained by the honest in heart. It is the process of perfection. Attaining perfection while living in a system of houses, stores, streets and divisive devilish influences of this present age is impossible. We believe the only way to effectively live in the world but not be part of it, is in the stake; the stake as revealed by God through Joseph Smith, Jr., not those promoted by the RLDS or Utah churches. The Stakes divinely organized always start with the building of the House of the Lord (temple) first. This church has prepared for five years to do this and at this writing (1975) are very near to commencing such a work in obedience to His word and to His glory.

"The obligation upon the saint (member of the church) is to become independent above every other creature or system beneath the Celestial world. Practicing daily the attributes of God is a way of life in the Stake. The Law of Preference is taught and lived.

"We believe in being good stewards over all God gives us. Sacrifice is expected and desired by members in this church so that God's final glorious chapter of His strange act might be completed. There is no perfection without sacrifice and where there is no perfection there is no church. Man must not fail to please God. Jesus willingly sacrificed all for His Father. So must we.

"We believe heaven is a place of varied glories. There is the Celestial, Terrestrial and Telestial glory that man may attain. We believe that when this earth has fulfilled itself in the present system of things that it will be changed and provide for the righteous the greatest glory of all— Celestial glory.

"We believe there are no authoritative High Priests on the earth today (1975) but that very soon this ministry will be restored to the salvation of man, the redemption of Zion and the everlasting glory of God.

"There is historical support for Presidencies in the Church of Christ. We do believe they are acceptable to God and necessary for the church to function orderly.

"There are other tenets of faith that make up the fullness of the doctrine of Jesus such as Ministerial Authority (who really are the servants of God?), the gifts and fruits of God's Holy Spirit, Baptism for the dead (by revelation through a prophet), Endowments, and other temple ordinances, Celestial Priesthood Education (School of the Prophets), equality, the gathering of scattered Israel, plus many many more."

Notes: *The Church of Jesus Christ Restored, a recent splinter from the Reorganized Church of Jesus Christ of Latter-Day Saints, has based its statement upon that of the parent body.*

* * *

A BRIEF STATEMENT OF FAITH
(REORGANIZED CHURCH OF JESUS CHRIST
OF LATTER-DAY SAINTS)

There is no official creed endorsed as such by the Church of Jesus Christ. It has been well stated that the creed of the church is "all Truth." We believe fundamentals leading to all truth are stated in the Bible, Book of Mormon, and Doctrine and Covenants.

Certain of the basic truths, however, have stood out in bold relief because of their very nature and have been gathered together in a statement or Epitome of Faith. This basic list is worthy of study and understanding which, of course, can only come as a member searches diligently in the Scriptures just mentioned and in the standard literary works of representative church writers.

We Believe:

In God the Eternal Father, creator of the heavens and the earth.

In the divine Sonship of Jesus Christ the Savior of all men who obey his gospel;

In the Holy Ghost whose function it is to guide all men unto the truth.

In the Gospel of Jesus Christ which is the power of God unto salvation.

In the six fundamental doctrinal principles of the gospel: Faith; Repentance; Baptism by immersion in water; the Baptism of the Holy Ghost; Laying on of the Hands for the healing of the sick, for conferring of the Holy Ghost, ordination, blessing of children, and other special blessings; Resurrection of the dead, and the Eternal Judgment.

In the justice of God who will reward or punish all men according to their works, and not solely according to their profession.

In the same kind of organization that existed in the primitive church: apostles, prophets, evangelists, pastors, teachers, elders, bishops, seventies, etc.

In the word of God contained in the Bible, as far as it is correctly translated.

In the word of God contained in the Book of Mormon, being a record of divine dealings with men in the new world as in the old.

In the word of God revealed today and recorded in the Doctrine and Covenants of the church.

In the willingness and ability of God to continue his revelation of his will to men to the end of time.

In the powers and gifts of the gospel: faith, discernment of spirits, prophecy, revelation, healing, visions, tongues, and their interpretation, wisdom, charity, temperance, brotherly love, etc.

In marriage as instituted and ordained of God whose law provides for but one companion in wedlock, for either man or woman, excepting in case of death. When the marriage contract is broken by trangression, the innocent party is free to remarry.

In the Book of Mormon declaration: "There shall not any man among you have save it be one wife; and concubines he shall have none."

In the Doctrine of Stewardships; that is, that every man is accountable to God for the conduct of his life and the use of his material blessings.

In the Divine Commission to the church to establish a Christian Community called Zion built upon the basis of stewardship and the principle of equality of opportunity, and where each member shall give according to his capacity and receive according to his needs.

Notes: *The statement of the Reorganized Church of Latter-Day Saints, the second largest of the Mormon groups, is much closer to that of the other Missouri groups than to that of the Church of Jesus Christ of Latter-Day Saints. The ordinances, here considered as "fundamental doctrinal principles," differ in number. There is no statement on pacifism, and polygamy is explicitly opposed.*

* * *

STATEMENT OF FAITH AND BELIEF (REORGANIZED CHURCH OF JESUS CHRIST OF LATTER-DAY SAINTS)

We believe in God the eternal Father, source and center of all love and life and truth, who is almighty, infinite, and unchanging, in whom and through whom all things exist and have their being.

We believe in Jesus Christ, the Only Begotten Son of God, who is from everlasting to everlasting; through whom all things were made, who is God in the flesh, being incarnate by the Holy Spirit for man's salvation; who was crucified, died and rose again; who is mediator between God and man, and the judge of both the living and the dead, whose dominion has no end.

We believe in the Holy Spirit, the living presence of the Father and the Son, who in power, intelligence, and love works in the minds and hearts of men to free them from sin, uniting them with God as his sons, and with each other as brethren. The Spirit bears record of the Father and of the Son, which Father, Son, and Holy Ghost are one God.

We believe that the Holy Spirit empowers men committed to Christ with gifts of worship and ministry. Such gifts, in their richness and diversity, are divided severally as God wills, edifying the body of Christ, empowering men to encounter victoriously the circumstances of their discipleship, and confirming the new creation into which men are called as sons of God.

We believe that the Holy Spirit creates, quickens, and renews in men such graces as love, joy, peace, mercy, gentleness, meekness, forbearance, temperance, purity of heart, brotherly kindness, patience in tribulation, and faithfulness before God in seeking to build up his kingdom.

We believe that man is endowed with freedom and created to know God, to love and serve him, and enjoy his fellowship. In following the dictates of pride and in declaring his independence from God, man loses the power to fulfill the purpose of his creation and becomes the servant of sin, whereby he is divided within himself and estranged from God, and his fellows. This condition, experienced by our ancestors who first came to a knowledge of good and evil, is shared by all who are granted the gift of accountability.

We believe that man cannot be saved in the kingdom of God except by the grace of the Lord Jesus Christ, who loves us while we are yet in our sins, and who gave his life to reconcile us unto God. Through this atonement of the Lord Jesus Christ and by the gift of the Holy Spirit, men receive power to choose God and to commit their lives to him; thus are they turned from rebellion, healed from sin,

STATEMENT OF FAITH AND BELIEF (REORGANIZED CHURCH OF JESUS CHRIST OF LATTER-DAY SAINTS) (continued)

renewed in spirit, and transformed after the image of God in righteousness and holiness.

We believe that all men are called to have faith in God and to follow Jesus Christ as Lord, worshipping the Father in his name. In this life those who hear the gospel and repent should commit their lives to Christ in baptism by immersion in water and the laying on of hands. Through living by these principles they participate in God's promise of forgiveness, reconciliation, and eternal life.

We believe that the church was established by Jesus Christ. In its larger sense it encompasses those both living and dead, who, moved by the Spirit of God, acknowledge Jesus as Lord. In its corporate sense, it is the community of those who have covenanted with Christ. As the body of Christ through which the Word of God is tangibly expressed among men, the church seeks to discern the will of God and to surrender itself to him in worship and service. It is enlightened, sustained, and renewed by the Holy Spirit. It is to bring the good news of God's love to all people, reconciling them to God through faith in Jesus Christ. The church administers the ordinances through which the covenant is established, cares for all within its fellowship, ministers to the needy, wages war on evil, and strives for the kingdom of God.

We believe that all men are called to be stewards under God. They are accountable to him, in the measure of their perception of the divine purpose in creation and redemption, for managing all gifts and resources given their care. In the exercise of stewardship, men embody the divine will and grow in spiritual maturity through developing native powers and skills achieving dominion over the physical order and perfecting human relationships in the Spirit of Christ.

We believe that the kingdom of God sustains men as the stable and enduring reality of history, signifying the total Lordship of God over all human life and endeavor. The kingdom is always at hand in judgment and promise, confronting all men with the joyful proclamation of God's rule and laying claim upon them as they acknowledge the new Creation in Christ. The full revelation of the kingdom awaits the final victory over evil, when the will of God shall prevail and his rule shall extend over all human relations to establish the dominion of peace, justice, and truth. To this end the church proclaims the gospel of the kingdom both as present reality and future hope in the midst of a faithless world.

We believe that Zion is the means by which the prophetic church participates in the world to embody the divine intent for all personal and social relations. Zion is the implementation of those principles, processes, and relationships which give concrete expression to the power of the kingdom of God in the world. It affirms the concern of the gospel with the structures of our common life together and promotes the expression of God's reconciling love in the world, thus bringing forth the divine life in human society. The church is called to gather her covenant people into signal communities where they live out the will of God in the total life of society. While this concrete expression of the kingdom of God must have a central point of beginning it reaches out to every part of the world where the prophetic church is in mission.

We believe that all are called according to the gifts of God unto them to accept the commission and cost of discipleship. Some are chosen through the spirit of wisdom and revelation and ordained by those who are in authority in the church to serve in specialized ministries. These include ministry to persons, families, and community, as well as preaching, teaching, administering the ordinances, and directing the affairs of the church. The authority of every member of the body in this respective calling emerges out of divine endowment to him and his faithfulness in servanthood with Christ.

We believe that the ordinances witness the continuing life of Christ in the church, providing the experiences in which God and man meet in the sealing of covenant. In the ordinances God uses common things, even the nature of man, to express the transcendent and sacramental meaning of creation. God thereby provides the continuing means of investing his grace in human life for its renewal and redemption.

We believe that God reveals himself to man. He enters into the minds of men through the Holy Spirit to disclose himself to them and to open their understanding to the inner meaning of his revelation in history and in the physical order. Revelation centers in Jesus Christ, the incarnate word, who is the ultimate disclosure of truth and the standard by which all other claims to truth are measured.

We believe that the Scriptures witness to God's redemptive action in history and to man's response to that action. When studied through the light of the Holy Spirit they illumine men's minds and hearts and empower them to understand in greater depth the revelation in Christ. Such disclosure is experienced in the hearts of men rather than in the words by which the revelation is interpreted and communicated. The Scriptures are open because God's redemptive work is eternal, and our discernment of it is never complete.

We believe in the resurrection. This principle encompasses the divine purpose to conserve and renew life. It guarantees that righteousness will prevail and that, by the power of God, men move from death into life. In resurrection God quickens and transforms the soul, i.e. the body and spirit, bringing man into fellowship with his Son.

We believe in eternal judgment. It is the wisdom of God bringing the whole creation under divine judgment for good. This judgment is exercised through men as they are quickened by the Holy Spirit to comprehend the eternal implications of divine truth. Through the judgment of God the eternal destiny of men is determined according to divine wisdom and love and according to their response to God's call to them. The principle of eternal judgment acknowledges that Christ is the judge of all human aspiration and achievement and that he summons men to express truth in decision until all things are reconciled under God.

We believe that the inner meaning and end toward which all history moves is revealed in Christ. He is at work in the midst of history, reconciling all things unto God in order, beauty, and peace. This reconciliation brings to fulfillment the kingdom of God upon earth. Christ's presence guarantees the victory of righteousness and peace over the injustice, suffering, and sin of our world. The tension between our assurance that the victory has been won in Christ and our continuing experience in this world where God's sovereignty is largely hidden is resolved in the conviction that Christ will come again. The affirmation of his coming redeems us from futility and declares the seriousness of all life under the unfailing and ultimate sovereignty of God.

Notes: *This statement, one of several circulated by the church, is taken from a volume published by the church's publishing concern,* Exploring the Faith *(Independence, MO: Herald House, 1970).*

*   *   *

Miscellaneous Mormons

ARTICLES OF FAITH [CHURCH OF JESUS CHRIST (BICKERTONITE)]

1. We believe in God, the Eternal Father, and in His Son, Jesus Christ, and in the Holy Ghost.

2. We believe that man will be punished for his own transgressions, and not for Adam's.

3. We believe that through the Atonement of Jesus Christ, all people may be saved, through obedience to the ordinances of the Gospel.

4. We believe in the principles of the Gospel as taught by the Saviour, Faith in Jesus Christ; Repentance and then baptism by immersion for the remission of sins, and the Laying on of hands for the gift of the Holy Ghost.

5. We believe in Feet Washing. John 13:5.

6. We believe the angel has flown. Rev. 14:6,7.

7. We believe that a man must be called by God, by His Holy Spirit and by the laying on of hands, by those in authority to preach the Gospel and administer in the Holy Ordinances thereof.

8. We believe in the same organization as was instituted by Jesus Christ, namely apostles, prophets, pastors, teachers, evangelists, etc.

9. We believe in the various gifts of the Gospel such as the gifts of tongues, prophecy, revelation, visions, healing, interpretation of tongues, etc.

10. We believe the Bible to be the word of God as far as it is correctly translated, and we also believe the Book of Mormon to be the word of God.

11. We believe what God has revealed, and what He may yet reveal. We believe that He will reveal much pertaining to the building up of His Kingdom upon the earth.

12. We believe in the literal gathering of Israel, including the Ten lost Tribes, also the Seed of Joseph (American Indians) on this land of America; and that Christ will eventually come, and reign on the earth one thousand years, between the First and Second Resurrections. See Rev. 20-1 & 6 inclusive.

13. We believe in, and claim the privilege of worshipping God according to the dictates of our own conscience. We concede and allow all others the same right.

14. We believe in being subject to Kings, Queens, Presidents, Rulers and Magistrates; in obeying, honoring and sustaining the Laws.

15. In conclusion, we say "whatever things are true, and honest, and just, and pure, and lovely, and of good report," we seek to uphold and maintain: for the fruits of the Spirit are love, joy, peace, long suffering, gentleness, goodness, faith, meekness, and temperance; "against such there is no law." The apostle Paul says to "prove all things, and hold fast to that which is good," Amen.

Notes: *These articles are derived directly from those of the Church of Jesus Christ of Latter-Day Saints. The church has added several articles on foot washing (item 5) and the angel of Revelation 14:6-7 (item 6), and has made several minor changes in wording.*

*   *   *

STATEMENT OF BELIEF [RESTORED CHURCH OF JESUS CHRIST (WALTON)]

1. We believe in the Godhead there are two personages, God the Father and Christ the Son. They both dwell in Celestial glory. Man was created, male and female, in the image (likeness) of both the Father and the Son, by whom were all things created. (Genesis 1:2, 29; John 1:1, 10, 16 I.V.; 3 Nephi 4:44-48; D & C 17:4-5)

2. We believe there is a Devil-Satan and that he is also from the beginning and that he is a fallen angel spirit and that he has legions of fallen spirits with him, and their stated purpose is to destroy man both body and soul and our disobedience to God gives the Devil power over us. (Genesis 3:1, 4-5; Rev. 12:8 I.V.; 2 Nephi 1:101-103, 120-125; D & C 1:6, 28:10-11; 2 Cor. 4:4)

3. We believe in the Holy Ghost, the Spirit of Truth, which is the life and power of God, to lead men into all truth, and back into the likeness and image of God, even a life of holiness, which is eternal life with God and the Christ. (Genesis 6:59-65, 67-71 I.V.; John 16:13-15; 3 Nephi 5:32-38; D & C 32:3, 34:5b)

4. We believe that men will be punished for their own sins and not for Adam's transgression, and that as a consequence of the atonement of Christ "all little children are alive in Christ, and also all they that are without the law." (Moroni 8:25-26). We believe that through Christ's Law and His Ordinances of the Gospel administered by Priesthood called of God by Revelation.

5.　All of His Commandments must be kept! We believe that the Doctrine of Jesus Christ consists of the following laws and ordinances: 1. Faith toward God and in the Lord Jesus Christ; 2. Repentance from all sin; 3. Baptism by immersion, both men and women, and children after 8 years of age, for the remission of sins; 4. Laying on of hands for the gift of the Holy Ghost, according to the scriptures (Acts 2:38, 8:14-19, 19:2-6 and Hebrews 6:1-3); 5. Resurrection of the dead; 6. Eternal judgement.

6.　We believe that the "Kingdom Order" can exist without the church, but the church cannot be without the "Keys of the Kingdom" and through priesthood ordained of God. (Matthew 16:19-20 I.V.; D & C 65 and 87:1-3)

7.　We believe Jesus Christ is the same today as He was yesterday, and we believe in the principle of continuous revelation; that the canon of scripture is not full, that God raises up Prophets and inspires them in every age and among all people, and that He speaks when, where and through whom He may choose. (Isaiah 28:10, 13; Hebrews 13:8; Amos 3:7)

8.　We believe in the "Holy Order of Enoch" and in sharing all things equal in order to establish Zion. (D & C 51, 77:1). We Believe Zion will be established before Christ returns (D & C 49:4-5) and that only those who keep all of His commandments will be authorized of God. (D & C 81:3b)

9.　We believe in the same kind of organization that existed in the primitive church, viz. apostles, evangelists, pastors, teachers, and all other officers provided for in the scriptures. (Ephesians 4:11-15). We believe in the powers and gifts of the everlasting gospel, viz: wisdom, knowledge, faith, healing, and miracles, prophecy, tongues and interpretation of tongues, etc.

10.　We believe that a man must be called of God by prophecy and by the laying on of hands, by those in authority to do so, to entitle him to preach the gospel and administer in the ordinances thereof. And that men only are to be ordained to preach the gospel and function in the priesthood ordinances. (Exodus 40:15, John 15:16, Galatians 1:11-12, Hebrews 5:1-6)

11.　We believe that in all matters of controversy upon the duty of man toward God, and in reference to preparation and fitness for the world to come, the word of God should be decisive and the end of dispute; and that when God directs, man should obey. We believe in the doctrine of the resurrection of the body, that man will be judged and rewarded or punished according to his works; according to the good or degree of evil he shall have done. (Matthew 7:18-29, 1 Cor. 15:34-42, Rev. 20:12-13)

12.　We believe in the Inspired Version of the Bible, and in the Stick of Joseph commonly known as the Nephite Record and in the 1835 first edition of the Doctrine and Covenants containing the Lectures on Faith accepted by the Church in General Assembly at Kirtland, Ohio.

13.　We believe a temple will be built in Independence, Missouri, wherein Christ will reveal himself and endow his servants whom He chooses with power to preach the gospel in all the world to every kindred, tongue and people, that the promises of God may be fulfilled and the tribes of Israel gathered. This temple will be recognized as God's temple by a celestial cloud over it. (D & C 83:2)

14.　We believe that marriage is ordained of God; and that the law of God provides for but one companion in wedlock for either man or woman. In cases where the contract of marriage is broken by death the remaining one is free to marry again, and in case of breach of the marriage covenant the innocent one is free to remarry. We believe that the doctrine of a plurality and a community of wives are heresies, and are opposed to the Law of God. (Mark 10:2-12, Jacob 2:36, D & C 49:3a-c)

15.　We believe that men should worship God in spirit and in truth; and we claim the privilege for ourselves and all men of worshipping Almighty God according to the dictates of their conscience providing that such worship does not require a violation of the constitutional law of the land. (John 4:23-24) (From an undated tract published by the church.)

SETTING THE CHURCH IN ORDER

The underlying theme and mission of the church is to bring about a reunited restoraton movement. The church teaches that this disunity has been allowed by God in order for believers to see that things must be done God's way and that a recognition of errors must take place in order to reunite and build Zion together on these points:

1.　Taking as our standard of faith the Inspired Version of the Holy Scriptures, the Nephite Record, and the divine revelations given to Joseph Smith, Jr.

2.　Affirming that the Nephite Record is a divine record written by men inspired of God, delivered by an angel of God and interpreted by Joseph Smith, Jr., by command of God with the use of ancient instruments of interpretation called the Urim and Thummim.

3.　That God has designated Independence, Missouri, as the center place of Zion. That the honest in heart, the saints of God, will begin their gathering here.

4.　That Israel shall be gathered and God shall restore the ten lost tribes.

5.　That the Law of Consecration is necessary to the establishment of Zion, with God's Bishop, directing a people pure in heart, by sacrifice and covenant.

6.　That God is unchangeable and speaks His divine will yesterday, today and forever to an obedient people, and that Christ will reign personally upon the earth, and that the earth will be restored to its paradisiacal glory.

7.　That in order to accomplish the work of the Lord committed to his people, it is necessary for them to unite in "one" organization, in harmony with the Holy and Sacred Law of God. (*Let's Together Set the Church in Order*, published by the church, nd)

Notes: *This statement is unique among Mormon groups for its assertion of a bipartite Godhead (rather than a tripartite one). As in the state of the Church of Christ (Temple Lot), the temple lot in Independence is affirmed as the center of a coming kingdom. Like the Reorganized Church of Jesus Christ of Latter-Day Saints, the Restored Church of Jesus Christ uses the Inspired Version of the Bible, produced by Joseph Smith, Jr. The "Record of the Nephites" is what is commonly known as the Book of Mormon.*

* * *

BELIEFS OF THE TRUE CHURCH OF CHRIST, RESTORED (ROBERTS)

1. We believe in God the eternal father, and his son Jesus Christ, and in the Holy Ghost, which is the glory and power of God. It is neither a person nor a personage in the Godhead.

2. We believe that men and women will be punished for their own sins, and not for Adam's transgressions.

3. We believe that through the atonement of Jesus Christ all of the human race is saved by obedience to the laws and ordinances of the true gospel of Jesus Christ.

4. We believe and practice these ordinances of the true gospel of Jesus Christ are: 1st, faith in the Lord Jesus Christ; 2nd, Repentance: 3rd, water baptism for the remission of sins by immersion: 4th, laying on of hands for the true gift of the Holy Ghost, with the physical evidence of speaking in other tongues and the baptism of fire with the evidence of gloven tongues of fire coming upon our physical body in order to receive divine health: 5th, the Lord's supper by the miracle of consubstantiation, communion and washing of the saints' feet during the new moon sabbaths and the seven annual feasts of the Lord our God.

5. We believe that men and women must be called of God by inspiration and ordained by laying on of hands by those who are duly commissioned to preach the true gospel of Jesus Christ and administer in the ordinances thereof.

6. We believe in the same organization that existed in the primitive church of Jesus Christ, viz., apostles, prophets, evangelists, pastors, teachers, etc.

7. We believe and practice the powers and gifts of the everlasting gospel, viz., the word of wisdom, the word of knowledge, the gift of great faith, the gifts the healing, the gift of mighty miracles, the gift of prophesy, the gift of beholding of angels and ministering spirits, the gift of all kinds of tongues, the gift of the interpretation of languages and of divers kinds of tongues, dreams, visions, the gift of revelation, and the fruit of spirit is love, joy, peace, longsuffering, gentleness, goodness, faith, meekness and temperance.

8. We believe in the word of God recorded in the Holy Bible and the word of God recorded in the book of Mormon (The Nephite Record), and in the revelations of the prophets Joseph Smith, Jr., and James J. Strang.

9. We believe all that God has revealed; all that he does now reveal; and all that God will yet reveal many more great and important things pertaining to the theocratic kingdom of God, and the second coming of Jesus Christ.

10. We believe in the literal gathering of Israel, and in the restoration of the ten tribes, that Zion (New Jerusalem) will be established upon the western continent; that Jesus Christ will reign personally upon the earth a thousand years; and that the earth will be renewed, and receive its paradisiacal glory.

11. We believe in the literal resurrection of the body, and that the dead in Jesus Christ will rise first, and that the rest of the dead live not again until the thousand years are expired.

12. We claim the privilege of worshipping almighty God according to the dictates of our conscience unmolested, and allow all men and women the same privilege, let them worship how or where they may.

13. We believe in being subject to Kings, Queens, Presidents, Rulers, and Magistrates, in obeying, honoring, and sustaining the law according to the word of God.

14. We believe in being honest, true, chaste, temperate, benevolent, virtuous, and upright, and in doing good to all; indeed, we may say that we follow the admonition of Paul, we believe all things, we hope all things, we have endured very many things, and hope to be able to endure all things. Everything virtuous, lovely, praiseworthy, and of good report, we seek after, looking forward to the recompense of reward.

15. We believe that the seventh day is the true sabbath of the Lord our God and the seventh day sabbath begins at sunset Friday to sunset Saturday and all believers in Christ Jesus must keep this day as the true sabbath day and no other day ever.

16. We believe that the new moon sabbaths, the seven annual feasts, the seventh year sabbath, and the jubilee year sabbath of the Lord our God must be observed and kept by all believers in Christ Jesus forever.

17. We believe that the law of clean and unclean meats and all other laws of health must be observed and kept by all believers in Christ Jesus forever.

18. We believe in salvation for the living and the dead and in building temples and in performing temple ordinances for both the living and the dead, such as, the baptism for the dead, washings, anointings, sealings and marriage for time and for all eternity, etc.

19. We believe in the virgin birth of Jesus Christ. We believe that he was conceived by the power of the Holy Spirit and that neither the seed of Mary nor the

BELIEFS OF THE TRUE CHURCH OF CHRIST, RESTORED (ROBERTS) (continued)

seed of Joseph was used in the virgin birth. Also that the Virgin Mary only encompasseth the child Jesus. Read St. Matt. 1:18-25: St. Luke 1:26-38; Isaiah 66:7 and Jeremiah 31:22.

20. We believe and practice all things common, even the united firm of Zion in all our stakes of Zion, according to the Holy Scriptures.

21. We believe in the translation of the Saints, such as Enoch, Elijah, John the beloved and the three Nephite disciples; also that the faithful Saints on earth will obtain complete Christ-like righteousness and be caught up in the air to meet our Lord Jesus Christ at his second coming.

Notes: *This statement is derived from that of the Church of Jesus Christ of Latter-Day Saints, but contains numerous additions such as the reference to James J. Strang, who claimed to be the successor to Joseph Smith, Jr., founder of the Mormon movement. The church is sabbatarian and keeps the Old Testament holy days and dietary practices.*

Chapter 3
Communal Family

TWENTY-FOUR RULES (AMANA CHURCH SOCIETY)

Buedingen, July 4, 1716

A most important revelation of the Spirit of the Lord through Johann Adam Gruber in accordance with which the new communities were established and received into "the gracious covenant of the Lord." These rules remain the basis of the faith of the community and are, indeed, the foundation on which the whole edifice of the community is erected.

Hear yea, Hear yea, the word of the Lord, you who are still here and profess to be members of the community! So speaketh the Lord: You have seen what I have begun among you and how my servants have, to some extent, prepared the ground to lay the foundation stones on which the whole structure shall be founded.

But do you consider this sufficient? That would be far from my justice. I have only, to some extent, revealed your motives as far as you were able to bear it. I, who have stepped in your midst, have heard all your words, all your promises, which you have given me although I find amongst you only a very few who have a heart as I wish to find it. These, and all of you, shall know, however, that all your words have been recorded in my book, and in accordance with this and your innermost thoughts you shall be judged.

You shall then once more avow openly before My holy face and the presence of My holy angels and of the members of your community with hand and mouth to My servant, the Elder given unto you, what I shall speak unto you and also what you have promised with words in your heart. And if you break this vow then this and all your words shall stand against you as a quick witness and all my promises will become, instead of a blessing, a fiery and heavy burden.

Is there still anybody among you who is still fearful and lacks courage and is afraid not to be able to live up to my commandments which may seem to him difficult at this time in spite of the grace given by me? Such a one may still step aside, for I know that there are still some whose hearts are hard and unbroken and who consider my wonders and my ways too lightly but of whom I expect that they hold them in fitting respect.

(Here followed a brief pause.)

Are they all willing?

Hear then what I say unto you. I, the Lord your God am holy! And therefore you, too, shall be and become a holy community, if I am to abide in your midst as you desire. And therefore you shall henceforth resolve:

I. To tear all crude and all subtle idols out of your hearts, that they may no longer befool you and mislead you further to idolatry against your God, so that His name be not defamed and He not suddenly go forth and avenge and save the glory of His name.

II. I desire that you shall have naught in common with the fruitless work of darkness; neither with grave sins and sinners, nor with the subtle within and without you. For what relationship and likeness has My holy temple with the temples of pride, unchasteness, ambition, seeking for power; and of the useless superfluous, condemning prattling, which steals the time away from Me. How could the light unite with the darkness? How can you as children of the light unite with the ungodly, the liars and their works, the scoffers and blasphemers, who are nothing but darkness?

III. You shall henceforth in your external life conduct yourself so that those standing without find no longer cause for ill reports and for defaming My name. Suffer rather the wrong if you are abused. But above all flee from associations which hinder you from growing in godliness. All mockers and scoffers and those who recommend you unto vanity, you shall shun and have no dealings with them.

IV. You shall also perform your earthly task the longer the more according to the dictates of your conscience; and gladly desist from that which My spirit shows you to be sinful—not heeding your own loss, for I am the Lord, who can and will care and provide

35

for the needs of your body—that through this you may not give cause for censure to the scoffer. The time which I still grant you here is very short; therefore, see to it well that My hand may bring forth and create within you a real harvest.

V. Let, I warn you, be far from you all falseness, lying, and hypocrisy. For I say unto you that I will give the spirit of discernment and will lay open unto you through the Spirit of Prophecy such vices. For to what end shall clay and metal be together? Would it not make for Me a useless vessel, which I could not use and should have to cast away with the rest. Behold, My children, I have chosen before many, many, many, and have promised to be unto you a fiery entrenchment against the defiance of your inner and outer enemies. Verily! Verily! I shall keep my promises, if only you endeavor to fulfill what you have promised and are promising.

VI. You shall therefore, none of you, strive for particular gifts and envy the one or the other to whom I give perchance the gift of prayer or maybe of wisdom. For such the enemy of My glory seeks ever to instill into you, especially into the passionate and fickle souls, to impart to you thereby a poison destructive to the soul. You shall, all, all, all of you be filled with My pure and holy spirit when the time will come to pass, if you will let yourself be prepared in humility and patience according to My will. Then you too shall speak with tongues different from the tongues you now speak with. Then I shall be able to communicate with you most intimately.

VII. Put aside henceforth all slander, and all malice of the heart toward each other, which you have harbored hitherto! None of you are free from it!

Behold I shall command the Spirit of my Love that He as often as you assemble in true simplicity of heart and in humility for prayer be in your very midst with His influence and may flow through the channels of His Love into the hearts He finds empty.

VIII. You must make yourself willing for all outer and inner suffering. For Belial will not cease to show unto you his rancor through his servants and through his invisible power. It is also pleasing to Me and absolutely necessary for you that you be tried through continuous sorrow, suffering, and cross, and to be made firm and precious in My crucible. And he who does not dare (but none must be indolent himself in this) to exert all his physical and spiritual powers through My strength, let him depart that he may not be later a blemishing spot upon My glory.

IX. Do not lend in future your ears to suspicion and prejudice and take, because of your lack of self-knowledge, offense at each other where there is none. But each one among you shall become the mirror for the other. You shall, moreover, also endeavor to stand every day and hour before the Lord as a

oneness, as a city or a light on a high mountain, which near and far shines bright and pure.

X. At the same time practice the longer the more outer and inner quiet. Seek ever, though it will be for the natural man which is inexperienced in this a hard death, to hide yourself, in humility in the inner and undermost chamber of your nothingness, that I may bring in this soil to a befitting growth My seed which I have concealed therein.

XI. Behold, my people! I make with you this day a covenant which I bid you to keep faithfully and sacredly. I will daily wander amongst you and visit your place of rest, that I may see how you are disposed toward Me.

XII. Guard yourself. I, the Lord, warn you against indifference towards this covenant of grace and against negligence, indolence, and laziness which thus far have been for the most part your ruler and have controlled your heart. I shall not depart from your side nor from your midst, but shall Myself on the contrary reveal Myself ever more powerfully, holier, and more glorious through the light of My face in and among you, as long as you will bring forth to meet Me the honest and sincere powers of your will. This shall be the the tie with which you can bind and hold Me. Behold I accept you this day as slaves of My will, as free-borns of My kingdom, as possessors, of My heart! Therefore let yourself gladly and willingly be bound with the ties of My love, and the power of love shall never be wanting unto you.

XIII. And you who are the heads and fathers of households hear what I say unto you: The Lord has now chosen you as members of His Community with whom He desires to associate and dwell day by day. See, therefore, to this that you prove truly heads and lights of your households, which, however, always stand under their faithful head, your King; see that you may bring your helpmates to true conduct and fear of God through your own way of living, which you shall strive to make ever more faultless, more earnest and manly.

XIV. Your children, you who have any, you shall endeavor with all your power to sacrifice to Me and to lead to Me. I shall give you in abundance, if you only inwardly keep close to Me, wisdom, courage, understanding, bravery, and earnestness mingled with love, that you yourself may be able to live before them in the fear of God and that your training may be blessed—that is, in those who want to submit to My hand in and through Me. But those who scorn you and do not heed my voice in and through you and otherwise, shall have their blood come upon their own heads. But you shall never abandon hope but wrestle for them with earnest prayer, struggle, and toil, which are the pangs of spiritual birth. But if you neglect them through indifference, negligence, half-heartedness, and laziness, then every such soul shall verily be demanded of such a father.

XV. Do now your part as I command you from without and frequently inwardly through My Spirit; do not desist, just as I never cease to work on you my disobedient children; then you will abide in my grace and save your souls. And such women and children shall bear the fruits of their sins as do not want to bow themselves under you and Me. I will henceforth no longer tolerate those grave offenses among you and in your houses about which the world and the children of wrath and disbelief have so much to say; but I have commanded the Spirit of My living breath, that He pass through all your houses and breathe upon every soul which does not wantonly close itself to Him. The dew of blessing shall flow from the blessed head of your high priest and prince of peace upon every male head among you, and through them it shall flow upon and into your helpmates, and through both man and wife into the offspring and children, so that all your seed shall be acceptable, pure, and holy before the Lord, since He has nourished and will nourish the same among you.

XVI. And none of your grown up children shall be permitted to attend your meetings, who have not previously received from their parents a good testimony according to the truth, not appearance, and without self-deception, as also from the Elders and leaders especially from the one who with his fellow workers has to watch over the training of the children, which is to be carried on with earnestness and love, but without all severity and harshness. This training is to be watched over with all earnestness; and should the parents be negligent and the case require it, so shall the latter be temporarily excluded (from the prayer-meetings) for their humiliation.

XVII. Prove yourselves as the people whom I have established for an eternal monument to Me, and whom I shall impress upon My heart as an eternal seal, so that the Spirit of My love may dwell upon you and within you, and work according to His desire.

XVIII. And this is the word which the Lord speaks of these strangers who so often visit you and cause so much disturbance: None, whom you find to be a scoffer, hypocrite, mocker, sneerer, derider, and unrepenting sinner, shall you admit to your Community and prayer-meetings. Once for all they are to be excluded that My refreshing dew and the shadow of My Love be never prevented from manifesting themselves among you. But if some should come to you with honest intentions who are not knowingly scoffers, hypocrites, and deriders, though it be one of those whom you call of the world, if he to your knowledge does not come with deceitful intentions, then you may well admit him. I shall give you My faithful servants and witnesses especially the spirit of discrimination and give you an exact feeling, whether they are sincere and come with honest intentions or otherwise.

XIX. If they then desire to visit you more frequently, you shall first acquaint them with your rules and ask them whether they will submit to these rules and to the test of the Elders. And then you shall read to them My laws and commands, which I give unto you; and if you see that they are earnestly concerned about their souls, then you shall gladly receive the weak, and become weak with them for a while, that is, you shall with them and for them repent and make their repentance your own. But if a scoffer or mocker declares that he repents, him you should only admit after considerable time and close scrutiny and examination of his conduct, if you find the latter to be righteous. For Satan will not cease to try to launch at you his fatal arrows through such people. Be therefore on your guard and watch that not the wolf come among you and scatter or even devour the sheep.

XX. And those who pledge themselves with hand and mouth after the aforesaid manner to you shall make public profession before the Community and also make an open confession of their resolve, and I shall indeed show you if this latter comes from their hearts; the conduct of those you shall watch closely, whether they live according to their profession and promise or not, lest the dragon defile your garments with his drivel.

XXI. (To the Elders.) Thus My Elder and his fellow-workers shall frequently visit the members of the Community and see how things are in their homes and how it stands about their hearts. I shall give to you my servant (E.L. Gruber) and to your Brothers keen eyes, if you only pray for it. And if you find that one is in uncalled sadness, or lives in negligence, impudence, boisterousness, or the like, then you shall admonish him in love. If he repents you shall rejoice. But if after repeated admonition he does not mend his ways, then you shall put him to shame openly before the Community; and if even this does not help then you shall exclude him for a while. Yet I shall ever seek my sheep, those who are already excluded and those who in the future because of their own guilt must be excluded, and I shall ever try to lead them in their nothingness into my pasture.

XXII. And to all of you I still give this warning: Let none of you reject brotherly admonition and punishment, so that secret pride grows not like a poisonous thorn in such a member and torment and poison his whole heart.

XXIII. You shall not form a habit of anything of the external exercises (forms of worship) and the duties committed to you, or I shall be compelled to forbid them again; on the contrary, you shall make your meetings ever more fervent, more earnest, more zealous, in the true simple love towards each other, fervent and united in Me, the true Prince of Peace.

XXIV. This the members and brethren of the Community shall sincerely and honestly pledge with hand and mouth to my Elders, openly in the assembly, after they have carefully considered it, and it shall be kept sacred ever after.

Notes: *These rules, which still govern the religious life of the Amana community, originated with Johann A. Gruber, the prophet who led the group during the eighteenth century.*

TWENTY-FOUR RULES (AMANA CHURCH SOCIETY) (continued)

They were revealed during a session in which he spoke as one inspired by a spirit of prophecy. The entire text of that session is reproduced here.

*   *   *

ACCOUNT OF OUR RELIGION, DOCTRINE AND FAITH (HUTTERITE BRETHREN)

I. DOCTRINE OF THE CHURCH AND OF THE SPIRIT

An assembly of children of God who have separated themselves from all unclean things is the church. It is gathered together, has being, and is kept by the Holy Spirit. Sinners may not be members unless and until they have repented of their sins. The essence of the church is its bearing of the Light; it is a lantern of righteousness in a world of unbelief, darkness, and blindness. It is a pillar and ground of the truth, which is confirmed, ratified, and brought to pass in her by the Holy Spirit. The "power and key" to forgive sins which was received by Christ from the Father is given to the church as a whole and not to individual persons. In its nature the church is spiritual, but concretely it is known as the pure sacred community. Church assembly and community are equated together.

II. DOCTRINE OF REDEMPTION AND ENTRANCE INTO THE CHURCH

Redemption means the working of the Spirit in the individual and his preparation for entrance into the church. It is the Spirit of Christ that leads into the church. ("The Christ of Ridemann is the inwardly experienced and fought-for Christ.") The work of Christ in man means a complete conversion and rebirth. Salvation and redemption consists in the liberation from the dominion of sin. Apart from Christ there is no goodness. Salvation also is a new covenant. God has cast out from our heart evil, sin, and the lust to sin, and we are to seek, love, hear, and keep His Word.

III. DOCTRINE OF FAITH

Faith is a real divine power which renews man and makes him like God in nature, ardent in love and in keeping His commandments.

IV. DOCTRINE OF BAPTISM

Baptism means the entrance into the covenant of grace of God and the incorporation into the Church of Christ. The "right and necessary" sequence is preaching, faith, rebirth, and baptism. Children cannot be baptized in the right way because they are not reborn through preaching, faith, and the Spirit.

V. DOCTRINE OF THE FELLOWSHIP OF THE LORD'S TABLE

The Supper is a sign of the community of Christ's body, in that each member thereby declares himself to be of the one mind, heart, and Spirit of Christ. It is an act of remembrance at which God's children become aware again of the grace which they have received. Only a true member of Christ may participate. The unity of the fellowship of the Lord's Table must already exist prior to the celebrating.

VI. DOCTRINE OF ORIGINAL SIN

The inheritance that we have from our Father Adam is inclination to sin. Original sin means that all of us have by nature a tendency toward evil and have pleasure in sin. This inheritance removes, devours, and consumes all that is good and of God in man; so that none may attain it again except to be born again.

VII. THE FORMULA FOR BAPTISM

The baptizer first testifies to the baptizand and asks if he believes in God, the Father, the Son, and the Holy Spirit. The baptizand confesses. He then is asked if he desires to yield himself to God to live for Him and His church. If so, he is told to kneel before God and the church, and water is poured upon him. If baptism cannot be performed before the entire church, the baptizer may perform the ordinance alone.

Notes: *Long before the Hutterite Brethren divided into three distinct groups in North America in the twentieth century, a confession of faith accepted by all was written by Peter Riederman in 1540 and published in 1565. It is a lengthy document of over 200 pages, and hence, is not reproduced here. Theologically the document, still accepted as authoritative by contemporary Hutterites, follows the Anabaptist-Mennonite tradition (see the Schleitheim and Dordrecht Confessions). It covers all of the major Christian doctrinal emphases, and in traditional fashion advocates adult baptism, separation from the world, and the use of the ban. It forbids participation in war and war industries (the manufacture of swords), litigation, swearing, and any association with strong drink (selling and/or consuming).*

An English translation by Kathleen Hasenburg was published in 1950 (London: Hodder and Stoughton; Rifton, NY: Plough Publishing House). Commentaries summarizing the content have been published in several Mennonite sources. See, for example, Robert Friedman, Hutterite Studies *(Goshen, IN: Mennonite Historical Society, 1961).*

The summary of the Riederman Account reproduced here was originally published in Baptist Confessions of Faith *by William L. Lumpkin (Chicago: Judson Press, 1959). It covers seven major points of the group's doctrine.*

*   *   *

SYNOPTICAL OUTLINE OF KORESHAN THEOLOGY (KORESHAN UNITY)

KORESHANITY DIFFERENTIATED FROM THE FALLACIOUS PANTHEISM OF MODERN TIMES

First, Pantheism is the all-God, the God of the Shepherds. The Lord Jesus Christ is Jehovah, the Shepherd of the sheep, and the Father-Mother of the Shepherds who stand on Mount Zion and sing the song of Moses and the Lamb. Jesus the Shepherd, the God Jehovah of the Shepherds, when coming again, comes not in sacrifice as the Lamb of God, for He must have a new name. He comes to sacrifice for the cleansing of the sanctuary, and is the goat Shepherd. It is the goat that is sacrificed for the cleansing of the sanctuary. Pan was the god of the "hollow earth."

The word "pan" signifies "a concavity or depression," and as all life develops in the shell, or from within the shell, the common order of development will not be violated in the development of the life proceeding toward the maturity of the Sons of God.

Second. Pantheism, as accepted today by the superficial thinker, supposes that the universe is, as it were, a body, and that its soul is Deity. The universe, conceived as circumference and center, furnishes the idea of a pivot or central point, which in Koreshanity is regarded as the Astral or Stellar Center. This, being the pivot and focal point of all influx from the pediment, rind or periphery, provides a demonstration or astronomical proof of a localized conscious point, affectional and intellectual, of the system of integralism. It furnishes such a demonstration because the physical universe, being center and circumference, and necessarily the expression of mind or cause, must be correspondentially like it. It will be noticed that the Deity of the Koreshan syntheticism is not a universal Deity, but, as the nucleus of the alchemico-organic cosmos, is a comparatively minute focal point, so the Astral Center of the anthropostic cosmos is the personal, individual and microcosmic Man. Such a Man was the Lord Jesus, who was and is Jehovah.

Third. It will be seen that there is a divine and a diabolic pantheism; and that while God (Elohi) is all and in all, the Lord, the Son of God, the Bridegroom in whom was the Bride, is the personal Deity, and, therefore, that the personal Deity of the Koreshan syntheticism is the God-Man and Man-God. When the process of regeneration is complete, in which the Sons of God (of the Lord Jesus) are manifest, these Sons also will be like the parent, namely, Father-Mother, and they each will be also Bride and Bridegroom, for they will be male and female—not dual, but biune in the image and likeness of God. "It doth not yet appear what we shall be: but we know that, when he shall appear, we shall be like him" (I John 3:2). "But as many as received him, to them gave he power to become the sons of God, even to them that believe on his name" (John 1:12).

Fourth. When this development is complete it will necessarily be the production of a new genus. This genus we denominate Theo-Anthropos—the God-Man genus.

CONTRAST BETWEEN MORTAL AND IMMORTAL LIFE

First. Man, as now existing, is mortal. He is mortal because the male and female are in two parts; and because of this, life does not form a cycle or wheel of perpetual being. Man is ignorant of the law of life; therefore he dies or goes to corruption. Whatsoever his profession, "Christian" and "pagan" alike, he passes to a corruptible decay.

Second. Man cannot become immortal but by obedience to the law of immortality.

Third. The science of immortal life is involved in the ten precepts of the Decalogue. These comprise the ten categories of natural immortality. The Lord Jesus kept these laws, and overcame the tendency to corruption. When He departed this existence, or life in the natural, He became spiritual; He dematerialized and passed out alive. This is the new and living way.

Fourth. No man can be saved but by the process that saved the Lord Jesus.

Fifth. Natural immortality does not mean that man will live in this earth eternally. Man, then, becomes immortal as the fruit of the Tree of Life, passes out of the natural into the invisible, but leaves behind a lower and subsequent form of human life in which the Seed of the Sons of God is planted for another fruitage at the end of another Grand Cycle.

Sixth. Time is divided into long and shorter cycles, consisting of solar, lunar, planetary and stellar cycles or periods. We are now terminating a lunar period of about twenty-four thousand years. In it we are reaching the greatest crisis of the world's history. From it will unfold the Kingdom of Righteousness. In a lunar period of twenty-four thousand years there are four ages of six thousand years each, designated: Gold, Silver, Brass, and Iron Ages. Each age is also divided into four periods or dispensations gold, silver, brass, and iron. We are now in the iron portion of the last or Iron Age.

The world enjoyed a period of greatest light and goodness for six thousand years, beginning twenty-four thousand years ago, and ending with the beginning of the Silver Age, eighteen thousand years ago. The world then entered into its grand Silver Age, and remained there for six thousand years. It then entered the Brass Age, and at the end of that, the Iron Age. The last six thousand, the Iron Age, has been the degenerate and degenerating period of the world's history. We are just now emerging from the darkest period of the most benighted age of all the ages, and about to enter, again, the Golden Age.

THE NEW KORESHAN DISPENSATION

The Koreshan system is inaugurated for the purpose of restoring normal states and relations, and insuring their permanency through their scientific regulation of all the functions of life. The want of equilibrium in the social fabric has its inception in the radical and willful violation of organic law, actuated either through the conscious disregard of religious, moral, political, social and physiological obligations, or through ignorance of the science of law, and lack of application because of such ignorance. The attainment and maintenance of a state of equibalance can accrue only as the result of a thorough comprehension of the principles of both life and death; and these may be resolved to a simple and unitary radix, whose quality may be stated in a brief but inclusive formulary.

Love is the fulfilling of the law. Is argument required for the demonstration of the distinctive virtue of love to God and the neighbor, as differentiated from the love of self, which now comprises the basis of nearly every impulse to human enterprise and activity? Life and death are two antithetical states involving properties of diametric force, whose "energies" are so at variance as to insure a perpetual opposition and struggle for supremacy and perpetuity. We mean by life and death, the two states properly denominated "immortality" and "mortality."

SYNOPTICAL OUTLINE OF KORESHAN THEOLOGY (KORESHAN UNITY) (continued)

The ultimate of man's natural destiny is in reaching such a degree of development and control of the functions of his physical organism, as to insure to him a passage from the natural to the spiritual or heavenly domain without the death of the body. The Lord Jesus in His earthly career—fraught with a succession of triumphal combats against the hells and final achievement of victory over the grave—conquered death in His own organism, and became the promise of a corresponding victory for all such as will obey the same law with the same fidelity, overcoming in themselves the power of corruptible dissolution as He overcame and entered through theocrasis into Glory.

Mortality is man's birthright through propagation from his sensual and lower origin. Immortality is the birthright of man through regeneration from God, by virtue of the divine planting or impregnation by the operation of the Holy Spirit. "I am from above," said Jesus; and this annunciation was proclaimed pursuantly to the central law of His conception by the divine overshadowing or spiritual impregnation. "Ye are from beneath," was uttered upon the basis of human origin through sensuous propagation, a propagation which involves inevitably a final corruptible dissolution through decay. (See John 8:23.)

The present system of religious, political and social activity has its momentuations in the central potency and force of self love. It is opposed to the law of God, as theoretically stated and practically applied by the Lord; and its career and termination are essentially mortal. In the presentation of two diametrically opposite determinations of human purpose as the two rival potencies of being, namely, love to the neighbor and self love, we have denoted the foundation stones of both life and death, or of immortality and mortality.

Love to God, manifest in love to the neighbor, is the keynote to the concord of harmonies soon to vibrate the octaves of terrestrial resonance, as the Deific respiration fills the body with God's eternal, vital Presence. "And the Lord God . . . breathed into his nostrils the breath of life; and man became a living soul" (Gen. 2:7), was true when, in the first Eden, the Sons of God awoke to the consciousness of divine origin, inception, birth, and destiny. Again God is about to breathe into man's nostrils the breath of life, through the coming theocrasis; and Eden restored will confirm the testimony of the sacred witnesses of God's humanity and humanity's Godhood and celestial origin.

The Kingdom of God established in the earth will fulfill the hope of consummate aspiration. This Kingdom established will verify God's promises, and also human expectation as predicated upon, and resting in, His purpose to reclaim the earth (man's body), and His power to achieve the victory over death, and make His triumphal entry into a domain hitherto under the jurisdiction of His Satanic Majesty. Nothing less than God's own Kingdom, inaugurated with men, will satisfy the longings of the chosen race; nothing less than this will fulfill the expectations of humanity as built upon the verity of the Word of God's annunciation. Nothing less than this can verify man's predication of the omnipotence, omniscience, and omnipresence of Deity, and the immortal destiny of the race—the hope of which is fixed in his confidence in the promised purpose of the Eternal.

If the Kingdom of Righteousness, involving the immortality of man, and with it his resurrection or restoration to his Edenic state, must exist by virtue of the dominance of love to the neighbor as originating in supreme love to God, then with the building of such a Kingdom must depart the system of competitive activity originating in self love, and concomitant with the evils of unwholesome agitation. If the promises of God are of any import, there is coming an adjustment of human affairs, the basis of which will be the plenary adjudication of the righteous claims and prerogatives of the downtrodden.

The wail of human degradation has reached the ears of the God of Sabaoth; the cry for bread, fuel, and shelter from those who are ground into the dust of despair by the unrelenting heel of affluent and imperialistic despotism, under the cloak of a democracy prostituted to the interests of an illegitimate aggrandizement and supremacy, has ascended, until, responsive to its pleadings, the God of Justice hurls back the thunderbolts of retributive wrath, the keen-edged sword of a divine vengeance and prosecuting force of a holy equation.

We behold with prophetic prescience the coming retribution, and therefore list the note of warning, both to the oppressor and the oppressed, who, in the struggle for supremacy, constitute Gog and Magog; that is, the roof and floor of a conflict, the inevitable culmination of which will be the overthrow of both parties to the contest. There is but a single remedy to the evils now afflicting society—the eradication of selfishness; and this can be insured only through the fulfillment of the divine purpose to inaugurate the Everlasting Kingdom, to be ushered in through the coming overshadowing and outpouring of the divine fire.

Notes: *Not a creed, this statement is one of the most recent attempts to restate the Koreshan religious perspective without mentioning the more controversial aspects of the cellular cosmology for which founder Cyrus Teed is best remembered.*

* * *

A CONCISE STATEMENT OF THE PRINCIPLES OF THE ONLY TRUE CHURCH, ACCORDING TO THE PRESENT APPEARANCE OF CHRIST [UNITED SOCIETY OF BELIEVERS IN CHRIST'S SECOND APPEARANCE (THE SHAKERS)]

We believe that the first light of salvation was given or made known to the patriarchs by promise; and they that believed in the promise of Christ, and were obedient to the command of God made known unto them, were the people of God and were accepted of God as righteous, or perfect in their generations; according to the measure of light and truth manifested unto them; which was as waters to the ankles signified by Ezekiel's vision of the holy waters (chapter 47). And altho' they could not receive regeneration or the fulness of salvation, from the fleshly or fallen nature in this life; because the fulness of time was not yet come, that they should receive the baptism of the Holy Ghost and fire; for the destruction of the body of sin, and purification of the soul; but Abram being [4] called, and chosen of God as the father of the faithful; was received into covenant relation with God by promise; that in him (and his seed which was Christ) all the families of the earth should be blessed, and these earthly blessings, which were promised to Abram, were a shadow of gospel or spiritual blessings to come: and circumcision, though it was a seal of Abram's faith, yet it was but a sign of the mortification and destruction of the flesh by the gospel in a future day. Observe, circumcision, or outward cutting of the foreskin of the flesh, did not cleanse the man from sin; but was a sign of the baptism of the Holy Ghost and fire: which is by the power of God manifested in divers operations and gifts of the spirit, as in the days of the apostles; which does indeed destroy the body of sin, or fleshly nature, and purify the man from all sin both soul and body. So that Abram, though in the [5] full faith of the promise; yet, as he did not receive the substance of the thing promised, his hope of eternal salvation was in Christ, by the Gospel to be attained in the resurrection from the dead.

The second dispensation was the law that was given of God to Israel, by the hand of Moses; which was a further manifestation of that salvation which was promised through Christ by the gospel, both in the order and ordinances which was instituted and given to Israel, as the church and people of God according to that dispensation; which was as waters to the ankles, Ezekiel XLVII. by which they were distinguished from all the families of the earth. For, while they were strictly obedient to all the commands, ordinances, and statutes, that God gave them, they were approbated of God according to the promise for life; and blessing was promised [6] unto them in the line of obedience: Cursing and death, in disobedience: for God, who is ever jealous for the honor and glory of his own great name, always dealt with them according to his word; for while they were obedient to the command of God, and purged out sin from amongst them, God was with them, according to his promise. But when they disobeyed the command of God, and committed sin, and became like other people, the hand of the Lord was turned against them; and those evils came upon them which God had threatened; so we see that they were wholly obedient to the will of God made known in that dispensation, were accepted as just, or righteous: yet, as the dispensation was short, they did not attain that salvation which was promised in the gospel; so that as it respected the new-birth, or real purification of the man from all sin; the law made nothing perfect, but was a [7] shadow of good things to come; their only hope of eternal redemption was in the promise of Christ, by the gospel to be attained in the resurrection from the dead. Acts of the Apostles XXVI. 6, 7.

The third dispensation was the gospel of Christ's first appearance, in the flesh: and that salvation which took place in consequence of his life, death, resurrection, and ascension at the right hand of the father being accepted in his obedience, as the first born among many brethren; he received power and authority to administer the power of the resurrection and eternal judgment to all the children of men: so that he has become the author of eternal salvation to all that obey him; and as Christ has this power in himself, he did administer power and authority to his church at the day of Pentecost, as his body: with all the gifts that he had promised them, which was the first [8] gift of the Holy Ghost, as an in-dwelling comforter to abide with them forever: and by which they were baptised into Christ's death; death to all sin; and were in the hope of the resurrection from the dead, through the operation of the power of God, which wrought in them. And as they had received the substance of the promise of Christ come in the flesh, by the gift and power of the Holy Ghost; they had power to preach the gospel in Christ's name to every creature;—and to administer the power of God to as many as believed, and were obedient to the gospel which they preached; and also to remit and retain sin in the name and authority of Christ on earth: so that they that believed in the gospel, and were obedient to that form of doctrine which was taught them; by denying all ungodliness and worldly lusts; and became entirely dead to the law by the body of Christ, [9] or power of the Holy Ghost, were in the travel of the resurrection from the dead; or the redemption of the body. So that they who took up a full cross against the world, flesh, and devil; and who forsook all for Christ's sake; and followed him in the regeneration, by preserving in that line of obedience to the end; found the resurrection from the dead, and eternal salvation in that dispensation was only as water to the loins; the mystery of God not finished; but there was another day prophesied of, called the second appearance of Christ, or final and last display of God's grace to a lost world: in which the mystery of God should be finished as he has spoken by his prophets since the world began: which day could not come, except there was a falling away from that faith and power that the church then stood in; in which time anti-christ was to have [10] his reign, whom Christ should destroy with the spirit of his mouth and brightness of his appearance: which falling away began soon after the apostles, and gradually increased in the church, until about four hundred and fifty seven years from Christ's birth (or thereabouts) at which time the power of the Holy People, or church of Christ, was scattered or lost by reason of transgression: and anti-christ, or false religion, got to be established. Since that time the witnesses of Christ have prophesied in sackcloth or under darkness; and altho' many have been faithful to testify against sin; even to the laying down of their lives for the testimony which they held; so that God accepted them in their obedience; while they were faithful and just to live or walk up to the measure of light and truth of God, revealed or made known unto them, but as it is written, that all they that will live godly in Christ [11] Jesus, shall suffer persecution: and so it has been, and those faithful witnesses lost their lives, by those falsely called the church of Christ: which is anti-christ; for the true church of Christ never persecuted any; but were inoffensive, harmless, separate from sin, living in obedience to God they earnestly contend for the fame. Therefore it may be plainly seen and known, where the true church of Christ is: but as it is writen anti-christ or false churches should prevail against the saints and overcome them, before Christ's

A CONCISE STATEMENT OF THE PRINCIPLES OF THE ONLY TRUE CHURCH, ACCORDING TO THE PRESENT APPEARANCE OF CHRIST [UNITED SOCIETY OF BELIEVERS IN CHRIST'S SECOND APPEARANCE (THE SHAKERS)] (continued)

second appearance, 2 Thess. II. 3. Let no man deceive you by any means for that day shall not come except there come a falling away first; and that man of sin be revealed, the son of perdition, Rev. XIII. 7. And it was given unto him to overcome them, and power was given him [12] over all kindreds, tongues, and nations; and this is the state Christ prophesied the world of mankind should be in, at his second appearance, Luke XVII. 26. And as it was in the day of Noe, so shall it be in the days of the son of man, verse 30. Even so shall be in the day when the son of man is revealed; plainly referring to his second appearance to consume or destroy anti-christ, and make a final end of sin; and establish his kingdom upon earth: but as the revelation of Christ must be in his people, whom he had chosen to be his body, to give testimony of him and to preach his gospel to a lost world.

The fourth dispensation or day is the second appearance of Christ, or final, or last display of God's grace to a lost world, in which the mystery of God will be finished and a decisive work, to the final salvation, or damnation of all the children [13] of men. (Which according to the prophecies rightly calculated, and truly understood, began in the year of our Saviour Jesus Christ, 1747.) See Daniel and the Revelations. In the manner following, 1st. To a number, in the manifestation of great light—and mighty trembling by the invisible power of God, and visions, and revelations, and prophecies; which has progressively increased, with administration of all those spiritual gifts, that was administered to the apostles at the day of Pentecost: which is the comforter that has led us into all truth: which was promised to abide with the true church of Christ unto the end of the world, and by which we find baptism into Christ's death; death to all sin, become alive to God, by the power of Christ's resurrection, which worketh in us mightily; by which a dispensation of the gospel is committed unto us; and woe be unto us if we [14] preach not the gospel of Christ. (For in finding so great a salvation and deliverance from the law of sin and death in believing and obeying this gospel which is the gospel of Christ, in confessing and forsaking all sin, and denying ourselves and bearing the cross of Christ, against the world, flesh, and devil.) We have found repentance of all our sins; and are made partakers of the grace of God wherein we now stand: which all others in believing and obeying, have acceptance with God, and find salvation from their sins as well as we; God being no respecter of persons but willing that all should come to the knowledge of the truth, and be saved. Thus we have given a short information of what we believe of the dispensations of God's grace to mankind, both past and present: and in what manner the people of God have found justification, or acceptance of God, which was and is still in believing [15] and obeying the light and truth of God, revealed or made known, in the day or dispensation in which it is revealed: for as the wrath of God is revealed from heaven against all ungodliness, and unrighteousness of men, who

hold the truth in unrighteousness or live in any known sin against him; so his mercy and grace is towards all them that truly fear him, and turn from all their sins, by confessing, and forsaking, and repenting, which is the way and manner in which all must find the forgiveness of their sins, and acceptance with God through our Lord Jesus Christ, or finally fail of the grace of God; and that salvation which is brought to light by the gospel. But to conclude, in short, as we believe, and do testify, that the present gospel of God's grace unto us is the day which in the scripture, is spoken or prophesied of, as the second appearing of Christ to consume [16] or destroy anti-christ, or false religion, and to make an end of the reigning power of sin (for he that committeth sin is the servant of sin and satan) over the children of men: and to establish his kingdom, and that righteousness that will stand forever: and that the present display of the work and power of God, will increase until it is manifest to all; which it must be in due time: for every eye shall see him; and he will reward every man according to his deeds: and none can stand in sin or unrighteousness; but in that righteousness which is pure and holy: even without fault before the throne of God which is obtained by grace, through faith in obedience to the truth of the everlasting gospel of our Lord Jesus Christ, in denying all ungodliness and worldly lusts; by confessing all sin, and taking up the cross of Christ, against the world, flesh, and devil: we desire therefore, that the children [17] of men would believe the testimony of truth, and turn from their sins by repentance, that they might obtain the mercy of God, and salvation from sin before it be too late.

Notes: *This statement written by Joseph Meacham appeared in 1790. It centers upon the understanding of history's successive dispensations as seen by the Shaker community. As a full statement of Shaker belief, it assumes an understanding of older Protestant confessions, elements of which are hastily affirmed in the closing section.*

* * *

TENETS (UNIVERSAL PEACE MISSION MOVEMENT)

POLITICALLY

We greet all mankind with Peace. We are Americans. We believe in the Declaration of Independence and the Constitution with its Bill of Rights and Amendments.

We respect and revere the American flag.

We are interracial, interdenominal, nonsectarian and nonpartisan.

We believe that all men and nations should be independent, pay all just debts and return all stolen goods or the equivalent.

This includes:

Restitution by individual nations for all territories taken by force.

Restitution by all individuals of mobs for all damage, injury or looting by the mob, and if murder is committed, payment of the full penalty of the law.

Also the county wherein the crime is committed should justly pay the heirs of the deceased.

SOCIALLY

We are all equal to and independent of each other in the sight of GOD. We believe that all men are entitled to not only equal but the same inalienable rights to Life, Liberty and the Reality of Happiness.

We believe that self control is birth control.

We believe that every man has the responsibility to protect his fellowman from being denied any right or freedom guaranteed by the Constitution.

We believe that nothing good will be restrained from man when all live together in the unity of Spirit, Mind, Aim and Purpose and that all men who are worthy to live shall live well.

We live FATHER DIVINE's International Modest Code:

No Smoking. No Drinking. No Obscenity. No Vulgarity. No Profanity. No Undue Mixing of Sexes. No Receiving of Gifts, Presents, Tips or Bribes.

EDUCATIONALLY

We believe in the Public School System.

We believe that the doors of all educational institutions should be open and free for universal education, with the same rights for all to higher education and professional training, according to ability.

We believe in English as the Universal Language and that it should be taught in the educational institutions of all nations.

We believe that a man is a man and not a so-called color, creed or race.

Therefore, we have deleted from all books in the Peace Mission Free Schools and recommend abolishing in all educational institutions every qualifying adjective that tends to low-rate or produce inequality between man and man. We do not use expressions such as N-people, B-people, C-people or W-people.

ECONOMICALLY

We believe in individual independence. We believe in serving the Cause of humanity through the Cooperative System, individually cooperating to purchase, own and manage hotels, apartment houses and businesses.

We believe in full employment for all able-bodied persons.

No true follower of FATHER DIVINE is on relief.

Social Security and compulsory insurance are not only unconstitutional but unnecessary when men express their individual independence as true Americans.

We pay our way as we go, pay cash on the spot and refuse to purchase on credit or on the instalment plan.

We believe in mass production as the best means of eliminating poverty and want universally.

We believe that all men have the right to be safe and secure in any possession permitted under the Constitution.

RELIGIOUSLY

We believe that the Scripture is being fulfilled as recorded in the King James Version of the Old and the New Testaments of the Holy Bible.

We believe that FATHER DIVINE fulfils the Scriptural Prophecy of the Second Coming of CHRIST for the Christian world and the Coming of the Messiah for the Jewish world.

We have ONE FATHER and ONE MOTHER — GOD Personified in FATHER DIVINE and HIS SPOTLESS VIRGIN BRIDE, MOTHER DIVINE.

We live in the Brotherhood of man under the FATHER-HOOD of GOD, therefore, we are one family indivisible.

We believe that the Principles of all true religion are synonymous.

True religion is faith in ONE INDIVISIBLE GOD.

We have the Ten Commandments and the precepts given in Jesus' Sermon on the Mount.

We believe that Heaven is a State of Consciousness to be universally established in fulfillment of Jesus' prayer: "Let Thy Kingdom come and Thy Will be done on earth . . . "

We believe that America is the Birthplace of the Kingdom of GOD on earth and IT shall be fully realized when all men live the synonymous Principles of true Americanism, Brotherhood, Democracy, Christianity, Judaism and all true religion.

We believe that GOD is Eternally Present with or without a Body.

True followers of FATHER DIVINE refuse to fight their fellowman for any cause whatsoever. However, if any individual will fight physically for himself in self-defense, then he has a right to fight physically in the defense of his country.

Under The Peace Mission Movement there are six incorporated Churches with branches in the U.S.A. and throughout the world of which FATHER DIVINE is the Bishop, Founder and Pastor.

The Church Services are without ritual and the general public is welcome to attend and participate harmoniously.

We believe in the serving of Communion daily after the manner of the Lord's Supper, as practical service for the sustenance of the body and benefit of the soul.

Neither FATHER DIVINE or MOTHER DIVINE, nor Officers and Co-workers in the Churches receive salary, compensation or remuneration.

No collections are ever taken for any Spiritual Service rendered, but all are requested to donate for material services received, such as for meals, lodging and other services provided.

We do not proselyte because the Life of CHRIST, when lived, is magnetic.

We believe that WOODMONT fulfils the prophecy of the Mount of the House of the Lord from which shall go forth the Law to all nations, spoken of in Isaiah 2:2, 3 and Micah 4:1, 2.

Notes: *Father Divine, founder of the Universal Peace Mission, is popularly remembered as a flamboyant, unconventional black religious figure of the Depression years. In more recent years, however, he has been recognized for his efforts to respond positively to a number of important issues for the black community. In light of recent historical reevaluation, Father Divine, divorced from exclusive focus upon his claims of divine status, has emerged as a leader articulating a meaningful approach to interracial harmony. The Tenets of the mission he founded outline the program still being followed by members today.*

*   *   *

Communal—After 1960

ARTICLES OF FAITH (JESUS PEOPLE U.S.A.)

(1) The undersigned believe in one eternal existent infinite God, Sovereign of the Universe; that He only is God, creative and administrative, Holy in Nature, attributes and purpose.

(2) The undersigned believe in the one true God who has revealed Himself as the externally self-existent, self-revealed "I AM," and has further revealed Himself as embodying the principles of relationship and association, i.e., Father, Son, and Holy Ghost, Deuteronomy 6:4; Mark 12:29; Isaiah 43:10, 11; Matthew 28:19; Luke 3:22.

(3) The undersigned believe the Bible is the inspired Word of God, a revelation from God to men, the infallible rule of faith and conduct, and is superior to conscience and reason, but not contrary to reason. 2 Timothy 3:15, 16; 1 Peter 2:2.

(4) The undersigned believe in the Holy Spirit, ever present and active in convicting souls of their sins and regenerating those who repent and believe on the Lord Jesus Christ; and that he also sanctified all believers who consecrate themselves unto God; that the Holy Scriptures are truly inspired Words of God, revealing God's will concerning us in all things necessary to our salvation and Holy living; and whatsoever is not contained therein is not to be enjoined as essential to salvation. We also believe that inasmuch that we do unto others, we do unto Christ, and will be rewarded accordingly.

Notes: *These brief articles are taken from those of the Full Gospel Church in Christ, a Pentecostal church which originally chartered the Jesus People U.S.A.*

THE SEVEN IMMUTABLE LAWS OF THE UNIVERSE (RENAISSANCE CHURCH OF BEAUTY)

1. The order of mind, the expansion of deepening of mind, to attain an even balance of mind that is not swayed by the devils of scorn and judgment, for where there is not order in the universe, there is chaos of the atomic law.

2. The balance of mind positive, and the balance of the brain negative. Through thought force you bring a discipline within the brain and mind so that there will be a constant flow of balance to all that your life touches upon. To express a true understanding that encompasses all progressions of life, this is the attainment of balance.

3. Harmony means a direct alignment with all vibration of electrical energy. It is harmony that flows over the earth and through it. It is what changes the layers of the universe into different patterns, that forces a change in all vibrational structures, and thus, as mankind enters into a new condition, this new condition is only brought about by the consistency of the thoughts which connect the mind of man and the mind of eternity.

4. Growth is needed from the carnal to the celestial. And it is the will of a person that decides what that growth will be. And this is the free will of true expression, where man assumes a spiritual attitude toward his material body, and looks ever deeper into the spirit to find the order and balance of which we have spoken.

5. The fifth law of the universe is god-perception. That is to perceive the shape of a cloud or of a tree, or of how many legs can be found upon the little ant that travels over the vast surface of the earth. It is to perceive the full vibration, to give a fuller interpretation to the various rooms within the mansion of the soul. The word "perception" means to look ahead into that which does operate, but does not control the free will of an individual spirit.

6. Love is that substance, that electrical force, that want, that gives to people the restlessness, the uncertainties, and the desire for a higher expression. It is truly found that that love must be given in accordance with the celestial law of full giving. It must be a total love, not limited by conditions of a material nature, but given to each person in a constant consideration of what each life expresses. And it is through the giving of the fullness of your all-in-all being that you come into the growth that gives you the fullness of life.

7. Man must now realize the true structure of the universe, the true energy that animates his physical structure, that gives him the precious flow of life, and allows him the very understanding of his full expression upon this earth. Life is simplicity, compounded by this great word, compassion. And wise is the man who not only sits in meditation, but also gives full realization, a true definition, to his life.

Compassion holds a true theme, through all his previous lives, his present, and aye, even his future.

Notes: *This document was received as a revelation by Michael Metelica, founder of the church.*

*   *   *

THE SYNANON PHILOSOPHY (SYNANON CHURCH)

The Synanon Philosophy is based on the belief that there comes a time in everyone's life when he arrives at the conviction that envy is ignorance; that imitation is suicide; that he must accept himself for better or for worse as is his portion; that though the wide universe is full of good, no kernel of nourishing corn can come to him but through his toil bestowed on that plot of ground which is given to him to till. The power which resides in him is new in nature, and none but he knows what it is that he can do, nor does he know until he has tried. Bravely let him speak the utmost syllable of his conviction. God will not have his work made manifest by cowards.

A man is relieved and gay when he has put his heart into his work and done his best; but what he has said or done otherwise shall give him no peace. As long as he willingly accepts himself, he will continue to grow and develop his potentialities. As long as he does not accept himself, much of his energies will be used to defend rather than to explore and actualize himself.

No one can force a person towards permanent and creative learning. He will learn only if he wills to. Any other type of learning is temporary and inconsistent with the self and will disappear as soon as the threat is removed. Learning is possible in an environment that provides information, the setting, materials, resources, and by his being there. God helps those who help themselves.

THE NEW COVENANT, THE WORLD BILL OF RIGHTS [UNIVERSAL INDUSTRIAL CHURCH OF THE NEW WORLD COMFORTER (ONE WORLD COMMUNE)]

Let each of us share all the world—the kingdom of God—and call one place of our choosing our own and be free to come and go in the world and stay at any dwelling place accommodating travelers.

Let each of us give of ourselves to the extent of our abilities to the One World Company, and in return all things shall be added unto us.

Let each person be judged only by his conscience in God and let no one judge his fellow beings, but rather judge himself.

Let no person or group hold any authority over another except that person be willingly led by wisdom and true personality.

Let the government be of the people, where the people are self-governed; by the people, where the people enjoy perfect freedom; for the people, where the people give themselves abundant living.

Let the Government seat be only the storehouse and inventory of the people's products.

Let all things be done unto edification, for God is not the author of confusion.

Notes: *This document was promulgated by Allan Noonan, founder of the One World Commune. It is illustrative of their planetary vision.*

Chapter 4

Christian Science-Metaphysical Family

Christian Science

THE TENETS OF CHRISTIAN SCIENCE (CHURCH OF CHRIST, SCIENTIST)

1. As adherents of Truth, we take the inspired Word of the Bible as our sufficient guide to eternal Life.

2. We acknowledge and adore one supreme and infinite God. We acknowledge His Son, one Christ; the Holy Ghost or divine Comforter; and man in God's image and likeness.

3. We acknowledge God's forgiveness of sin in the destruction of sin and the spiritual understanding that casts out evil as unreal. But the belief in sin is punished so long as the belief lasts.

4. We acknowledge Jesus' atonement as the evidence of divine, efficacious Love, unfolding man's unity with God through Christ Jesus the Way-shower; and we acknowledge that man is saved through Christ, through Truth, Life, and Love as demonstrated by the Galilean Prophet in healing the sick and over-coming sin and death.

5. We acknowledge that the crucifixion of Jesus and his resurrection served to uplift faith to understand eternal Life, even the allness of Soul, Spirit, and the nothingness of matter.

6. And we solemnly promise to watch, and pray for that Mind to be in us which was also in Christ Jesus; to do unto others as we would have them do unto us; and to be merciful, just, and pure.

Notes: *The tenets of the Church of Christ, Scientist, are found on p. 497 of the authorized edition of Mary Baker Eddy's* Science and Health with Key to the Scriptures. *This statement highlights the essential Christian element in Christian Science. It affirms several of the major ideas for which the church is well known: the unreality of evil, the nothingness of matter, and the allness of Soul or Spirit.*

New Thought

DECLARATION OF PRINCIPLES (INTERNATIONAL NEW THOUGHT ALLIANCE)

DECLARATION OF PRINCIPLES, 1917

We affirm the freedom of each soul as to choice and as to belief, and would not, by the adoption of any declaration of principles, limit such freedom. The essence of the New Thought is Truth, and each individual must be loyal to the Truth he sees. The windows of his soul must be kept open at each moment for the higher light, and his mind must be always hospitable to each new inspiration.

We affirm the Good. This is supreme, universal and everlasting. Man is made in the image of the Good, and evil and pain are but the tests and correctives that appear when his thought does not reflect the full glory of this image.

We affirm health, which is man's divine inheritance. Man's body is his holy temple. Every function of it, every call of it, is intelligent, and is shaped, ruled, repaired, and controlled by mind. He whose body is full of light is full of health. Spiritual healing has existed among all races in all times. It has now become a part of the higher science and art of living the life more abundant.

We affirm the divine supply. He who serves God and man in the full understanding of the law of compensation shall not lack. Within us are unused resources of energy and power. He who lives with his whole being, and thus expresses fullness, shall reap fullness in return. He who gives himself, he who knows and acts in his highest knowledge, he who trusts in the divine return, has learned the law of success.

We affirm the teachings of Christ that the Kingdom of Heaven is within us, that we are one with the Father, that we should not judge, that we should love one another, that we should heal the sick, that we should return good for evil, that we should minister to others, and that we should be perfect even as our Father in Heaven is perfect. These are not only ideals, but practical, everyday working principles.

47

DECLARATION OF PRINCIPLES (INTERNATIONAL NEW THOUGHT ALLIANCE) (continued)

We affirm the new thought of God as Universal Love, Life, Truth and Joy, in whom we live, move, and have our being, and by whom we are held together; that His mind is our mind now, that realizing our oneness with Him means love, truth, peace, health and plenty, not only in our own lives but in the giving out of these fruits of the Spirit to others.

We affirm these things, not as a profession, but practice, not on one day of the week, but in every hour and minute of every day, sleeping and waking, not in the ministry of a few, but in the service that includes the democracy of all, not in words alone, but in the innermost thoughts of the heart expressed in living the life. "By their fruits ye shall know them."

We affirm Heaven here and now, the life everlasting that becomes conscious immortality, the communion of mind with mind throughout the universe of thoughts, the nothingness of all error and negation, including death, the varity in unity that produces the individual expressions of the One-Life, and the quickened realization of the indwelling God in each soul that is making a new heaven and a new earth.

We affirm that the universe is spiritual and we are spiritual beings. This is the Christ message to the twentieth century, and it is a message not so much of words as of works. To attain this, however, we must be clean, honest and trustworthy and uphold the Jesus Christ standards as taught in the Four Gospels. We now have the golden opportunity to form a real Christ movement. Let us build our house upon this rock, and nothing can prevail against it. This is the vision and mission of the ALLIANCE.

These principles were adopted and made unanimous at the Congress held in St. Louis, in 1917.

DECLARATION OF PRINCIPLES, 1957

What We Believe . . .

We affirm the inseparable oneness of God and man, the realization of which comes through spiritual intuition, the implications of which are that man can reproduce the Divine perfection in his body, emotions, and in all his external affairs.

We affirm the freedom of each person in matters of belief.

We affirm the Good to be supreme, universal, and eternal.

We affirm that the Kingdom of Heaven is within us, that we are one with the Father, that we should love one another, and return good for evil.

We affirm that we should heal the sick through prayer, and that we should endeavor to manifest perfection "even as our Father in Heaven is perfect."

We affirm our belief in God as the Universal Wisdom, Love, Life, Truth, Power, Peace, Beauty, and Joy, "in whom we live, move, and have our being."

We affirm that man's mental states are carried forward into manifestation and become his experience through the Creative Law of Cause and Effect.

We affirm that the Divine Nature expressing Itself through man manifsts Itself as health, supply, wisdom, love, life, truth, power, peace, beauty, and joy.

We affirm that man is an invisible spiritual dweller within a human body, continuing and unfolding as a spiritual being beyond the change called physical death.

We affirm that the universe is the body of God, spiritual in essence, governed by God through laws which are spiritual in reality even when material in appearance.

(Adopted by 42nd Congress, July 25, 1957)

Notes: *The International New Thought Alliance (INTA) is an ecumenical group to which many New Thought groups belong. It adopted two statements, one in 1917 and another in 1957. The older statement is longer and makes specific reference to the teachings of Christ, identifying New Thought with "the Christ message to the twentieth century." In the second version, all specific mention of Christ and/or Christianity have been deleted. In both statements an impersonal God, prosperity, and life after death are affirmed. In 1916 a committee was appointed by INTA to prepare a declaration of principles. A number of people submitted proposed statements, among them Alliance president James A. Edgerton. His proposed statement was largely adapted without change, although a paragraph was added identifying New Thought as a Christ movement in order to answer criticisms of the INTA from the Unity School of Christianity. In spite of these references, Unity soon withdrew from the Alliance. When a revised declaration was adopted in 1957, no references to Christianity were made.*

*   *   *

A NEW THOUGHT CREED (ELIZABETH TOWNE)

We affirm that God, the All Wise, All Powerful, All Present Spirit, is the Life, Wisdom, and Power of every human being.

We affirm that all humans are "members one of another," that in and through each God "works to will and to do of his good pleasure," which is the Good and the Pleasure of each and all.

We affirm that the Desire for Good, and the Desire to Do Good, found in every human soul, is God's Will working in him.

We affirm that by constant recognition of God in all and through all, man co-operates with God to fulfill his destiny, his individual desires for Being Good, Doing Good and Having the Good Things of the world.

We affirm that God's nature is Love and His Universe One Living Organism, all its individual members made to function in Freedom and Loving kindness, each after its own pattern.

We affirm that through constant recognition of man as One with God, man comes to realize and manifest God, or Love, in increasing measure, each after his own soul's pattern.

We affirm that in truth all soul patterns are equally indispensable to the working out of God's Good Pleasure for all; that all souls are equally valuable to the world, equally entitled to the world's Opportunities and Good Things.

We affirm that man's nature is Love, and that Self-Expression in Lovingkindness is the Way of Enjoyment of Peace and Prosperity of mind, body and conditions.

We affirm that, as God is the Infinite One, so mankind is Infinite, and One, able through recognition, realization and manifestation of God within, and by co-operation with all men to think out and work out on this earth heavenly conditions such as are beyond those dreamed of in the imaginations of seers and prophets.

Notes: *Elizabeth Towne, as editor of the* Nautilus *and head of her own publishing company, was one of the most powerful figures in early New Thought. She was elected president of the International New Thought Alliance (INTA) in 1924. She was also one of four persons appointed on the committee to draft a Declaration of Principles for the INTA in 1916. She was one of several who wrote personal statements on New Thought for use by the committee. While not adopted by the INTA, A New Thought Creed summarizes the meaning of New Thought for one who was a significant leader in the movement for over half a century.*

* * *

WHAT THE NEW THOUGHT STANDS FOR (HORATIO DRESSER)

The New Thought is a practical philosophy of the inner life in relation to health, happiness, social welfare and success.

It stands for the inner life first of all because the life within is found to be the source of power, the basis of health and happiness, the clue to success, individuality and freedom.

It stands for an affirmative attitude in contrast with older types of thought, for optimism instead of pessimism, and for the unity of life instead of any teaching which separates the forces of the universe into hostile powers. To understand its practical values and its sphere of activity one needs to consider both its essential principles and its special methods.

As a philosophy the New Thought starts with the principle that all power is essentially one—the Universal Life or Infinite Spirit.

The world is regarded as an expression or manifestation of this Life, disclosed in the orderly processes of creation. The world exists for spiritual ends.

Man as a spiritual being is living an essentially spiritual life, for the sake of the soul His life proceeds from within outward, and makes for harmony, health, freedom, efficiency, service.

Health and freedom, individuality and success are his birthright privileges.

It is natural and right to be well and prosperous. What man needs, in his ignorance and bondage is THE TRUTH concerning this, his spiritual being and birthright. He needs to learn that he is a soul or spirit possessing the physical body as an instrument of experience and expression. He needs to REALIZE this, the spiritual truth of his being, that he may rise above all ills and all obstacles into fullness of power. Every resource he could ask for is at hand, in the omnipresent divine wisdom. Every individual can learn to draw upon the divine resources.

The special methods of the New Thought grow out of this central spiritual principle. Much stress is put upon inner or spiritual meditation, through the practice of silence, concentration and inner control, because each of us needs to become still to learn how to be affirmative, optimistic.

Great emphasis is also put upon the subconscious mind as the agency for the realization of ideals, the execution of affirmations. Suggestion or affirmation is employed to banish ills and errors and establish spiritual truth in their place. Silent or mental treatment is employed to overcome disease and secure freedom and success.

The New Thought teaches that every individual can use its method of spiritual meditation and mental healing. What is required is that one shall gain the inner point of view, get the impetus, become aware that the spirit is supreme. To some this comes as a sense of the newness and freshness of life, in contrast with the old idea that the world is a field of warfare between good and evil. To others it comes as an awakening that man is a spirit, not a body; that he can acquire inner self-mastery and control the flesh. It comes to many as a theory and method of mental healing at first, and when illness is banished as a theory of the whole of life. Whatever the starting point the end is the same. The important point is to learn to apply here and now the best that has been lived and taught concerning the things of the spirit.

The New Thought then is not a substitute for Christianity, but an inspired return to the original teaching and practice of the gospels. It is not opposed to the churches, but aims to make religion immediately serviceable and practical. It is not hostile to science, but wishes to spiritualize all facts and laws. It encourages each man to begin wherever he is, however conditioned, whatever he may find to occupy his hands; and to learn the great spiritual lessons taught by this present experience. Thus apparent failure may be turned into success, weakness to strength and an apparent curse into a blessing.

Notes: *This statement was one of many submitted to the International New Thought Alliance committee appointed in 1916 to draft a Declaration of Principles. Although Dresser was not a member of the committee that prepared the final statement presented to the Alliance in 1917, he was an intellectual leader in the movement for many years. He never identified with any of the several New Thought churches (he eventually joined the Swedenborgian Church of the New Jerusalem).*

THE NEW THOUGHT RELIGION AND PHILOSOPHY (ABEL L. ALLEN)

New Thought has been defined as the latest product of growing mind; also as an attitude of mind and not a cult. Neither definition is complete.

New Thought is a search for light and understanding of man's relations with the Infinite, and hence is not susceptible of definition in terms.

New Thought is old thought stated in modern terms of expression, adapted to man's spiritual development and welfare.

It is a philosophy and Religion of Life. It is a quest for truth and inner peace.

Its supreme purpose is to awaken the highest aspirations of the soul and lead man into conscious unity with God.

Its teachings are positive, constructive and optimistic.

It deals with life and reveals inner sources of power for man's essential needs.

It does not deny the existence of matter, but asserts the dominion of mind over matter.

It propounds no fixed creeds or ecclesiastical dogmas, because it sets no limitation to man's progress, and man is limited by the creeds and dogmas for which he stands.

It does not depend on a particular book or books for spiritual light or look outward for revelation, but to the soul within.

It recognizes no spiritual authority save the light of the individual soul.

It endeavors to keep pace with the progress of science and modern psychology.

It recognizes no conflict between true religion and real science, since truth is the ultimate goal of each.

A conception of God is the basis of every religion and philosophy.

The orthodox Christian Religions rest on the quality of God and man; New Thought on the unity of God and man.

New Thought is founded on primary, eternal and immutable principles. Thought may change, but principles are changeless.

These fundamental principles, boundless as infinity, may support a religion or philosophy that may expand to the full circle of truth—that may keep pace with man's development, as he reaches out towards the infinite.

PRINCIPLES OF NEW THOUGHT:

1. God is Unity, Universal Love, Life, Intelligence and Power, pervading and animating the Universe, existing with equal power at every point, manifesting in every created entity, reaching its highest expression in man, revealing to him his own individuality and the consciousness of his own Divine Soul.

2. The individual soul is an inlet to the Great Divine Soul. As man becomes conscious of his contact with Universal Life, Intelligence and Power, he realizes the unlimited potentialities within himself and that he may draw from his Infinite Source at will, for health, wisdom, life abundant and prosperity. The consciousness of this truth removes all limitations to man's possibilities.

3. The reign of universal law uniform in the mental and spiritual worlds as in the physical universe. Because of the unity of all things, whatsoever affects one part, affects all parts. The law of cause and effect enters into every thought, act and relationship in human life. Thought is the maker and molder of man's destiny. Thought is expressed in the life and personality of the individual. The consciousness of individual responsibility is necessary to man's development. Man is punished by every sin and rewarded by every virtue. Whatsoever he sows, that shall he also reap.

4. Nature is man's teacher and the revelation of the purposes of the Infinite Supreme wisdom. Power and Intelligence are in all entities from atoms to planes. Within man are the hidden meanings of creation. Through Nature and the voices of Intuition alone, God speaks to man. Man's life can be peaceful and harmonious only as he obeys Nature's laws.

5. Man is the result of the processes of evolution. He is an evolved and an evolving being. Evolution springs from within; it is a law of inner progress. Its trend is towards perfection. The ascent is the invisible spirit. The fruit of evolution is the unfolding and development of consciousness. Through the steps of evolution the soul of man is reaching up to a conscious union with the great Divine Soul.

6. Truth is the one reality. Every enduring religion must conform to the standard of truth. Truth is the only basis for right living. Truth alone sets man free. The only slavery is self-imposed through ignorance of man's Divine Inheritance. Truth dispels fear, man's greatest enemy. Truth alone brings Peace, Power and satisfaction to man.

7. The conscious identity of the soul after the event called death. This conclusion is written in man's nature; he feels and knows this voiceless message of truth. The soul persists in expression and life knows no diminution.

8. That Jesus, the Christ, is the most illumined Prophet and Teacher of the ages and has given man the true message of life.

9. The brotherhood of man as the true foundation of every human relationship.

10. Man's highest duty to God is to live a constructive life, in harmony with the laws of nature and serve his fellowmen.

11. The good, the true and the beautiful as the highest ideals of right living.

12. The purpose of New Thought is to point the way to truth and not to limit or circumscribe it.

13. New Thought is unalterably opposed to all practices of Hypnotism.

14. It does not recognize the hypotheses of what are popularly known as Spiritualism, Astrology or Rein-

carnation as a part of the Philosophy and Religion of New Thought.

Notes: *Abel L. Allen, a judge, was one of four people appointed to the committee to draft a Declaration of Principles for the International New Thought Alliance in 1916. He used his legal mind to draft one of the longest statements dealt with by the committee. Notice his denunciation of hypnotism, spiritualism, astrology, and reincarnation.*

*　　*　　*

DECLARATION OF PRINCIPLES PROPOSED FOR THE INTERNATIONAL NEW THOUGHT ALLIANCE (CHARLES GILBERT DAVIS)

Eternal progress marks the destiny of the human race. Up through the ages of the misty past, man has been seeking for his God. Step by step through the phenomena of nature, through every branch of science and philosophy and the various expressions of religion he has been searching for eternal truth. The journey has been long, wearisome and full of pain. Often at different periods of the world's history and in different localities, the cry has gone forth that the great mystery had been revealed. These have only been stages of development revealing slight glimpses of truth along the evolutionary path. Now in the dawn of the twentieth century, the windows of the soul are again opened and a new revelation is given to mankind. It is a new life, a new birth, a new step toward infinite perfection. We are just beginning to realize that the evolutionary progress has arrived at the transition stage that marks the boundary between the physical and the spiritual in human development. It is like awakening from a troubled dream and the world is not yet adjusted to the new impulses that are throbbing through the hearts of man. Some have caught glimpses of the light and have felt the glorified radiance of the new environment. But the great multitudes are yet in ignorance, wandering through the dark forest where the haunting ghosts of fear and other depressing emotions fill the soul with terror and drive men to the madness of despair. In vain each nation, tribe and tongue reaches out with pleading, uplifted hands to the unknown God on his distant throne, claiming him as their very own according to each dogmatic, theological belief, and demanding his special effort in their deliverance.

Through the centuries and millenniums, man has been following an unreality. He has imagined his God far off in an imaginary heaven sitting in majesty on a kingly throne. But he has wakened from this nightmare. He has dismissed the unreal and at last embraced the real. He has looked into his own soul and found God. In a flood of joy, the truth has burst upon his vision and he is awakened to the realization that he is an emanation from the Divine, that he and the Father are one. The joy of the discovery of this divine inheritance has renewed the life currents and lifted man up and sent him rejoicing on his journey to carry the glad tidings to all the world. In this new enlightenment, man has discovered God immanent in His world. We who have grasped the full significance of this new revelation and being desirous that all the earth should understand

and join with us in this great evolutionary advance toward infinite life and love, make the following declaration of principles:

1. We believe in the existence of an Infinite power of Life and Love and Beauty behind all the physical universe, which now and forevermore is working through evolutionary law for the betterment of all things.

2. The soul of man is immortal and co-existent with Divine Spirit.

3. A full recognition of the brotherhood of mankind is essential to all progress, all development and all unity of purpose.

4. Science is the handwriting of the Infinite Spirit on the walls of time. Hence all verified and classified wisdom must be recognized as the footprints of the Almighty and be followed and utilized for the betterment of the world.

5. God is imminent in humanity and every living soul is not only a reservoir of Divine Energy but also a distributing center from whence emanates the creative power that makes manifest the evolutionary law.

6. Our bodies are the instruments of the soul, hence it devolves upon us to keep them clean and undefiled.

7. Divine Spirit is creative, and when manifested through the individual may be utilized for the uplift of man physically, mentally and spiritually.

8. The subjective mind or soul of man is dynamic, and while directed along the currents of evolutionary progress, it may send forth and distribute the universal energy for the healing of humanity: physically, mentally and spiritually. Neither time nor distance can interpose against the working of this law.

9. All life is existent on a progressive plane. The materializations of the Divine Spirit are evidence of eternal progress. No creed of philosophy or religion that aims at truth can be forever stationary. As the light is thrown upon the pathway of the soul, new facts are revealed and a new door is opened for a greater revelation.

10. Christ is the manifestation of the fulfillment of the law. He and the Father are one-God manifest in the flesh. He points the way to life, truth and evolution. Let us follow Him.

Darkness shadows the earth and through the violation of law man has wandered far from the highway that leads to the perfection of the soul. It is time for a new revelation There must be a new adjustment of human vision. God and his world are inseparable. Science and religion must join hands to rescue mankind.

Notes: *Charles Gilbert Davis was a member of the committee to draft a Declaration of Principles for the International New Thought Alliance in 1916. As part of his work for the committee, he wrote and submitted a personally written article.*

ARTICLES OF FAITH AND ALTRURIAN BELIEF (ALTRURIAN SOCIETY)

ARTICLES OF FAITH

I accept as a working hypothesis, "The Spirit of God dwelleth in me," therefore I covenant to love and serve God in and through inner consciousness.

I accept universal brotherhood as a means to God attainment.

I promise to pay debts, be moral, adjust difficulties, back up when wrong and do all things necessary to God attainment.

I promise to introspect my daily acts, and to follow the outline in "The Four Keys" as a means to Health, Happiness and Prosperity.

I promise to make the laws, acts and experiences of Jesus Christ, my guide and to live them to the best of my ability.

ALTRURIAN BELIEF

We believe in Jesus Christ as the way to Salvation all can follow, and His way as law and not "Blood Atonement." Nothing left out,—no creed or dogma put in. We believe that man must control his body, and therefore "Penances and Restraints" consisting of Prayer, Love, Fasting and Service are the principles of attainment.

We believe in the Corruptible and the Incorruptible body, one temporary and the other everlasting. As we control the one, the other becomes free,—and freedom of the Incorruptible means everlasting life. The means of control is in strict morality, probity, truth, freedom from evil and devotion to the inner consciousness of God.

We believe the Love gift at the Altar is necessary before prayer, and prayer to be effective must be silent in introspection; consisting of paying debts and freedom from evil, in which the body and mind becomes purged and clean. Then the asking will result in an answer,—the petitioner getting what is needed.

We believe in a Brotherhood without caste, and in one God, Omnipotent, Omniscient and Omni-present and we as individuals can by strict obedience to law, become conscious of God within. We believe Jesus Christ as the Son of God, and potentially every man a "Son of God."

We believe Jesus Christ healed the Sick, cast out Devils and performed mighty works as a demonstration of His work and the means of salvation. We believe the same works and the same plan is applicable now, and the means of salvation. What He did we can do, and must do, if there is realization.

We believe in the Ordinances of God, the First of which must be Belief, Second—Faith, Third—Surrender or Repentance, Fourth—Baptism, Fifth—Remission of Sin through confession and work, Sixth—Divine consciousness and the descent of the "Holy Ghost," Seventh—Transmission from one to another of the power of the "Holy Ghost" by "laying on of hands."

We believe in Prophecy, Divine inspiration. Gifts and the power to demonstrate them. We believe in Vision and Divine direction. We believe in law and order of things, and man must experience Religious fervor in order to be true to his Vision. We believe it is through Vision and Prophecy given to Master men that have given and is giving man an understanding of Divine law. We believe these laws are given to mankind through revelation,—the spoken word—or laying on of hands, through which sickness, sin and death are banished.

We believe Healing the Sick,—creating Abundance and Happiness are ordinances of God and should be a part of Christian inheritance. We believe the Signs of "The Christian" are those given in the last Chapter of St. Mark, and include them in our ordinance.

We believe that Christians should be Healthy, Happy and Prosperous: debt payers, giving no offense, save in a cause righteous. We believe in obedience to law, all law whether Divine or man made. We believe all church organizations are seeking correct principles of living and so ask for humble privilege to demonstrate our plans.

We believe "The Kingdom of God" is here and everywhere, when man is ready to comply with the law of God understanding. This is in belief, Acceptance, Faith, Intention, Contemplation, Meditation and Conviction that mellow objective intelligence into abeyance while arousing the "Hidden and latent" within belonging to God into control of body function.

We believe in being honest, sober, true, moral, clean in our dealings, just in account, loving, generous, forgiving, kind, and obedient to our vision of usefulness. We accept the new Testament as the direct revelation of the later dispensation, the Four Gospels as Christ's direction and all other writing of an inspired nature as collateral.

Notes: *New members of the Altrurian Society were asked to sign a card subscribing to the brief Articles of Faith. The longer statement of belief provides a fuller understanding of the society's broad perspective.*

* * *

FUNDAMENTAL PRINCIPLES (CHRISTIAN ASSEMBLY)

The fundamental principles of the teaching of the Christ form the basis of all the teaching presented. Some of these are as follows:

1. God is Spirit, Whose nature is love and wisdom. As Spirit, God is One: Omnipotent, Omniscient, and Omnipresent.

2. The kingdom of God is within the soul of every one. The real creation of God is spiritual humanity. As God did not create man a carnal being, it is necessary for him to regenerate in order to enter the kingdom. The kingdom of heaven is for the living, for the Christ said: "He is not God of the dead, but of the living; for all are alive to him" (Luke 20:38 lit.).

3. Jesus is the Christ, the Son of the living God, the Saviour of the world. As the Son of God He is divine; and as the Son of man He is human. In Him the divine and human are a perfect unit. Jesus Christ, the

risen Lord, abides in His kingdom within the hearts and souls of His disciples.

4. True faith comes from God and makes all things possible to them that believe. Divine faith is, therefore, a mighty power which one may use in prayer and in all good works into which the Holy Spirit leads him with most gratifying results.

5. Evil has no power from God; the power it seems to have, unregenerate man through ignorance and fear has given it.

6. Divine love is the fulfillment of the law which is constitutional with man. It is the only sovereign power in time, as well as in eternity. The power of love works for the good of man, and when he believes and trusts in it, he is helped in his every need.

7. Christian healing is properly part of the gospel.

8. Through works of faith and love, and the renunciation of the false selfhood, regenerate man comes to know that the kingdom of heaven is within. He also realizes that as he does the will of God he becomes one with him, and joint heir with the Christ in all the Father has.

Notes: *This small body centered in San Jose, California, is a specifically Christian branch of the New Thought movement. Its position, as distinct within New Thought, is found in item 3.*

*　　*　　*

BASIC TENETS OF THEOLOGIA 21 [CHURCH OF THE TRINITY (INVISIBLE MINISTRY)]

We believe that . . .

The Presence of God, as Father, Son and Holy Spirit, fills all space and time. There is no spot where God is not. (Psa. 90:2; 139:7-12)

The nature of God is forever perfect in every way, for in him there is no darkness at all. (Mat. 5:48; 1 John 1:5)

Christ-Jesus, the only begotten Son, shares the divine Nature of The Father, and is therefore indestructible, omniscient, omnipotent, immutable and eternal. (Mal. 3:6; Mat. 28:18; Heb. 13:8; Jas. 1:17; 1 John 4:9)

By divine Grace, The Christ-Jesus Consciousness indwells every man in potentia, and that potential may be cultivated and developed in unlimited degree. (Eph. 2:5; Phi. 2:5; Col. 1:27)

Man's awareness and acceptance of the gift of Grace fulfills God's will. It is The Father's good pleasure to give us the kingdom, and our spiritual destiny to be perfect, as he is perfect. (Luke 12:32; Eph. 2:8)

The power of God flows outward, radiating from the secret place of the most High at the center of every man. (Zep. 3:17; Luke 17:21; 1 John 4:4)

This power is therefore available to all, and is always available now. (Psa. 46:1; Mark 11:24; Acts 10:34; 2 Cor. 6:2)

Faith in this power, through Christ-Jesus, sets man free from the law of sin and death, and aligns him with the royal Law of eternal Life. Amen. (Mat. 14:13-14; John 1:12; John 3:15; Rom 8:2; Jas. 2:8)

Notes: *Theologia 21 is the name given to the Church of the Trinity's theological teachings. It is aligned to the common New Thought perspective.*

*　　*　　*

STATEMENTS BY THE CHURCH OF THE TRUTH

THE CHURCH OF THE TRUTH BELIEVES

That always there is perfect guidance for each one in any and every time of uncertainty.

That always there is healing power greater than the seeming power of disease.

That always conditions and events are working toward a great and ultimate good surpassing the most extravagant hopes of man.

That always there is a way out.

That always the attitude of alert calmness and of steadfast expectation makes easy the demonstration of needed good.

That always we may think new thoughts about old conditions, and thereby set new forces into action.

That always the TRUE MAN is good and beautiful and kind and just and loving and strong and divine.

That always God is available to man for wisdom, supply, good will, strength, self-confidence, health, efficiency and happiness.

THE STATEMENT OF THE TRUTH

To outline the vision of the Truth as it is revealed to us, but not as a finality, we utter this statement of the Truth:

God is all and God is Spirit.

Man is the child of God, inheriting His nature.

Jesus, the Christ, entered into the fullness of his God-heritage.

God's world and man's world are thought created.

To think in harmony with God is to enter God's Good.

The Kingdom of Heaven is within the soul.

What faith shapes in the within God manifests in the without.

When man thinks God's thought, God's power is with his thought.

To know this Divine Omnipresence and realize its power is eternal life.

The essence of Divine Omnipresence is love.

And Love is Heaven in every realm.

THE CHURCH OF THE CHURCH

Our universal mission is to make this Church so great and so beautiful and so filled with transforming and healing power, to make it such a demonstration of what the life lived in God may mean, that all mankind will hasten to establish just such places as this throughout the hungry, sin-sick, suffering world.

Each church is feeding a certain state of consciousness in man, and so we can bless, without one thought of condemnation, every organization, every religious movement in the world. But if we did not believe, if we did not know that there is a line of Truth, a hair-breadth line, which no other church has ever followed, there would be no excuse for this new denomination, the Church of the Truth. If I did not believe with my whole soul that it gives expression in fuller and truer outline to the vision of Jesus the Christ, I should not have dared to assist you in its organization. I am so cognizant of the fact that a peculiar and absolutely divine mission has been placed in our hands, that nothing can shake that conviction in my soul. And it is because I see this, that I say these words, and because many of you also realize it, you will understand me.

I want to tell you now that the ultimate goal of the Church of the Truth of this ministry, is the discovering and establishing for the future of mankind that platform, broad enough so that no one who may ever come to it will be crowded off.

I am seeking a kind of healing power a kind of philosophy big enough to last mankind for all time; and if not one of you follows me, if not one of you believes as I do, I can go alone. I see that which is a thousand years from the present time, and I am speaking the word not only for you, but every man who comes into the world for all future generations.

This Church is the biggest thing on earth. If anyone asks me the question: "What is the ultimate work of your organization?" I want to bear testimony to this thing, that its purpose, regardless of present opinions of man, is to build a church so big and so broad, so universal and so absolutely true, that no evolution of man, no progress of the souls of man, no discovery of the mind of man shall be so vast that it cannot stand upon this platform which we are uncovering—for we are uncovering the Truth of Almighty God. We are trying to get at the secret of God, to find the very kernel of the thought of Jesus, to get hold of the lines of power of Infinite Intelligence, and we are striving to make them so clear that a little child can understand them. Is not that a great work to do? Oh, the glory of a church that brings up its children to the knowledge of the mighty program of the Father!

To this Church, in addition to all its potency in the way of healing men's bodies, in the way of healing the circumstances of their lives, in the way of giving them a power through which they may make life's pathway smooth and ascend to the heights of God to this Church has been given the shaping of a religion so broad, so universal, so absolutely true that all the discoveries of all future times shall not find one flaw or one break in its structure. We are to state for men and women, today, the ultimate and absolute and perfect Truth of the Christ, so that wounds shall be healed, hearts shall be made whole, tears shall be wiped from all faces; we are to place in the hand of man the power of the God-life, and in addition to that, we are to state, for all time that Truth of God on which the hope of the future of humanity rests. I am endeavoring, in the silence and in all the work which I do, to let the Holy Spirit of Truth speak to me the word that shall live throughout the ages, as the word of Christ has lived since Jesus spoke upon this earth. And I pray that God will give me wisdom and power and fineness of spirit to discern, that I may lead you to the uncovering of this marvelous platform on which by and by, at the great white throne of God, shall be gathered all the nations of the earth, all of the children of our Father.

Notes: *Growing out of the mystical vision of founder Albert Grier, the Church of the Truth has a variety of guiding and confessional statements. H. Edward Mills wrote The Church of the Truth Believes, while Grier wrote the church's Statement of the Truth and the missional statement, The Church of the Church. The Statement of the Truth describes Christ as a person who entered into the "fullness of his God-heritage," a possibility for each person.*

*　　*　　*

STATEMENT OF BEING (DIVINE SCIENCE FEDERATION INTERNATIONAL)

God is all, both invisible and visible.

One Presence, One Mind, One Power is all.

This One that is all is perfect life, perfect love, and perfect substance.

Man is the individualized expression of God and is ever one with this perfect life, perfect love, and perfect substance.

*　　*　　*

PRINCIPLES OF MIRACLES (MIRACLES EXPERIENCES, INC.)

1. There is no order of difficulty in miracles. One is not "harder" or "bigger" than another. They are all the same. All expressions of love are maximal.

2. Miracles as such do not matter. The only thing that matters is their Source, Which is far beyond evaluation.

3. Miracles occur naturally as expressions of love. The real miracle is the love that inspires them. In this sense everything that comes from love is a miracle.

4. All miracles mean life, and God is the Giver of life. His Voice will direct you very specifically. You will be told all you need to know.

5. Miracles are habits, and should be involuntary. They should not be under conscious control. Consciously selected miracles can be misguided.

6. Miracles are natural. When they do not occur something has gone wrong.

7. Miracles are everyone's right, but purification is necessary first.

8. Miracles are healing because they supply a lack; they are performed by those who temporarily have more for those who temporarily have less.

9. Miracles are a kind of exchange. Like all expressions of love, which are always miraculous in the true sense, the exchange reverses the physical laws. They bring more love both to the giver and the receiver.

10. The use of miracles as spectacles to induce belief is a misunderstanding of their purpose.

11. Prayer is the medium of miracles. It is a means of communication of the created with the Creator. Through prayer love is received, and through miracles love is expressed.

12. Miracles are thoughts. Thoughts can represent the lower or bodily level of experience, or the higher or spiritual level of experience. One makes the physical, and the other creates the spiritual.

13. Miracles are both beginnings and endings, and so they alter the temporal order. They are always affirmations of rebirth, which seem to go back but really go forward. They undo the past in the present, and thus release the future.

14. Miracles bear witness to truth. They are convincing because they arise from conviction. Without conviction they deteriorate into magic, which is mindless and therefore destructive; or rather, the uncreative use of mind.

15. Each day should be devoted to miracles. The purpose of time is to enable you to learn how to use time constructively. It is thus a teaching device and a means to an end. Time will cease when it is no longer useful in facilitating learning.

16. Miracles are teaching devices for demonstrating it is as blessed to give as to receive. They simultaneously increase the strength of the giver and supply strength to the receiver.

17. Miracles transcend the body. They are sudden shifts into invisibility, away from the bodily level. That is why they heal.

18. A miracle is a service. It is the maximal service you can render to another. It is a way of loving your neighbor as yourself. You recognize your own and your neighbor's worth simultaneously.

19. Miracles make minds one in God. They depend on cooperation because the Sonship is the sum of all that God created. Miracles therefore reflect the laws of eternity, not of time.

20. Miracles reawaken the awareness that the spirit, not the body, is the altar of truth. This is the recognition that leads to the healing power of the miracle.

21. Miracles are natural signs of forgiveness. Through miracles you accept God's forgiveness by extending it to others.

22. Miracles are associated with fear only because of the belief that darkness can hide. You believe that what your physical eyes cannot see does not exist. This leads to a denial of spiritual sight.

23. Miracles rearrange perception and place all levels in true perspective. This is healing because sickness comes from confusing the levels.

24. Miracles enable you to heal the sick and raise the dead because you made sickness and death yourself, and can therefore abolish both. *You* are a miracle, capable of creating in the likeness of your Creator. Everything else is your own nightmare, and does not exist. Only the creations of light are real.

25. Miracles are part of an interlocking chain of forgiveness which, when completed, is the Atonement. Atonement works all the time and in all the dimensions of time.

26. Miracles represent freedom from fear. "Atoning" means "undoing." The undoing of fear is an essential part of the Atonement value of miracles.

27. A miracle is a universal blessing from God through me to all my brothers. It is the privilege of the forgiven to forgive.

28. Miracles are a way of earning release from fear. Revelation induces a state in which fear has already been abolished. Miracles are thus a means and revelation is an end.

29. Miracles praise God through you. They praise Him by honoring His creations, affirming their perfection. They heal because they deny body-identification and affirm spirit-identification.

30. By recognizing spirit, miracles adjust the levels of perception and show them in proper alignment. This places spirit at the center, where it can communicate directly.

31. Miracles should inspire gratitude, not awe. You should thank God for what you really are. The children of God are holy and the miracle honors their holiness, which can be hidden but never lost.

32. I inspire all miracles, which are really intercessions. They intercede for your holiness and make your perceptions holy. By placing you beyond the physical laws they raise you into the sphere of celestial order. In this order you *are* perfect.

33. Miracles honor you because you are lovable. They dispel illusions about yourself and perceive the light in you. They thus atone for your errors by freeing you from your nightmares. By releasing your mind from the imprisonment of your illusions, they restore your sanity.

34. Miracles restore the mind to its fullness. By atoning for lack they establish perfect protection. The spirit's strength leaves no room for intrusions.

35. Miracles are expressions of love, but they may not always have observable effects.

36. Miracles are examples of right thinking, aligning your perceptions with truth as God created it.

37. A miracle is a correction introduced into false thinking by me. It acts as a catalyst, breaking up erroneous perception and reorganizing it properly. This places you under the Atonement principle,

PRINCIPLES OF MIRACLES (MIRACLES EXPERIENCES, INC.) (continued)

where perception is healed. Until this has occurred, knowledge of the Divine Order is impossible.

38. The Holy Spirit is the mechanism of miracles. He perceives both God's creations and your illusions. He separates the true from the false by His ability to perceive totally rather than selectively.

39. The miracle dissolves error because the Holy Spirit identifies error as false or unreal. This is the same as saying that by perceiving light, darkness automatically disappears.

40. The miracle acknowledges everyone as your brother and mine. It is a way of perceiving the universal mark of God.

41. Wholeness is the perceptual content of miracles. They thus correct, or atone for, the faulty perception of lack.

42. A major contribution of miracles is their strength in releasing you from your false sense of isolation, deprivation and lack.

43. Miracles arise from a miraculous state of mind, or a state of miracle-readiness.

44. The miracle is an expression of an inner awareness of Christ and the acceptance of His Atonement.

45. A miracle is never lost. It may touch many people you have not even met, and produce undreamed of changes in situations of which you are not even aware.

46. The Holy Spirit is the highest communication medium. Miracles do not involve this type of communication, because they are *temporary* communication devices. When you return to your original form of communication with God by direct revelation, the need for miracles is over.

47. The miracle is a learning device that lessens the need for time. It establishes an out-of-pattern time interval not under the usual laws of time. In this sense it is timeless.

48. The miracle is the only device at your immediate disposal for controlling time. Only revelation transcends it, having nothing to do with time at all.

49. The miracle makes no distinction among degrees of misperception. It is a device for perception-correction, effective quite apart from either the degree or the direction of the error. This is its true indiscriminateness.

50. The miracle compares what you have made with creation, accepting what is in accord with it as true, and rejecting what is out of accord as false.

Notes: *These statements from the first pages of* A Course in Miracles *summarize the content of the book around which the organization is built. See:* A Course in Miracles *(New York: Foundation for Inner Peace, 1975).*

STATEMENT OF BELIEF [PHOENIX INSTITUTE (CHURCH OF MAN)]

The Church of Man is established because we believe:

There is only One Presence: God;

That God and man cannot be separated;

That every man is hungering for the experience of Oneness with the Self of his own being;

That this One acts in only one way;

That this way is a reciprocal action according to man's belief;

That man is the evidence of this action of the One;

That there is a way for man to experience this satisfaction of finding HimSelf;

That this occurs within man and then outer man is at peace with himself, his world, and his God;

That every man is the church;

That the teaching "Ye are gods" is verified by esoteric as well as exoteric knowledge synthesizing the principles of Science, Art, and Religion.

* * *

BASIC TENETS OF THE TRUTH OF LIFE MOVEMENT, SUMMARY OF TEACHINGS, AND THE SEVEN PROMULGATIONS OF LIGHT (SEICHO-NO-IE)

BASIC TENETS

WE ARE ALL CHILDREN OF GOD

The Truth of Life philosophy teaches that mankind is created in the image of God, and that we already possess the perfection of divine nature within us, whether we recognize it or not. As children of God, we are heirs to all of God's power and abundance. We are in reality without sin, disease, poverty, pain, or suffering. This is one of the most important points of the teachings.

Man is a spiritual being. Once we come to this realization, all negative delusions disappear and we naturally manifest perfect health, love, harmony, and abundance.

We believe that we can live God-like, profound lives now, and achieve a heavenly existence while still living in this world. We need only awaken to that which we already possess.

POWER OF THE WORD

Word is the creator of our spiritual universe. What we think and say has a profound effect on our lives and on others. We believe that prayer, words of love, and praise nourish our souls and provide the means to bring out the indwelling divinity within ourselves and others.

ONENESS OF ALL RELIGIONS

The Truth of Life philosophy embraces all religions, races, and creeds. It incorporates the teachings of Christianity, Buddhism, and Shintoism and emphasizes the truth that all major religions emanate from one universal God.

We encourage members to maintain their original beliefs and affiliations and do not seek to replace any religion or one's own image of God. The Truth of Life philosophy is intended to enhance what one has already learned and to shed additional light upon the path so that the individual may progress more rapidly.

THE SOUL OF EACH INDIVIDUAL IS IMMORTAL

Each of us comes to this school of life for our soul's development. We are given opportunities to learn to overcome obstacles, to develop our character, and to increase our ability to love, thereby gaining spiritual growth. It is our purpose to awaken to our true identities as divine beings, and to unfold the inner perfection, love, spirituality, and God-given potential which are inherent within each of us.

DELIVERANCE FROM SIN CONSCIOUSNESS

The Truth of Life philosophy teaches that in reality there is no sin; that we do not have to be redeemed because we do not carry the burden of "original sin." A sense of guilt has concealed the divinity of the human race for a long, long time. The mission of the Truth of Life Movement is to awaken mankind to the truth that we are in reality children of God, and, as such, perfect in nature.

THE PHENOMENAL WORLD DULY REFLECTS OUR OWN THOUGHTS

The physical world is a reflection of the mind. Our environment will appear according to our thoughts—dark or bright. To be healthy, we must have healthy thoughts and harmonious feelings. Here the law, "Like attracts like," works precisely; once we change our attitudes, the world around us changes.

RECONCILIATION AND PERFECT HARMONY

Since our environment is a reflection of our thoughts, as long as we possess a deep-rooted discordant feeling, our inner perfection will never be able to manifest in this world. Therefore, it is essential that we become reconciled with everyone and everything in the universe in order to be able to manifest genuine peace and happiness. We are not truly reconciled until we are grateful; therefore, we are taught to be grateful to all people and all things.

SUMMARY OF TEACHINGS

The teachings of SEICHO-NO-IE are summarized as follows:

1. Man is a child of God. This is one of the most important points of the teaching. Man is really created in the image of God in the world of Truth, and already has the divine quality within himself, whether he recognizes it or not. All we have to do is to manifest this perfect quality in this phenomenal world, then we can enjoy genuine happiness.

2. The power of Word is applied as a means of manifesting this indwelling infinite quality. For Word is the Creator of *the Spiritual Universe*. (Here Word implies Divine thought or Spiritual vibration at the same time.) Prayer or the recitation of Holy Sutra—these are another example of the power of Word.

3. The phenomenal world duly reflects our own thoughts (mind). If you wish to be really happy, therefore, you have to change your mind. According to your thoughts (mind), dark or bright, your environment will appear so, often concealing the real phase of the Spiritual Universe. In order to be healthy, you must have a healthy thought and harmonious feeling. Here the law, "Like attracts like" works precisely.

4. In Absolute Truth, all religions are basically one and same. This One Truth has appeared in the different forms such as Christianity, Buddhism, Shintoism and others according to the difference of time, race and place. We have to know the oneness of Truth. Through this understanding, people will be united regardless of the difference of their religions. One of the *raison d'etre* of Seicho-No-Ie lies here.

5. Deliverance from the Sense of Guilt. Sense of Guilt has concealed the Divinity of human race for a long, long time. With deep-rooted feeling of sin, man can never be saved forever. The mission of Seicho-No-Ie is to deliver humanity by letting them know that man is, in Reality, a child of God and already immaculate and redeemed.

6. Reconciliation, Perfect Harmony. Since our environment is the reflection of our thoughts (mind) as long as we possess a deep-rooted discordant feeling, the inner perfectness will never be made manifest in this world. Therefore, it is essential to reconcile with everyone and all things in the universe in order to manifest genuine peace and happiness. It is revealed in the Divine Revelation, "Spiritual Teachings Written on the Seven Golden Candlesticks to Light the Path of life." (See the Truth of Life, vol. I, p. 4-6)

7. Shinsokan (Prayerful Meditation). In order to realize oneness with God, Seicho-No-Ie teaches this unique meditation called "Shinsokan." This is also spiritually initiated through Dr. MASAHARU TANIGU-CHI. Those who clearly realize their own divinity through this meditation can manifest their inner perfectness upon him. Numerous healings through Shinsokan are reported.

THE SEVEN PROMULGATIONS OF LIGHT

1. We resolve to transcend religious and sectarian differences, to worship Life, and to live in accordance with the laws of Life.

2. We believe that the laws governing the manifestation of Life constitute the path to infinite spiritual growth and that the Life dwelling within the individual is also immortal.

3. We study and make known to others the creative laws of Life so that humanity may tread the true path, which leads to infinite spiritual growth.

4. We believe that the proper nourishment for Life is love, and that prayer, words of love, and praise express the creative power of the Word necessary for the realization of love.

BASIC TENETS OF THE TRUTH OF LIFE MOVEMENT,
SUMMARY OF TEACHINGS, AND THE SEVEN
PROMULGATIONS OF LIGHT (SEICHO-NO-IE) (continued)

5. We believe that we as children of God, harbor within
us infinite potentiality and that we can reach a state
of magnificent freedom through the correct utiliza-
tion of the creative power inherent in words.

6. We shall propagate our doctrines by writing and
publishing good words, holding classes and lectures,
broadcasting on radio and television, and by utilizing
other cultural facilities, so that we may improve the
destiny of mankind through the creative power of
good words.

7. We shall organize an actual movement to conquer
diseases and other afflictions of life through a proper
outlook on life, a proper way of living and proper
education and thereby establish a heaven, here on
earth, that is based on spiritual fellowship.

Notes: *The Seicho-No-Ie is a Japanese version of Religious
Science. It has published three "creedal" documents which
summarize its beliefs.*

* * *

DECLARATION OF PRINCIPLES (UNITED
CHURCH OF RELIGIOUS SCIENCE)

LEADER: We believe in God, the Living Spirit Almighty;
one, indestructible, absolute, and self-existent Cause.

CONGREGATION: This One manifests Itself in and
through all creation but is not absorbed by Its creation.

LEADER: The manifest universe is the body of God; it is
the logical and necessary outcome of the infinite self-
knowingness of God.

CONGREGATION: We believe in the incarnation of the
Spirit in man and that all men are incarnations of the One
Spirit.

LEADER: We believe in the eternality, the immortality,
and the continuity of the individual soul, forever and ever
expanding.

CONGREGATION: We believe that the Kingdom of
Heaven is within man and that we experience this
Kingdom to the degree that we become conscious of it.

LEADER: We believe the ultimate goal of life to be a
complete emancipation from all discord of every nature,
and that this goal is sure to be attained by all.

CONGREGATION: We believe in the unity of all life,
and that the highest God and the innermost God is one
God.

LEADER: We believe that God is personal to all who feel
this Indwelling Presence.

CONGREGATION: We believe in the direct revelation of
Truth through the intuitive and spiritual nature of man,
and that any man may become a revealer of Truth who
lives in close contact with the Indwelling God.

LEADER: We believe that the Universal Spirit, which is
God, operates through a Universal Mind, which is the
Law of God.

CONGREGATION: We are surrounded by this Creative
Mind, which receives the direct impress of our thoughts
and acts upon it.

LEADER: We believe in the healing of the sick through
the Power of this Mind. We believe in the control of
conditions through the Power of this Mind.

CONGREGATION: We believe in the eternal Goodness,
the eternal Loving-kindness, and the eternal Givingness of
Life to all.

LEADER: We believe in our own soul, our own spirit, and
our own destiny.

CONGREGATION: We understand that the life of man
is God.

WHAT I BELIEVE (1965)

This topic naturally divides itself into three parts: What I
believe about God, what I believe about man, and what I
believe about the relationship between God and man.

First, I believe that God is Universal Spirit, and by Spirit I
mean the Life-Essence of all that is, that subtle Intelligence
which permeates all things and which, in man, is self-
conscious mind. I believe that God is present in every
place, conscious in every part, the Intelligence or Mind of
all that is.

I believe that man is the direct representative of this
Divine Presence on this plane of existence. Man is the
most highly evolved intelligence of which we have any
knowledge. Man, being the highest representation of God
here, is more nearly like God than any other manifestation
on earth.

I believe that the relationship between God and man,
between the Infinite and the finite, is a direct one; and that
the avenue through which the Mind of God expresses to
the mind of man is through the mind of man himself. We
have the ability to think, to know, to perceive, to receive,
and to act. What are these attributes other than a direct
channel through which the Universal Spirit flows to us?

I do not feel that we approach God through any formula,
sacred prayer, or intermediary, but rather that the Spirit of
God, the eternal Mind, is the Power by which we think
and know. It is self-evident that the only God whom we
can know is the only God whom we do know, and that this
knowing is an interior process of our own belief and
perception. We can know no God other than the God
whom our consciousness perceives.

But, some will say, while it is true that we cannot think
outside of ourselves, we can know that which is outside of
ourselves, because we do know things that are not within
us. This is true, as it is true that we have a city hall; but to
me that city hall would have no existence unless I were
first aware of the fact. It has no existence to those who
never heard of it. This is true of everything; and, while the
possibility of knowledge may and must expand, we cannot
know that which we do not perceive.

Therefore, I feel that God is to each one what each is to
God. The Divine nature must be, and is, infinite; but we
can know only as much of this nature as we permit to flow
through us. In no other way can God be known to us. I

believe the relationship between God and man is hidden within, and that when we discover a new truth, or find out something further about an old truth, it is really more of this infinite Mind revealing Itself through us.

I believe, then, in a direct communication between the Spirit of God and man—God personifying Himself through each and all. This is a beautiful as well as a logical concept, and an unavoidable conclusion. This makes of the human being a Divine being, a personification of the Infinite.

But if we are Divine beings, why is it that we appear to be so limited, so forlorn, so poor; so miserable, sick, and unhappy? The answer is that we are ignorant of our own nature, and also ignorant of the Law of God which governs all things.

I believe that all things are governed by immutable and exact laws; these laws cannot be changed or violated. Our ignorance of any law will offer no excuse for its infringement and we are made to suffer; not because God wills it, but because we are ignorant of the truth. We are individuals and have free will and self-choice. We shall learn by experience about things mental and spiritual just as we do about things physical and material. There is no other way to learn, and God Himself could not provide any other way without contradicting His own nature.

But if everything is governed by Law, is there any spontaneous Mind in the universe? Yes, but this spontaneous Mind, which is God, never contradicts Its own nature; It never violates Its own Law. We shall cease to misuse the Law as we learn more about ourselves and our relationship to the Whole. Experience alone will do this for us. We are made free, and because we are made free we shall have to abide by our nature and gradually wake up to the truth of our being.

Since I believe that everything is governed by exact laws, I believe all that the scientific world teaches, provided it is true in theory and principle. But should anyone in the scientific world, realizing that all is governed by law, thereby exclude the necessity of a spontaneous Spirit pervading all things, I would ask him this question: By what power of intelligence do you recognize that all things are governed by exact laws? And he would be compelled to answer that he knew by the power of a spontaneous intelligence welling up within him.

We are living in a universe governed by mechanical laws which have no conscious intelligence or personal volition. Of this we are sure. But the very fact that we can make this declaration proves that we are not governed by mechanical law alone, for mechanical law cannot, by reason of its very nature, recognize itself. When we come to self-recognition we have already arrived at spontaneous self-knowingness.

We are subject to the Law of our being, but this Law is not a Law of bondage, but one of liberty—liberty under Law.

I can conceive of a spontaneous Spirit and an immutable Law, the Spirit, and the way It works. This position has been accepted by deep thinkers of every age. It is self-evident. Spirit can never contradict Itself. Neither can It violate Its creative action through Its own Law.

God works through what we call the principle of evolution or unfoldment and we are subject to the laws involved. It is not a limitation, but is the only way through which our freedom and individuality can be guaranteed to us. There is an unfolding principle within us which is ever carrying us forward to greater and greater expressions of life, in freedom, love, and joy.

Each one of us is, I feel, at a certain level of evolution, and on the pathway of an endless expression of Life, Truth, and Beauty. Behind us is the All, before us is the All, and within, or expressing through us, is as much of this All as we are ready to receive. I believe absolutely in the immortality and the continuity of the individual stream of consciousness, which is what we mean by the individual life-stream. Humanity is an ascending principle of life, individuality, and expression through experience and unfoldment.

I do not believe in hell, the devil, damnation, or in any future state of punishment; or any other of the fantastic ideas which have been conceived in the minds of those who are either morbid, or who have felt the need of a future state of damnation to which to consign the immortal souls of those who have not agreed with their absurd doctrines. God does not punish people. There is, however, a Law of Cause and Effect which governs all and which will automatically punish, impartially and impersonally, if we conflict with the fundamental Harmony. This is bad enough, but it seems to me to be necessary, else we could not learn. It is one thing to believe in hell and damnation and quite another proposition to believe in a Law of just retribution.

The Law of retribution is the Law of balance, compensation, and equilibrium which is necessary to the universe. As we sow we shall, no doubt, reap. But I am sure that full and complete salvation will come alike to all. Heaven and hell are states of consciousness in which we now live according to our own state of understanding. We need not worry about either reward or punishment, for both are certain. In the long run, all will be saved from themselves through their own discovery of their Divine nature, and this is the only salvation necessary and the only one that could really be.

I believe in every man's religion for it is the avenue through which he worships God. I believe in my own religion more than in that of anyone else because this is the avenue through which I worship God.

I do not believe that there is anything in the Universe which is against us but ourselves. Everything is and must be for us. The only God who exists, the "Ancient of Days," wishes us well, knows us only as being perfect and complete. When we shall learn to know as God knows, we shall be saved from all mistakes and all troubles. This is heaven.

The apparent imperfection is but a temporary experience of the soul on the pathway of unfoldment. Man is a creature of time and of the night, but the day will break and the dawn of an everlasting morning of pure joy is in store for all. Meantime, God is with us and we need have no fear for He doeth all things well. I feel that we have reason to rejoice in what truth we now have; and that we

DECLARATION OF PRINCIPLES (UNITED CHURCH OF RELIGIOUS SCIENCE) (continued)

may look toward the future in confident expectancy, with gratitude and certainty that as we gain greater understanding we shall receive greater illumination.

I believe that we are surrounded by a mental or spiritual law—the Law of Mind—which receives the impress of our thought and acts upon it. This is the Law of all life and we may consciously use It for definite purposes. I am not superstitious about this Law anymore than I would be about the law of electricity or any other natural law, for nature is always natural.

I believe in a religion of happiness and joy. There is too much depression and sorrow in the world; these things were never meant to be and have no real place in God's world of Love. Religion should be like the morning sun, sending forth its glorious rays of light; it should be like the gently falling dew covering all, like the cool of the evening and the repose of the night. It should be a spontaneous song of joy and not a funeral dirge. From the fullness of the heart the mouth should speak.

I believe in the brotherhood of man, the Fatherhood of God, and the bond of Unity that binds all together in One Perfect Whole. I believe that God speaks to us in the wind and the wave and proclaims His Presence to us through all nature, but most completely through our own minds and in our hearts which proclaim His Life and Love.

Notes: *In 1927 Ernest Holmes, founder of United Church of Religious Science, published a statement entitled "What I Believe" in the first issue of* Science of Mind Magazine *(October 1927). This statement has been frequently republished as a summary of the church's belief (as well as that of Religious Science International). In January 1965, a lengthier statement with the same title was published in* Science of Mind Magazine. *This statement has been reprinted as a leaflet by the church. In 1954, the original statement was adapted with only slight modifications as the "Declaration of Principles" of the International Association of Religious Science Churches. It was printed in the* Religious Science Hymnal *in the format of a responsive reading. The declaration from the* Hymnal *and the statement published in 1965 are reproduced here.*

Chapter 5

Spiritualist, Psychic, and New Age Family

Swedenborgian Groups

THE NEW JERUSALEM AND ITS HEAVENLY DOCTRINE

OF THE NEW HEAVEN AND NEW EARTH, AND WHAT IS MEANT BY THE NEW JERUSALEM.

1. It is written in the Apocalypse, "I saw a new heaven and a new earth; for the first heaven and the first earth had passed away. And I saw the holy city, New Jerusalem, coming down from God out of heaven, prepared as a bride adorned for her husband. The city had a wall great and high, which had twelve gates, and at the gates twelve angels, and names written thereon, which are the names of the twelve tribes of the children of Israel. And the wall of the city had twelve foundations, and in them the names of the twelve apostles of the Lamb. And the city lieth four square, and the length is as large as the breadth. And he measured the city with the reed twelve thousand furlongs; and the length, and the breadth, and the height of it were equal. And he measured the wall thereof, a hundred and forty and four cubits, the measure of a man, that is, of an angel. And the wall of it was of jasper; but the city itself was pure gold, like unto pure glass; and the foundations of the wall of the city were of every precious stone. And the twelve gates were twelve pearls; and the street of the city was pure gold, as it were transparent glass. The glory of God enlightened it, and its lamp was the Lamb. And the nations of them which are saved shall walk in the light of it, and the kings of the earth shall bring their glory and honor into it." Ch. xxi. ver. 1, 2, 12 to 24. When man reads these words, he does not understand them otherwise than according to the sense of the letter, thus, that the visible heaven and earth will be dissolved, and a new heaven be created, and that the holy city Jerusalem will descend upon the new earth, and that it will be, as to its measures, according to the description. But the angels understand these things very differently; that is, what man understands naturally, they understand spiritually. And as the angels understand them, such is their signification; and this is the internal or spiritual sense of the Word. According to this internal or spiritual sense, in which the angels are, by a new heaven and a new earth is meant a new church, both in the heavens and the earths, which shall be spoken of hereafter; by the city Jerusalem descending from God out of heaven, is signified its heavenly doctrine; by the length, breadth, and height, which are equal, are signified all the goods and truths of that doctrine, in the complex; by its wall are meant the truths which protect it; by the measure of the wall, which is a hundred and forty-four cubits, which is the measure of a man, that is, of an angel, are meant all those defending truths in the complex, and their quality; by the twelve gates which are of pearls, are meant introductive truths; which are likewise signified by the twelve angels at the gates; by the foundations of the wall, which are of every precious stone, are meant the knowledges whereupon that doctrine is founded; by the twelve tribes of Israel, and also by the twelve apostles, are meant all things of the church in general and in particular; by gold like unto pure glass, whereof the city and its streets were built, is signified the good of love, from which the doctrine and its truths are made transparent; by the nations who are saved, and the kings of the earth who bring glory and honor into the city, are meant all from the church who are in goods and truths; by God and the Lamb is meant the Lord, as to the essential Divine and the Divine Human. Such is the spiritual sense of the Word, to which the natural sense, which is that of the letter, serves as a basis; nevertheless these two senses, the spiritual and the natural, make one by correspondences. It is not, however, the design of the present work to prove, that such a spiritual meaning is involved in the forementioned passages, but it may be seen proved at large in the ARCANA CŒLESTIA, in the following places. That by EARTH, in the Word, is meant the church, particularly when it is applied to signify the land of Canaan, n. 662, 1066, 1067, 1262,

1413, 1607, 2928, 3355, 4447, 4535, 5577, 8011, 9325, 9643. Because by earth, in the spiritual sense, is signified the nation inhabiting it, and its worship, n. 1262. That the people of the land signify those who belong to the spiritual church, n. 2928. That a new heaven and new earth signify something new in the heavens and the earths, with respect to goods and truths, thus with respect to those things that relate to the church in each, n. 1733, 1850, 2117, 2118, 3355, 4535, 10373. What is meant by the first heaven and the first earth, which passed away, may be seen in the small Treatise on the last Judgment and the Destruction of Babylon, throughout, but particularly from n. 65 to 72. That by JERUSALEM is signified the church with regard to doctrine, n. 402, 3654, 9166. That by cities [*urbes*] and cities [*civitates*] are signified the doctrines which belong to the church and religion, n. 402, 2450, 2712, 2943, 3216, 4492, 4493. That by the WALL of a city is signified the defensive truth of doctrine, n. 6419. That by the GATES of a city are signified such truths as are introductory to doctrine, and thereby to the church, n. 2943, 4478, 4492, 4493. That by the twelve TRIBES OF ISRAEL were represented and thence signified all the truths and goods of the church, in general and in particular, thus all things of faith and love, n. 3858, 3926, 4060, 6335. That the same is signified by the Lord's TWELVE APOSTLES, n. 2129, 2329, 3354, 3488, 3858, 6397. That when it is said of the apostles, *that they shall sit upon twelve thrones, and judge the twelve tribes of Israel*, it is signified that all are to be judged according to the goods and truths of the church, and of consequence by the Lord, from whom those truths and goods proceed, n. 2129, 6397. That by TWELVE are signified all things in their complex, n. 577, 2089, 2129, 2130, 3272, 3858, 3913. The same is also signified by a hundred and forty-four, inasmuch as that number is the product of twelve multiplied by twelve, n. 7973. That twelve thousand has likewise the same signification, n. 7973. That all numbers in the Word signify things, n. 482, 487, 647, 648, 755, 813, 1963, 1988, 2075, 2252, 3252, 4264, 6175, 9488, 9659, 10217, 10253. That the products arising from numbers multiplied into each other have the same signification with the simple numbers so multiplied, n. 5291, 5335, 5708, 7973. That by MEASURE is signified the quality of a thing with respect to truth and good, n. 3104, 9603, 10262. That by the FOUNDATIONS of a wall are signified the knowledges of truth whereupon doctrinals are founded, n. 9642. That by a QUADRANGULAR figure, or SQUARE, is signified what is perfect, n. 9717, 9861. That by LENGTH is signified good and its extension, and by BREADTH is signified truth and its extension, n. 1613, 9487. That by PRECIOUS STONES are signified truths from good, n. 114, 9863, 9865. What is signified, both in general and particular, by the precious stones in the URIM and THUMMIM, may be seen, n. 3862, 9864, 9866, 9905, 9891, 9895. What is signified by the JASPER, of which the wall was built, may be seen, n. 9872. That by the STREET of the city is signified the truth of doctrine from good, n. 2336. That by GOLD is signified the good of love, n. 113, 1551, 1552, 5658, 6914, 6917, 9510, 9874, 9881. That by GLORY is signified divine truth, such as it is in heaven, with the intelligence and wisdom thence derived, n. 4809, 5292, 5922, 8267, 8427, 9429, 10574. That by NATIONS are signified those in the church who are in good, and in an abstract sense the goods of the church, n. 1059, 1159, 1258, 1260, 1288, 1416, 1849, 4574, 7830, 9255, 9256. That by KINGS are signified those in the church who are in truths, and in an abstract sense the truths of the church, n. 1672, 2015, 2069, 4575, 5044. That the rites at the coronations of kings involve such things as are of divine truth, but that the knowledge of them at this day is lost, n. 4581, 4966.

2. Before the new Jerusalem and its doctrine are treated of, some account shall be given of the new heaven and new earth. It was shown in the small Treatise concerning the last Judgment and the Destruction of Babylon, what is meant by the first heaven, and the first earth, which have passed away. After this event, that is, when the last judgment was finished, a new heaven was created or formed by the Lord; which heaven was formed of all those who, from the advent of the Lord even to this time, had lived a life of faith and charity; as these alone are forms of heaven. For the form of heaven, according to which all consociations and communications there exist, is the form of divine truth from divine good, proceeding from the Lord; and man puts on this form, as to his spirit, by a life according to divine truth. That the form of heaven is thence derived, may be seen in the Treatise concerning Heaven and Hell, n. 200 to 212, and that all the angels are forms of heaven, n. 51 to 58, and 73 to 77. Hence it may be known of whom the new heaven is formed, and thereby what is its quality, viz. that it is altogether unanimous. For he that lives a life of faith and charity loves another as himself, and by love conjoins him with himself, and this reciprocally and mutually; for love is conjunction in the spiritual world. Wherefore when all act in like manner, then from many, yea, from innumerable individuals consociated according to the form of heaven, unanimity exists, and they become as one; for there is then nothing which separates and divides, but every thing conjoins and unites.

3. Inasmuch as this heaven was formed of all those who had been of such a quality from the coming of the Lord until the present time, it is plain that it is composed as well of Christians as of Gentiles, but chiefly of infants, from all parts of the world, who have died since the Lord's coming; for all these were received by the Lord, and educated in heaven, and instructed by the angels, and then reserved, that they, together with the others, might constitute a new heaven; whence it may be concluded how great

that heaven is. That all who die infants are educated in heaven, and become angels, may be seen in the Treatise concerning Heaven and Hell, n. 329 to 345. And that heaven is formed as well of Gentiles as of Christians, n. 318 to 328.

4. Moreover, with respect to this new heaven, it is to be observed, that it is distinct from the ancient heavens which were formed before the coming of the Lord; and yet there is such an orderly connection established between them, that they form together but one heaven. The reason why this new heaven is distinct from the ancient heaven is, because in the ancient churches there was no other doctrine than the doctrine of love and charity, and at that time they were unacquainted with any doctrine of faith separated from those principles. Hence also it is that the ancient heavens constitute superior expanses, whilst the new heaven constitutes an expanse below them; for the heavens are expanses one above another. In the highest expanses are they who are called celestial angels, many of whom were of the most ancient church; they are called celestial angels from celestial love, which is love towards the Lord; in the expanses below them are they who are called spiritual angels, many of whom were of the ancient church; they are called spiritual angels, from spiritual love, which is charity towards the neighbor: below these are the angels who are in the good of faith, who are they that have lived a life of faith; to live a life of faith, is to live each according to the doctrine of his particular church; and to live is to will and to do. All these heavens, however, make one by a mediate and immediate influx from the Lord. But a more full idea concerning these heavens may be obtained from what is shown in the Treatise concerning Heaven and Hell, and particularly in the article which treats of the two kingdoms into which the heavens in general are divided, n. 20 to 28; and in the article concerning the three heavens, n. 29 to 40; concerning mediate and immediate influx in the extracts from the ARCANA CŒLESTIA, after n. 603; and concerning the ancient and most ancient churches in a small Treatise on the last Judgment and the Destruction of Babylon, n. 46.

5. This may suffice concerning the new heaven; now something shall be said concerning the new earth. By the new earth is understood a new church upon earth: for when a former church ceases to be, then a new one is established by the Lord. For it is provided by the Lord that there should always be a church on earth, as by means of the church there is a conjunction of the Lord with mankind, and of heaven with the world; there the Lord is known, and therein are divine truths, by which man is conjoined to him. That a new church is at this time establishing, may be seen in the small Treatise concerning the last Judgment, n. 74. That a new church is signified by a new earth, is from the spiritual sense of the Word; for in that sense no particular earth is understood by earth, but the nation therein, and its divine worship; this being the spiritual thing whereof

earth is representative. Moreover by earth in the Word, without the name of any particular country affixed, is signified the land of Canaan; and in the land of Canaan a church has existed from the earliest ages, which was the reason why all the places therein, and in the adjacent countries, with their mountains and rivers, which are mentioned in the Word, are made representative and significative of those things which are the internals of the church, which are what are called its spiritual things; hence it is, as was observed, that by earth in the Word, inasmuch as the land of Canaan is understood, is signified the church, and in like manner here by a new earth. It is therefore usual in the church to speak of the heavenly Canaan, and by it to understand heaven. That by the land of Canaan, in the spiritual sense of the Word, is understood the church, was shown in the ARCANA CŒLESTIA in various places, of which the following shall be adduced: That the most ancient church which was before the flood, and the ancient church which was after the flood, were in the land of Canaan; n. 567, 3686, 4447, 4454, 4516, 4517, 5136, 6516, 9327. That then all places therein became representative of such things as are in the kingdom of the Lord and in the church, n. 1505, 3686, 4447, 5136. That therefore Abraham was commanded to go thither, to the intent that among his posterity, for Jacob, a representative church might be established, and the Word might be written whose ultimate should consist of representatives and significatives existing in that land, n. 3686, 4447, 5136, 6516. Hence it is that by earth and the land of Canaan, in the Word, is signified the church, n. 3038, 3481, 3705, 4447, 4517, 5757, 10658.

6. What is understood by Jerusalem in the Word, in its spiritual sense, shall also be briefly declared. By Jerusalem is understood the church with respect to doctrine, inasmuch as at Jerusalem in the land of Canaan, and in no other place, there were the temple, the altar, the sacrifices, and of consequence all divine worship; wherefore also three festivals were celebrated there every year, to which every male throughout the whole land was commanded to go: this, then, is the reason why by Jerusalem in its spiritual sense is signified the church with respect to worship, or, what is the same thing, with respect to doctrine; for worship is prescribed in doctrine, and is performed according to it. The reason why it is said *the holy city, new Jerusalem, descending from God out of heaven,* is, because, in the spiritual sense of the Word, by a city [*civitas*] and a city [*urbs*] is signified doctrine, and by a holy city the doctrine of divine truth, inasmuch as divine truth is what is called holy in the Word. It is called the New Jerusalem for the same reason that the earth is called new, because, as was observed above, by earth is signified the church, and by Jerusalem the church with respect to doctrine; and it is said to descend from God out of heaven, because all divine truth, from whence doctrine is, descends out of heaven from the Lord.

That by Jerusalem is not understood a city, although it was seen as a city, appears manifestly from hence, that it is said that *its height was* as its length and breadth, 12000 *furlongs,* ver. 16; *and that the measure of its wall, which was 144 cubits, was the measure of a man, that is, of an angel,* ver. 17; and also from its being said to be *prepared as a bride before her husband,* ver. 2; and afterwards, *the angel said, Come hither, I will shew thee the bride, the Lamb's wife,* and he shewed me the holy city, that Jerusalem, ver. 9. The church is what is called in the Word the bride and the wife of the Lord; the bride before conjunction, and the wife after conjunction, as may be seen in the ARCANA CŒLESTIA, n. 3103, 3105, 3164, 3165, 3207, 7022, 9182.

7. As to what particularly concerns the following doctrine, that also is from heaven, inasmuch as it is from the spiritual sense of the Word; and the spiritual sense of the Word is the same with the doctrine which is in heaven. For there is a church in heaven as well as on earth; for in heaven there is the Word, and doctrine from the Word; there are temples there and preaching in them; there are also both ecclesiastical and civil governments there: in short, there is no other difference between the things which are in heaven, and the things which are on earth, except that all things in the heavens are in a more perfect state; inasmuch as all who dwell there are spiritual, and things that are spiritual immensely exceed in perfection those that are natural. That such things exist in heaven may be seen in the work concerning Heaven and Hell throughout, particularly in the article concerning governments in heaven, n. 213 to 220, and also in the article on divine worship in heaven, n. 221 to 227. Hence it may plainly be seen what is meant by the holy city, New Jerusalem, being seen to descend from God out of heaven. But I proceed to the doctrine itself, which is for the new church, and which is called HEAVEN-LY DOCTRINE, because it was revealed to me out of heaven; for to deliver this doctrine is the design of this work.

INTRODUCTION TO THE DOCTRINE.

8. That the end of the church takes place when there is no faith because there is no charity, was shown in the little work concerning the last Judgment and the Destruction of Babylon, n. 33 to 39. Now forasmuch as the churches throughout Christendom have distinguished themselves solely by such things as relate to faith, and yet there is no faith where there is no charity, therefore I will here premise something concerning the doctrine of charity among the ancients, before I proceed to deliver the doctrine of the New Jerusalem. It is said THE CHURCHES IN CHRISTENDOM, and by them are understood the reformed or evangelical Churches, but not the popish or Roman Catholic church, inasmuch as that is no part of the Christian church; because wherever the church is, there the Lord is worshipped, and the Word is read; whereas, among the Roman Catholics, they worship themselves instead of the Lord, forbid the Word to be read by the people, and affirm the pope's decree to be equal, yea, superior to it.

9. The doctrine of charity, which is the doctrine of life, was the essential doctrine in the ancient churches; concerning which churches the reader may see more in the ARCANA CŒLESTIA, n. 1238, 2385; and that doctrine conjoined all churches, and thereby formed one church out of many. For they acknowledged all those to be members of the church, who lived in the good of charity, and called them brothers, howsoever they might differ in truths, which at this day are called matters of faith. In these they instructed one another which was among their works of charity; nor were they angry if one did not accede to another's opinion, knowing that every one receives truth in such proportion as he is in good. Forasmuch as the ancient churches were of such a quality, therefore the members of them were interior men, and forasmuch as they were interior men, they were wiser men. For they who are in the good of love and charity, are, with respect to the internal man, in heaven, and in an angelic society there which is in similar good; whence there is an elevation of their mind to interior things, and consequently they are in wisdom: for wisdom cannot come from any other source than from heaven, that is, through heaven from the Lord; and in heaven there is wisdom because those who are there are in good: wisdom consists in seeing truth from the light of truth, and the light of truth is the light which is in heaven. But in process of time that ancient wisdom decreased; for so far as mankind removed themselves from the good of love to the Lord, and the good of love towards the neighbor, which love is called charity, so far also they removed themselves from wisdom, because they so far removed themselves from heaven. Hence it was that man from internal became external, and this successively; and when man became external, he also became worldly and corporeal; and when this is his quality, he little cares for the things which are of heaven; for the delights of earthly loves, and the evils which are delightful to man from those loves, then occupy him entirely; and the things which he hears concerning a life after death, concerning heaven and hell, and concerning spiritual subjects in general, are then as it were without him and not within him, as nevertheless they ought to be. Hence it is that the doctrine of charity, which was of such estimation among the ancients, is at this day among the things which are lost; for who at this day knows what charity is, in a genuine sense, and what our neighbor is, in a genuine sense? when nevertheless that doctrine not only teaches this, but innumerable things beside, of which not a thousandth part is known at this day. The whole sacred scripture is nothing else than the doctrine of love and charity, which the Lord also teaches, saying. "Thou shalt love the Lord thy God from thy whole heart, and in

thy whole soul, and in thy whole mind; this is the primary and great commandment; the second is like unto it; thou shalt love they neighbor as thyself: on these two commandments hang all the law and the prophets." Matt. xxii. verses 37, 38, 39. The law and the prophets are the Word in general and in particular.

OF GOOD AND TRUTH.

11. All things in the universe, which are according to divine order, have relation to good and truth. Nothing exists in heaven, and nothing in the world, which does not relate to these two. The reason is, because both, as well good as truth, proceed from the Divine, from whom are all things.

12. Hence it appears, that nothing is more necessary for man than to know what good and truth are, and how each regards the other, and in what manner they are mutually conjoined. But it is most necessary for the man of the church; for as all things of heaven have relation to good and truth, so also have all things of the church, inasmuch as the good and truth of heaven are also the good and truth of the church. It is on this account that good and truth are first treated of.

13. It is according to divine order that good and truth should be conjoined, and not separated; thus that they should be one and not two: for they proceed in conjunction from the Divine, and they are in conjunction in heaven, and therefore they should be in conjunction in the church. The conjunction of good and truth is called in heaven celestial marriage, for all therein are in this marriage. Hence it is, that, in the Word, heaven is compared to marriage, and the Lord is called Bridegroom and Husband, but heaven bride and wife; in like manner the church. That heaven and the church are so called, is because they who are therein receive divine good in truths.

14. All the intelligence and wisdom which angels possess is from that marriage, and not any of it from good separate from truth, nor from truth separate from good. It is the same with men of the church.

15. Inasmuch as the conjunction of good and truth bears resemblance to marriage, it is plain that good loves truth, and that truth, in its turn, loves good, and that each desires to be conjoined with the other. The man of the church, who has not such love and such desire, is not in celestial marriage, consequently the church as yet is not in him; for the conjunction of good and truth constitutes the church.

16. Goods are manifold; in general there is spiritual good and natural good, and both conjoined in genuine moral good. As goods are manifold, so also are truths, inasmuch as truths are of good, and are the forms of good.

17. As is the case with good and truth, so it is in the opposite with evil and the false; for as all things in the universe, which are according to divine order, have relation to good and truth, so all things which are contrary to divine order have relation to evil and the false. Again, as good loves to be conjoined to truth, and *vice versa,* so evil loves to be conjoined to the false, and *vice versa.* And again, as all intelligence and wisdom are born of the conjunction of good and truth, so all insanity and folly are born of the conjunction of evil and the false. This conjunction of evil and the false is called infernal marriage.

18. From the circumstance that evil and the false are opposite to good and truth, it is plain that truth cannot be conjoined to evil, nor good to the false of evil; if truth be adjoined to evil, it becomes truth no longer, but the false, inasmuch as it is falsified; and if good be adjoined to the false of evil, it becomes good no longer, but evil, inasmuch as it is adulterated. Nevertheless the false which is not of evil may be conjoined to good.

19. No one who is in evil, and thence in the false from confirmation and life, can know what good and truth is, for he believes his own evil to be good, and thence he believes his own false to be truth; but every one who is in good and thence in truth may know what evil and the false is. The reason of this is, because all good and its truth is, in its essence, celestial, and what is not celestial in its essence is still from a celestial origin; but evil and its false is in its essence infernal, and what is not infernal in its essence has nevertheless its origin from thence; and every thing celestial is in light, but every thing infernal is in darkness.

OF WILL AND UNDERSTANDING.

28. Man has two faculties which constitute his life: one is called WILL, and the other UNDERSTANDING: they are distinct from each other, but so created that they may be one; and when they are one, they are called MIND: wherefore of these consists the human mind, and all the life of man is in them.

29. As all things in the universe; which are according to divine order, have relation to good and truth, so all things with man have relation to will and understanding; for good with man is of his will, and truth with him is of his understanding. These two faculties, or these two lives of man, are their receptacles and subjects; the will being the receptacle and subject of all things of good, and the understanding the receptacle and subject of all things of truth. Goods and truths have no other residence with man: and forasmuch as goods and truths have no other residence with man, so neither have love and faith; for love is of good, and good is of love; and faith is of truth, and truth is of faith.

30. Now forasmuch as all things in the universe have relation to good and truth, and all things of the church to the good of love and the truth of faith; and forasmuch as man is man from these two faculties; therefore they also are treated of in this doctrine; otherwise man could have no distinct idea concerning them, whereon to found his thought.

31. The will and understanding likewise constitute the spirit of man, for his wisdom and intelligence, and

his life in general, reside in them, the body being only obedience.

32. Nothing is more important to be known, than in what manner will and understanding make one mind. They make one mind as good and truth make one; for there is a similar marriage between will and understanding as there is between good and truth. What is the quality of that marriage may appear from what has been said above, concerning good and truth. As good is the very esse of a thing, and truth the existere of a thing thence derived, so the will with man is the very esse of his life, and the understanding the existere of life thence; for good, which is of the will, assumes a form, and renders itself visible, in the understanding.

33. They who are in good and truth have will and understanding, but they who are in evil and the false have not will and understanding; but, instead of will, they have cupidity, and, instead of understanding, they have science. For the truly human will is the receptacle of good, and the understanding the receptacle of truth; wherefore will cannot be predicated of evil, nor understanding of the false, because they are opposite, and opposites destroy each other. Hence it is that the man who is in evil, and thence in the false, cannot be called rational, wise, and intelligent. With the evil, also, the interiors which are of the mind, wherein the will and the understanding principally reside, are closed up. It is supposed that the evil also have will and understanding, because they say that they will and that they understand; but their will is mere lust, and their understanding is mere science.

OF THE INTERNAL AND EXTERNAL MAN.

36. Man is so created as to be, at one and the same time, in the spiritual world and in the natural world. The spiritual world is that in which angels are, and the natural world is that in which men are. And because man is so created, therefore he is endowed with an internal and an external; an internal by which he may be in the spiritual world, and an external by which he may be in the natural world. His internal is what is called the internal man, and his external is what is called the external man.

37. Every man has an internal and an external; but there is a difference in this respect between the good and the evil. The internal with the good is in heaven and its light, and the external is in the world and its light, which light with them is illuminated by the light of heaven, so that with them the internal and the external act in unity, as the efficient cause and the effect, or as what is prior and what is posterior. But with the evil the internal is in the world and its light, as is also the external; wherefore they see nothing from the light of heaven, but only from the light of the world, which light they call the light of nature. Hence it is that the things of heaven are to them in darkness, and the things of the world in light. It is

therefore manifest that the good have an internal man and an external man, but that the evil have no internal man, but only an external.

38. The internal man is what is called the SPIRITUAL MAN, because it is in the light of heaven, which light is spiritual; and the external man is what is called the NATURAL MAN, because it is in the light of the world, which light is natural. The man whose internal is in the light of heaven, and his external in the light of the world, is a spiritual man as to each; but the man whose internal is not in the light of heaven, but only in the light of the world, in which is also his external, is a natural man as to each. The spiritual man is he who is called in the Word ALIVE, but the natural man is he who is called DEAD.

39. The man whose internal is in the light of heaven, and his external in the light of the world, thinks both spiritually and naturally; but then his spiritual thought flows in into the natural, and is there perceived. But the man whose internal, together with his external, is in the light of the world, does not think spiritually, but materially; for he thinks from such things as are in the nature of the world, all which are material. To think spiritually is to think of things as they essentially are in themselves, to see truths from the light of truth, and to perceive goods from the love of good; also to see the qualities of things, and to perceive their affections, abstractedly from what is material: but to think materially is to think, see, and perceive them together with matter, and in matter, thus respectively in a gross and obscure manner.

40. The internal spiritual man, regarded in himself, is an angel of heaven; and, also, during his life in the body, notwithstanding his ignorance of it, is in society with angels; and after his separation from the body, he comes among them. But the merely natural internal man, regarded in himself, is a spirit, and not an angel; and, also, during his life in the body, is in society with spirits, but with those who are in hell, among whom he also comes after his separation from the body.

41. The interiors, with those who are spiritual men, are also actually elevated towards heaven, for that is what they primarily regard; but the interiors which are of the mind with those who are merely natural, are turned to the world, because that is what they primarily regard. The interiors, which are of the mind [*mens*], are turned with every one to that which he loves above all things; and the exteriors which are of the mind [*animus*], are turned the same way as the interiors.

42. They who have only a common [or general] idea concerning the internal and external man, believe that to be the internal man which thinks and wills, and that to be the external which speaks and acts; because to think and to will is internal, and to speak and to act thence is external. But it is to be observed, that when man thinks intelligently, and wills wisely,

he then thinks and wills from a spiritual internal; but when man does not think intelligently, and will wisely, he thinks and wills from a natural internal. Of consequence, when man thinks well concerning the Lord and those things which are of the Lord, and well concerning the neighbor, and those things which are of the neighbor, and wills well to them, he then thinks and wills from a spiritual internal, because he then thinks from the faith of truth and from the love of good, thus from heaven. But when man thinks ill concerning them, and wills ill to them, he then thinks and wills from a natural internal, because he thinks and wills from the faith of what is false and from the love of what is evil, thus from hell. In short, so far as man is in love to the Lord, and in love towards his neighbor, so far he is in a spiritual internal, from which he thinks and wills, and from which also he speaks and acts: but so far as man is in the love of self, and in the love of the world, so far he is in a natural internal, from which he thinks and wills, and from which also he speaks and acts.

43. It is so provided and ordered by the Lord, that so far as man thinks and wills from heaven, so far the internal spiritual man is opened and formed. It is opened into heaven even to the Lord, and it is formed according to those things which are of heaven. But, on the contrary, so far as man does not think and will from heaven, but from the world, so far his internal spiritual man is closed, and his external is opened; it is opened into the world, and it is formed according to those things which are of the world.

44. They, with whom the internal spiritual man is opened into heaven to the Lord, are in the light of heaven, and in illumination from the Lord, and thence in intelligence and wisdom; these see truth because it is truth, and perceive good because it is good. But they with whom the internal spiritual man is closed, do not know that there is an internal man, and much less what the internal man is; neither do they believe that there is a Divine, nor that there is a life after death; consequently they do not believe the things which are of heaven and the church. And forasmuch as they are only in light of the world and in illumination thence, they believe in nature as the Divine, they see the false as truth, and they perceive evil as good.

45. He whose internal is so far external, that he believes nothing but what he can see with his eyes and touch with his hands, is called a sensual man: this is the lowest natural man, and is in fallacies concerning all the things which are of faith and the church.

46. The internal and external, which have been treated of, are the internal and external of the spirit of man; his body is only an additional external, within which they exist; for the body does nothing from itself, but from its spirit which is in it. It is to be observed that the spirit of man, after its separation from the body, thinks and wills, speaks and acts, the same as before; to think and to will is its internal, and to speak and

to act is its external; concerning which, see the Treatise on Heaven, n. 234 to 245, 265 to 275, 432 to 444, 453 to 484.

OF LOVE IN GENERAL.

54. The very life of man is his love, and such as the love is, such is the life, yea, such is the whole man. But it is the governing or ruling love which constitutes the man. That love has many other loves subordinate to it, which are derivations from it. These appear under another form, but still they are all present in the ruling love, and constitute, with it, one kingdom. The ruling love is as their king and head; it directs them, and, by them, as mediate ends, it regards and intends its own end, which is the primary and ultimate end of them all; and this it does both directly and indirectly. The object of the ruling love is what is loved above all things.

55. That which man loves above all things is continually present in his thought, and also in his will, and constitutes his most essential life. As, for example, he who loves riches above all things, whether in money or in possessions, is continually revolving in his mind how he may obtain them. He rejoices exceedingly when he acquires them, and is equally grieved at their loss; his heart is in them. He who loves himself above all things regards himself in every thing: he thinks of himself, he speaks of himself, he acts for the sake of himself, for his life is the life of self.

56. Man regards that which he loves above all things as an end; he is governed by it in all and every particular of his conduct. It is in his will like the latent current of a river, which draws and bears him away, even when he is doing something else; for it is this which animates him. It is of such a quality, that one man explores and also discovers it in another, and either leads him, or regulates his dealings with him, according to it.

57. Man is altogether of such a quality as the ruling principle of his life is: by this he is distinguished from others; according to this is his heaven if he be good, and his hell if he be evil. It is his will itself, his proprium, and his nature, for it is the very esse of his life: this cannot be changed after death, because it is the man himself.

58. Every one enjoys delight, pleasure and happiness from his ruling love, and according to it; for man calls that delightful which he loves, because he perceives it; but that which he thinks and does not love, he may also call delightful, but it is not the delight of his life. That which is delightful to his love is what man esteems good, and that which is undelightful is what he esteems evil.

59. There are two loves, from which, as from their fountains, all goods and truths exist; and there are two loves, from which all evils and falses exist. The two loves, from which all goods and truths exist, are love to the Lord, and love towards the neighbor; and the two loves, from which all evils and falses exist,

THE NEW JERUSALEM AND ITS HEAVENLY
  DOCTRINE (continued)

are the love of self and the love of the world. These two loves are in direct opposition to the former.

60. The two loves from which are all goods and truths, which are, as was said, love to the Lord and love towards the neighbor, constitute heaven with man, wherefore also they reign in heaven; and forasmuch as they constitute heaven with man, they also constitute the church with him. The two loves from which are all evils and falses, which are, as was said, the love of self and the love of the world, constitute hell with man, wherefore also they reign in hell.

61. The two loves from which all goods and truths are, which as was said, are the loves of heaven, open and form the internal spiritual man, because they reside therein. But the two loves from which all evils and falses are derived, when they have the dominion, shut up and destroy the internal spiritual man, and render man natural and sensual, according to the extent and quality of their dominion.

OF THE LOVES OF SELF AND OF THE WORLD.

65. The love of self consists in willing well to ourselves alone, and not to others except for the sake of ourselves, not even to the church, to our country, to any human society, or to a fellow-citizen; and also in doing good to them only for the sake of our own fame, honor and glory; for unless it sees that these will be promoted by the goods which it does to others, it says in its heart, What matters it? why should I do this? and what advantage will it be to me? and so it passes them over. Whence it is plain that he who is in the love of self does not love the church, nor his country, nor society, nor his fellow-citizen, nor anything good, but himself alone.

66. Man is in the love of self, when, in those things which he thinks and does, he has no respect to his neighbor, nor to the public, much less to the Lord, but only to himself and his own connections; consequently when every thing which he does is for the sake of himself and his own connections, and when, if he does any thing for the public and his neighbor it is only for the sake of appearance.

67. It is said for the sake of himself and his own connections, because he who loves himself also loves his own connections, who are, in particular, his children and relations, and in general, all who make one with him, and whom he calls his own. To love these is still to love himself, for he regards them as it were in himself, and himself in them:—among those whom he calls his own, are also all they who praise, honor, and pay their court to him.

68. That man is in the love of self, who despises his neighbor in comparison with himself, who esteems him his enemy if he does not favor him, and if he does not respect and pay his court to him: he is still more in the love of self who for such reasons hates his neighbor and persecutes him; and he is still more

so who for such reasons burns with revenge against him, and desires his destruction: such persons at length delight in cruelty.

69. From a comparison with celestial love, it may plainly appear what is the quality of the love of self. Celestial love consists in loving uses for the sake of uses, or goods for the sake of goods such as man should perform to the church, to his country, to human society, and to his fellow-citizens. But he who loves them for the sake of self, loves them no otherwise than he loves his domestics because they are serviceable to him. Hence it follows that he who is in the love of self, would that the church, his country, human societies, and his fellow-citizens, should serve him, and not that he should serve them. He places himself above them, and them below himself.

70. Moreover, so far as any one is in celestial love, which consists in loving uses and goods, and in being affected with delight of heart when he performs them, so far he is led by the Lord, because that is the love in which the Lord is, and which is from Him. But so far as any one is in the love of self, so far he is led by himself; and so far as he is led by himself, so far he is led by his own proprium; and the proprium of man is nothing but evil; for it is his hereditary evil, which consists in loving self more than God, and the world more than heaven.

71. The love of self is also of such a quality, that so far as the reins are given to it, that is, so far as external restraints are removed, which are fears on account of the law and its penalties, and on account of the loss of fame, of honor, of gain, of office, and of life, it rushes on till it would not only extend its empire over the universal globe, but also over heaven, and over the Divine itself; it has no bound nor end. This propensity lurks in every one who is in the love of self, although it does not appear before the world, on account of the checks and restraints before mentioned. Besides, every one who is of such a quality, when he meets with an insuperable obstacle in his way, waits till it is removed; hence it is that the man who is in such love does not know that such a mad, unbounded cupidity is latent within him. Nevertheless, any one may see that this is the case, who observes the conduct of potentates and kings, who are not withheld by such checks, restraints, and insuperable obstacles; who rush on and subjugate provinces and kingdoms as long as success attends them, and aspire after power and glory without bounds. And it may be seen still more clearly from the case of those who extend their dominion into heaven, and transfer to themselves all the divine power of the Lord, and are continually lusting after more.

72. There are two kinds of dominion, that of love towards our neighbor, and that of the love of self. These two kinds of dominion are in their essence entirely opposite to each other. He who rules from love towards his neighbor, wills good to all, and loves nothing more than to perform uses, consequently to

serve others; (to serve others consists in doing them good from good will, and in performing uses;) this is his love, and this is the delight of his heart. He is also rejoiced in proportion as he is exalted to dignities, not for the sake of the dignities, but for the sake of uses, which he is thereby enabled to perform in more abundance and in a greater degree; such is the quality of dominion in the heavens. But he who rules from the love of self, wills good to none except to himself and his own connections: the uses which he performs are for the sake of his own honor and glory, which he esteems the only uses: when he serves others, it is in order that he may be served, honored and exalted: he seeks dignities, not for the sake of the goods which he might perform, but that he may be in eminence and glory, and thence in the delight of his heart.

73. The love of dominion also remains with every one after the termination of his life in the world. They who have ruled from love towards their neighbor, are then intrusted with dominion in the heavens; but then it is not they that rule, but the uses and goods which they love; and when uses and goods rule, the Lord rules. But they who have ruled in the world from the love of self, are after the termination of their life in the world, in hell, where they are vile slaves.

74. Hence it may be known who they are that are in the love of self. It is of no importance how they appear externally, whether elate or submissive; for such things reside in the interior man, and the interior man is concealed by many, whilst the exterior is instructed to assume the contrary appearance of love for the public and the neighbor. And this is also done for the sake of self: for they know that the love of the public and the neighbor has a power of interiorly affecting all men, and that they shall be loved and esteemed in proportion. The reason why that love has such a power is, because heaven flows in into it.

75. The evils which belong to those who are in the love of self, are, in general, contempt of others, envy, enmity against those who do not favor them, hostility on that account, hatreds of various kinds, revenge, cunning, deceit, unmercifulness, and cruelty; and where such evils exist, there is also contempt of the Divine, and of divine things, which are the truths and goods of the church: if these are honored by such persons, it is only with the mouth, and not with the heart. And because such evils are thence, so there are similar falses, for falses proceed from evils.

76. But the love of the world consists in wishing to appropriate the wealth of others to ourselves by any artifice, in placing the heart in riches, and in suffering the world to draw us back, and lead us away from spiritual love, which is love towards the neighbor, consequently, from heaven. They are in the love of the world who desire to appropriate the goods of others to themselves by various artifices, particularly they who do so by means of cunning and deceit, esteeming their neighbor's good as of no importance.

They who are in that love covet the goods of others, and so far as they do not fear the laws and the loss of reputation, which they regard for the sake of gain, they deprive others of their property, and even commit depredations.

77. But the love of the world is not opposite to celestial love in the same degree that the love of self is, inasmuch as such great evils are not concealed in it. This love is manifold: there is the love of riches as the means of obtaining honors; there is the love of honors and dignities as the means of obtaining riches; there is the love of riches for the sake of various uses with which people are delighted in the world; there is the love of riches for the sake of riches alone, which is avarice, and so on. The end for the sake of which riches are desired, is called their use, and it is the end or use from which the love derives its quality; for the quality of the love is the same as that of the end which it has in view, to which other things only serve as means.

78. In a word, the love of self and the love of the world are altogether opposite to love to the Lord and love towards the neighbor; wherefore the love of self and the love of the world are infernal loves, for they reign in hell, and also constitute hell with man; but love to the Lord and love towards the neighbor are heavenly loves, for they reign in heaven, and also constitute heaven with man.

79. From what has been now said, it may be seen that all evils are in and from those two loves; for the evils which were enumerated at n. 75 are common; the others, which were not enumerated, because they are specific, originate in and flow from them. Hence it may appear, that man, forasmuch as he is born into these two loves, is born into evils of every kind.

80. In order that man may know what evils are, he ought to know their origin; and unless he knows what evils are, he cannot know what good is, consequently cannot know of what quality he himself is: this is the reason that these two origins of evils are treated of here.

OF LOVE TOWARDS THE NEIGHBOR, OR CHARITY.

84. It shall first be shown what the neighbor is, as it is the neighbor who is to be loved, and towards whom charity is to be exercised. For unless it be known what our neighbor is, charity may be exercised in a similar manner, without distinction, towards the evil as well as towards the good, whence charity ceases to be charity: for the evil, from the benefactions conferred on them, do evil to their neighbor, but the good do good.

85. It is a common opinion at this day, that every man is equally a neighbor, and that benefits are to be conferred on every one who needs assistance; but it is the business of Christian prudence to examine well the quality of a man's life, and to exercise charity to him accordingly. The man of the internal church exercises his charity with discrimination, conse-

THE NEW JERUSALEM AND ITS HEAVENLY
DOCTRINE (continued)

quently with intelligence; but the man of the external church, forasmuch as he is not able thus to discern things, does it indiscriminately.

86. The distinctions of neighbor, which the man of the church ought well to know, depend upon the good which is with every one; and forasmuch as all goods proceed from the Lord, therefore the Lord is our neighbor in a supreme sense and in a supereminent degree, and the origin is from Him. Hence it follows that so far as any one is receptive of the Lord, in that degree he is our neighbor; and forasmuch as no one receives the Lord, that is, good from Him, in the same manner as another, therefore no one is our neighbor in the same manner as another. For all who are in the heavens, and all the good who are on the earths, differ in good; no two ever received a good that is altogether one and the same; it must be various, that each may subsist by itself. But all these varieties, consequently all the distinctions of neighbor, which depend on the reception of the Lord, that is, on the reception of good from Him, can never be known by any man, nor indeed by any angel, except in a general manner, or with respect to their kinds and species: neither does the Lord require any more of the man of the church, than to live according to what he knows.

87. Forasmuch as good is different with every one, it follows, that the quality of his good determines in what degree and in what proportion any one is our neighbor. That this is the case is plain from the Lord's parable concerning him that fell among robbers, whom, when half dead, the priest passed by, and also the Levite; but the Samaritan, after he had bound up his wounds, and poured in oil and wine, took him up on his own breast, and led him to an inn, and ordered that care should be taken of him: he, forasmuch as he exercised the good of charity, is called neighbor, Luke x. 29 to 37; whence it may be known that they are our neighbor who are in good: oil and wine, which the Samaritan poured into the wounds, also signify good and its truth.

88. It is plain, from what has now been said, that, in a universal sense, good is the neighbor, forasmuch as a man is neighbor according to the quality of the good that is with him from the Lord; and forasmuch as good is the neighbor, so is love, for all good is of love; consequently every man is our neighbor according to the quality of the love which he receives from the Lord.

89. That love is what causes any one to be a neighbor, and that every one is a neighbor according to the quality of his love, appears manifestly from the case of those who are in the love of self, who acknowledge for their neighbor those who love them most; that is, so far as they belong to themselves they embrace them, they treat them with kindness, they confer benefits on them and call them brothers; yea, forasmuch as they are evil, they say, that these are

their neighbor more than others: they esteem others as their neighbor in proportion as they love them, thus according to the quality and quantity of their love. Such persons derive the origin of neighbor from self, by reason that love constitutes and determines it. But they who do not love themselves more than others, as is the case with all who belong to the kingdom of the Lord, will derive the origin of neighbor from Him whom they ought to love above all things, consequently, from the Lord; and they will esteem every one as neighbor according to the quality of his love to Him and from Him. Hence it appears from whence the origin of neighbor is to be drawn by the man of the church; and that every one is neighbor according to the good which he possesses from the Lord, consequently that good itself is the neighbor.

90. That this is the case, the Lord also teaches in Matthew, "for he said to those who were in good that they had given him to eat, that they had given him to drink, that they had gathered him, had clothed him, had visited him, and had come to him in prison; and afterwards that, so far as they had done it to one of the least of their brethren, they had done it unto him," xxv. 34 to 40; in these six kinds of good, when understood in the spiritual sense, are comprehended all the kinds of neighbor. Hence, likewise, it is evident, that when good is loved the Lord is loved, for it is the Lord from Whom good is, Who is in good, and Who is good itself.

91. But the neighbor is not only man singly, but also man collectively, as a less or greater society, our country, the church, the Lord's kingdom, and, above all, the Lord Himself; these are the neighbor to whom good is to be done from love. These are also the ascending degrees of neighbor, for a society consisting of many is neighbor in a higher degree than a single man is; in a still superior degree is our country; in a still superior degree is the church; and in a still superior degree is the Lord's kingdom; but in the supreme degree is the Lord: these ascending degrees are as the steps of a ladder, at the top of which is the Lord.

92. A society is our neighbor more than a single man, because it consists of many. Charity is to be exercised towards it in a like manner as towards a man singly, that is, according to the quality of the good that is with it; consequently in a manner totally different towards a society of well-disposed persons, than towards a society of ill-disposed persons; the society is loved when its good is provided for from the love of good.

93. Our country is our neighbor more than a society, because it is like a parent; for a man is born therein, and is thereby nourished and protected from injuries. Good is to be done to our country from a principle of love according to its necessities, which principally regard its sustenance, and the civil and spiritual life of those therein. He who loves his country, and does good to it from good will, in the other life loves the

Lord's kingdom, for there the Lord's kingdom is his country, and he who loves the Lord's kingdom loves the Lord, because the Lord is all in all in His kingdom.

94. The church is our neighbor more than our country, for he who provides for the church, provides for the souls and eternal life of the men who dwell in his country; wherefore he who provides for the church from love, loves his neighbor in a superior degree, for he wishes and wills heaven and happiness of life to eternity to others.

95. The Lord's kingdom is our neighbor in a still superior degree, for the Lord's kingdom consists of all who are in good, as well those on the earths as those in the heavens; thus the Lord's kingdom is good with all its quality in the complex: when this is loved, the individuals are loved who are in good.

96. These are the degrees of neighbor, and love ascends, with those who are principled in love towards their neighbor, according to these degrees. But these degrees are degrees in successive order, in which what is prior or superior is to be preferred to what is posterior or inferior; and forasmuch as the Lord is in the supreme degree, and He is to be regarded in each degree as the end to which it tends, consequently He is to be loved above all persons and things. Hence, now, it may appear in what manner love to the Lord conjoins itself with love towards the neighbor.

97. It is a common saying, that every one is his own neighbor; that is, that every one should first consider himself; but the doctrine of charity teaches how this is to be understood. Every one should provide for himself the necessaries of life, such as food, raiment, habitation, and other things which the state of civil life, in which he is, necessarily requires, and this not only for himself, but also for his family, and not only for the present time, but also for the future; for, unless a man procures himself the necessaries of life, he cannot be in a state to exercise charity, for he is in want of all things.

98. But in what manner every one ought to be his own neighbor may appear from this comparison: every one ought to provide food and raiment for his body; this must be the first object, but it should be done to the end that he may have a sound mind in a sound body. And every one ought to provide food for his mind, viz. such things as are of intelligence and wisdom, to the end that it may thence be in a state to serve his fellow-citizens, human society, his country, and the church, thus the Lord. He who does this provides for his own good to eternity; whence it is plain that the first thing is to discover the end in view, for all other things look to this. The case is like that of a man who builds a house: he first lays the foundation; but the foundation is for the house, and the house is for habitation, he who believes that he is his own neighbor in the first place, is like him who regards the foundation as the end, not the house and habitation: when yet the habitation is the very first

and ultimate end, and the house with the foundation is only a medium to this end.

99. The end declares in what manner every one should be his own neighbor, and provide for himself first. If the end be to grow richer than others only for the sake of riches, or for the sake of pleasure, or for the sake of eminence, and the like, it is an evil end, and that man does not love his neighbor, but himself: but if the end be to procure himself riches, that he may be in a state of providing for the good of his fellow-citizens, of human society, of his country, and of the church, in like manner if he procure himself offices for the same end, he loves his neighbor. The end itself, for the sake of which he acts, constitutes the man; for the end is his love, forasmuch as every one has for a first and ultimate end, that which he loves above all things.

What has hitherto been said is concerning the neighbor; love towards him, or CHARITY, shall now be treated of.

100. It is believed by many, that love towards the neighbor consists in giving to the poor, in assisting the indigent, and in doing good to every one; but charity consists in acting prudently, and to the end that good may result. He who assists a poor or indigent villain does evil to his neighbor through him, for, through the assistance which he renders, he confirms him in evil, and supplies him with the means of doing evil to others: it is otherwise with him who gives support to the good.

101. But charity extends itself much more widely than to the poor and indigent; for charity consists in doing what is right in every work, and our duty in every office. If a judge does justice for the sake of justice, he exercises charity; if he punishes the guilty and absolves the innocent, he exercises charity, for thus he consults the welfare of his fellow-citizens, and of his country. The priest who teaches truth, and leads to good, for the sake of truth and good, exercises charity. But he who does such things for the sake of self and the world, does not exercise charity, because he does not love his neighbor, but himself.

102. The case is the same in all other instances, whether a man be in any office or not; as with children towards their parents, and with parents towards their children; with servants towards their masters, and with masters towards their servants; with subjects towards their king, and with a king towards his subjects: whoever of these does his duty from a principle of duty, and what is just from a principle of justice, exercises charity.

103. The reason why such things belong to the love towards the neighbor, or charity, is, because, as was said above, every man is our neighbor, but in a different manner. A less and greater society is more our neighbor; our country is still more our neighbor; the Lord's kingdom still more; and the Lord above all; and in a universal sense, good, which proceeds from the Lord, is our neighbor; consequently sincerity and justice are so too. Wherefore he who does any

good for the sake of good, and he who acts sincerely and justly for the sake of sincerity and justice, loves his neighbor and exercises charity; for he does so from the love of what is good, sincere, and just, and consequently from the love of those in whom good, sincerity, and justice are.

104. Charity therefore is an internal affection, from which man wills to do good, and this without remuneration; the delight of his life consists in doing it. With them who do good from internal affection, there is charity in every thing which they think and speak, and which they will and do: it may be said that a man or angel, as to his interiors, is charity, when good is his neighbor. So widely does charity extend itself.

105. They who have the love of self and of the world for an end, cannot in any wise be in charity; they do not even know what charity is, and cannot at all comprehend that to will and do good to the neighbor without reward as an end, is heaven in man, and that there is in that affection a happiness as great as that of the angels of heaven, which is ineffable; for they believe, if they are deprived of the joy proceeding from the glory of honors and riches, that nothing of joy can be experienced any longer; when yet it is then that heavenly joy first begins, which infinitely transcends the other.

OF FAITH.

108. No man can know what faith is in its essence, unless he know what charity is, because where there is no charity there is no faith, forasmuch as charity makes one with faith as good does with truth. For what man loves or holds dear, this he esteems good, and what man believes, this he esteems truth; whence it is plain that there is a like union of charity and faith, as there is of good and truth; the quality of which union may appear from what has been said above concerning GOOD and TRUTH.

109. The union of charity and faith is also like that of will and understanding with man; for these are the two faculties which receive good and truth, the will receiving good and the understanding truth; thus, also, these two faculties receive charity and faith, forasmuch as good is of charity and truth is of faith. No one is ignorant that charity and faith reside with man, and in him, and forasmuch as they are with him and in him, they must be in his will and understanding, for all the life of man is therein, and from thence. Man has also memory, but this is only the outer court, where those things are collected together which are to enter into the understanding and the will: whence it is plain that there is a like union of charity and faith, as there is of will and understanding; the quality of which union may appear from what has been said above concerning WILL and UNDERSTANDING.

110. Charity conjoins itself with faith with man, when man wills that which he knows and perceives; to will is of charity, but to know and perceive is of faith. Faith enters into man, and becomes his, when he wills and loves that which he knows and perceives; otherwise it is without him.

111. Faith does not become faith with man, unless it become spiritual, and it does not become spiritual, unless it become of the love, and it then becomes of the love, when man loves to live truth and good, that is, to live according to those things which are commanded in the Word.

112. Faith is the affection of truth originating from willing truth because it is truth; and to will truth because it is truth is the very spiritual principle of man; for it is abstracted from the natural principle, which consists in willing truth not for the sake of truth, but for the sake of one's own glory, reputation or gain. Truth abstractedly from such things is spiritual, because it is from the Divine: that which proceeds from the Divine is spiritual, and this is conjoined to man by love, for love is spiritual conjunction.

113. Man may know, think, and understand much, but when he is left to himself alone, and meditates, he rejects from himself those things which do not agree with his love; and thus he rejects them also after the life of the body, when he is in the spirit, for that only remains in the spirit of man which has entered into his love: other things after death are regarded as foreign, and because they are not of his love he casts them out. It is said in the spirit of man, because man lives a spirit after death.

114. An idea concerning the good which is of charity, and concerning the truth which is of faith, may be formed from the light and heat of the sun. When the light which proceeds from the sun is conjoined to heat, as is the case in the time of spring and summer, then all the productions of the earth germinate and flourish; but when there is no heat in the light, as in the time of winter, then all the productions of the earth become torpid and die: the truth of faith is also spiritual light, and love is spiritual heat. Hence an idea may be formed concerning the man of the church, what his quality is when faith with him is conjoined to charity—that he is indeed as a garden and paradise; and what his quality is when faith with him is not conjoined to charity—that he is as a desert and earth covered with snow.

115. The confidence or trust, which is said to be of faith, and is called indeed saving faith, is not spiritual confidence or trust, but natural, when it is of faith alone. Spiritual confidence or trust has its essence and life from the good of love, but not from the truth of faith separate. The confidence of faith separate is dead; wherefore true confidence cannot be given with those, who lead an evil life: the confidence also of obtaining salvation on account of the Lord's merit with the Father, whatever a man's life may have been, is likewise not from truth. All those who are in

spiritual faith have confidence that they are saved by the Lord, for they believe that the Lord came into the world to give eternal life to those who believe, and live according to the precepts which He taught, and that He regenerates them, and renders them fit for heaven, and that He alone does this from pure mercy, without the aid of man.

116. To believe those things which the Word teaches, or which the doctrine of the church teaches, and not to live according to them, appears as if it were faith, and some also fancy that they are saved by it, but by this alone no one is saved, for it is persuasive faith, the quality of which shall now be declared.

117. Faith is persuasive, when the Word and the doctrine of the church are believed and loved, not for the sake of truth and of a life according to it, but for the sake of gain, honor, and the fame of erudition, as ends; wherefore they who are in that faith, do not look to the Lord and to heaven, but to themselves and the world. They who aspire after great things in the world, and covet many things, are in a stronger persuasive principle that what the doctrine of the church teaches is true, than they who do not aspire after great things and covet many things: the reason is, because the doctrine of the church is to the former only a medium to their own ends, and so far as the ends are coveted, so far the means are loved, and are also believed. But the case in itself is this: so far as any persons are in the fire of the loves of self and of the world, and from that fire speak, preach, and act, so far they are in the above persuasive principle, and then they know no other than that it is so: but when they are not in the fire of those loves, then they believe but little, and many not at all; whence it is evident, that persuasive faith is a faith of the mouth and not of the heart, and that in itself it is not faith.

118. They who are in persuasive faith do not know, from any internal illustration, whether the things which they teach be true or false; yea, neither do they care, provided they be believed by the vulgar; for they are in no affection of truth for the sake of truth. Wherefore they recede from faith, if they are deprived of honors and gains, provided their reputation be not endangered. For persuasive faith is not inwardly with man, but stands without, in the memory only, out of which it is taken when it is taught. Wherefore that faith with its truths vanishes after death; for then there remains only that faith which is inwardly in man, that is, which is rooted in good, thus which has become of the life.

119. They who are in persuasive faith are understood by these persons in Matthew: "Many will say to me in that day, Lord, Lord, have we not prophesied by Thy name, and by Thy name cast out demons, and in Thy name done many virtues? but then I will confess to them, I have not known you, ye workers of iniquity." vii. 22, 23. Also in Luke: "Then will ye begin to say, We have eaten before Thee, and have drunk, and Thou hast taught in our streets; but He will say, I say to you, I have not known you whence you are; depart from Me, all ye workers of iniquity." xiii. 26,27. They are understood also by the five foolish virgins who had no oil in their lamps, in Matthew: "At length came those virgins, saying, Lord, Lord, open to us; but He answering will say, Verily I say unto you, I have not known you." xxv. 11, 12: oil in lamps is the good of love in faith.

OF PIETY.

123. It is believed by many, that spiritual life, or the life which leads to heaven, consists in *piety,* in *external sanctity,* and in the *renunciation of the world:* but piety without charity, and external sanctity without internal sanctity, and a renunciation of the world without a life in the world, do not constitute spiritual life: but piety from charity, external sanctity from internal sanctity, and a renunciation of the world with a life in the world, constitute it.

124. Piety consists in thinking and speaking piously, in spending much time in prayer, in behaving humbly at that time, in frequenting temples and attending devoutly to the preaching there, in frequently every year receiving the sacrament of the supper, and in performing the other parts of worship according to the ordinances of the church. But the life of charity consists in willing well and doing well to our neighbor, in acting in all our works from justice and equity, and from good and truth, and in like manner in every office; in a word, the life of charity consists in performing uses. Divine worship primarily consists in this life, but secondarily in the former; wherefore he who separates one from the other, that is, who lives the life of piety, and not that of charity at the same time, does not worship God. He thinks indeed of God, but not from God, but from himself; for he thinks of himself continually, and not at all of his neighbor; and if he does think of his neighbor, he regards him as vile, if he be not of such a quality also. He likewise thinks of heaven as a reward, whence his mind entertains the idea of merit, and also the love of self, together with a contempt or neglect of uses, and thus of his neighbor; and at the same time he cherishes a belief that he is blameless. Hence it may appear that the life of piety, separate from the life of charity, is not the spiritual life which should be in divine worship. Compare Matt. vi. 7,8.

125. External sanctity is like such piety, and is not holy with man unless his internal be holy; for such as man is as to his internal, such he also is as to his external, as this proceeds from the former as action does from its spirit; wherefore external sanctity without internal sanctity is natural and not spiritual. Hence it is that external sanctity is found with the evil as well as with the good; and they who place the whole of worship therein are for the most part void; that is, without knowledges of good and truth. And yet goods and truths are the real sanctities which are to be known, believed and loved, because they are from the Divine, and thus the Divine is in them. Internal sanctity, therefore, consists in loving good and truth for the sake of good and truth, and justice and

THE NEW JERUSALEM AND ITS HEAVENLY
DOCTRINE (continued)

sincerity for the sake of justice and sincerity. So far
also as man thus loves them, so far he is spiritual,
and his worship too, for so far also he is willing to
know them and to do them; but so far as man does
not thus love them, so far he is natural, and his
worship too, and so far also he is not willing to know
them and do them. External worship without internal may be compared with the life of the respiration
without the life of the heart; but external worship
from internal may be compared with the life of the
respiration conjoined to the life of the heart.

126. But to proceed to what relates to the renunciation of
the world. It is believed by many, that to renounce
the world, and to live in the spirit and not in the
flesh, is to reject worldly things, which are chiefly
riches and honors; to be continually engaged in pious
meditation concerning God, concerning salvation,
and concerning eternal life; to spend one's life in
prayer, in the reading of the Word and pious books;
and also to afflict one's self: but this is not renouncing the world; but to renounce the world is to love
God and to love the neighbor; and God is loved
when man lives according to His commandments,
and the neighbor is loved when man performs uses.
In order, therefore, that man may receive the life of
heaven, it is necessary that he should live in the
world, and in offices and business there. A life
abstracted from worldly things is a life of thought
and faith separate from the life of love and charity, in
which life the principle of willing good and doing
good to the neighbor perishes. And when this
perishes, spiritual life is as a house without a
foundation, which either sinks down successively
into the ground, or becomes full of chinks and
openings, or totters till it falls.

127. That to do good is to worship the Lord, appears from
the Lord's words. "Every one who heareth my words
and doeth them, I will liken to a prudent man who
built a house upon a rock; but he who heareth my
words and doeth them not, I will liken to a foolish
man who built a house upon the sand, or upon the
ground without a foundation," Matt. vii. 24 to 27;
Luke vi. 47, 48, 49.

128. Hence now it is manifest, that a life of piety is of
value, and is acceptable to the Lord, so far as a life of
charity is conjoined to it; for this is the primary, and
such as the quality of this is, such is that of the
former. Also, that external sanctity is of value, and is
acceptable to the Lord, so far as it proceeds from
internal sanctity; for such as the quality of this is,
such is that of the former. And also, that the
renunciation of the world is of value, and is
acceptable to the Lord, so far as it is practised in the
world; for they renounce the world who remove the
love of self and the world, and act justly and
sincerely in every office, in every business, and in
every work, from an interior, thus from a celestial
origin; which origin dwells in that life when man acts

well, sincerely, and justly, because it is according to
the divine laws.

OF CONSCIENCE.

130. Conscience is formed with man from the religious
principle in which he is, according to its reception
inwardly in himself.

131. Conscience, with the man of the church, is formed by
the truths of faith from the Word, or from doctrine
out of the Word, according to their reception in the
heart; for when man knows the truths of faith, and
apprehends them in his own manner, and then wills
them and does them, he acquires conscience. Reception in the heart is reception in the will, for the will
of man is what is called the heart. Hence it is that
they who have conscience, speak from the heart the
things which they speak, and do from the heart the
things which they do: their mind also is undivided,
for according to that which they understand and
believe to be true and good they do.

132. A more perfect conscience can be given with those
who are enlightened in the truths of faith more than
others, and who are in a clear perception above
others, than with those who are less enlightened, and
who are in obscure perception.

133. The real spiritual life of man resides in a true
conscience, for his faith, conjoined to his charity, is
therein; wherefore, with those who are possessed of
it, to act from conscience is to act from their own
spiritual life, and to act contrary to conscience is,
with them, to act contrary to their own spiritual life.
Hence it is that they are in the tranquility of peace,
and in internal blessedness, when they act according
to conscience, and in intranquility and pain, when
they act contrary to it: this pain is what is called
remorse of conscience.

134. Man has a conscience of what is good, and a
conscience of what is just: the conscience of what is
good is the conscience of the internal man, and the
conscience of what is just is the conscience of the
external man. The conscience of what is good
consists in acting according to the precepts of faith
from internal affection, but the conscience of what is
just consists in acting according to civil and moral
laws from external affection. They who have the
conscience of what is good, have also the conscience
of what is just; and they who have only the
conscience of what is just, are in a faculty of
receiving the conscience of what is good; and they
also do receive it when they are instructed.

135. Conscience, with those who are in charity towards
the neighbor, is the conscience of truth, because it is
formed by the faith of truth; but with those who are
in love to the Lord, it is the conscience of good,
because it is formed by the love of truth. The
conscience of these is a superior conscience, and is
called the perception of truth from good. They who
have the conscience of truth, are of the Lord's
spiritual kingdom; but they who have the superior

conscience, which is called perception, are of the Lord's celestial kingdom.

136. But let examples illustrate what conscience is. If a man be in possession of another man's goods, whilst the other is ignorant of it, and thus can retain them without fear of the law, or of the loss of honor and reputation, and he still restores them to the other, because they are not his own, he has conscience, for he does what is good for the sake of what is good, and what is just for the sake of what is just. Again, if a person has it in his power to obtain an office, but knows that another, who also desires it, would be more useful to his country, and gives way to him, for the sake of the good of his country, he has a good conscience. So in other cases.

137. From these instances it may be concluded, what quality they are of who have not conscience; they are known from the opposite. Thus, they who for the sake of any gain make what is unjust appear as just, and what is evil appear as good, and *vice versa,* have not conscience. Neither do they know what conscience is, and if they are instructed what it is, they do not believe; and some are not willing to know. Such is the quality of those, who, in all their actions, have respect only to themselves and the world.

138. They who have not received conscience in the world, cannot receive it in the other life; thus they cannot be saved. The reason is, because they have no plane into which heaven, that is, the Lord through heaven, may flow in, and by which He may operate, and lead them to Himself. For conscience is the plane and receptacle of the influx of heaven.

OF FREEDOM.

141. All freedom is of love, for what man loves, this he does freely; hence also all freedom is of the will, for what man loves, this he also wills; and forasmuch as love and the will constitute the life of man, so also does freedom. From these considerations it may appear what freedom is, namely, that it is that which is of the love and the will, and thence of the life of man: hence it is, that what a man does from freedom, appears to him as if he did it from his own proprium.

142. To do evil from freedom, appears as if it were freedom, but it is bondage, because that freedom is from the love of self and from the love of the world, and these loves are from hell. Such freedom is actually turned into bondage after death, for the man who has been in such freedom then becomes a vile servant in hell. But to do good from freedom is freedom itself, because it proceeds from love to the Lord and from love towards the neighbor, and these loves are from heaven. This freedom also remains after death, and then becomes freedom indeed, for the man who has been in such freedom, becomes in heaven like a son of the house. This the Lord thus teaches: "Every one that doeth sin is the servant of sin; the servant abideth not in the house forever: the son abideth forever; if the Son shall have made you free, you shall be truly free," John viii. 34, 35, 36. Now, forasmuch as all good is from the Lord, and all

evil from hell, it follows, that freedom consists in being led by the Lord, and slavery in being led by hell.

143. That man has the liberty of thinking what is evil and false, and also of doing it, so far as the laws do not withhold him, is in order that he may be capable of being reformed; for goods and truths are to be implanted in his love and will, so that they may become of his life, and this cannot be done unless he have the liberty of thinking what is evil and false as well as what is good and true. This liberty is given to every man by the Lord, and so far as he does not love evil and the false, so far, when he thinks what is good and true, the Lord implants them in his love and will, consequently in his life, and thus reforms him. What is inseminated in freedom, this also remains, but what is inseminated in a state of compulsion, this does not remain, because what is from compulsion is not from the will of the man, but from the will of him who compels. Hence also it is, that worship from freedom is pleasing to the Lord, but not worship from compulsion; for worship from freedom is worship from love, but worship from compulsion is not so.

144. The liberty of doing good, and the liberty of doing evil, though they appear alike in the external form, are as different and distant from each other as heaven and hell are: the liberty of doing good also is from heaven, and is called heavenly liberty; but the liberty of doing evil is from hell, and is called infernal liberty; so far, likewise, as man is in the one, so far he is not in the other, for no man can serve two lords, Matt. vi. 24; which also appears from hence, that they who are in infernal liberty believe that it is slavery and compulsion not to be allowed to will evil and think what is false at their pleasure, whereas they who are in heavenly liberty abhor willing evil and thinking what is false, and would be tormented if they were compelled to do so.

145. Forasmuch as acting from freedom appears to man like acting from his own proprium, therefore heavenly freedom may also be called the heavenly proprium, and infernal freedom may be called the infernal proprium. The infernal proprium is that into which man is born, and this is evil; but the heavenly proprium is that into which man is reformed, and this is good.

146. Hence it may appear what *Free-will* is; that it consists in doing good from choice or will, and that they are in that freedom who are led by the Lord; and they are led by the Lord who love good and truth for the sake of good and truth.

147. Man may know what is the quality of the liberty in which he is, from the delight which he feels when he thinks, speaks, acts, hears, and sees; for all delight is of love.

OF MERIT.

150. They who do good with a view to merit, do not do good from the love of good, but from the love of

**THE NEW JERUSALEM AND ITS HEAVENLY
DOCTRINE** (continued)

reward, for he who wills to have merit, wills to be rewarded; they who do thus, regard and place their delight in the reward, and not in good; wherefore they are not spiritual, but natural.

151. To do good, which is good, must be from the love of good, thus for the sake of good. They who are in that love are not willing to hear of merit, for they love to do, and perceive satisfaction therein, and, on the other hand, they are sorrowful if it be believed that what they do is for the sake of any thing of themselves. The case herein is nearly the same as with those who do good to their friends for the sake of friendship; to a brother for the sake of brotherhood, to wife and children for the sake of wife and children, to their country for the sake of their country, thus from friendship and love. They who think well, also say and insist, that they do not do good for the sake of themselves, but for the sake of them to whom the good is done.

152. They who do good for the sake of reward do not do good from the Lord, but from themselves, for they regard themselves in the first place, inasmuch as they regard their own good; and the good of their neighbor, which is the good of their fellow-citizens, of human society, of their country, and of the church, they regard no otherwise than as means to this end. Hence it is, that the good of the love of self and of the world lies concealed in the good of merit and that good is from man and not from the Lord, and all good which is from man is not good; yea, so far as self and the world lies concealed in it, it is evil.

153. Genuine charity and genuine faith disclaim all merit, for good itself is the delight of charity, and truth itself is the delight of faith; wherefore they who are in that charity and faith know what good not meritorious is, but not they who are not in charity and faith.

154. That good is not to be done for the sake of reward, the Lord himself teaches in Luke: "If ye love those who love you what grace have ye, for sinners do the same: rather love your enemies, and do good, and lend, hoping for nothing; then shall your reward be great, and ye shall be the sons of the Most High," vi. 32, 33, 34, 35. That man cannot do good that is good from himself, the Lord also teaches in John: "A man cannot take any thing, unless it be given him from heaven," iii. 27; and in another place, "Jesus said, I am the vine, ye are the branches: as the branch cannot bear fruit from itself, unless it shall abide in the vine, so neither can ye unless ye shall abide in Me: He who abideth in Me and I in him, he beareth much fruit, for except from Me ye cannot do any thing," xv. 4 to 8.

155. Forasmuch as all good and truth is from the Lord, and nothing of them from man, and forasmuch as good from man is not good, it follows that merit belongs to no man, but to the Lord alone; the merit of the Lord consists in this, that from His own proper power He has saved the human race, and also, that He saves those who do good from Him. Hence it is that in the Word, he is called just to whom the merit and justice of the Lord are ascribed, and he is called unjust to whom are ascribed his own justice and the merit of self.

156. The delight itself, which is in the love of doing good without regard to reward, is a reward which remains to eternity, for heaven and eternal happiness are insinuated into that good by the Lord.

157. To think and believe that they who do good will come into heaven, and also that good is to be done in order that they may come into heaven, is not to regard reward as an end, nor yet to place merit in words; for even they who do good from the Lord think and believe so, but they who thus think, believe and do, and are not in the love of good for the sake of good, have regard to reward as an end, and place merit in works.

OF REPENTANCE AND THE REMISSION OF SINS.

159. He who would be saved must confess his sins, and do the work of repentance.

160. To *confess sins*, is to know evils, to see them in ourselves, to acknowledge them, to make ourselves guilty, and to condemn ourselves on account of them. This, when it is done before God, is the confession of sins.

161. *To do the work of repentance*, is to desist from sins after a man has thus confessed them, and from an humble heart has made supplication for remission, and to live a new life according to the precepts of charity and faith.

162. He who only acknowledges generally that he is a sinner, and makes himself guilty of all evils, and yet does not explore himself, that is, see his own evils, makes confession indeed, but not the confession of repentance; he, forasmuch as he does not know his own evils, lives afterwards as he did before.

163. He who lives the life of charity and faith does the work of repentance daily; he reflects upon the evils which are with him, he acknowledges them, he guards against them, he supplicates the Lord for help. For man of himself continually lapses towards evil, but he is continually raised by the Lord, and led to good. Such is the state of those who are in good; but they who are in evil lapse continually, and are also continually elevated by the Lord, but are only withdrawn from falling into the most grievous evils, to which of themselves they tend with all their power.

164. The man who explores himself in order to do the work of repentance, must explore his thoughts and the intentions of his will, and must there examine what he would do if it were permitted him, that is, if he were not afraid of the laws, and of the loss of reputation, honor and gain. There the evils of man reside, and the evils which he does in the body are all from thence. They who do not explore the evils of

their thought and will, cannot do the work of repentance, for they think and will afterwards as they did before, and yet to will evils is to do them. This is self-examination.

165. Repentance of the mouth and not of the life is not repentance, and sins are not remitted by means of repentance of the mouth, but by repentance of the life. Sins are indeed continually remitted to man by the Lord, for He is mercy itself, but still they adhere to man, however he may suppose that they are remitted; nor are they removed from him but by a life according to the precepts of true faith. So far as he lives according to those precepts, so far sins are removed; and so far as they are removed, so far they are remitted.

166. It is supposed that sins are wiped away, or are washed off, as filth is by water, when they are remitted; but sins are not wiped away, but they are removed; that is, man is withheld from them when he is kept in good by the Lord; and when he is kept in good, it appears as if he were without them, thus as if they were wiped away; and so far as man is reformed, so far he is capable of being kept in good. How man is reformed will be shown in the following doctrinal on regeneration. He who supposes that sins are in any other manner remitted, is much deceived.

167. The signs that sins are remitted, that is, removed, are these which follow. They whose sins are remitted, perceive a delight in worshiping God for the sake of God, and in serving their neighbor for the sake of their neighbor, thus in doing good for the sake of good, and in speaking truth for the sake of truth; they are unwilling to claim merit by any thing of charity and faith; they shun and are averse to evils, as enmities, hatreds, revenges, adulteries, and the very thoughts of such things with intention. But the signs that sins are not remitted, that is, removed, are these which follow. They whose sins are not remitted, worship God not for the sake of God, but serve their neighbor not for the sake of their neighbor, thus they do not do good and speak truth for the sake of good and truth, but for the sake of themselves and the world; they wish to claim merit by their deeds; they perceive nothing undelightful in evils, as in enmity, in hatred, in revenge, in adulteries; and from these evils they think of them in all licentiousness.

168. The repentance which takes place in a free state is of avail, but that which takes place in a state of compulsion is of no avail. States of compulsion are states of sickness, states of dejection of mind in consequence of misfortune, states of imminent death, as also every state of fear which takes away the use of reason. He who is evil, and in a state of compulsion promises repentance, and also does good, when he comes into a free state returns to his former life of evil; the case is otherwise with one who is good.

169. After a man has explored himself, and acknowledged his sins, and done the work of repentance, he must remain constant in good even to the end of life. For if he afterwards relapses into his former evil life, and

embraces it, he commits profanation, for he then conjoins evil with good; whence his latter state becomes worse than his former, according to the words of the Lord: "When the unclean spirit goes out from a man, he walks through dry places, seeking rest, but doth not find; then he says, I will return into my house whence I went out; and when he comes and finds it void, and swept, and adorned for him, then he goes away, and adjoins to himself seven other spirits worse than himself, and, entering in, they dwell there, *and the latter things of the man become worse than the first*," Matt. xii. 43, 44, 45.

OF REGENERATION.

173. He who doth not receive spiritual life, that is, who is not begotten anew by the Lord, cannot come into heaven; which the Lord teaches in John, "Verily, verily, I say unto thee, except any one be begotten again, he cannot see the kingdom of God," iii. 3.

174. Man is not born of his parents into spiritual life, but into natural life. Spiritual life consists in loving God above all things, and in loving his neighbor as himself, and this according to the precepts of faith, which the Lord taught in the Word. But natural life consists in loving ourselves and the world more than our neighbor, yea, more than God Himself.

175. Every man is born of his parents into the evils of the love of self and of the world; for every evil, which by habit has acquired as it were a nature, is derived into the offspring; thus it descends successively from parents, from grand-fathers, and from great-grandfathers, in a long series backwards; whence the derivation of evil at length becomes so great, that the whole of man's proper life is nothing else but evil. This continual derivation of evil is not broken and altered, except by the life of faith and charity from the Lord.

176. Man continually inclines to, and lapses into, what he derives from his hereditary principle: hence he confirms with himself that evil, and also superadds more of himself. These evils are altogether contrary to spiritual life, and destroy it; wherefore, unless man receives new life, which is spiritual life, from the Lord, thus unless he is conceived anew, is born anew, is educated anew, that is, is created anew, he is damned, for he wills nothing else, and thence thinks nothing else, but what is of self and the world, in like manner as they do who are in hell.

177. No man can be regenerated unless he knows such things as belong to the new life, that is, to spiritual life; and the things which belong to the new life, which are the spiritual life, are truths which are to be believed and goods which are to be done; the former are of faith, the latter of charity. These things no one can know from himself, for man apprehends only those things which are obvious to the senses, from which he procures to himself a light which is called natural light, by virtue of which he sees nothing else than what relates to the world and to self, but not the things which relate to heaven and to God. These he must learn from revelation; as that the Lord, who is

THE NEW JERUSALEM AND ITS HEAVENLY DOCTRINE (continued)

God from eternity, came into the world to save the human race; that He has all power in heaven and in earth; that the all of faith and the all of charity, thus all truth and good, is from Him; that there is a heaven, and that there is a hell; and that man is to live to eternity in heaven if he have done well, in hell if he have done evil.

178. These and many other things belong to faith, and ought to be known by the man who is to be regenerated, for he who knows them, may think them, afterwards will them, and lastly do them, and so have new life, whilst he who does not know that the Lord is the Saviour of the human race, cannot have faith in Him, love Him, and thus do good for the sake of Him. He who does not know that all good is from Him, cannot think that his own salvation is from Him, still less can he will it to be so, thus he cannot live from Him. He who does not know that there is a hell and that there is a heaven, nor that there is eternal life, cannot even think about the life of heaven, nor apply himself to receive it, and so in other cases.

179. Every one has an internal man and an external man; the internal is what is called the spiritual man, and the external is what is called the natural man, and each is to be regenerated, that the man may be regenerated. With the man who is not regenerated, the external or natural man rules, and the internal serves; but with the man who is regenerated, the internal or spiritual man rules, and the external serves. Whence it is manifest that the order of life is inverted with man from his birth, namely, that that principle serves which ought to rule, and that that principle rules which ought to serve. In order that man may be saved, this order must be inverted; and this inversion can by no means exist, but by regeneration from the Lord.

180. What it is for the internal man to rule and the external to serve, and *vice versa*, may be illustrated thus:—If a man places all his good in voluptuousness, in gain, and in pride, and has delight in hatred and revenge, and inwardly in himself seeks for reasons which confirm such evils, then the external man rules and the internal serves. But when a man perceives good and delight in thinking and willing well, sincerely, and justly, and in outwardly speaking and doing in like manner, then the internal man rules and the external serves.

181. The internal man is first regenerated by the Lord, and afterwards the external, and the latter by means of the former. For the internal man is regenerated by thinking those things which are of faith and charity, but the external by a life according to them. This is understood by the words of the Lord, "Unless any one be begotten of water and the spirit, he cannot enter into the kingdom of God," John iii. 5. Water, in the spiritual sense, is the truth of faith, and the spirit is a life according to it.

182. The man who is regenerated, is, as to his internal man, in heaven, and is an angel there with the angels, among whom he also comes after death; he is then able to live the life of heaven, to love the Lord, to love his neighbor, to understand truth, to relish good, and to perceive the blessedness thence derived.

OF TEMPTATION.

187. They alone who are regenerated undergo spiritual temptations; for spiritual temptations are pains of the mind, induced by evil spirits, with those who are in goods and truths. Whilst these spirits excite the evils which are with such persons, there arises an anxiety which is that of temptation; man knows not whence it comes, because he is unacquainted with this its origin.

188. For there are evil spirits and good spirits attendant on every man; the evil spirits are in his evils, and the good spirits are in his goods. When the evil spirits approach, they draw forth his evils, and the good spirits, on the contrary, draw forth his goods, whence collision and combat take place, from which the man perceives an interior anxiety, which is temptation. Hence it is plain that temptations are not from heaven, but are induced by hell, which is also according to the faith of the church, which teaches that God tempts no one.

189. Interior anxieties also take place with those who are not in goods and truths, but these are natural anxieties, not spiritual ones; they are distinguished by this, that natural anxieties have worldly things for their objects, but spiritual anxieties have heavenly things for their objects.

190. In temptations, the dominion of good over evil, or of evil over good, is what is contended for. The evil which desires to have the dominion, is in the natural or external man, and the good is in the spiritual or internal; if evil conquers, then the natural man has dominion, but if good conquers, then the spiritual man has dominion.

191. Those combats are fought by means of the truths of faith, which are from the Word. It is from these that man must fight against evils and falses; for if he combats from any other principles than these, he does not conquer, because the Lord is not in any other principles. Forasmuch as the combat is fought by means of the truths of faith, therefore man is not admitted into that combat before he is in the knowledges of good and truth, and has thence obtained some spiritual life; wherefore those combats do not take place with man until he has arrived at years of maturity.

192. If man falls in temptation, his state after it becomes worse than his state before it, inasmuch as evil has thereby acquired power over good, and the false over truth.

193. Inasmuch as at this day faith is rare because there is no charity, the church being at its end, therefore few at this day are admitted into any spiritual tempta-

tions; hence it is that it is scarcely known what they are and to what end they conduce.

194. Temptations conduce to acquire for good, dominion over evil, and for the truth, dominion over the false; also to confirm truths, and to conjoin them to goods, and at the same time to disperse evils and the falses thence derived. They conduce likewise to open the internal spiritual man, and to subject the natural thereto, as also to break the loves of self and the world, and to subdue the concupiscences which proceed from them. When these things are effected, man acquires illustration and perception respecting what truth and good are, and what the false and evil are; whence man obtains intelligence and wisdom, which afterwards continually increase.

195. The Lord alone combats for man in temptations; if man does not believe that the Lord alone combats and conquers for him, he then only undergoes an external temptation, which does not conduce to his salvation.

OF BAPTISM.

202. Baptism was instituted for a sign that the man belongs to the church, and for a memorial that he is to be regenerated; for the washing of baptism signifies nothing else than spiritual washing, which is regeneration.

203. All regeneration is effected by the Lord, by means of the truths of faith and of a life according to them; therefore baptism testifies that the man is of the church, and that he is capable of being regenerated; for in the church, the Lord, who regenerates, is acknowledged, and therein is the Word, which contains the truths of faith, by means of which regeneration is effected.

204. This the Lord teaches in John, "Except a man be begotten of water and the spirit, he cannot enter into the kingdom of God," iii.5; water, in the spiritual sense, is the truth of faith from the Word: the spirit is a life according to it, and to be begotten is to be regenerated thereby.

205. Forasmuch as every one who is regenerated also undergoes temptations, which are spiritual combats against evils and falses, therefore by the waters of baptism those temptations are also signified.

206. Since baptism is for a sign and for a memorial of those things, therefore a man may be baptized when an infant, and if he be not baptized then, he may be baptized when he is an adult.

207. Let it be known therefore to those who are baptized, that baptism itself gives neither faith nor salvation, but that it testifies that they will receive faith, and that they will be saved, if they are regenerated.

208. Hence it may appear what is understood by the Lord's words in Mark, "He who shall believe and be baptized shall be saved, but he who shall not believe shall be condemned," xvi. 16; he who shall believe is he who acknowledges the Lord, and receives divine truths from Him by means of the Word; he who shall

be baptized is he who by means of those truths is regenerated by the Lord.

OF THE HOLY SUPPER.

210. The Holy Supper was instituted by the Lord, that by means thereof there may be a conjunction of the church with heaven, thus with the Lord; it is therefore the most holy thing of worship.

211. But in what manner conjunction is effected by it is not apprehended by those who do not know any thing concerning the internal or spiritual sense of the Word, for they do not think beyond the external sense, which is the sense of the letter. From the internal or spiritual sense of the Word it is known what is signified by body and blood, and what by bread and wine, also what is signified by eating.

212. In that sense, the body or flesh of the Lord is the good of love, as is the bread likewise; and the blood of the Lord is the good of faith, as is the wine likewise; and eating is appropriation and conjunction. The angels, who are attendant on man when he receives the sacrament of the supper, understand those things in no other manner; for they perceive all things spiritually. Hence it is that a holy principle of love and a holy principle of faith then flows in with man from the angels, thus through heaven from the Lord; hence there is conjunction.

213. From these considerations it is evident, that when man takes the bread, which is the body, he is conjoined to the Lord by means of the good of love to Him from Him; and when he takes the wine, which is the blood, he is conjoined to the Lord by means of the good of faith in Him from Him. But it is to be noted, that conjunction with the Lord by means of the sacrament of the supper is effected solely with those who are in the good of love to, and faith in, the Lord from the Lord; with these there is conjunction by means of the holy supper; with others there is presence, but not conjunction.

214. Besides, the holy supper includes and comprehends all the divine worship instituted in the Israelitish church; for the burnt-offerings and sacrifices, in which the worship of that church principally consisted, were called, in a single word, bread; hence also the holy supper is its completion.

OF THE RESURRECTION.

223. Man is so created, that as to his internal he cannot die, for he is capable of believing in God, and also of loving God, and thus of being conjoined to God by faith and love; and to be conjoined to God is to live to eternity.

224. This internal is with every man who is born; his external is that by means of which he brings into effect the things which are of faith and love. The internal is what is called the spirit, and the external is what is called the body. The external, which is called the body, is accommodated to uses in the natural world; this is rejected when man dies; but the internal, which is called the spirit, is accommodated to uses in the spiritual world; this does not die. This

internal is then a good spirit and an angel, if the man had been good when in the world, but an evil spirit, if the man had been evil when in the world.

225. The spirit of man, after the death of the body, appears in the spiritual world in a human form, altogether as in the world; he enjoys also the faculty of seeing, of hearing, of speaking, of feeling, as in the world; and he is endowed with every faculty of thinking, of willing, and of acting as in the world. In a word, he is a man as to all things and every particular, except that he is not encompassed with that gross body which he had in the world; he leaves that when he dies, nor does he ever re-assume it.

226. This continuation of life is what is understood by the resurrection. The reason why men believe that they are not to rise again before the last judgment, when also every visible object of the world is to perish, is because they have not understood the Word; and because sensual men place their life in the body, and believe that unless this were to live again, it would be all over with the man.

227. The life of man after death is the life of his love and the life of his faith, hence such as his love and such as his faith had been, when he lived in the world, such his life remains to eternity. It is the life of hell with those who have loved themselves and the world above all things, and the life of heaven with those who have loved God above all things and their neighbors as themselves. The latter are they that have faith, but the former are they that have not faith. The life of heaven is what is called eternal life, and the life of hell is what is called spiritual death.

228. That man lives after death, the Word teaches, as that God is not the God of the dead, but of the living, Matt. xxii. 31; that Lazarus after death was taken up into heaven, but the rich man cast into hell, Luke xvi. 22, 23, and the following verses; that Abraham, Isaac, and Jacob are there, Matt. viii. 11; chap. xxii. 31, 32; Luke xx. 37, 38; that Jesus said to the thief, To-day shalt thou be with me in Paradise, Luke xxiii. 43.

OF HEAVEN AND HELL.

230. There are two things which constitute the life of man's spirit, love and faith; love constituting the life of his will, and faith the life of his understanding. The love of good, and the faith of truth thence derived, constitute the life of heaven; and the love of evil, and the faith of what is false thence derived, constitute the life of hell.

231. Love to the Lord and love towards the neighbor constitute heaven, and so does faith, so far as it has life from those loves; and forasmuch as each of those loves and the faith thence derived is from the Lord, it is evident from hence that the Lord constitutes heaven.

232. Heaven is with every one according to his reception of love and faith from the Lord; and they who receive heaven from the Lord whilst they live in the world, come into heaven after death.

233. They who receive heaven from the Lord are they who have heaven in themselves; for heaven is in man, as the Lord also teaches: "They shall not say, The kingdom of God, lo it is here! or lo there! for behold the kingdom of God is in you," Luke xvii. 21.

234. Heaven with man resides in his internal, thus in willing and thinking from love and faith, and thence in his external, which consists in acting and speaking from love and faith. But it does not reside in the external without being in the internal; for all hypocrites are capable of acting and speaking well, but not of willing well and thinking well.

235. When man comes into the other life, which takes place immediately after death, it is then manifest whether heaven is in him, but not whilst he lives in the world. For in the world the external appears, and not the internal; but in the other life the internal is made manifest, because man then lives as to his spirit.

236. Eternal happiness, which is also called heavenly joy, is imparted to those who are in love and faith to the Lord, from the Lord; that love and that faith have in them that joy, into which the man who has heaven in himself comes after death; in the mean time it lies stored up in his internal. In the heavens there is a communion of all goods; the peace, the intelligence, the wisdom, and the happiness of all, are communicated to every one therein, yet to every one according to his reception of love and faith from the Lord. Hence it appears how great peace, intelligence, wisdom and happiness are in heaven.

237. As love to the Lord, and love towards our neighbor, constitute the life of heaven with man, so the love of self and the love of the world, when they reign, constitute the life of hell with him, for these latter loves are opposite to the former. Wherefore they with whom the loves of self and of the world reign, are incapable of receiving any thing from heaven; but the things which they receive are from hell; for whatever a man loves, and whatever he believes, is either from heaven or from hell.

238. They with whom the loves of self and of the world reign, do not know what heaven and the happiness of heaven are; and it appears incredible to them that happiness should be given in any other loves than in those, when yet the happiness of heaven only enters, so far as those loves, as ends, are removed. The happiness which succeeds on their removal is so great, that it exceeds all human comprehension.

239. The life of man cannot be changed after death, but remains then such as it had been in the world; for the whole spirit of man is such as his love is, and infernal love cannot be transcribed into heavenly love, because they are opposite: this is understood by the words of Abraham to the rich man in hell: "There is a great gulf between us and you, so that they who would pass to you cannot, neither can they pass from

thence to us." Luke xvi. 26. Hence it is plain that they who come into hell remain there to eternity, and that they who come into heaven remain there to eternity.

OF THE CHURCH.

241. That which constitutes heaven with man, also constitutes the church; for as love and faith constitute heaven, so also love and faith constitute the church. Hence, from what has been said before concerning heaven, it is evident what the church is.

242. Where the Lord is acknowledged, and where the Word is, the church is said to be; for the essentials of the church are love to, and faith in, the Lord from the Lord; and the Word teaches how man is to live, in order that he may receive love and faith from the Lord.

243. In order that there may be a church, there must be doctrine from the Word, since without doctrine the Word is not understood. But doctrine alone does not constitute the church with man, but a life according to it; whence it follows that faith alone does not constitute the church, but the life of faith, which is charity. Genuine doctrine is the doctrine of charity and of faith together, and not the doctrine of faith without that of charity; for the doctrine of charity and of faith together, is the doctrine of life, but not the doctrine of faith without the doctrine of charity.

244. They who are without the church, and still acknowledge one God, and live according to their religious principles in a certain charity towards their neighbor, are in communion with those who are of the church, for no one, who believes in God and lives well, is damned. Hence it is evident that the church of the Lord is every where in the universal globe, although it is specifically where the Lord is acknowledged, and where there is the Word.

245. Every one with whom the church is, is saved, but every one with whom the church is not, is condemned.

OF THE SACRED SCRIPTURE, OR THE WORD.

249. Without a revelation from the Divine, man cannot know any thing concerning eternal life, nor even any thing concerning God, and still less any thing concerning love to, and faith in Him: for man is born into mere ignorance, and must therefore learn every thing from worldly things, from which he must form his understanding. He is also born hereditarily into every evil which proceeds from the love of self and of the world; the delights from thence prevail continually, and suggest such things as are diametrically contrary to the Divine. Hence it is that man knows nothing concerning eternal life; wherefore there must necessarily be a revelation to communicate such knowledge.

250. That the evils of the love of self and of the world induce such ignorance concerning the things which are of eternal life, appears manifestly from those within the church, who, although they know from revelation that there is a God, that there is a heaven

and a hell, that there is eternal life, and that that life is to be acquired by means of the good of love and faith, still lapse into denial concerning those subjects, as well the learned as the unlearned. Hence it is further evident how great ignorance would prevail, if there were no revelation.

251. Since therefore man lives after death, and then lives to eternity, and a life awaits him according to his love and faith, it follows that the Divine, out of love towards the human race, has revealed such things as may lead to that life, and conduce to man's salvation. What the Divine has revealed, is with us the Word.

252. The Word, forasmuch as it is a revelation from the Divine, is divine in all and every particular part; for what is from the Divine cannot be otherwise. What is from the Divine descends through the heavens even to man; wherefore in the heavens it is accommodated to the wisdom of the angels who are there, and on earth it is accommodated to the apprehension of the men who are there. Wherefore in the Word there is an internal sense, which is spiritual, for the angels, and an external sense, which is natural, for men; hence it is that the conjunction of heaven with man, is effected by means of the Word.

253. No others understand the genuine sense of the Word but they who are enlightened; and they only are enlightened who are in love to, and faith in, the Lord; for their interiors are elevated by the Lord into the light of heaven.

254. The Word in the letter cannot be understood, but by means of doctrine drawn from the Word by one who is enlightened; for the literal sense thereof is accommodated to the apprehension even of simple men, wherefore doctrine drawn from the Word must serve them for a lamp.

OF PROVIDENCE.

267. The government of the Lord in the heavens and in the earths is called Providence; and forasmuch as all the good of love and all the truth of faith, which give salvation, are from Him, and nothing at all of them from man, it is evident that the Divine Providence of the Lord is in all and singular the things which conduce to the salvation of the human race. This the Lord thus teaches in John: "I am the way, the truth, and the life," xiv. 6; and in another place, "As the branch cannot bear fruit of itself, unless it shall abide in the vine, so neither can ye, unless ye shall abide in Me; except from Me ye cannot do any thing," xv. 4, 5.

268. The Divine Providence of the Lord extends to the most singular things of the life of man; for there is only one fountain of life, which is the Lord, from whom we are, live, and act.

269. They who think from worldly things concerning the Divine Providence, conclude from them that it is only universal, and that singulars appertain to man. But such persons do not know the arcana of heaven, for they form their conclusions only from the loves of self and of the world, and their pleasures; wherefore,

when they see the evil exalted to honors, and acquire wealth more than the good, and that success attends them according to their artifices, they say in their hearts, that this would not be the case if the Divine Providence were in all things and singulars; not considering that the Divine Providence does not regard that which briefly passes away, and ends with the life of man, in the world, but that it regards that which remains to eternity, thus which has no end. What has no end, that Is; but what has an end, that respectively Is not. Let him who is capable consider, whether a hundred thousand years be any thing to eternity, and he will perceive that they are not; what then are some years of life in the world?

270. Every one who rightly considers it, may know, that eminence and opulence in the world are not real divine blessings, notwithstanding man, from the pleasure he finds in them, calls them so; for they pass away, and also seduce many, and turn them away from heaven; but that eternal life, and its happiness, are real blessings, which are from the Divine: this the Lord also teaches in Luke: "Make to yourselves a treasure that faileth not in the heavens, where the thief cometh not, nor the moth corrupteth; for where your treasure is, there will your heart be also."

271. The reason why success attends the evil according to their arts is, because it is according to divine order that every one should act what he acts from reason, and also from freedom; wherefore, unless man were left to act from freedom according to his reason, and thus unless the arts which are thence derived were to succeed, man could by no means be disposed to receive eternal life, for this is insinuated when man is in freedom, and his reason is enlightened. For no one can be forced to good, forasmuch as nothing that is forced inheres with him, for it is not his own; that becomes a man's own, which is done from freedom according to his reason, and that is done from freedom which is done from the will or love, and the will or love is the man himself. If a man were forced to that which he does not will, his mind would continually incline to that which he does will; and besides, every one strives after what is forbidden, and this from a latent cause, because every one strives to be in freedom. Whence it is plain, that, unless man were kept in freedom, good could not be provided for him.

272. To leave man from his own freedom also to think, to will, and, so far as the laws do not restrain him, to do evil, is called permission.

273. To be led to felicities in the world by means of arts, appears to man as if it were from his own proper prudence, but still the Divine Providence incessantly accompanies by permitting and continually withdrawing from evil. But to be led to felicities in heaven is known and perceived to be not from man's own proper prudence, because it is from the Lord,

and is effected of his Divine Providence by disposing and continually leading to good.

274. That this is the case, man cannot comprehend from the light of nature, for from that light he does not know the laws of divine order.

275. It is to be noted that there is providence, and prævidence; good is what is provided by the Lord, but evil is what is prævided. The one must accompany the other, for what comes from man is nothing but evil, but what comes from the Lord is nothing but good.

OF THE LORD.

280. There is one God, who is the Creator and Conservator of the universe; thus, who is the God of heaven and the God of the earth.

281. There are two things which constitute the life of heaven with man, the good of love and the truth of faith. Man has this life from God, and nothing at all of it is from man; wherefore the primary principle of the church is, to acknowledge God, to believe in God, and to love Him.

282. They who are born within the church ought to acknowledge the Lord, His Divine, and His Human, and to believe in Him, and to love Him; for from the Lord is all salvation. This the Lord teaches in John: "He who believeth in the Son hath eternal life, but he who believeth not the Son shall not see life, but the anger of God abideth with him," iii. 36. Again, "This is the will of him who sent me, that every one who seeth the Son, and believeth in Him, should have eternal life, and I will resuscitate Him in the last day," vi. 40. Again, "Jesus said, I am the resurrection and the life; he who believeth in Me, although he dies, shall live; but every one who liveth and believeth in Me, shall not die to eternity," xi. 21, 23.

283. Wherefore they within the church who do not acknowledge the Lord, and His divine, cannot be conjoined to God, and thus cannot have any lot with the angels in heaven, for no one can be conjoined to God but from the Lord and in the Lord. That no one can be conjoined to God but from the Lord, the Lord teaches in John, "No one hath ever seen God; the only-begotten Son, who is in the bosom of the Father, He hath shown Him," i.20. Again, "Ye have never heard the voice of the Father, nor seen His shape," v. 37. Again, "No one knoweth the Father but the Son, and to whom the Son shall be willing to reveal Him," xi. 27. And again, "I am the way, the truth, and the life; no one cometh to the Father but by Me," xiv. 6. The reason why no one can be conjoined to God but in the Lord, is because the Father is in Him, and they are one, as He also teaches in John: "If ye know Me, ye know my Father also; he who seeth Me seeth the Father; Philip, believest thou not that I am in the Father and the Father in Me? believe Me that I am in the Father and the Father in Me," xiv. 7 to 11. And again, "The Father and I are One; that ye may know and believe

that I am in the Father and the Father in Me," x. 30, 38.

284. Forasmuch as the Father is in the Lord and the Father and the Lord are One; and forasmuch as He ought to be believed in, and he that believes in Him has eternal life, it is evident that the Lord is God. That the Lord is God, the Word also teaches, as in John: "In the beginning was the Word, and the Word was with God, and GOD WAS THE WORD: all things were made by Him, and without Him was not any thing made which was made; and THE WORD WAS MADE FLESH, and dwelt among us, and we saw His glory, the glory as of the only-begotten of the Father," i. 1, 3, 14. In Isaiah, "A child is born to us, a Son is given to us, on whose shoulder is the government, and His name shall be called GOD, HERO, THE FATHER OF ETERNI-TY, the Prince of Peace," ix. 5. Again, "A virgin shall conceive and bring forth, and His name shall be called GOD WITH US," vii. 14; Matthew i. 23. And in Jeremiah, "Behold the days shall come when I will raise up to David a just branch, who shall reign a king, and shall prosper; and this is His name which they shall call Him, JEHOVAH OUR JUSTICE," xxiii. 5, 6; chap. xxxiii. 15, 16.

285. All they who are of the church, and in light from heaven, see the Divine in the Lord; but they who are not in light from heaven, see nothing but the Human in the Lord; when yet the Divine and Human are in Him so united, that they are one; as the Lord also taught in another place, in John: "Father, all Mine are Thine, and all Thine Mine," xvii. 10.

286. That the Lord was conceived from Jehovah the Father, and was thus God from conception, is known in the church; and also that He rose again with His whole body, for He left nothing in the sepulchre; of which he also afterwards confirmed the disciples, saying, "See My hands and My feet, that it is I Myself; feel Me and see; for a spirit hath not flesh and bones as ye see Me have," Luke xxiv. 39. And although He was a man as to the flesh and bones, still He entered through the closed doors, and, after He had manifested himself, became invisible, John xx. 19, 26; Luke xxiv. 3. The case is otherwise with every man, for man only rises again, as to the spirit, and not as to the body, wherefore when He said, "that He is not as a spirit," He said that He is not as another man. Hence it is evident that the Human in the Lord is also Divine.

287. Every man has his esse of life, which is called his soul, from his father; the existere of life thence derived is what is called the body; hence the body is the effigy of its soul, for the soul, by means of the body, exercises its life at pleasure. Hence it is that men are born into the likeness of their parents, and that families are distinguished from each other; from this circumstance it is evident what was the quality of the body or Human of the Lord, viz. that it was as the Divine Itself, which was the esse of His life, or

the soul from the Father; wherefore he said, "He that seeth Me, seeth the Father," John xiv. 9.

288. That the Divine and Human of the Lord is one person, is agreeable to the faith received in the whole Christian world, which is to this effect: "Although Christ is God and man, still He is not two, but one Christ; yea, He is altogether one and a single person; because as body and soul are one man, so God and man are one Christ." This is from the Athanasian creed.

289. They who, respecting the Divinity, have an idea of three persons, cannot have an idea of one God; if with the mouth they say one, still they think three; but they who, respecting the Divinity, have an idea of three principles in one person, can have an idea of one God, and can say one God, and also think one God.

290. An idea of three principles in one person is attained, when it is thought that the Father is in the Lord, and that the Holy Spirit proceeds from Him; there is then a trine in the Lord, the Divine itself which is called the Father, the Divine Human which is called the Son, and the Divine Proceeding which is called the Holy Spirit.

291. Forasmuch as all the Divine is in the Lord, therefore He has all power in the heavens and in the earths; which he also says in John: "The Father hath given all things into the hands of the Son," ii.35. Again, "The Father hath given to the Son power over all flesh," xvii. 2. In Matthew, "All things are delivered to Me by the Father," xi. 27. Again, "All power is given to Me in heaven and in earth," xxviii. 16. Such power is divine.

292. They who make the Human of the Lord like the human of another man, do not think of His conception from the Divine Itself, nor do they consider that the body of every thing is the effigy of its soul. Neither do they reflect on His resurrection with the whole body, nor of His appearance at His transformation, when His face shone as the sun. Neither do they think, respecting those things which the Lord said concerning faith in Him, concerning His unity with the Father, concerning His glorification, and concerning His power over heaven and earth, that these are divine, and were mentioned in relation to His Human. Neither do they remember that the Lord is omnipresent also as to His human, Matthew xxviii. 20, although the faith of His omnipresence in the sacred supper is derived from this consideration: omnipresence is divine. Yea, perhaps they do not think that the Divine principle which is called the Holy Spirit, proceeds from His Human; when yet it proceeds from His glorified Human, for it is said, "The Holy Spirit was not yet, because Jesus was not yet glorified," John vii. 39.

293. The Lord came into the world that He might save the human race, who would otherwise have perished in eternal death; and He saved them by this, that He subjugated the hells, which infested every man coming into the world and going out of the world;

and at the same time by this, that he glorified His Human: for thus He can keep the hells in subjugation to eternity. The subjugation of the hells, and the glorification of His Human at the same time, were effected by means of temptations admitted into the human which He had from the mother, and by continual victories therein. His passion on the cross was the last temptation and full victory.

294. That the Lord subjugated the hells, He Himself teaches in John: when the passion of the cross was at hand, then Jesus said, "Now is the judgment of this world; *now the prince of this world shall be cast out* ," xii. 27, 28, 31; again, "Have confidence, *I have overcome the world* ," xvi. 33. And in Isaiah, "Who is this that cometh from Edom, going on in the multitude of His strength, great to save? My own arm brought salvation to Me; so He became to them for a Saviour," lxiii, 1 to 20; chap. lix. 16 to 21. That He glorified His Human, and that the passion of the cross was the last temptation and full victory, by means of which He glorified it, He teaches also in John: "After Judas went out, Jesus said, Now is the Son of Man glorified, and God will glorify Him in Himself, and will immediately glorify Him," xiii. 31, 32. Again, "Father, the hour has come; glorify Thy Son, that Thy Son also may glorify Thee," xvii. 1, 5. Again, "Now is My soul troubled; Father, glorify Thy Name; and a voice came out from heaven, saying, I have both glorified it, and will glorify it again," xii. 27, 28. And in Luke, "Ought not Christ to suffer these things, and to enter into His glory," xxiv. 30. These words were said in relation to His passion: to glorify is to make Divine. Hence, now, it is manifest, that, unless the Lord had come into the world, and been made a man, and in this manner had liberated from hell all those who believe in Him and love Him, no mortal could have been saved; this is understood by the saying, that without the Lord there is no salvation.

295. When the Lord fully glorified His Human, He then put off the human from the mother, and put on the human from the Father, which is the Divine Human, wherefore he was then no longer the son of Mary.

296. The first and primary principle of the church is, to know and acknowledge its God; for without that knowledge and acknowledgment there is no conjunction; thus, in the church, without the acknowledgment of the Lord. This the Lord teaches in John: "He who believeth in the Son hath eternal life, but he who believeth not the Son shall not see life, but the anger of God abideth with him," iii. 36. And in another place, "Except ye believe that I am, ye shall die in your sins," viii. 24.

297. That there is a trine in the Lord, viz. the Divine Itself, the Divine Human, and the Divine Proceeding, is an arcanum from heaven, and is for those who shall be in the Holy Jerusalem.

OF ECCLESIASTICAL AND CIVIL GOVERNMENT.

311. There are two things which ought to be in order among men, viz. the things which are of heaven, and the things which are of the world: the things which are of heaven are called ecclesiastical things, and those which are of the world are called civil things.

312. Order cannot be maintained in the world without governors, who are to observe all things which are done according to order, and which are done contrary to order; and are to reward those who live according to order, and to punish those who live contrary to order. If this be not done, the human race must perish; for the will to command others, and to possess the goods of others, is hereditarily connate with every one, whence proceed enmities, envyings, hatreds, revenges, deceits, cruelties, and many other evils: wherefore, unless men were kept under restraint by the laws, and by rewards suited to their loves, which are honors and gains for those who do good things; and by punishments contrary to those loves, which are the loss of honor, of possessions, and of life, for those who do evil things; the human race would perish.

313. There must therefore be governors to keep the assemblages of men in order, who should be persons skilled in the laws, wise, and men who fear God. There must also be order among the governors, lest any one, from caprice or inadvertence, should permit evils which are against order, and thereby destroy it: which is guarded against when there are superior and inferior governors, among whom there is subordination.

314. Governors over those things among men which relate to heaven, or over ecclesiastical matters, are called priests, and their office is called the priesthood. But governors over those things among men which relate to the world, or over civil concerns, are called magistrates, and their chief, where such a form of government prevails, is called king.

315. With respect to the priests, they ought to teach men the way to heaven, and also to lead them; they ought to teach them according to the doctrine of their church derived from the Word, and they ought to lead them to live according to it. Priests who teach truths, and thereby lead to the good of life, and so to the Lord, are the good shepherds of the sheep; but they who only teach, and do not lead to the good of life, and so to the Lord, are the evil shepherds.

316. Priests ought not to claim to themselves any power over the souls of men, inasmuch as they do not know in what state the interiors of a man are; still less ought they to claim the power of opening and shutting heaven, since that power belongs to the Lord alone.

317. Dignity and honor ought to be paid to priests on account of the sanctity of their office; but they who are wise give the honor to the Lord, from whom all sanctity is derived, and not to themselves, whilst they

who are not wise attribute the honor to themselves, whereby they take it from the Lord. They who attribute honor to themselves, on account of the sanctity of their office, prefer honor and gain to the salvation of souls, which they ought to provide for; but they who give the honor to the Lord, and not to themselves, prefer the salvation of souls to honor and gain. The honor of any employment is not in the person, but is adjoined to him according to the dignity of the thing which he administers; and what is adjoined does not belong to the person himself, and is also separated from him with the employment. All personal honor is the honor of wisdom and the fear of the Lord.

318. Priests ought to teach the people, and to lead them by means of truths to the good of life, but still they ought to force no one, since no one can be forced to believe contrary to what he thinks from his heart to be truth. He who believes otherwise than the priest, and makes no disturbance, ought to be left in peace; but he who makes disturbance ought to be separated; for this also is agreeable to order, for the sake of which the priesthood is established.

319. As priests are appointed to administer those things which relate to the divine law and worship, so kings and magistrates are appointed to administer those things which relate to civil law and judgment.

320. Forasmuch as the king alone cannot administer all things, therefore there are governors under him, to each of whom a province is given to administer, where the administration of the king cannot be extended. These governors, taken collectively, constitute the royal function, but the king himself is the chief.

321. Royalty itself is not in the person, but is adjoined to the person. The king who believes that royalty is in his own person, and the governor who believes that the dignity of government is in his own person, is not wise.

322. Royalty consists in administering according to the laws of the realm, and in judging according thereto, from justice. The king who regards the laws as above himself, is wise, and he who regards himself as above the laws, is not wise. The king who regards the laws as above himself, places royalty in the law, and the law has dominion over him, for he knows that the law is justice, and that all justice which is justice, is divine. But he who regards himself as above the laws, places royalty in himself, and either believes himself to be the law, or the law, which is justice, to be derived from himself; hence he arrogates to himself that which is divine, to which nevertheless he ought to be in subjection.

323. The law, which is justice, ought to be enacted in the realm by persons skilled in the law, wise, and men who fear God; and the king and his subjects ought afterwards to live according to it. The king who lives according to the law so enacted, and therein sets an example to his subjects, is truly a king.

324. A king who has absolute power, and believes that his subjects are such slaves that he has a right to their possessions and lives, and exercises such a right, is not a king, but a tyrant.

325. The king ought to be obeyed according to the laws of the realm, and by no means to be injured either by word or deed; for on this the public security depends.

Notes: *Emanuel Swedenborg, whose voluminous writings fill several shelves, prepared a condensation of his teachings into a small volume which was published in English in a paperback volume. It summarizes the teachings of this religious teacher, now largely forgotten, whose role in the development of nineteenth-century American thought was vast. This document also serves as a creedal statement for the several Swedenborgian churches.*

* * *

CONFESSIONS OF THE GENERAL CHURCH OF THE NEW JERUSALEM

1

I believe in the Lord Jesus Christ, the almighty and everlasting God, the Maker of heaven and earth, the Redeemer and Savior of the world.

I believe in the Sacred Scripture, the Word of God, the Fountain of wisdom, the Source of life, and the Way to heaven.

I believe in the Second Coming of the Lord, in the Spiritual Sense of the Word, and in the Heavenly Doctrine of the New Jerusalem.

I believe in the New Angelic Heaven, in the New Christian Church, in the communion of angels and men, in repentance from sin, in the life of charity, in the resurrection of man, in the judgment after death, and in the life everlasting.

2

I believe that the Lord from eternity, who is Jehovah, came into the world to subdue the hells, and to glorify His Human; and that without this no mortal could have been saved; and they are saved who believe in Him. (F 34)

3

I believe that God is One in person and in essence, in whom is the Trinity, and that the Lord is that God.

I believe that no mortal could have been saved unless the Lord had come into the world.

I believe that the Lord came into the world in order to remove hell from man, and He removed it by combats against it and by victories over it; thus He subdued it, and reduced it into order and under obedience to Himself.

I believe that the Lord came into the world to glorify the Human which He took upon Him in the world, that is, in order to unite it to the all-originating Divine (the Divine itself).

I believe that in this way the Lord to eternity holds the hells in order and under obedience to Himself.

CONFESSIONS OF THE GENERAL CHURCH OF THE NEW
JERUSALEM (continued)

I believe that these mighty works could not have been
accomplished except by means of temptations even to the
uttermost, which was the passion of the cross; and that is
why the Lord underwent that most grievous temptation.
(F 35)

4

I believe that the Lord came into the world to reduce into
order all things in heaven and on the earth.

I believe that this was accomplished by means of combats
against the hells, which were then infesting every man that
came into the world and that went out of the world.

I believe that thereby the Lord became righteousness, and
saved men, who otherwise could not have been saved.
(Lord 14)

5

I believe that the Lord from eternity, who is Jehovah,
came into the world to subdue the hells and to glorify His
Human; and that without this no flesh could have been
saved, and those are saved who believe in Him.

I believe that man is conjoined with the Lord by faith in
Him, and through conjunction with the Lord he is saved.

I believe that to have faith in the Lord is to have
confidence that He will save; and because none can have
such confidence except he who leads a good life, therefore
this also is understood by having faith in the Lord.

I believe that Jehovah God is love itself and wisdom itself,
or good itself and truth itself.

I believe that as the Divine truth, which is the Word, and
which was God with God, He came down and took on the
Human for the purpose of reducing to order all things that
were in heaven, and all things in hell, and all things in the
church.

I believe that Jehovah God did this because at that time
the power of hell prevailed over the power of heaven, and
upon the earth the power of evil over the power of good,
and in consequence a total damnation stood threatening at
the door.

I believe that Jehovah God removed this threat by means
of His Human which was Divine truth, and thus He
redeemed angels and men; for He united in His Human,
Divine truth with Divine good, or Divine wisdom with
Divine love; and so, with and in His glorified Human, He
returned into His Divine in which He was from eternity.

6

I believe that the Lord came into the world, and assumed a
Human, in order to put Himself into the power of
subjugating the hells, and of reducing all things to order
both in the heavens and on the earths.

I believe that He superinduced this Human over His
former Human, and that that which was superinduced was
like the human of a man in the world.

I believe that both these Humans are Divine, and therefore
infinitely transcend the finite humans of angels and men.

I believe that because the Lord fully glorified the natural
Human even to its ultimates, therefore He rose again with
the whole body, therein differing from any man.

I believe that by the assumption of this Human the Lord
put on Divine omnipotence, not only for subjugating the
hells and reducing the heavens to order, but also for
holding the hells in subjection to eternity, and thus saving
mankind.

7

I believe that without the coming of the Lord into the
world no mortal could have been saved, and they are saved
who believe in Him, and who live well.

8

I believe that Jehovah God Himself came into the world to
deliver men and angels from the assault and violence of
hell, and thus from damnation.

I believe that He did this by means of combats against hell
and by victories over it, whereby He subjugated it, reduced
it to order, and brought it under obedience to Himself.

I believe that He also formed a new heaven, and through
this instaurated a new church.

By this means Jehovah God put Himself in the power of
saving all who believe in Him and who do His precepts.
Thus He redeemed all in the whole world, and all in the
whole heaven. (Can. Redemption VI)

Notes: *A contemporary branch of the Swedenborg churches,
the General Church of the New Jerusalem has published
seven brief confessions of faith in addition to the lengthy
creedal-confessional statement written by Emanuel Swedenborg, which summarizes the creeds of the church he
founded. All eight confessions are used primarily for
liturgical purposes and are reproduced here from the
church's hymnal.*

* * *

Spiritualism

WHAT AQUARIANS BELIEVE (AQUARIAN FOUNDATION)

THE AQUARIAN FOUNDATION does not hold to any
specific creeds or dogmas, for Aquarians themselves do not
believe in "belief" so much as in knowledge. How and
where such knowledge has been gained, they feel is not as
important as how it is applied in one's life. Any fixed creed
or statement of belief, therefore, might tend more to
"crystallize" philosophy and thought than to allow "room
for growth."

There can be no single word or descriptive phrase which
fully categorizes the Aquarian teachings; for human
language itself is, at best, a conveyor of "half-truths."
Some of the terms often applied to various phases of our

study can be considered appropriate, however, so long as no one of them—nor all of them together—are ever considered all-encompassing.

Some *AQUARIANS* consider themselves to be *CHRISTIANS*; some consider themselves *BUDDHISTS*; and others, good members of certain other great religious faiths. Yet, all or nearly all Aquarians are aware of the values and truths, as well as the distortions and half-truths brought to the group-consciousness by EACH of these movements. Aquarians are aware, too, of the many similarities which may be found in the spiritual and moral precepts of Jesus, Gautama Buddha, Krishna, Babaji and many other teachers.

AQUARIANS are SPIRITUALISTS, to the extent that they believe in and practice communication with the so-called dead, some of whom serve as "guides" or "guardian angels," through human instruments called "mediums." This would seem to presuppose a belief in the continuity of life beyond the grave, and in other planes of life than this physical plane. Aquarians are not content, however, with presupposing alone, but tend to investigate thoroughly the field of psychic phenomena and mediumship until absolute proof is found to the satisfaction of each one of them.

On the other hand, Aquarians do not allow the belief and practice of contacting loved ones and guides in spirit to become the main focal point of their religion. Neither do they seek psychic phenomena for the sake of phenomena alone; for they know that when such a thing is sought after as an end in itself, it becomes injurious rather than beneficial. Only when psychic phenomena is used as a means to a greater benefit, such as the giving of helpful service or the stimulation of needed truths, is it worthwhile.

AQUARIANS are THEOSOPHISTS to the extent that they continue the studying and sharing with those on earth ready to receive such knowledge, the teachings of the Masters of the Great Brotherhood of Cosmic Light, as was received in the West nearly a century ago by Madame H.P. Blavatsky and her successors. These include teachings on soul evolution, reincarnation, the law of cause and effect, or "Karma," the attainment of personal Mastership, or mastery over life and death, and a great many not-so-obvious facets of nature.

Aquarians also, continuing the Theosophical principle, embrace the idea of continuous service to humanity and of striving to establish world brotherhood, without regard to race, creed or nationality. On the other hand, Aquarians, like many other students of the occult, are aware that no book or library or lecture course can ever contain the "last word" on any subject, and that any such materials which are general enough to be given to the public may be prone to man-made error and distortion.

AQUARIANS are YOGA PHILOSOPHERS in a sense, inasmuch as they recognize the "yoke" to God, or pathway to Divine Realization, in its various forms. They have been taught in the Eastern Yoga schools throughout the ages, and the Aquarian recognizes the validity and worth of each of these pathways, be it one of advanced exercises and postures, special meditations, mental development through meditations, mental development through

concentration and study, or of some related type of activity. Aquarians are not inclined to follow any one of the others, however, unless it is so indicated by their development and by advice from their spiritual Gurus, or Master Teachers.

AQUARIANS are FREE-THINKERS in their approach to life and morals, knowing the truth of cause-and-effect, the need for personal independent action, the merit of the Golden Rule: "Do unto others as you would have others do unto you" and the worth of the Aquarian New Age Commandment: "You shall love and respect yourself."

AQUARIANS are TRANSCENDENTALISTS, continuing the line of thought advanced by Ralph Waldo Emerson, who was surely inspired in turn by numerous others who had gone before him. Transcendentalists, like Emerson, affirm the truth, not only that the higher meanings of life are to be perceived by means other than the five physical senses, but also that the Divine Life exists in all things. They note with interest the fact that one of the means of perception developed and used AFTER one's transition into the spirit world is called the "organs of transcendence"; also that the great universities in that plane of life are called "Schools of Transcendentalism."

AQUARIANS are UNIVERSALISTS in the original meaning of that term, Universal in that they acknowledge a kinship with everything that exists, and a *SURETY OF ULTIMATE UNIVERSAL SALVATION*, for all members of the human race.

Notes: *Rooted in Spiritualism, the Aquarian Foundation has become extremely eclectic, as its statement of belief amply demonstrates. The foundation is gnostic, with an emphasis upon the member's acquisition of cosmic knowledge over any communal agreement upon a set of specific beliefs. Nevertheless, the foundation has reached a unique perspective that sets it apart from similar organizations.*

* * *

WHAT DOES THE OLD CHRISTIAN INITIATE TEACH? AS TAUGHT BY THE CHURCH OF REVELATION

1. The Old Christian Initiate as taught by the Master Jesus, is the Messenger from the inner soul to humanity, linking earth and heaven, bringing the only proof of immortality. It is the broad Educator, the great Revealer, the Comforter.

2. It teaches that death is not the cessation of life, but a mere change of conditions.

3. It teaches a personal responsibility.

4. It removes all fear of death, which is really the portal of the spirit world.

5. It teaches not only that a man has a soul, but that man is spirit with a soul which is the spiritual house in which the spirit dwells.

6. That a man is a spiritual being now, even while incased in the flesh.

7. That as man sows on the earth he reaps in the life to come.

WHAT DOES THE OLD CHRISTIAN INITIATE TEACH? AS TAUGHT BY THE CHURCH OF REVELATION (continued)

8. That those who have passed on are conscious—not asleep.

9. The Old Christian initiate is the world religion, non-sectarian Philosophy based upon Scientific Truth, shows how to find spirit, understand the "Natural Law" and have life everlasting without death.

10. That communion between the living and the so-called dead, is scientifically proven.

11. The Old Christian Initiate is based upon the full teaching of the Master Jesus consisting of three facts; the spirit ability after the physical death to communicate with mortals.

12. The Old Christian Initiate is the Science, Philosophy and Religion of continuous life, based upon the demonstrated fact of communication by means of mediumship, with those who live in the Spirit World.

13. It brings to the surface man's spiritual powers, gifts such as inspiration, clairvoyance, clairaudience and healing powers.

14. It teaches that the spark of divinity dwells in all.

15. That as a flower gradually unfolds in beauty, so the spirit of man unfolds and develops in the spirit Phores.

16. The Old Christian Initiate is God's message to mortals, declaring that there is no death. That all who have passed on still live. That there is hope in the life beyond for the most sinful. Jesus said "Why marvel at the things I do, Ye shall do these things and even greater things, because I go to my Father to prepare a place for you and if I go I will come again."

17. That every soul will progress through thes to heights, sublime and glorious, where God is Love and Love is God.

18. The Old Christian Initiate is both a religion and a rule of life, based upon fundamental truth, explained and amplified by revelation from the wiser ones who have passed through death.

19. The Old Christian Initiate is the only science, religion and philosophy, which furnishes positive proof (by oft-repeated mental and Physical Phenomena through mediumship) of the knowledge of spirit life, spirit return and imortality.

20. It demonstrates the many spiritual gifts which mankind is endowed but which through want of knowledge have been allowed to lay dormant, or through prejudice have been violently and unjustly suppressed.

21. The Old Christian Initiate does not create truth, but is a living witness of the truth of a future existence. It reveals, it demonstrates it, describing its inhabitants, their occupations and characteristics.

22. The Old Christian Initiate, the teaching of spirit and those who worship in spirit are some times called Spiritualist or a teacher of Spiritualism. The "Ist" and "Ism" is merely a phrase or expression. It is used in the same manner as we use the Word "Americanism."

23. The Old Christian Initiate is not spiritism, that is talking to the dead for curiosity, for fleshly gratification, for selfish gain, for ambitious end, or for unworthy amusing and irreligious purposes. If this was the witch-spiritism that Moses condemned or disapproved of he did well. It should be discouraged, condemmed today as unworthy of rational, royal-souled men and women.

24. The Old Christian Initiate as taught by Jesus, brings a sweet reward for welldoing and certain punishment for every wrong action, and that the good and divine that is attained here will be retained when entering the spiritual world: that we are building now, by our conduct and characters, our homes in the future state of immortality.

25. The teaching of spirit does not say "Goodnight" in the hour of death but rather gives the glad assurance of a most welcome "Good morning" just across the crystal river. It does not drape the mourners home in gloom, but lifts the grim curtain, permitting us to hear responsive words of undying affection from those we love. The future life is a social life, a constructive life, a progressive life, where the soul sweeps onward and upward, in glory transcending glory, through ages into eternal progression.

26. The Old Christian Initiate brings comfort to all who know the law. It aims at the unfoldment and upliftment of the race. It is the best key with which to unlock the store house of spiritual knowledge. It brings all realms of nature under the law and asserts that Man's whole duty in life is to find out the laws of Nature and conform to them.

27. War is regarded with Horror by all true believers of spirit. All whom believe in peace and brotherhood between man and man, and world wide peace among nations.

28. All aggressive wars, wars of conquest, wars of extension, of territory or commercial privilege or trade or colonization, are absolutely condemned by the ethics of spirit truth or teaching of the Old Christian Initiate.

29. Wars of self defense, wars of liberation for the oppressed, wars for the privilege vital to human life and happiness are justified reluctantly on the ground that a nation has the same right to fight in defense of its national life and in defense of human liberty as an individual has to fight in defense of his life and liberty under attack.

30. The Old Christian Initiate brings through the development of the moral consciousness in man, and through the ministry of Unseen angels and Spirits; the touch of a vanished hand, the sound of a voice that is still. That is why out of all the churches today, members are going in Secret like Nicodemeus, to the Medium for comfort.

The organized seekers of truth recognize the good the churches are doing in various ways and the student of truth is taught the great lesson continually to grant freely to others the same right of independent thinking and judging which they claim for themselves.

Ministers of the Old Christian Initiate do not employ speakers to tour the country in order to preach against anybody's religion.

They do not get money under false pretenses, by instilling into human minds, fear of Hell and perdition. The old deceptions of Hell have fallen out of the minds of all reasonable people of modern thinking.

Notes: *This statement combines Spiritualist, Christian, and esoteric traditions.*

* * *

ARTICLES OF OUR FAITH (INTERNATIONAL CHURCH OF AGELESS WISDOM)

1. WE BELIEVE that God is our Father and the Creator of all that is. That because He is our Father, all men everywhere are our Brothers and therefore no discrimination can be tolerated, for we are all His offspring. We acknowledge our relationship with all Kingdoms: mineral, vegetable, animal and that of man.

2. WE BELIEVE that we must depend on God for all things, but we must do our part in making our desires manifested.

3. WE BELIEVE that all souls are immortal; that no soul can ever be lost, for the opportunity for reformation is always open.

4. WE BELIEVE in the progression of the soul through successive incarnations whereby man eventually learns the meaning of "As you sow, so shall ye reap," thereby leading every soul to ultimate perfection.

5. WE BELIEVE this earthly life is the effect of the cause we have set into motion, either in this or in previous live Earth acts as a school where we learn the qualities of Godliness.

6. WE BELIEVE that we are all children of God, created in His spiritual image for the body contains within it replicas of the Universe and the steps in the life of Christ as taught through the spiritual anatomy of man. We do not believe in an anthropomorphic God.

7. WE BELIEVE that we must spiritually progress to the point where we will be able to follow the commandment of the Master Teacher Jesus, "The things I do must ye do and even greater things must ye do." We will be given the Christ Power to do these things when we have raised ourselves, through study, meditation and Service to mankind to the Christ Consciousness.

8. WE BELIEVE in the Power of Love to conquer all so-called evil. We believe in the Power of Prayer to save the human race and our beloved planet Earth.

9. WE BELIEVE that if we conscientiously practice the Golden Rule, we can be instrumental in uplifting mankind from their material bondage. We believe in teaching by example.

10. WE BELIEVE that it is possible and necessary to communicate with Spiritual Beings on the Higher Planes of life and that communion of the Saints, as said in the Apostle's Creed means communion with those who have left the world of flesh and entered the Heaven or Spirit worlds. The early Church taught this and Jesus exemplified this teaching, for He communed with the Saints on the mountain top and in the garden.

Notes: *This church believes in reincarnation. It also lives with the tension of affirming God as Father while denying a belief in an anthropomorphic deity.*

* * *

PRINCIPLES OF SPIRITUALISM (INTERNATIONAL SPIRITUALIST ALLIANCE)

1. The Fatherhood of God

2. The Brotherhood of Man

3. The immortality of the soul and its personal characteristics

4. Communion between departed human spirits and mortals

5. Personal responsibility

6. Compensation and retribution for all the good and evil deeds done here

7. A path of eternal progress open to every soul

WE BELIEVE IN ONE GOD WHO IS LOVE, Father of all souls, of the just and of the unjust; creator and sustainer of all worlds, visible and invisible; manifest in the holy breath, supreme emanation of truth and power, whereby we and all creation move forward unto perfection.

AND IN JESUS, OUR SPIRITUAL LORD, who was incarnated for the salvation of men, and in simplicity and with supreme courage, in obedience to His Heavenly Father, was perfected after much suffering, and is become unto us both Lord and Christ.

WE ACKNOWLEDGE the guardianship of the Holy Angels; the ministry of just men made perfect.

WE REJOICE in the fellowship and communion with our loved departed, and

WE LOOK for full reunion with them in the joy of life everlasting.

Notes: *These brief documents present a mildly Christian-Spiritualist perspective.*

* * *

BELIEFS OF THE LOTUS ASHRAM

Our beliefs have proven themselves to be true to many thousands of persons. They are wide, undogmatic and universal in principle. The old adage, "there is no teaching,

BELIEFS OF THE LOTUS ASHRAM (continued)

only learning," plays an important part in our lives. In other words, knowledge may be imparted but unless the self is out of the way, it falls on stoney ground.

The teachings have a kinship with the world religions, although they are basically Christian. To us God is dual, both male and female, a creative as well as a sustaining power. The link between our spirits and God's spirit is made through the ability to meditate perfectly. We believe in developing the Fruits and Gifts of the Spirit as St. Paul writes in the Bible.

FRUITS OF THE SPIRIT: Love, joy, peace, longsuffering, gentleness, goodness, faith, meekness, temperance. Corinthians 1, v 8-10

GIFTS OF THE SPIRIT: Wisdom, knowledge, faith, healing, working of miracles, prophecy, discerning of spirits, speaking in tongues, interpretation of tongues. Galatians 5, v 22-23

A part of the Lotus philosophy is that one's spirit returns to earth and other planets again and again in order to learn the necessary experiences in life and so attain perfection. You will find it explained in Revelations, Chapter 3, v 12, "Him that overcometh will I make a pillar in the temple of God, and he shall go no more out."

Another important belief is that cleanliness is next to Godliness. Our bodies must be kept clean and healthy through exercise, especially yoga, and natural eating habits. Several Lotus publications are directed towards this area. The body, after all is the temple of the soul.

Notes: *This small group presents a popular Spiritualist notion of the dual sexual nature of God.*

* * *

DECLARATION OF FAITH (NATIONAL FEDERATION OF SPIRITUAL SCIENCE CHURCHES)

ARTICLE I.

We believe in GOD ALMIGHTY, whose existence, power and wisdom nature proclaims; and the human soul recognizes His Love and Goodness.

ARTICLE II.

We declare that the foundation of our Science and Philosophy is based on the teachings of the Master, JESUS the Christ.

ARTICLE III.

The Bible contains inspirational truths, worthy of careful study, all of which are to be tested by reason and the Laws of GOD, which are in the human soul.

ARTICLE IV.

JESUS announced the great truth about human salvation when He said: "Ye shall know the truth and the truth shall make you free." Salvation is not a gift but a reward of living in accord with truth and Divine Law.

ARTICLE V.

We declare that the Spiritual and Divine Healing practiced in churches of the Federation is accomplished with prayer and faith in the power and love of GOD.

ARTICLE VI.

History proves that religion is inherent in the human soul, is normal and beneficial, when practiced in harmony with reason and natural Law.

ARTICLE VII.

Spiritual Science teaches the immortality of the soul, and that the spiritual life is abundantly demonstrated by the reappearance of the departed in their communication with Mortals.

ARTICLE VIII.

Man is a Creation of GOD and an inheritor of all His Divine Attributes; and is destined to eternal progression and ultimate happiness.

ARTICLE IX.

The great purpose of Spiritual Science is to demonstrate that Life's manifestations are continuous, and teach man the Harmonial Philosophy; and help him to spiritualize his human character.

Notes: *This federation was one of the more Christian of the Spiritualist organizations.*

* * *

SPIRITUAL SCIENCE GUIDELINES (NATIONAL SPIRITUAL SCIENCE CENTER)

1. God, the Universal Creative Energy, the creator and sustainer of the universe, permeates all within it.

2. The universe is a whole in a dynamic state of constant growth.

3. The life drive of every entity aims at complete unification with the Universal Creative Power.

4. Man, as an immortal spirit and a co-creator, is the master of his own destiny, completely responsible for his every thought, word and deed.

5. Individual free will embodies a relationship to Universe Will. Growth of awareness and spirituality is directly coupled to the increase of role of Universal Will.

6. Wisdom, the secret of all religion, the power of the mysteries, and the essence of all philosophy, lies latent in man awaiting the discovery and realization of the light and power of God within.

7. Communication at spirit levels is a fact and everyone is psychic. The path of wisdom however, is seeking first the kingdom of God and his righteousness. All things are added to man as he grows.

8. Soul unfoldment is the purpose of life. Fraternal service is the way of life.

9. The God Force is just, impersonal and totally accepting, drawing all the perfection.

Notes: *The Christian Science roots of the center have almost completely disappeared, as can be seen in this thoroughly Spiritualist affirmation.*

* * *

DECLARATION OF PRINCIPLES (NATIONAL SPIRITUALIST ASSOCIATION OF CHURCHES)

1. We believe in Infinite Intelligence.
2. We believe that the phenomena of nature, both physical and spiritual, are the expression of Infinite Intelligence.
3. We affirm that a correct understanding of such expression and living in accordance therewith constitute true religion.
4. We affirm that the existence and personal identity of the individual continue after the change called death.
5. We affirm that communication with the so-called dead is a fact, scientifically proven by the phenomena of Spiritualism.
6. We believe that the highest morality is contained in the Golden Rule: "Whatsoever ye would that others should do unto you, do ye also unto them."
7. We affirm the moral responsibility of the individual, and that he makes his own happiness or unhappiness as he obeys or disobeys Nature's physical and spiritual laws.
8. We affirm that the doorway to reformation is never closed against any human soul here or hereafter.
9. We affirm that the precept of Prophecy contained in the Bible is a divine attribute proven through Mediumship.

DEFINITIONS (Adopted by the National Spiritualist Association of Churches: Adopted October, 1914, 1919, 1930, 1951.)

1. Spiritualism is the Science, Philosophy and Religion of continuous life, based upon the demonstrated fact of communication, by means of mediumship, with those who live in the Spirit World.
2. A Spiritualist is one who believes, as the basis of his or her religion, in the communication between this and the spirit world by means of mediumship, and who endeavors to mould his or her character and conduct in accordance with the highest teachings derived from such communion.
3. A Medium is one whose organism is sensitive to vibrations from the spirit world and through whose instrumentality intelligences in that world are able to convey messages and produce the phenomena of Spiritualism.
4. A Spiritualist Healer is one who, either through his own inherent powers or through his mediumship, is able to impart vital, curative force to pathologic conditions.
5. The Phenomena of Spiritualism consist of Prophecy, Clairvoyance, Clairaudience, Gift of Tongues, Lay-ing on of Hands, Healing, Visions, Trance, Apports, Revelation, Levitation, Raps, Automatic and Independent Writing and Paintings, Photography, Materialization, Psychometry, Voice and any other manifestation proving the continuity of life as demonstrated through the physical and Spiritual Senses and faculties of Man.

"Spiritualism Is a Science" because it investigates, analyzes and classifies facts and manifestations demonstrated from the spirit side of life.

"Spiritualism Is a Philosophy" because it studies the laws of nature both on the seen and unseen sides of life and bases its conclusions upon present observed facts. It accepts statements of observed facts of past ages and conclusions drawn therefrom, when sustained by reason and by results of observed facts of the present day.

"Spiritualism Is a Religion" because it strives to understand and to comply with the Physical, Mental and Spiritual Laws of Nature, "which are the laws of God."

Notes: *The National Spiritualist Association of Churches is the oldest and largest of the Spiritualist churches. The association's statement has been adopted in a modified form by several other Spiritualist associations and has exerted great influence throughout the movement. The association has also adopted a set of basic definitions which explain the terms used in the declaration.*

The International General Assembly of Spiritualists has adopted the association's declaration, using the first eight items as its Tenets. The Universal Church of the Master has rewritten the association's declaration to form its Basic Principles.

* * *

CONFESSION OF FAITH (PROGRESSIVE SPIRITUAL CHURCH)

We believe in the communion of Spirits; man's restoration to an everlasting life; the resurrection of the soul, not flesh: acknowledging God as Absolute Divine Spirit, whose voice and presence is always with us, and that of the Angels who are departed spirits who communicate and materialize with the living by means of mediums; manifesting by demonstration in origin and in phenomena all Biblical phases or reading, and the relation between God and soul and between the soul and the body, and bridging the hitherto "impassable gulf" between the dead and the living.

We believe that Jesus Christ was a medium, controlled by the Spirit of Elias and the Spirit of Moses and the Spirit of John the Baptist * * *, who after His death and resurrection materialized before His disciples * * *. That Moses communicated with the Divine Spirit, God. That the celebrated Nun of Kent received communications direct from God.

We believe that all these Spirits have desires; that the Spiritual body and the material body can commune together through the mouthpiece of another in harmony with the Spiritual; that through this channel we can receive the desires of the Spirit forces, concerning all

CONFESSION OF FAITH (PROGRESSIVE SPIRITUAL
CHURCH) (continued)

human affairs; that we are obligated to these desires, and
their fulfillment is pleasing to God.

We believe that the fingers of the hand of a medium under
control can write and deliver divine messages and visions
* * *. That a divine understanding of dreams can be had
* * *. That God revealeth secrets that should be made
known * * *. That the stars divine the pathway of life of
every character * * *. That the rewards of divinations are
in the hand of every character * * *. That the length of our
days, riches, and honor are shown in the hands * * *.

We believe that Divine Metaphysics are designed by God,
guiding the mind of the medium from the visible to the
invisible, and that it is only through this channel that the
cause of disease can be detected and over-powered. That
God has a fixed law for the preservation of the Spiritual
body until death itself shall die, and that a departed spirit
can be relieved from this death through prayer to a higher
state or sphere of Spirituality.

We acknowledge the Holy Bible to be the inspired word of
God, a guide to Spirit life, and all phases of Spiritualism
such as prophecies, spiritual palmistry, spiritual automatic
writing, spiritual suggestions and radiations, spiritual
materialization, spiritual trumpet speaking, spiritual healing by magnetized articles, spiritual levitation and spiritual
tests * * *, and as so practiced was and is a real science.
That it is present with us now and does not belong to a
dispensation now ended. That when a person does not
possess the necessary understanding of either of the above,
a Teacher or Reader may be employed for compensation
to explain and teach the Truth relating to these mental and
spiritual thought forms as revealed to him or her through
the Divine Spirit.

We believe that heaven and hell are conditions, not
locations. That it is necessary that we hold personal
communication with the spirits of the departed and their
forces, to confess to them the renunciation of our material
wills and intelligence that we may be properly guided in
our daily life by messages received from the Spiritual realm
according to the strength of our harmony with the spirits
of the departed and their Spiritual love and desires. That it
is necessary for us in consulting Spiritual mediums to place
ourselves in harmony with such belief.

We believe that the change called death should be met
without fear; that our sins stay with us forever; provided,
that we have not lived in obedience to the law of spiritual
harmony. That man is perfection, the image and likeness
of God. That he exists independent of human will,
controlled by the Spirit forces free from malicious magnetic elements.

Notes: *The doctrine of the Progressive Spiritual Church was
conceived to be that of conventional Christianity, modified
by the revelations of spiritualist mediums in the late-
nineteenth century. These revelations affirmed the immortality of the soul, the existence of angels, and a spiritual
hierarchy including the angels and Christ.*

OUR SPIRITUAL DOCTRINE (ROOSEVELT SPIRITUAL MEMORIAL BENEVOLENT ASSOCIATION)

This organization is the association of its Members as a
Religious, Non-profit, Self-supporting, Educational, Civic,
Fraternal, Charitable and Benevolent Corporation, dedi-
cated to the Glory of God and the reality of His Truth,
and for the Spiritual emancipation and Salvation of all
Humanity.

To help those in need, to visit the sick and afflicted, those
in the prisons, care of the dying, to comfort those who
mourn, defend the helpless, to awaken to realization those
who are Spiritually unconscious of The Truth, Love and
Power of God.

To spread, broadcast, among all Mankind, the everlasting
gospel of Christ Jesus and the Truth from the Holy Bible
as He taught it and in accordance with the proved and
demonstrated knowledge of Reason, Science and Spirituality.

To teach, preach, and practice the Religion, Philosophy
and Science of Truth as found in the Holy Bible (which is
the Truth of all Religion) including the provable and
demonstrable knowledge of the Continuity of Life in the
Spiritual World after the Change (called death).

To communicate with persons (so-called dead) in the
Spiritual World as Jesus did through Spiritual Gifts of
God and harmoniously with the statements of such
Communications, which are contained both in the Old and
New Testaments of the Holy Bible.

To teach, practice and conduct investigations in Psychic
Research, Extrasensory Perception, Clairvoyance, Clairaudience, prognosis and other constructive and helpful forms
of Spiritual, Mental, Psychic phenomena, as manifestations in such light and upon such conditions that anyone
present may see or hear, for themselves, whatever physical
phenomena and manifestations may occur.

To teach and practice Spiritual Healings through the
Almighty Power of Prayer and the Spiritual Gifts of God
in accordance with, and not against, the Laws of the State
of Florida or other states or countries in which this
association and churches may operate.

To teach, train, ordain and issue charters for Churches,
Clubs, Associations, Seminaries, organizers, etc.; to issue
Certificates to Doctors of Divinity. Teachers, Ministers,
Healers, Class Leaders and all others found worthy
according to their duties and their teachings of Truth and
of the Religion as taught by Our Saviour, Jesus the Christ.
Provided such persons are qualified (by the Board of
Directors) to receive said diplomas, degrees (etc.) either
because of having successfully completed the study of
prescribed Scholastic, Theological or Ecclesiastical subjects, or courses, of instruction and training, or because of
the excellence of their knowledge or because of their
accomplishments in the Service of God.

The membership of this organization shall consist of any
and all persons, regardless of nationality, race or creed, or
membership in any other churches, who shall conform to
the Charter, Constitution and By-Laws of this organiza-

tion, and who have been accepted by its Board of Directors.

Notes: *This statement is more a program for action than a statement of belief. However, it does manifest a Christian Spiritualist perspective while remaining silent on most controversial subjects.*

*   *   *

THIS WE BELIEVE (TEMPLE OF UNIVERSAL LAW)

"There is one body and one Spirit; just as you were called to the one hope there belongs to your call; one Lord, one faith, one baptism, one God and Father of us all, who is above all and through all and in all." (Eph. 4:4-6)

"One Lord, one faith, one God." This is the foundation of Universal Law. There is only one Lord, the indwelling Christ Spirit that seeks to guide and inspire our every action, word and thought. There is only one faith and the many religions in the world today are but different manifestations of that faith. There is only one Eternal Spirit who lives, moves and has His Being within all of the universe.

We believe that Deity expresses as a Trinity, which we call God the Father, God the Son and God the Holy Spirit. God the Father is Spirit. God the Son is the manifested creative expression of Spirit. God the Holy Spirit is the action of Spirit through created manifestation.

We believe that God the Father is the infinite Universal Law of life which creates and sustains all manifestation, both large and small, through evolution of progression to eternal life.

We believe that God the Son is the Christ Principle, the perfect demonstration of Divine Mind. We believe that this Christ has come to earth many times in human form. We believe that Jesus, the Son of God, most perfectly manifested this Principle and that by following his example, we awaken the Christ power that dwells within us. Thus we are able to become a great light to mankind, as he was and is.

We believe that God the Holy Spirit is the action of Divine Mind which leads us to expression of the God Power within us.

We believe in the worship of God, no matter what name he may be given by man, and regardless of the kind of ritual performed by the different religions. We can worship God in the quiet of a sanctuary or in the hustle of our busy, daily life. We can worship God in communion with many others, or in the silent secret place of our soul. Man has devised many and varied forms to express his worship of the Divine, and all are good insofar as they lead men to find their innate oneness with all of life.

We seek to interpret the teachings of the Bible and the utterances of all prophets and spiritual teachers, for it is only through study and understanding that the glowing words and ideas of the religious scriptures of the world can be made to apply to each person as an individual.

We strive to guide and help our fellow man in understanding his relationship to God and to the universe around him. By awakening our soul consciousness to a complete awareness of the unity of all life, we lift our minds to the higher spiritual realms of thought and realize our oneness with God.

We believe that all life is immortal and there is no death. That which is called death is merely a change from a material body to a spiritual body. That which God has created cannot be destroyed. The outer form may change and decay but that which is the real you, the divine Spirit within, is eternal. Life is a school in which we advance from one grade to the next, evolving upward and onward.

We believe that man is the highest evolved creature on the earth, made after the spiritual image of God, gifted with creative reasoning power and the ability to worship Deity. We believe man is an immortal soul clothed in a physical form; a spark of infinite Divine Spirit.

We recognize Universal Law in all faiths for we believe that God is universal. He manifests to different peoples in different ways at different times. All faiths have their deep wells of spiritual truth which shine forth in the lives and teachings of the great prophets and leaders of those religions.

In our worship, we use the Christian Bible as a record of man's search for God and an attempt to explain our life on the earth. We believe that the basic teachings of the Christ are to be found in the Sermon on the Mount.

We are aware that in order to survive in this world of ours, man must begin to practice universal brotherhood. We must learn to see our fellow man as our brother, regardless of race, creed or color. We must cast out all forms of discrimination and strive to love our fellow man without judging according to his nationality, his belief or the color of his skin. All are created by one Spirit, instilled with the same Divine Life Force.

We believe the way to accomplish these goals is by studying the operations of nature around us and by looking deep within our own being to awaken the Christ Spirit which dwells in each and every one. Only by realizing those goals and by manifesting the Spirit within us will we attain health, strength, wisdom, understanding, peace, prosperity and happiness now and forever. Only by learning and understanding the Universal Law which rules our lives can we consciously come into complete oneness with God.

We present no new religion or new ideals to strive to attain. These are the oldest truths known to man. We seek only to inspire those we contact to begin now to travel on the pathway of wisdom and understanding of the Law of God, the Universal Law of life.

We cannot erase the thought habits of centuries that have led man to his present state of existence. Further, we would not, for we believe that all of life is an evolution of progression to eternal life. We are all on the path that leads to eventual oneness with Spirit. If we could realize it, we are one in Spirit right now.

The path of life we offer is not an easy one. It requires study and concentration. It hold many pitfalls for those

THIS WE BELIEVE (TEMPLE OF UNIVERSAL LAW) (continued)

whose aims are selfish and shallow. Many scoff at those who seek to improve and elevate their soul consciousness. But the reward is well worth the effort involved. The peace of mind, the silent joy, the overflowing love for all of life are, in themselves, reward enough. But the greatest reward is the sure knowledge that we are one with God, and that His Spirit dwells within us, guiding and inspiring us along life's pathway.

Your faith, your belief, can blend with the teachings of Universal Law, for we believe there is truly one Lord, one faith and one God, now and forever.

Notes: *This church teaches reincarnation.*

* * *

BASIC PRINCIPLES (UNIVERSAL CHURCH OF THE MASTER)

1. We believe in the Fatherhood of God and the Brotherhood of man.

2. All Phenomena that occur within the realms of nature, both physical and spiritual, are manifestations of Infinite Intelligence.

3. True religion is discovered by understanding correctly the Laws of Nature and of God, and by living in harmony therewith.

4. Individual existence, personal identity and memory continue after the transitional experience called death.

5. Communication with the "Living Dead" is a scientific fact, fully proven under test conditions by the phenomena of psychical research.

6. The Golden Rule, "Whatsoever ye would that others should do unto you, do ye also unto them," is the essence of morality.

7. Every individual is morally self-responsible. Happiness flows from consonance with the Laws of Nature and God.

8. The genuine improvement and reformation of the human soul are always possible in this world and the next.

9. Prophecy exists in our times as in Biblical Days, and is proven scientifically through mediumistic powers of divination.

10. The Universe, as a spiritual system expressing Divine Wisdom, makes possible the eternal progress of the aspiring soul who loves truth and goodness.

Notes: *Although derived from the Declaration of Principles of the National Spiritualist Association of Churches, these principles were heavily edited and revised. The last item is a reference to reincarnation.*

SEVEN AFFIRMATIONS OF THE LIVING SPIRIT (UNIVERSAL HARMONY FOUNDATION)

The Universal Harmony Foundation is a Religious Non-Profit Organization. Its Philosophy, a union of Religion-and-Science, promulgates the following Seven Affirmatives of the Living Spirit.

1. I AFFIRM the Fatherhood of God and the Brotherhood of Man.

2. I AFFIRM the Eternality of Life-and-Living.

3. I AFFIRM the Power of Prayer.

4. I AFFIRM the Practice of Spiritual Healing.

5. I AFFIRM the Reality of the Psychic Principle.

6. I AFFIRM Soul Growth—as the Purpose of Life.

7. I AFFIRM Fraternal Service—as the Way of Life.

Notes: *These affirmations present only the most basic statement of belief.*

* * *

PRACTICE AND FAITH (UNIVERSAL SPIRITUALIST ASSOCIATION)

SECTION 1. The Universal Spiritualist Association is an organization of believers in and practitioners of the religion of Spiritualism as understood in the following:

A. Spiritualism is the Science, Philosophy and Religion of continuous life, based upon the demonstrated fact of communication, by means of mediumship, with those who live in the spirit world.

B. A Spiritualist is one who believes, as the basis of his or her religion, in the communication between this and the spirit world by means of mediumship, and who endeavors to mould his or her character and conduct in accordance with the highest teachings derived from such communion.

C. A medium is one whose organism is sensitive to vibrations from the spirit world, and through whose instrumentality intelligences in that world are able to convey messages and produce the psychic phenomena of Spiritualism.

D. A Healer is one who, through his own inherent power, or through his mediumship, is able to impart vital curative force to pathologic conditions.

E. The psychic phenomena on which Spiritualism is based are of two types. Mental and Physical. Mental phenomena are subjective experiences in which mental energy is expended and include those phases of mediumship known as Impressional Mediumship, Prophecy, Inspirational Mediumship, Psychometry, Clairvoyance, Clairaudience, Clairsentience, Clairgustience, Trance Speaking, and Xenoglossis or Polyglot Mediumship. Physical phenomena are objective phenomena in which physical energy is expended and include those phases of mediumship known as Concussion or Rapping, Parakinesis, Telekinesis, Precipitation, Direct Writing and/or Drawing, Direct Voice including Independent Voice and Trumpet, Transfiguration, Materialization including Etherealization, Apport, Skotograph, and Spirit Photography.

F. The Precepts, Confession and Acts of Faith to be acceptable and binding upon the associates forming this organization shall be:

(a) The Precepts of Faith.

1. The Lord is Almighty God.

2. Thou shalt worship the Lord thy God.

3. There is a natural world and there is a spiritual world.

4. Divine Law is holy, and just, and good.

5. The gift of God to all men is eternal life.

6. Man in the natural world and man in the spiritual world can communicate, one with the other.

7. All men shall turn to righteousness and dwell in the house of the Lord forever.

(b) The Confession of Faith

We believe in the Fatherhood of God, the brotherhood of all life everywhere, the leadership of Christ, salvation by character, and the progression of man upward and onward forever.

(c) The Acts of Faith

1. We believe that God is Love, and Power, and Truth, and Light; that perfect justice rules the worlds; that all His sons shall one day reach His feet, however far they stray. We hold the Fatherhood of God, the brotherhood of man; we know that we do serve Him best when best we serve our brother man. So shall His blessings rest on us and peace for evermore. Amen.

2. We place our trust in God, the holy and all-glorious Trinity, who dwelleth in the Spirit of man. We place our trust in Christ, the Lord of love and wisdom, first among many brethren, who leadeth us to the glory of the Father, and is Himself the Way, the Truth, and the Life. We place our trust in the Law of Good which rules the worlds; we strive towards the ancient narrow path that leads to life eternal; we know that we do serve our Master best when best we serve our brother man. So shall His blessing rest on us and peace for evermore. Amen.

G. Spiritualists accept, practice and promulgate spiritual truths; as recorded in the Holy Bible, as revealed in the life and teachings of Jesus the Christ, and as manifested in modern times through mental and physical mediumship.

Notes: *The Universal Spiritualists have expressed their faith through a series of documents grouped together in their association's constitution.*

THE PRINCIPLES OF THE CHURCH OF THE WHITE EAGLE LODGE

The White Eagle Lodge teaches:

1. That God, the Eternal Spirit, is both Father and Mother.

2. That the Son—the Cosmic Christ—is also the light which shines in the human heart. By reason of this divine sonship, all are brothers and sisters in spirit, a brotherhood which embraces all life visible and invisible, including the fairy and angelic kingdom.

3. The expression of these principles in daily life, through service.

4. The awareness of the invisible world, which bridges separation and death and reveals the eternal unity of life.

5. That life is governed by five cosmic laws: Reincarnation : Cause and Effect : Opportunity : Correspondences : Compensation (Equilibrium and Balance).

6. The ultimate goal of mankind is that the inner light should become so strong and radiant that even the cells of the physical body are transmuted into finer substances which can overcome mortality. This is known as the Christing of Man, or in the words of the Ancient Brotherhood, the blooming of the Rose upon the Cross of matter.

Notes: *The Principles of the Church of the White Eagle Lodge tie the lodge broadly to both popular Spiritualism and the more exclusive occult orders, especially Rosicrucianism and Theosophy. Of particular notice is the lodge's belief in ascension, the idea that the body's cells can be transformed into a fine immortal substance.*

* * *

Teaching Spiritualism (Channeling)

THE LAWS AND PRECEPTS (COSMIC AWARENESS COMMUNICATIONS)

THE UNIVERSAL LAW is that knowledge that awareness, that all living things, all life has within it that vitality, that strength to gather into it all things necessary for its growth and its fruition.

THE LAW OF LOVE is that law which places the welfare and the concern and the feeling for others above self. The Law of Love is that close affinity with all forces that you associate with as good. The Law of Love is that force which denies the existence of evil in the world, that resists not evil.

THE LAW OF MERCY is that law which allows one to forgive all error, to forgive equally those who err against you as you err against them. This is to be merciful. To be merciful is akin to the Law of Love, and if one obeys the Law of Mercy, there can be no error in the world.

THE LAW OF GRATITUDE is that sense of satisfaction where energy which has been given receives a certain reward.

THE LAWS AND PRECEPTS (COSMIC AWARENESS
COMMUNICATIONS) (continued)

JUDGE NOT. BE HUMBLE. DENY SELF. NEVER
DO ANYTHING CONTRARY TO THE LAW OF
LOVE. RESIST NOT EVIL. DO NOTHING WHICH IS
CONTRARY TO THE LAW OF MERCY.

Notes: *This brief statement is not only used by Cosmic
Awareness Communications, but has been assumed by the
splinter groups that emerged after the death of William
Ralph Duby (d. 1967), the original channel for the spiritual
entity, Cosmic Awareness. These groups include the Anthro-
pological Research Foundation and the several branches of
the Organization of Awareness.*

* * *

CREDO (FELLOWSHIP OF THE INNER LIGHT)

JOHN 1:1-5

In the beginning God expressed Himself, and the expression of God is Love and Love is God expressing Himself.

The Love that is God expressing Himself was with God
when all things were made. Love made all things and all
things were made of Love.

In Love is Life and without Love there is no Life. It is
Love that gives Light and consciousness to all who are
born. Love shines out in the darkness as the Source of Life
and awareness though there are some who do not know it.

A gift of those who become aware that it is Love that gives
Life and Light is the ability to know themselves to be Sons
and Daughters of God.

We believe that at least once, in the life of Jesus the Christ,
man has so perfectly expressed God as to be Love
personified and God incarnate.

We believe that Love has an opposite and the opposite of
Love is fear. Just as Life is the expression of Love, so death
is the expression of fear. Without Love there is no Life and
without fear there is no death.

While it is true that all things were made by God and
nothing exists that is not made of Love, yet God did not
make fear or death. For death is no more than the absence
of what is and fear is a fantasy entertained in minds of
those who do not believe in and depend upon Love for life
and security.

Fear is nothing more than an expression of faith in evil and
evil is loss of Life. Just as faith in good and faith in God
will increase life and vitality, so faith or believing in lack,
limitation and evil will take away life, love and vitality, so
bringing about death.

We believe that Love heals and can repair both mind and
body. Love is the key to communication with both God
and mankind.

It is our ideal to become the perfect Love which casts out
fear.

We believe it is not necessary to consider others wrong to
make ourselves right. It is likely that every prophet
throughout time had something valuable to share. It is
likely that every religion has a gift to give to those who

have ears to hear. We shall therefore, welcome all who
wish to worship with us in Love and we will love those
who choose not to worship with us. Amen.

Notes: *This statement begins with a metaphysical para-
phrase of the opening verses of the biblical Gospel of John. It
emphasizes the popular metaphysical affirmation of the
unreality of fear and death.*

* * *

TENETS (INNER CIRCLE KETHRA E'DA FOUNDATION)

"The tenets of our organization are: That man is born in
love and is a free agent: that knowledge is cosmic honey
and man should not only be permitted to gather this
honey, but should be aided and abetted in doing so."

—Yada di Shi'ite

* * *

OUR CREED (LIGHT OF THE UNIVERSE)

Man is lost amid a myriad of stars which feign their glory
and engulf Man's soul, and the One Star, which is the
brightest, is shunned because its brilliance and glorious
radiance cannot be borne by the weak, cowardly heart of
Man. The Light of this Star shines so brilliantly that only
those with a soul as Powerful and as brilliant as the Light
of this single Star can face it and receive its well-hidden
secrets. This Star rules all the Universe including Man,
who so conceitedly states that he is the ruler of the
Universe.

What then, is this Glorious Star, which has the Power to
engulf Man, body and soul into this zone?

The Star is Man, not Man as we know him with his
dictatorial spirit, but Man's True Self.

"Man's Soul, the True Divine Soul of Man, rules the
Universe. The True Divine Soul of every wisp of the
breeze, the True Divine Soul in every blade of grass and
every leaf of every tree. This Divine Soul, which is within
all, animate and inanimate, organic and inorganic, rules
the Universe. This Divine Soul, this Omniscient, Omnipotent, Omnipresent Being, which is within all, rules the
Universe.

"This Divine Soul is the maker and Creator of us all. This
Soul, this Divine Presence, which has created all, every
race, every religion, black and white, rich and poor, this
Divine Soul has created everything, everyone, every Being.
This Divine Soul is All."

"DEUS OMNIS EST"

Notes: *This creed affirms the single metaphysical reality of
God. The true self of individuals participates in the divine
and could even be thought of as God.*

STATEMENT OF THE RADIANT SCHOOL OF SEEKERS AND SERVERS

I believe, God has a Divine Plan for all to follow. This Plan is never separated from anyone and each can be "conscious" of this Plan.

I believe, this Plan is wrapped into the folds of every Life Pattern and is permanent, perfect and indestructible. If you relax yourself in the presence of this Divine Plan, it will work to manifest all good, so that you may recognize it in action, leaving you filled with Joyful Thoughts and that Inner Peace—all is well with the Soul.

I believe, as each seeks to unfold their Divine Plan, co-operating with the urge to receive Truth, they will learn to serve their fellowman, helping them to find the way to unfold their Divine Plan.

I believe, that all Divine Life Patterns are connected, and they are interwoven in a Great Universal Pattern, so that each Pattern depends upon another to find complete success (as you give, so shall you receive), thus unfolding together, God's Great Universal Plan for all mankind.

I believe, God expects each to unfold his own Divine Plan in full, not choosing only those parts which pleases or appeals to the mental mind.

I believe, God has given to each the opportunity to meet all other Divine Plans in which we have interfered, by creating against the Law of Truth, leaving sin or Karma—instead of Perfection. This is the opportunity to learn perfection. When each realizes that none are the select or chosen by God, but that the Laws of God help each to select that part of their Pattern which they alone must work out on their Path of Perfection.

I believe, that each Divine Plan includes three Divine Rights. These Divine Rights are: Health, Happiness and prosperity. These Divine Rights reflect upon man (as he thinketh, so he will be), so his Divine Plan will be made.

I believe, each should realize that the Physical Body is the "Temple" and through it all contacts are made manifest to our Higher Self.

I believe, that all should remember these words, found in the 91st Psalm: "I shall give my Angels charge over thee, and they shall keep thee in all thy ways." When realization comes, that no man is ever alone, then each will strive to perfect his own Life Pattern.

I believe, Happiness is the KEY of attraction and all who come in contact with this reflection will receive Faith overcoming fear, Love overcoming hate, Strength that overcomes weariness and Understanding that will overcome doubt.

I believe, that the act of Praying, should be the expression of desires, and by longing to know "The Great Love of God" will bring about abundance. Prayers should be the Soul expressing from the God Mind to the physical mental mind. When this is the way of Praying, the door to Peace and Understanding will open and Praying will become a daily practice.

I believe, to be patient, forgiving, willing and enduring, through the effort of seeking, is the KEY to perfection.

TEACHINGS OF THE SCHOOL OF NATURAL SCIENCE

The School of Natural Science Teaches:

That there exists a Universal Intelligence which is revealed in Nature by the establishment of an intelligent order governed by certain inexorable, immutable Laws;

That all life is endowed with the same potential of growth and refinement. Nature is absolutely and unconditionally just and is engaged in the evolvement of individual intelligences;

That man's Essential Self or Soul is an immortal, evolving entity possessing, simultaneously, a body of physical material and a body of spiritual material;

That there is a principle in Nature that impels the individual to attain higher and higher levels of consciousness;

That man is invested with Free Will and Choice and is held personally responsible and morally accountable for his deeds within the scope of his knowledge, The Law of Compensation is acknowledged and the standard of values is personal effort;

That prayer is a means of communication with other individuals from whom response may be expected if the need is genuine, the attitude unselfish and the motives worthy;

That knowledge of and willing conformity to the Laws of Nature are rewarded by the attainment of Self Mastery, Poise and Happiness;

That by persistent application of intelligent effort to the "living of a life" in conformity to the laws of Nature, an individual may personally demonstrate that there is a spiritual existence and a continuity of Life.

Notes: *These affirmations of the underlying Universal Intelligence, human free will under the reign of Law, the necessary progress of the soul, and the soul's accountability to the Law of Compensation (generally called "karma"), are common to occult philosophies.*

*   *   *

CREDO OF AMBER/CRYSTAL LIGHT BEARERS (SISTERS OF AMBER)

CREDO: He who abuses power, loses power; and he who loves and serves his fellow-man with all his compassionate understanding—as well as all his strength so loves and serves his God. For God is in all—and for all—and the reason for all . . . be it high or low or here or there or coming or going . . . in the eyes of those who, as yet, can see the Whole only in fragmentary bits. PEACE! BE STILL AND KNOW THAT I AM GOD! And that I shall forever reign supreme over the Universal Scheme and teach My children Life and Growth and Love and Laughter . . . and the darkness shall disappear in the Light of Truth!

THE DECLARATION (UNIVERSAL BROTHERHOOD OF FAITHISTS)

I declare unto Thee, JEHOVIH, in the presence of the Faithists here assembled, that henceforth I will worship none but Thee, Thou All Highest Creator. Who art variously named by mortals, Jehovih, The Great Spirit, The Almighty, The Eternal Father, The I Am, The All Light, Eolin, Ormazd. The Architect of the Universe, Ever Present in all and yet above all, unto Whom none can attain for ever.

I declare that I will henceforth turn from evil and strive to do good, that I may come into at-one-ment with Thee, Thou All Father, Life of all life, and Soul of all souls, Who art to the understanding of all the living even as the sun is to the light of day.

I promise to abnegate self and dwell in harmony with my brother and sister Faithists, also to respect the authority of the Chief of the Community.

I promise to put aside the uncharitable tongue, and not to perceive evil in any man, woman, or child, but only the limitations of their birth and surroundings. In Thee, O Jehovih, is my trust. Amen.

Notes: *The Declaration is taken from the Kosmon Church Service Book, where it is an important liturgical element. It is frequently repeated in the various church rituals.*

* * *

Flying Saucer Groups

THE SPIRITUAL AIMS (AETHERIUS SOCIETY)

1. To spread the teachings of the Master Aetherius, Jesus and other Cosmic Masters.
2. To administer Spiritual Healing.
3. To prepare the way for the coming of the next Master.
4. To organize the Society so as to create favourable conditions for closer contact with and ultimately meetings with people from the other Planets.
5. To tune in and radiate the Power transmitted during a Holy time or Spiritual Push, in order to enhance all Spiritual practices, irrespective of one's religious beliefs.
6. To form a Brotherhood based on the teachings and knowledge of the Cosmic Masters.
7. To spread the Spiritual Operation known as Operation Starlight throughout the World, as directed by the Space People.

* * *

SPIRITUAL CREED FOR LIGHT WORKERS (MARK-AGE)

We all are of the one Spirit.
Spirit is Divine Mind.

We all think (send and receive thoughts) through the one Mind, therefore what you think about others is received by them through one Mind Source.

What you wish for them or believe of them is received and returned (re-acted) to you by the same Energy Source, Mind.

As you think, so it is manifested in your life now or later.

What you think about, you form.

As thought is energy and mind is force, so you create your own life, relationships, supply, services, love.

As you think, so you are, bad or good, ugly or beautiful, ill or healthy, hated or loved.

This is divine law in action.

Notes: *Not a statement of Mark-Age belief, this creed is a liturgical affirmation representative of a general New Age perspective. It nevertheless affirms some basic opinions about the supremacy of Mind and Spirit, common to New Age groups.*

* * *

DECALOG, THE TWELVE BIDS FROM PETALE (SEMJASE SILVER STAR CENTER)

1. You ought have no other powers and no gods, idols and saints besides The Creation.
2. You ought keep holy the Name of The Creation and not misuse it.
3. You ought make every day a holiday and keep it holy (control it).
4. You ought not be in violation to your bond with The Creation; contained therein: you ought not commit adultery.
5. Honor The Creation as you honor, respect and love your father and mother.
6. You ought not kill by degeneration.
7. You ought not be depriving or expropriating.
8. You ought not bear false witness against The Creation and the Life.
9. You ought never ever speak an untruth.
10. You ought not desire with greediness material treasures and the possessions of your fellow creatures.
11. You ought not swear at the truth.
12. Never ever place The Creation's Laws and The Creations Bids into unworthy cults.

Notes: *With an obvious reliance upon the traditional Ten Commandments, the Twelve Bids [or Commandments] were given to Edmund "Billy Meier" by the space brothers (spiritual teachers believed to have come from outer space). Ultimate reality is named the Creation, which has both a male and female aspect. "Bid" is a translation of the German word "Gebote," meaning to command or to bid.*

PRINCIPLES (SOLAR LIGHT CENTER)

1. Belief in an Infinite Creator (the All-Knowing One. Our Radiant One, of the Space beings) and in the Cosmic Christ, the Spiritual Hierarchy, and the Great White Brotherhood.

2. Belief in the expression of universal love, compassion and understanding as the true basis for world peace and the healing of all mankind's ills. This embodies reverence for all life and non-violence toward man and animals.

3. Acceptance of the eternal truths given by World Avatars (Jesus, Buddha, Krishna) and spiritual Masters as taught in most esoteric schools of thought. These include Man's spiritual evolution through many embodiments on an ever-ascending spiral path of consciousness under the Laws of Cause and Effect (Karma) and Rebirth. They outline methods whereby the individual may speed up spiritual unfoldment by attunement with the higher self, the "god-self" within, and by the transmutation of old Karma utilizing the higher frequencies.

4. Belief that other planets are inhabited by advanced beings who have attained mastery over space travel, hence they are called Space Beings. (Their civilization is far superior to any found on Earth. They have ended war, disease, poverty, taxes, and famine; they control the weather and gravity and provide free energy.)

5. Belief in communication with advanced Space Beings by such means as direct physical contact, tele-thought, telepathy, tensor beam, light beam, and other means. Recognition that such communications provide information of vital importance to Earth man and should be given out to all New Age souls who are ready to accept such teachings.

6. Belief that a spiritual Light is being sent to uplift Earth and raise the frequency level of all cells, all atoms, in preparation for the coming change, and this Light can be focused through certain Light Centers in Vortex areas. Space Beings are assisting at this time of change in many ways. They are concerned for Earth-man's welfare and are prepared to prevent complete destruction of the planet through a nuclear holocaust or gigantic geological change.

7. Belief that our Freedom of Attitude toward: (1) the Infinite Creator, (2) Self (ego), (3) Other beings, are the deciding factors on the path to the All Highest, and service in the Universal Program is the key to this.

8. Belief that as the end of a Great Cycle of approximately 26,000 years approaches, a "cleansing" is taking place due to Light energies received, and the planet is being prepared for a density level transition into a higher frequency. Such a change heralds the Second Coming of Christ and the beginning of a Golden Age.

WHAT IS UNDERSTANDING (UNDERSTANDING, INC.)

Begin with this: to know yourself is to begin to understand others, who thereby increase their understanding of you.

To communicate is to understand. Communicate.

To truly desire to understand is to begin to understand the person, matter, condition or situation desired.

To pray to understand is to approach understanding; but prayer must have wings or feet provided by you to be increasingly efficient.

To understand another, listen to his words with the true desire to understand them and him/her. If you don't begin to understand you're not listening or being heard.

Love Understanding is the law of magnetic attraction in the Universe which maintains its parts in their Divine-Law relation to one another. If you're not thus related to your environment and its inhabitants, you are imbalancing or contributing to imbalance. If your environment is sick you cannot be wholly well.

Understanding begins with you, me, our families, our political sub-divisions, extending gradually from you and me, endlessly in *all* directions. Not to seek beyond ourselves is to ourselves remain lost.

Understanding is love, graduated through acquaintance, friendship, cooperation, collaboration *wherever indicated,* listening and being heard, talking with intent to contribute and clearly transmit sincere motive, mutual understanding being the intent and desire.

Understanding balances you/he/him/it/they, exalting all.

Understanding is a sincere attempt to expand consciousness, never wholly by yourself alone.

"Understanding" is the best definition of "love."

"The love that passeth (or seeth through) understanding," is the love-understanding which Understanding, Inc., Understanding Magazine, Understanding Units and individual members, seek to awaken in all men.

Nations are no more different from one another than any two individuals. To understand the individual is to approach understanding of the nation, any nation. Each nation is an aggregate individual composed of its people.

Understanding units are forums for discussion. Discussion, even heated if positive, leads to understanding.

Individual members of Units and members-at-large are volunteer counsellors. They will listen to individual misunderstanding to the nearest member of Understanding, Inc., who will listen and comment as inspired.

Notes: *According to Understanding, Inc., its philosophy is best expressed in the belief that there are more areas of agreement than disagreement between all men and that finding those areas will bring about understanding, cooperation, and peace to all. A more substantive statement, What Is Understanding, was written by Arthur J. Burks and published in the organization's periodical.*

THE CREED OF FAHSZ (UNIVERSE SOCIETY CHURCH)

I am Fahsz. I am the servant of the Father and Brsgv and the Master of Anahsz who permeates, the universe on the physical plain of existence. On my right hand there are seven stars and on my left hand seven golden pyramids. The seven pyramids are the seven steps to Fahsz through Anahsz, and the seven stars the seven Inner teachers. Write of the things I have told you and the Things you have seen in the Kingdom or marveled at during the Shel. There are two great forces in the universe of which only my deserving acceptors can be aware. These are HAL and SHEL; the Force of Light and The Creative Force. You are to create a temple of many pyramids which is ordered to be opened unto all who receive Anahsz and the one who is at the right hand of Anahsz. These two have received Shel; no others have. Follow my teachings and you shall live, obey my acceptors and you shall permeate the universe. The one who sits at the right hand of Anahsz is his opposite number; each of these has an opposite number who acts as a mirror.

Notes: *Fahsz is the extraterrestrial contacted by Hal Wilcox, founder of the Universe Society Church. His creed is a cryptic document that requires some deciphering as it uses jargon and symbols peculiar to the church.*

* * *

Drug-Related Groups

AFFIRMATIONS (CHURCH OF THE AWAKENING)

1. WE AFFIRM the unity of all mankind, of whatever nation, race or religion.

2. WE AFFIRM the reality of man's spiritual nature, called Christ, Light, Life, Atman or Buddha, and the importance of our recognition of this Light or Christ as our real Being, rather than the physical or intellectual form.

3. WE AFFIRM the importance of achieving a personal experience of this Reality and its oneness with Universal Reality, through the Unitive Experience.

4. WE AFFIRM the importance of a properly directed psychedelic sacrament (through the use of peyote or other sacramental substance approved by the Board of Directors) as a means toward the achievement of the Unitive Experience.

5. WE AFFIRM the importance of the practical application of the Unitive Experience in our daily lives, through the loving acceptance of each person, and the recognition of the Being of each as this Reality or Christ.

6. WE AFFIRM the importance of extending the awareness of the reality of man's spiritual Being, both in ourselves and in others, as a major factor in the solution of both personal and world problems.

Notes: *This statement simply explains the church's mystical approach to life through the ingestion of psychedelic sacramental substances.*

* * *

PRINCIPLES OF THE NEO-AMERICAN CHURCH

Members of the NEO-AMERICAN CHURCH subscribe to the following principles:

(1). Everyone has the right to expand his consciousness and stimulate visionary experience by whatever means he considers desirable and proper without interference from anyone.

(2). The psychedelic substances, such as LSD, are the True Host of the Church, not "drugs". They are sacramental foods, manifestations of the "the Grace of God", of the infinite imagination of the Self, and therefore belong to everyone.

(3). We do not encourage the ingestion of psychedelics by those who are unprepared.

Notes: *The principles of the church are much more a manifesto for the religious use of psychedelic substances than a full statement of the church's teaching.*

* * *

Miscellaneous Psychic New Age Groups

CREED (CHURCH OF DIVINE MAN)

We the church believe in: limitless space, timeless endurance, neverending acceptance, everlasting patience, and continuous comprehension. "What if a man gain the whole world and lose his own soul?" asks Jesus. To a mystic, with eyes turned inward to infinity and cosmic consciousness, His words have great meaning. Psychic freedom creates no ideologies, no isms, no dissenting philosophies which divide, corrupt and destroy communication between human souls. No governments are upturned, no faiths cut down by the sword, no sects or types eliminated: only a one to one contact between the cosmic and a living soul, which flames quietly, bringing a lifetime of contentment and a realization that nothing in this world is worth exchanging for that attainment.

Notes: *This creed is not so much a statement of beliefs (it denies the need of ideologies and isms) as an assertion of the freedom necessary for a psychically atuned person to develop. The church strives not for agreement of opinion, but the provision of a context in which personal contact with the divine can be most easily realized.*

* * *

DOCTRINE (CHURCH OF MERCAVAH)

1. Man is a spiritual being with a physical classification. All forms of life are spiritual; all of life itself is

spiritual. If life is born of action and action born of abstract ideas, then all of existence is abstract. That factor which moves life, which moves it beyond the abstract into application, is spiritual.

2. Since man is a spiritual being, those paths we each walk, our individual lives, must be defined and refined spiritually. "The search to know is a spiritual path, whether it be science or religion." (R. O. M.)

3. Each individual is a light within the universe. Each is a star.

4. Each individual must find both within and without himself the path to self-knowledge.

5. This path will ultimately lead to harmony. Discord is a part of the balance within the equilibrium of all. We can not achieve harmony until we see the harmony within the discord. Discord is nothing but imperfect harmony.

6. Our responsibility is first to that flame within each of us. Our responsibility is then to let our light shine before all men.

7. When we limit the truth of others we cast shadows on our own path.

8. To allow others the freedom of search and the freedom of error is to increase the light on our own way.

9. Within everything is Truth, and within Truth is born responsibility.

10. Life IS. Life is the plane of spirit and the plane of reality.

Notes: *Like the Church of Divine Man, the statement of the Church of Mercavah does not strive to present a whole perspective but to argue for the freedom of individuals to find a path to self-knowledge within the context of spiritual attainment.*

*   *   *

CREED (CHURCH OF SCIENTOLOGY)

We of the Church believe:

That all men of whatever race, color or creed were created with equal rights.

That all men have inalienable rights to their own religious practices and their performance.

That all men have inalienable rights to their own lives.

That all men have inalienable rights to their sanity.

That all men have inalienable rights to their own defence.

That all men have inalienable rights to conceive, choose, assist and support their own organizations, churches and governments.

That all men have inalienable rights to think freely, to talk freely, to write freely their own opinions and to counter or utter or write upon the opinions of others.

That all men have inalienable rights to the creation of their own kind.

That the souls of men have the rights of men.

That the study of the mind and the healing of mentally caused ills should not be alienated from religion or condoned in non-religious fields.

And that no agency less than God has the power to suspend or set aside these rights, overtly or covertly.

And we of the Church believe:

That man is basically good.

That he is seeking to survive.

That his survival depends upon himself and upon his fellows, and his attainment of brotherhood with the Universe.

And we of the Church believe that the laws of God forbid Man:

To destroy his own kind.

To destroy the sanity of another.

To destroy or enslave another's soul.

To destroy or reduce the survival of one's companions or one's group.

And we of the Church believe:

That the spirit can be saved *and*

That the spirit alone may save or heal the body.

Notes: *The Creed of the Church of Scientology is not only a statement of beliefs, but a statement of human rights. While the doctrine of the Scientology religion is contained in the written and spoken words of its founder, L. Ron Hubbard, the creed affirms basic Church tenets.*

*   *   *

STATEMENT OF BELIEFS (CONGREGATIONAL CHURCH OF PRACTICAL THEOLOGY)

PREAMBLE

You will notice in number 14 of the following statement of beliefs that it is our contention that a person should not be restricted to a specific creed or set of beliefs. Our minds should be like an "open book" through which we are constantly seeking to find God's truth in all of life, and therefore, we should be growing spiritually each day. If we try to restrict ourselves to a certain creed or a specific set of beliefs, we may at the same time be restricting our spiritual growth.

The following statement of beliefs has been written by the Administrative Committee, approved by the Executive Committee and the General Assembly of The Congregational Church of Practical Theology, however, we emphasize the fact that they are not, and will not be adopted as final, for we are still seeking spiritual enlightenment, and as we learn new truths, those which are presented here may be changed or completely disregarded.

1. We believe that God is our loving Father, and the loving Father of all mankind.

2. We believe that God is the power and energy which brought the worlds into being, has made man and has given man that part of Himself which we call life, and has set before man the way which will enable him to walk free and secure.

3. We believe that God is Spirit. God is not a being, separate and far away, but is a Spirit within us. God is part of us and we are part of Him. God is right where we are at all times. We have constant access to Him.

4. We believe that God made man as a manifestation of His love, for part of love is sharing, and God wanted to share even a part of Himself, therefore, man was made through the love of God, thus all men are equal in God's sight.

   NOTE! We emphasize the dignity and love of all mankind, people of all races, colors, religions, social backgrounds, and economic levels. Therefore, we are dedicated to living service to all individuals, society, and the world at large, with no restrictions or prejudice based on race, color, religion, social background or economic level.

5. We believe that God is love, God's will is good for all mankind; Joy, not pain or sorrow; Life, not death or destruction; wholeness, not imperfection; plenty, not lack; peace, not fear and anxiety.

6. We believe that God will supply everything we need for a full, happy life, if we trust His love and let ourselves be used by His wisdom. When we let ourselves be used by the wisdom of God, we believe that every adversity, every failure, every disappointment, every error of judgment, and every defeat can be used as stepping stones of priceless value.

7. We believe that God's will for all persons is good, and that behind all appearances the goodness of God stands, that through every change His good is unchanging, that through every experience His power is present to help and to bless. God kindles anew the dead hope of all who tune themselves to Him and draw upon the great reservoir of His unlimited intelligence.

8. We believe that whatever man needs will come to him through the love of God. When we are willing to give our efforts to make a worthwhile contribution to live, our prosperity will be supplied by our loving Father.

9. We believe that God has provided us with the power to shape our own thoughts, and the privilege of fitting them to the pattern of our choice.

   In other words, God has placed before us the possibility of attaining the riches of life. The riches of true friendship; the riches of achievement; the riches of harmony in home relationships; the riches of sound physical health; the riches of freedom from fear; the riches of enthusiasm; the riches of song and laughter; the riches of self-discipline; the riches of play; the riches of discovery; the riches of faith; the riches of meditation; the riches of understanding; and the riches of economic security.

   Buddha taught "all that we are is the result of what we have thought." The Bible says, "As a man thinketh in his heart, so is he."

   We believe this means we have the power to form our own character and to create our own happiness. This is the reason it is so important to be careful about the thoughts we permit to permeate our minds.

   "Whatsoever things are true, whatsoever things are honest, whatsoever things are just, whatsoever things are pure, whatsoever things are lively, whatsoever things are of good report . . . think on these things." Philippians 4:8.

   We are literally what we think. Our character is the sum of all our thoughts. A noble character is not a thing of favor or chance, but the natural result of continued effort in right thinking, the effect of long-cherished association with noble thoughts.

10. We believe that we become spiritually rich when we discover the reality of God within; when we are conscious of the oneness of all life; when we know the power of meditation, and when we experience kinship with nature.

11. We believe that life is an eternal unfoldment; an existence which has no end. In other words, we do not believe that God made man just for the purpose of living in a body for a few minutes or a few years, then to die and cease to exist. Nor do we believe that, if man fails to fulfill his life now he is everlastingly damned. The life which God put into man is a part of God Himself, and is for eternity. We are constantly growing, learning, unfolding—failing, perhaps many times—but eventually attaining the stature of the fullness of God.

    NOTE! We suggest reincarnation as a possible explanation concerning the way in which this unfoldment may take place, but, we by no means insist that this idea be accepted. In fact, we believe the present is more important to us now than the past or the future. The important thing is what we are making of the present moment.

18. We believe in the divinity of Jesus Christ, but we also believe that, like Jesus, each of us is a child of God and therefore, we are all divine in nature.

19. We believe that Jesus Christ came to earth and shared the common lot of man. In doing this, he lived an outstanding life of love, which revealed to us an example of the true Spirit of God, and He calls for us to follow His example of love.

20. We believe that love is the most important characteristic we can possess. We accept the definition of love as it has been recorded in I Corinthians the 13th chapter, believing that love does not pass away. Nor does it fail those who live by it.

21. We believe that God calls us to be His Church, to accept the cost and joy of discipleship, as it is

revealed through us when we show true love to all mankind.

22. We believe that God calls us to be His servants in the service of men, and that we are to be channels through which God's will is done.

23. We believe there can be no richer man than he who is devoted to a labor of love and who keeps himself busy serving others, for this type of labor is the highest form of human expression which reveals the God-part of man.

24. We believe that every person we meet in our daily life, regardless of his race, color, religion, social background or economic level, is a child of God and we, therefore, should look to him as one worthy of our love, understanding and consideration.

25. We believe that love is the part of man which reveals God's image. Love is an outward expression of the spiritual nature of man. True love clears out selfishness, greed, jealousy, envy and prejudice. True greatness will not be found where love does not abide.

26. We believe that every change which comes into our life and world provides us with an opportunity to learn and grow. And whatever comes to us, we know that God can help us to meet it courageously, working through us to accomplish good.

27. We accept the Bible as a textbook of truth, and we believe it represents much of the truth which has been revealed to men in ages past, however, we believe Truth is never final and that it is still being revealed. Therefore, we accept statements of truth from all souces, secular and religious.

28. We believe it is our privilege and duty to praise and honor God whom we recognize as that creative Force, behind and in the universe, who reveals Himself as energy, as life, as order, as beauty, as thought as conscience, and as love.

Blessing and honor, glory and power be unto Him. Amen.

SUBMITTED AND APPROVED BY THE BOARD OF DIRECTORS OF THE CONGREGATIONAL CHURCH OF PRACTICAL THEOLOGY, OCTOBER 17, 1970.

E. Arthur Winkler, Ph.D., Th.D., President, The Congregational Church of Practical Theology.

Notes: *This statement was written to be as inclusive of different opinions as possible.*

* * *

COPTIC BELIEFS (COPTIC FELLOWSHIP OF AMERICA)

1. That revelations of truth are ever present to all men and are understood as capacities are developed.

2. That these truths as they were perceived and passed on to the White Brotherhood, the Essenes and the Coptic Order are the foundation of our teachings.

3. That God's love, made evident by and through natural law, is universal and everlasting.

4. That life, creation, progress and evolution emanate from this God Love Expression—that it has ever been and ever will be.

5. That love, will and wisdom are natural attributes that guide individual and social destinies to perfection.

6. That each individual soul lives in eternal continuity, wherein the threshold of reformation can be crossed at any time in the here or hereafter by those who will it so. That continuity of life is an essential part of this belief.

7. That the law of Karma (cause and effect) is Nature's unavoidable mode of refinement of Man, his expressions and his environment.

8. That ignorance and misdirection obscure these realities from the majority of mankind.

9. That joy and happiness and health are the natural state of those who have achieved a harmonious God-Nature-Man relationship.

* * *

STATEMENT OF FAITH (FOUNDATION FAITH OF GOD)

GOD. THERE IS ONE GOD OVER ALL, WHO IS THE GOD OF LOVE. WE ARE HIS CHILDREN, AND HE IS OUR FATHER.

GOD created all things. He created matter, the universe, the world, and all that is in the world.

And he is before all things, and by him all things consist. Colossians 1:17

We can know GOD through His Works, the stars, the sky, the planets, the earth, the creatures, the seasons, the elements.

We can know GOD through His Word, the Scriptures of the Bible.

We can know GOD through Jesus Christ GOD the Son, through His life and the gift of the Holy Ghost.

Great is our Lord, and of great power: his understanding is infinite. Psalm 147:5

It is our duty to love and obey GOD.

Fear GOD, and keep his commandments: for this is the whole duty of man. Ecclesiastes 12:13

GOD AND THE SIN OF MAN.

Man is ashamed of his own sin. He is ashamed that he so freely lets Satan fill his heart with wickedness. The sin is Satan's, but man adopts it.

GOD is merciful and filled with compassion. He does not want man to suffer at the hand of Satan.

For I have no pleasure in the death of him that dieth, saith the Lord GOD. Ezekiel 18:32

But GOD's Love is a Love of Justice; justice requires that sin be accounted for.

> *But I say unto you, that every idle word that men shall speak, they shall give account thereof in the day of judgment.* Matthew 12:36

JESUS CHRIST.

Jesus Christ is the Son of GOD — GOD the Son. GOD, in His great mercy, sent into the world Jesus Christ, offering true salvation to man.

Jesus is the one link between GOD and fallen man. He is the only being who, as man, overcame the works of Satan. This He did in His life and in His triumph over death through His resurrection.

> *For there is one GOD, and one mediator between GOD and men, the man Christ Jesus.* Timothy 2:5

> *For GOD so loved the world, that he gave his only begotten Son, that whosoever believeth in him should not perish.* John 3:16

JESUS AND THE SINS OF MAN.

Jesus Christ, the Son of GOD, became man and took on the nature of man, facing and overcoming the temptations of Satan. By thus taking on man's sinful state to His death, and in triumph overcoming death (Satan) through His Resurrection, He made possible the redemption of man.

> *But GOD commendeth his love toward us, in that, while we were yet sinners, Christ died for us.* Romans 5:8

> *For GOD sent not his Son into the world to condemn the world; but that the world through him might be saved.* John 3:17

SALVATION FOR MAN.

Salvation for man, through the redemptive spirit of Jesus Christ, is a gift from GOD. Man alone, separated from GOD, cannot free himself from the wiles of Satan, nor can he alone make true recompense for the sins which he thereby assumes.

Jesus took on man's sins, and paid sufficient sacrifice for them.

Salvation is a gift from GOD, granted to those who confess Jesus as their only Savior, humbly, and in repentance, for their sin — for the sin of having let Satan rule their thoughts and actions.

> *Repent: for the kingdom of heaven is at hand.* Matthew 4:17

> *And this is the will of him that sent me, that every one which seeth the Son, and believeth on him, may have everlasting life: and I will raise him up at the last day.* John 6:40

THE HOLY GHOST.

Jesus, after His Ascension, gave His followers the gift of the Holy Ghost (Holy Spirit) — the lasting presence of GOD — to be our Comforter.

The Holy Ghost is the third person of the Trinity (Father, Son and Holy Ghost) and is available to all who believe in Jesus as Savior.

> *But the Comforter, which is the Holy Ghost whom the Father will send in my name, he shall teach you all things, and bring all things to your remembrance, whatsoever I have said unto you.* John 14:26

BAPTISM.

The Baptism of a believer (in the Name of the Father, Son and Holy Ghost) is a symbol of his rebirth in Christ — his repentance and acceptance of Jesus as Savior.

> *He that believeth and is baptized, shall be saved; but he that believeth not shall be damned.* Mark 16:16

DUTIES OF THE BELIEVER.

Rebirth in Jesus, being "born again," is a gift of GOD's Grace. For this we are thankful and resolve to work, in Jesus's Name, to cast out Satan, both as a tempter to ourselves and to the lives of others. Jesus has given us the strength to do this and made it possible by His atonement for our former sin.

JESUS LIVES.

Jesus was raised from the dead, a miracle and a demonstration of His ascent over Satan — who would that all men come to death.

In the Resurrection He appeared to men, and in particular His Disciples, granting them the gift of the Holy Ghost, that GOD's work might continue in the world.

Jesus ascended into Heaven, returning to GOD the Father.

> *Who is gone into heaven, and is on the right hand of GOD; angels and authorities and powers being made subject unto him.* I Peter 3:22

JESUS WILL COME AGAIN.

There will be trials and hardships in the world, for Satan still lives. Satan is conquered by Jesus and may be overcome by Christians, but he still has much to work with.

> *And ye shall hear of wars and rumours of war: see that ye be not troubled; for all these things must come to pass, but the end is not yet. For nation shall rise against nation, and kingdom against kingdom: . . .* Matthew 24:6-7

But Jesus will come again to earth to judge all men in justice and to rule in peace. He will honor those who have acknowledged Him as Savior and have truly served Him. He will come in GODly righteousness, and works of iniquity will be to no avail. This will be His true hour of glory, when the cycle of this world will be ended, and the people of GOD will return to GOD whence they came.

> *. . . this same Jesus, which is taken up from you into heaven, shall so come in like manner as ye have seen him go into heaven.* Acts 1:11

> *And if I go and prepare a place for you, I will come again, and receive you unto myself; that where I am, there ye may be also.* John 14:3

SATAN CAST OUT.

At the end time, when Jesus will rule on earth in righteousness, the devil, Satan, will be cast out, and have no more influence, seen or unseen, upon GOD's people.

Now is the judgement of this world: now shall the price of this world* be cast out. *Satan John 12:31

And the devil that deceived them was cast into the lake of fire and brimstone . . . and shall be tormented day and night for ever and ever. Revelation 20:10

THE GLORY OF GOD.

The Glory of GOD's Kingdom will be seen, both on earth and in Heaven. For that which is of GOD in the world must return to Him.

The works of man, however inspired, are small when compared to the immensity of the universe and the Greatness of the Creator.

Man's struggles for existence and attempts at an understanding of the great mysteries are of little avail when compared to the Will of the Lord.

GOD is to be praised, for the highest hope of man is to walk in peace with his GOD. In Jesus Christ we have this opportunity and have only to reach out in true repentance and trust to be received in Grace.

It is right that man should praise the Lord, and spend his days in worship and thanksgiving.

Praise ye the LORD. Praise GOD in his sanctuary: praise him in the firmament of his power.

Let every thing that hath breath praise the LORD. Praise ye the LORD. Psalm 150:1, 6

Notes: *The Foundation Faith of God was founded in the mid-1970s by a group of individuals, many of whom had been members and/or leaders of the Church of the Final Judgment. Since its founding, the church has moved consistently toward an orthodox Christian position.*

*   *   *

THIRTEEN PURPOSES (WORLD CATALYST CHURCH)

1. To be a Light unto the feet of all men.

2. To lead mankind to the truth that all wisdom, all the Kingdom, is within HIMSELF.

3. To point the way to that inner door where man may find himself.

4. To open the way to that inner wisdom of the soul through meditation and self-searching . . . without any false bait to appease sensual cravings or desires for idle amusements.

5. To be a church of the road, with no expensive buildings but an earnest response to wherever the need may be.

6. To give spiritual enlightenment or counselling to all who truly seek, regardless of race, color or creed.

7. A church that condemns no other religion or church but one that is willing to work with all toward the one goal.

8. To be a church that recognizes all things are evolving, including truth and the need to work harmoniously with both spiritual and scientific efforts.

9. To be a church that exerts no pressure or persuasion but one that grants free choice to all as to whether they wish to follow us or not.

10. A church that relies entirely upon the freewill effort and financial assistance of all men.

11. To gain an understanding of the fixed laws of the universe and how to conform to them in joy and harmony, and *not* to flatter, coax or cajole God to grant our impossible whims.

12. To awaken all men to the only enemy that obstructs and darkens our doorway to glory . . . the greatest of all deceivers, MAN'S SELF!

13. To abolish anger, self-desire and ignorance.

Chapter 6

Ancient Wisdom Family

Rosicrucianism

OBJECTIVES OF THE ROSICRUCIAN ANTHROPOMORPHIC LEAGUE

To investigate the occult laws of nature and the super physical powers of man;

To promote the principles which will eventually lead to recognition of the truth of the universal brotherhood of man, without distinction as to sex, creed, race or color;

To acquire, disseminate, and exemplify a knowledge of spiritual truth as given to the world by the Elder Brothers of the White Lodge;

To study and teach ancient religion, philosophy and astrology in the light of modern needs;

To encourage the study of science and art in the hope that religion, art and science—which are a veritable trinity, the equilateral triangle which has always been used as a symbol of the Divine—may again be recognized as portals through which egos must pass in attaining to the mastery of self;

And, finally, to attain to self-conscious immortality, which is the crowning feat of evolution.

The Path is not strewn with roses, but thereon only can self-conscious immortality be won—THERE IS NO OTHER WAY.

Notes: *Rosicrucian groups are part of a secret occult tradition and, as a whole, have refrained from making any public statements concerning their position. The principles of the Rosicrucian Anthropomorphic League were published occasionally in the League's periodical.*

*   *   *

Occult Orders

TENETS (HOLY ORDER OF MANS)

1. The Holy Order of MANS is a non-denominational, non-sectarian group of people, banded together for the purpose of a more thorough understanding of the Universal Laws of the Creator, so they might better manifest His Creation, and thus, promote Peace and Harmony among men.

2. We accept the basic law of the Triangle and the spoken word, as tools given to us by the Creator to fulfill our needs in this life and the one to come.

3. We accept that there is both a seen and unseen plane of the Life Force as set down by the Creator when It created us.

4. We accept that Life is continuous, uninterrupted, and ever evolving at the point of Being.

5. We accept that Man has the ability as an instrument of healing, as given by the Creator, to heal the sick, the lame and the halt, as well as the mentally ill, of the spirit, as vouched for by the Master Man, Jesus.

6. We accept the giving of Communion, both materially and spiritually.

7. We accept Baptism of the child, the adult, as the baptism of the Holy Spirit, as the lifting of consciousness.

8. We accept the confession of sins, through the confessional, if it is so desired by the individual, by and through the Word given as a divine edict to every truly ordained Priest.

9. We accept the unity of the Great Creator in God, Mind and matter, throughout this solar system.

10. We accept that all men and women be accepted on an equal basis in the eyes of the Creator and the Holy Order of MANS.

11. We accept that, above all things, man must be free to choose the things in this life, both spiritual and material, which are one.

12. We accept man as an Evolving Being of unlimited resources and unlimited expansion, with a God of Infinite Wisdom.

Notes: *The Holy Order accepts the Nicene Creed as a full statement of the community's faith. It has also published a set of tenets which cover matters not mentioned in the creed.*

Theosophy

THE THREE OBJECTS OF THE THEOSOPHICAL SOCIETY

FIRST. To form a nucleus of the Universal Brotherhood of Humanity, without distinction of race, creed, sex, caste or color.

SECOND. To encourage the study of Comparative Religion, Philosophy and Science.

THIRD. To investigate the unexplained laws of Nature and the powers latent in man.

Notes: *Common to all branches of theosophy are the three objectives which gave direction to its early program.*

* * *

THE TEMPLE AS A WORLD MOVEMENT (TEMPLE OF THE PEOPLE)

In order to do anything well we must have a plan, a program. Therefore, it is well to outline what the Temple program for the world consists of. This can be summed up in five definite objectives:

FIRST: To formulate the truths of religion as the fundamental factor in human evolution. This does not mean the formulation of a creed, but rather the recognition of the religious instinct in human beings. Every religion that the world has ever known has been an attempt to interpret this primary impulse in human nature. To the extent that we are able to interpret wisely this impulse, are we able to undersand what true religion is.

SECOND: To set forth a philosophy of life that is in accord with natural and Divine Law.

THIRD: To promote the study of the sciences and the fundamental facts and laws on which the sciences are based. This will permit us to extend our belief and knowledge from what is known to the unknown, from the physical to the super-physical. When accomplished, such will corroborate those spiritual teachings which have been given to mankind from time to time by the Masters of Light.

FOURTH: To promote the study and practice of the Arts on Fundamental lines, showing that the Arts are in reality the application of knowledge to human good and welfare. The Christos can speak to humanity through art as well as through any other fundamental line of manifestation.

FIFTH: The promotion of knowledge of a true social science based on immutable law, the law showing the relationship between man and man, man and God, and man and nature. When these relationships are once understood, we will instinctively formulate and follow the Law of true Brotherhood. It is ignorance that perpetuates separateness, and once humanity can spiritually see the relation of all things, the Law of Unity begins to operate instantaneously.

Remember, the Temple as a principle includes the whole world. We become a mighty power for good as we keep attuned to the ideal of unselfish service, and with minds open and receptive to truth from every angle.

Notes: *Within this statement are references to theosophical basics such as reliance on natural and Divine law and the teachings of the masters.*

* * *

SOME PRINCIPLES OF THEOSOPHY (THEOSOPHICAL SOCIETY OF AMERICA)

1. One Life pervades the universe and keeps it in being.

2. The phenomenal universe is the manifestation of an eternal, boundless and Immutable Principle beyond the range of human understanding.

3. Spirit (or consciousness) and matter are the two polar aspects of the ultimate Reality. These two with the interplay between them comprise a trinity from which proceed innumerable universes, which come and go in an endless cycle of manifestation and dissolution, all being expressions of the Reality.

4. Every solar system is an orderly scheme governed by laws of nature that reflect transcendental intelligence. 'Deity is Law,' said H.P. Blavatsky. The visible planets of the solar system are its densest parts; it also contains invisible worlds of exceedingly tenuous matter interpenetrating the physical. The entire system is the scene of a great scheme of evolution.

5. The spirit of man (often called the soul) is in essence identical with the one supreme Spirit, 'that Unity (as Emerson put it), that Oversoul, within which every man's particular being is contained and made one with all other.' The gradual unfolding of this latent divinity takes place by means of a process of reincarnation, in accordance with the Cyclic Law, seen everywhere in Nature, of periods of activity alternating with periods of rest and assimilation.

6. 'Whatsoever a man soweth, that shall he also reap.' This is the Law of Karma under which men weave their own destiny through the ages. This is the great hope for humanity, for man can indeed become the master of his future fate by what he does in the present.

7. Man's pilgrimmage takes him from his source in the One through his experience of the many back to union with the One Divine Source. The goal for man is thus to complete the cosmic cycle of manifestation in full conscious realization of his self, no longer as polarized between consciousness and matter—self and other—but as both all and one with the Source of all. This realization constitutes Enlightenment.

Notes: *This unofficial statement published by the Theosophical Society of America attempts to summarize the society's teachings. These teachings identify the human and divine very closely and are centered upon progress through reincarnation.*

DECLARATION (UNITED LODGE OF THEOSOPHISTS)

The policy of this Lodge is independent devotion to the cause of Theosophy without professing attachment to any Theosophical organization. It is loyal to the great Founders of the Theosophical Movement, but does not concern itself with dissensions or differences of individual opinion.

The work it has on hand and the end it keeps in view are too absorbing and too lofty to leave it the time or inclination to take part in side issues. That work and that end is the dissemination of the Fundamental Principles of the philosophy of Theosophy, and the exemplification in practice of those principles, through a truer realization of the SELF; a profounder conviction of Universal Brotherhood.

It holds that the unassailable *Basis for Union* among Theosophists, wherever and however situated, is "similarity of aim, purpose and teaching," and therefore has neither Constitution, Bye-Laws nor Officers, the sole bond between its Associates being that basis. And it aims to disseminate this idea among Theosophists in the furtherance of Unity.

It regards as Theosophists all who are engaged in the true service of Humanity, without distinction of race, creed, sex, condition or organization, and

It welcomes to its association all those who are in accord with its declared purposes and who desire to fit themselves, by study and otherwise, to be the better able to help and teach others.

"The true Theosophist belongs to no cult or sect, yet belongs to each and all."

The following is the form signed by Associates of the United Lodge of Theosophists:

Being in sympathy with the purposes of this Lodge as set forth in its "Declaration," I hereby record my desire to be enrolled as an Associate, it being understood that such association calls for no obligation on my part other than that which I, myself, determine.

Notes: *Members of the United Lodge are required to sign a statement of "sympathy" with the Declaration at the time of their becoming an "associate" (member) of the United Lodge.*

* * *

Alice Bailey Groups

THE GREAT INVOCATION

From the point of Light within the Mind of God Let light stream forth into the minds of men. Let Light descend on Earth.

From the point of Love within the Heart of God Let love stream forth into the hearts of men. May Christ return to Earth.

From the centre where the Will of God is known Let purpose guide the little wills of men—The purpose which the Masters know and serve.

From the centre which we call the race of men Let the Plan of Love and Light work out. And may it seal the door where evil dwells.

Let Light and Love and Power restore the Plan on Earth.

Notes: *The Alice Bailey groups are non-creedal, but common to all the groups which have formed around Bailey's books is The Great Invocation. It is frequently repeated, and copies are widely disseminated. The invocation is similiar in intent to the Spiritual Creed for Light Workers.*

* * *

Liberal Catholic Churches

THE TEACHINGS OF THE AMERICAN CATHOLIC CHURCH

THE TEACHING OF AMERICAN CATHOLIC CHURCH is Catholic in scope. There are three immutable and fundamental truths of Christian Theosophy (1st Cor. Ch. 2, v. 6 and 7).

1. That our ignorance of God and Nature is the result of the want of the Spirit and Life of God in us.

2. The only way to the Divine Knowledge is the way of the Gospel, which calls and leads us to a new birth of the Divine Nature brought forth in us.

3. The Way of the New Birth lies wholly in man's will to it, and every step of it consists in a continual dying to the selfish, corrupt will, which man has in flesh and blood.

This teaching of the Church can be summarised as follows: First—The Words of Christ. Second—The Words of the Apostles. Third—The teaching of the Catholic Church. Any teaching that is contrary to the first two cannot be deemed to be the teaching of the True and Catholic Church.

All of this teaching can be summarised in the *Beatitudes.* (There are twelve. Matt. 5, v. 3-11; 11, v. 6; 13, v. 16 and 25, v. 34.)

Notes: *The American Catholic Church uses the Apostles' and Nicene creeds, but has also published a less formal statement which is more indicative of its theosophical teachings.*

* * *

STATEMENT OF PRINCIPLES (CHURCH OF ANTIOCH)

PREAMBLE: At the heart of our faith stands the conviction: That the universe is the visible body of God and that, therefore, in God all things live, and move, and have their being;

STATEMENT OF PRINCIPLES (CHURCH OF ANTIOCH) (continued)

That man is, in essence, a Divine being and was created to achieve a consciousness of oneness with the Creative Intelligence;

That man will realize this exalted achievement by a gradual unfolding of the powers that are latent within him and about him, through growth in understanding, through mastery of himself, and through the implementation of currents of Divine Grace operating in and about him;

That the purpose of the CHURCH OF ANTIOCH is to provide a priestly ministry of mature spiritual guidance for all who seek this ultimate goal of human perfection (Matthew 5:48).

ARTICLE I: Inasmuch as this our faith rests on universal principles observable in Nature, we have banded ourselves together to bring into manifestation an expression of the Church Universal, also to be known as The Church of Antioch, to proclaim and give witness to the world of this faith, by which:

1. We affirm that God is Love, Power, Truth, and Light; that His Law of Good rules the world; that all His sons shall one day reach His feet, however far they stray. We hold the Fatherhood of God, the Brotherhood of man. We know that we serve Him best, when best we serve our brother;

2. We place our faith in God, the Holy and All-Glorious Trinity, who dwelleth in the spirit of man;

3. And in the eternal and indwelling Christ, the Lord of Love and Wisdom, the first-born of every creature, Who leads us to the glory of the Father, Who is Himself the Way, the Truth, and the Life, without whose Way there is no going, without whose Truth there is no knowing, without whose Life there is no living;

4. We give recognition and allegiance to the Law of Good which rules the world, and

5. We strive toward that Wisdom which leads to the Fulfillment of Life, without discriminating against any Source that would reveal a further measure of that Wisdom.

Notes: *This statement is taken from the church's constitution. Because it contains essential doctrinal statements, the preamble to the constitution is also reproduced here.*

* * *

AN ACT OF GNOSIS (ECCLESIA GNOSTICA)

We know Thee
Thou eternal thought
immovable, unchangeable, unlimited and unconditioned
remaining unchanged in essential essence
while forever thinking the mystery of the universe
manifesting three extensions of cosmic power
creation, preservation and destruction -
Thou, Lord of all.

We know Thee

Father
Thou secret, supreme and ineffable Maker
unchanging in essence
yet ever-changing in appearance and manifestation
visualizing as an act of consciousness the mystery of
 creation
and by an act of will absorbed into life -
Creator.

We know Thee
Son
Thou Word, Thou Logos
divine manifestation of the Lord
alone-begotten of the great stillness
begotten by an act of consciousness alone
coming to the flesh to destroy incarnate error -
Sustainer.

We know Thee
Holy Spirit
Thou giver of life and goodness
principle of love, beauty and compassion
remaining here on earth to guide and care for us
Thou, with the Father and the Son
art the wholeness upon which the manifested universe is
 erected -
and Destroyed.

We know you
Messengers
custodians of the essential wisdom of the race
preachers of the great Law
containing within yourselves spiritual insight and courage
living and laboring unselfishly
mediating between the supreme source and its creation
dedicated to the advancement of all.
We look to the absorption of the self
into the universal Will
and thus liberation
from the infinite chain of attainment.

Notes: *Not from a creedal tradition, the Ecclesia Gnostica includes this Act of Gnosis [knowledge] in its major liturgy. Within the service it functions similarly to a creed in the more orthodox liturgical traditions. Within gnosticism, the emphasis is not placed on creedal assent, but on the gaining of cosmic wisdom by the individual members.*

* * *

STATEMENT OF FAITH (FEDERATION OF ST. THOMAS CHRISTIAN CHURCHES)

We believe in the True Light which enlightens all in the Holy One, the Lord Jesus Christ, who brought salvation to us from the Father by the power of the Holy Spirit.

We believe that we must make a personal committment to the Lord Jesus as the Savior of our lives and the Chief Bishop of the Church.

We receive the ancient priesthood by Apostolic Succession from the Lord Jesus, Our King of Kings and Lord of Lords.

We acknowledge the Levitical Order in our deacons.

We celebrate the Aaronic and the Melchizedek orders combined in our presbyters and bishops.

We look to the Universal Divine Gnosis and the life of the world to come. We believe that the gifts of the Holy Spirit and regeneration are necessary for spiritual growth.

Blessings eternal be upon the Sons and Daughters of Light in Christ Jesus.

Amen.

Notes: *This church is gnostic in its teachings, placing its faith in the "True Light" which brought the "Universal Divine Gnosis" (wisdom).*

*   *   *

ABRIDGEMENT OF DOCTRINE (INTERNATIONAL LIBERAL CATHOLIC CHURCH)

1. GOD IS—immanent, eternal, and transcendent. "In Him we live, and move, and have our being." (Acts 17:28)

2. God manifests in the universe under a triplicity expressed as the Father, the Son and the Holy Spirit—co-equal and co-eternal.

3. Man, created in the image and likeness of God, is divine in essence, an unfolding spiritual intelligence. Sharing in God's nature, he cannot cease to be, and his future is one whose glory and splendor are without limits.

4. Christ ever lives as a mighty spiritual Presence in the world, guiding and sustaining His people. The divinity manifest in Him is gradually being unfolded in man, until he shall become "unto a perfect man, unto the measure of the stature of the fulness of Christ." (Eph. 4:13)

5. The world is a stage of a Divine Plan in which the soul of man, by expressing himself in varied earthly experiences, continually unfolds his God-given potential. This evolution or spiritual development follows the inviolable law of causality. "Be not deceived; God is not mocked: for whatsoever a man soweth, that shall he also reap." (Gal. 6:7)

6. Man is a link in a vast chain of lives, from the lowest to the highest. As he helps those below him, he receives help from those above him on the ladder of lives, thus receiving the "free gift of Grace." A Communion of Saints and Ministry of Angels function to help mankind evolve.

7. Man has ethical responsibilities to himself and to his fellow men. "Thou shalt love the Lord thy God with all thy heart, and with all thy soul, and with all thy mind. This is the first great commandment. And the second is like unto it, thou shalt love thy neighbor as thy-self. On these two commandments hang all the law and the prophets." (Matt. 22:37-40)

8. It is the duty of man to discern the Divine Light in himself and others: that Light "which lighteth every man that cometh into the world." (John 1:9) Because men are sons of God, they are inseparably linked together as brothers. That which harms one harms the entire brotherhood. Service to humanity and the conscious alignment of the personality with the soul's high aspirations are the laws of spiritual growth.

9. The seven Sacraments of the Church have been instituted by the Christ, outward and visible signs of inward and spiritual grace, as potent aids for the unfoldment of the divine character of man—altruism, selflessness, creativity, wisdom, compassion and nobility. Christ, the Living Head of His Church, is the true Minister of the Sacraments wherein deacons, priests and bishops function as His channels of blessing and grace to mankind.

Notes: *This statement is derived from that of the Liberal Catholic Church, Province of the United States.*

*   *   *

SUMMARY OF DOCTRINE (LIBERAL CATHOLIC CHURCH, PROVINCE OF THE UNITED STATES)

1. The existence of God, infinite, eternal, transcendent and immanent. He is the one existence from which all other existences are derived. "In him we live and move and have our being." (Acts xvii, 28).

2. The manifestation of God in the universe under a triplicity called in the Christian religion, Father, Son and Holy Spirit; three Persons in one God, co-equal, co-eternal, the Son "alone-born" of the Father, the Spirit proceeding from the Father and the Son. The Father, the source of all; the Son, "The Word who was made flesh and dwelt among us"; the Holy Spirit, the life-giver, the inspirer and sanctifier.

3. Man, made in the image of God, is himself divine in essence—a spark of the divine fire. Sharing God's nature, he cannot cease to exist, therefore he is eternal and his future is one whose glory and splendour have no limit.

4. Christ ever lives as a mighty spiritual presence in the world, guiding and sustaining his people. The divinity that was manifest in him is gradually being unfolded in every man, until each shall come "unto a perfect man, unto the measure of the stature of the fulness of Christ." (Eph. iv, 13).

5. The world is the theatre of an ordered plan, according to which the spirit of man, by repeatedly expressing himself in varying conditions of life and experience, continually unfolds his powers. That evolution or spiritual unfoldment takes place under an inviolable law of cause and effect. "Whatsoever a man soweth, that shall he also reap." (Gal. vi, 7). His doings in each physical incarnation largely determine his experience after death in the intermediate world (or world of purgation) and the heavenly world and greatly influence the circumstances of his next birth. Man is a link in a vast chain of life extending from

SUMMARY OF DOCTRINE (LIBERAL CATHOLIC CHURCH, PROVINCE OF THE UNITED STATES) (continued)

the highest to the lowest. As he helps those below him, so also he is helped by those who stand above him on the ladder of lives, receiving thus a "free gift of grace." There is a "communion of saints" of "just men made perfect" or holy ones, who help mankind. There is a ministry of angels.

6. Man has ethical duties to himself and to others. "Thou shalt love the Lord thy God with all thy heart and with all thy soul and with all thy mind and with all thy strength. This is the first and great commandment, and the second is like unto it: Thou shalt love thy neighbor as thyself. On these two commandments hang all the law and the prophets." (Matt. 22, 37-40)

It is the duty of man to learn to discern the divine light in himself and others—that light "which lighteth every man" (St. John i, 9). Because men are sons of God they are brothers and inseparably linked together. That which harms one harms the entire brotherhood. Hence a man owes it as a duty to the God within himself and others: first, to endeavor constantly to live up to the highest that is in him, thereby enabling that God within himself to become more perfectly manifest, and, secondly, to recognize the fact of that brotherhood by constant effort towards unselfishness, love, consideration for, and service of, his fellowmen. Service of humanity and the sacrifice of the lower self to the higher are laws of spiritual growth.

7. Christ instituted various sacraments in which "an inward and spiritual grace" is given unto us through "an outward and visible sign." There are seven of these rites which may be ranked as sacraments, namely, Baptism, Confirmation, the Holy Eucharist, Absolution, Holy Unction, Holy Matrimony, Holy Orders.

Notes: *Both the Liberal Catholic Church, Province of the United States, and the International Liberal Catholic Church have the same summary statement of doctrine, and those Liberal Catholic jurisdictions that have not written a separate doctrinal statement accept the content if not the wording of this document. Individual members do not have to accept the statement, but it is considered the embodiment of "the distinctive contribution of the Liberal Catholic Church to Christian thought." Candidates for ordination must be in agreement with the statement.*

*　　*　　*

WHAT WE BELIEVE (NEW ORDER OF GLASTONBURY)

The New Order of Glastonbury is a mystically-oriented ecumenical religious Order. We espouse the following Principles:

1. To encourage the recognition that God, the Eternal Spirit, is One.

2. To encourage the recognition of the Triune Aspects of God as manifested in the Creator; The Son, the Cosmic Christ; and the Holy Spirit, the Comforter.

3. To encourage the recognition that the Son, the Cosmic Christ, is also the Light that shines in every human heart.

4. To encourage the celebration and preservation of the Christian Sacraments: Baptism; Confirmation; Holy Eucharist; Marriage; Holy Orders; Absolution; and Anointing for Healing.

5. To uphold and share the Apostolic Succession of the Western Christian Church and the Eastern Christian Church.

6. To provide pastoral care, the application of spiritual and Christian ideas and ideals to matters of life.

7. To encourage the study of the Bible, Comparative Religion, Philosophy and the other Spiritual Arts and Sciences.

8. To encourage the understanding of the life of Christ and human evolution.

9. To encourage the development of the gifts of the Spirit and the fruits of the Spirit.

10. To encourage the recognition that the spiritual can never be put into a rigid mold and so there will be diversities of emphasis, practice, and theology.

11. To encourage the expression of these principles in daily life, through practice and service to others.

*　　*　　*

SUMMARY OF BELIEF (OLD HOLY CATHOLIC CHURCH, PROVINCE OF NORTH AMERICA)

We believe that God is the creator of heaven and earth. We believe that He seeks one-ness with man that man might dwell in Him and He in man. Although God may not be understood by the finite mind, He can be experienced. We believe that during the celebration of the sacrifice of the Holy Eucharist, we become at-one with the Christ and unite our hearts and minds with Him, so that His will becomes our will.

We believe that Jesus Christ is God and man and that He is true and eternal. As we truly accept Him as our Saviour we become co-heirs with Him as sons of God. That He and He alone offers us the way, the Truth, and the Life and that no person comes unto the Father save by Christ.

We believe that the Holy Spirit is GOD and that He dwells among men and seeks to guide and instruct them that they might direct their affairs heavenward.

We believe that the church is the body of God. It is the community of the faithful and is governed by Jesus Christ. This body of God is composed of all baptized Christians who regularly participate in public worship.

We believe in the right of private judgement for members both lay and clergy in matters of doctrine as long as the judgement is in harmony with that of the undivided Catholic Church.

The Church's doctrinal position in all matters of faith and practice shall be in accordance with the Holy Scriptures, the Ecumenical Creeds, and the Holy Apostolic Tradition. We further accept, because they conform to the above, the doctrines embodied in the official liturgy of the church, its catechism, and the constitution and Canons of this church.

Notes: *Of the several juridictions in the Liberal Catholic orb, the Old Holy Catholic Church has the most orthodox Christian statement.*

* * *

"I AM" Groups

TENETS (CHURCH UNIVERSAL AND TRIUMPHANT)

I. FOUNDATION, HEAD, AND MEMBERS OF THE CHURCH UNIVERSAL AND TRIUMPHANT

We proclaim the Church Universal and Triumphant, founded by Almighty God upon the rock of the Christ consciousness, to be the true Church of Jesus the Christ, Guautama the Buddha, and all who have ever become one with the Christ and the I AM THAT I AM in the ritual of the ascension.

We declare Jesus the Christ to be the head of this Church, and we accept the one anointed by the Lord to be the Vicar of Christ as his representative on earth. We declare Gautama the Buddha to be the Lord of the World, and we accept the ones anointed by the hierarchy to be the messengers of the Great White Brotherhood as his representatives on earth.

We recognize the members of this Church to be those in heaven and on earth who have retained the essential flame of the way of the Christ and the way of the Buddha, having the cosmic cube within the heart, those who are one in heart, mind, and soul as the body of God on earth and in heaven.

We recognize affiliates of this Church to be those who show forth the quickening of that flame and that cube by allegiance and obedience to the ascended hierarchy, the Vicar of Christ, and the Messengers by becoming Communicants of this congregation, by regularly partaking of the sacraments and meeting their obligations to God and man in invocation to light, in service to life, and in fulfillment of the law of the tithe.

II. THE GOD FLAME, THE SOUL

We acknowledge and adore the one supreme God, the Creator of heaven and earth, and the individualization of the God flame in the I AM Presence as the I AM THAT I AM, the Source of life for each individual soul. We give allegiance to the Word that was made flesh, the only begotten of the Father, the eternal Logos, who is the universal Christ individualized as the Christed Self of the sons and daughters of God and the children of God.

We acknowledge the Kingdoms of the Elohim, the Archangels, and the Ascended Masters to be the manifestation of the Sacred Trinity of power, wisdom, and love—of Father, Son, and Holy Spirit—throughout the cosmos. And we acknowledge the Divine Mother, both in Spirit and in Matter, as the Mater-realization of the Trinity in the God flame.

We define the soul as the living potential of God and the purpose of the soul's evolution and its descent into the planes of Matter as the proving of the law of being through the correct exercise of free will, self-mastery in time and space, the balancing of karma, the fulfillment of dharma, including discipleship on the path of Christic and Buddhic initiation, followed by the return to the plane of Spirit through the union with the I AM Presence that was demonstrated by Jesus and Gautama in the ritual of the ascension.

III. ASCENDED MASTERS, HIERARCHY, THE GREAT WHITE BROTHERHOOD

Inasmuch as we acknowledge the goal of life to be the ascension, we recognize those who have attained that goal to be ascended masters (those who have ascended out of the planes of Matter, the kingdoms of this world, having mastered time and space); and we declare them to be the true teachers of mankind, inhabitants of the planes of Spirit (the kingdom of heaven), living masters in God's cosmic consciousness whose presence with and among us we affirm to be the communion of the Holy Spirit.

We therefore acknowledge the law of hierarchy in the ascending scale of being, from the lowest unto the highest, from the least in the kingdom unto the greatest, as individualizations of the God flame unfolding aspects of the identity of the one flame of life that is God. And we affirm our allegiance on earth and in heaven and our conscious cooperation with the cause of the fraternity of ascended and unascended beings known as the Great White Brotherhood.

IV. SACRED SCRIPTURES, PROGRESSIVE REVELATION, THE MESSENGERS

We accept the message of salvation and the statement of cosmic law contained in all of the sacred scriptures of the world according to the interpretation of the Holy Spirit given to the messengers Mark L. Prophet and Elizabeth Clare Prophet.

We accept the progressive revelation of God as dictated through his emissaries, the ascended masters, to their messengers Mark L. Prophet and Elizabeth Clare Prophet and their appointed successors. We accept this revelation as the word of God, The Everlasting Gospel, and the prophecy of the two witnesses (Rev. 11) set forth as sacred scripture for the two-thousand-year dispensation of Aquarius.

V. THE PATH OF BECOMING THE CHRIST AND THE BUDDHA

We accept the way of the Christ and the Buddha as the path of initiation defined by the messengers Mark I. Prophet and Elizabeth Clare Prophet according to the teachings of the ascended masters in the Holy Spirit's interpretation of the sacred scriptures of the world, the via dolorosa and the Eightfold Path, the words and works, the life and example of Jesus and Gautama, their profound teaching and their demonstration of many signs and wonders to their disciples.

We find in the lives of Jesus and Gautama examples of the life lived in God which we are compelled by the living flame to emulate. Above all, we find therein the calling to fulfill the promise which Jesus gave when he said, "He that believeth on me, the works that I do shall he do also; and greater works than these shall he do; because I go unto my Father," and of Gautama, who has said of man, "He may grow—oh, wondrous maturity—into the consciousness of becoming a true Buddha, an aspiring one, one who seeks by the process of budding to become a cosmic flower in the garden of God."

Therefore in obedience to the flame of living love we accept the cross of white fire of Jesus and Gautama as the sign of our attainment of the Christ consciousness, our enlightenment through the Buddhic consciousness, and our soul's victory through God Self-awareness over sin, disease, and death.

VI. MASCULINE AND FEMININE RAY, FATHER AND MOTHER OF THE CHURCH

As Jesus proclaimed himself to be the Son of God, thereby defining his mission to set the example of the Christ as the Real Self of every man and woman, so we accept our calling in the Aquarian age to be the challenge of defining our identity in and as the Mother—Mother as the feminine counterpart of God the Father, Mother as the materialization of the God flame, and Mother as the mastery within us of the planes of Matter.

We understand the raising-up of the feminine ray to be the challenge of the Aquarian age and the balancing of that ray with its masculine counterpart to be the fusion within being of the energies of the Father-Mother God for the birth of the Cosmic Christ and the advent of the Holy Spirit. To fulfill the goal of balancing the masculine and feminine rays of being for the fullness of the Holy Spirit to dwell in us bodily, we earnestly aspire to demonstrate the mastery of the energies of the chakras as centers of God Self-awareness through the recitation of Mary's Scriptural Rosary for the New Age, Jesus' "Watch with Me," and other meditations and invocations as shall be set forth from time to time by the Vicar of Christ and the Messenger.

We accept the example of the Virgin Mary in her ensoulment of the Mother ray as the supreme definition of our own opportunity to prove the Mother as the God flame where we are. Therefore, we do accept Mary not only as the Mother of the Word incarnate in Jesus and in all mankind, but also as the Mother of the Church, and her flame—anchored in the heart of the Mother of the Flame, her appointed representative on earth—nourishing and sustaining all life evolving in the planes of Matter.

We accept the flaming consciousness of Saint Germain, Hierarch of the Seventh Ray of the Holy Spirit and master of the Aquarian dispensation, as the open door to mankind's freedom in this age; and we do accept the Protector of Mary as the Father of the Church and the

example of God-freedom to all life through whose heart and mind we demonstrate self-mastery on the masculine ray even as the messenger Mark L. Prophet lived to the utmost the perfection of the fatherhood of God.

We accept and adore God in heaven and on earth in the planes of Spirit and in the planes of Matter, and God within the threefold flame anchored in the heart as Father, as Mother, as Christed Self in son and daughter and as Holy Spirit. And through the paths of Christic initiation and Buddhic attainment and enlightenment, we diligently pursue the converging of every aspect of the identity of God in the fiery core of being that is the I AM Presence.

VII. BAPTISM OF THE HOLY SPIRIT, FORGIVENESS OF SIN, BALANCE OF KARMA

We acknowledge the baptism of the Holy Spirit as the action of the sacred fire, and specifically of the violet flame, which is the power to forgive (hold in abeyance) the weight of sin and to transmute (transform) the misqualified energies of mankind's karma (cause-effect sequences in Matter) into the purified and perfected energies of the Holy Spirit.

We recognize this baptism of fire, prophesied by John the Baptist, as a dispensation of the Cosmic Christ implemented through the consciousness of Saint Germain as an altogether necessary component of our salvation in this age. Therefore do we vow to offer in the Spirit of Harmony daily invocations to Almighty God in the name of the Christ for the release of the violet flame as the action of Saint Germain's consciousness of God-freedom to a planet and a people. We acknowledge that this form of application results in (1) the transmutation of the records of sin, disease, and death and, when reinforced by active, selfless service to God and man, the fulfillment of the soul's divine plan and the obligations of sacred labor, in (2) the balancing of any and all karma necessary for the soul's liberation from the wheel of rebirth and its reunion with the I AM Presence in the ritual of the ascension.

VIII. CHILDREN OF GOD, SONS AND DAUGHTERS OF GOD

We recognize all mankind as children of the one God who become communicants of the one flame of the Holy Spirit when they acknowledge, adore, and give allegiance to the flame of God as the I AM THAT I AM, personified as the universal Christ, and, when they bow before the true nature of their own being, as the I AM Presence, personified in the individual Christ Self.

We recognize the sons and daughters of God to be those who have passed certain initiations on the path by entering into the God consciousness and accepting the responsibility for being, consciousness, energy, action and interaction in the planes of Spirit and Matter.

We define the creation of God to be the individualization of the God flame as twin flames of the masculine and feminine rays of the Godhead. Thus sons and daughters of God and children of God, as living souls clothed upon with spirals of God's consciousness, are endowed with the flame of life anchored in the heart known in the planes of Spirit and Matter as the threefold flame of the Christ. This flame distinguishes them from the children of the wicked one—soulless beings without flame or God-awareness whom Jesus described in his parable of the tares among the wheat.

IX. EIGHT SACRAMENTS, DEFENSE OF CONSCIOUSNESS

We accept and we agree to participate in, as we are able, the ritual of the eight sacraments of the rays as taught by the Vicar of Christ and administered by him and the ministers of the Church Universal and Triumphant.

We promise to watch and pray earnestly for the coming of the kingdom of God into manifestation on earth as it is in heaven and to hold perpetually within our hearts the surrender of the Lord Jesus made in the Garden of Gethsemane, "Nevertheless, not my will, but thine be done."

We pledge to defend the citadel of consciousness against all forms of evil and animal magnetism originating in the carnal mind; this defense we shall pursue most diligently through the methods of invocation, meditation, prayer, and decree taught by the ascended masters and the messengers and through the study and application of the teachings and example of the entire Spirit of the Great White Brotherhood.

In the name of Jesus the Christ and Gautama the Buddha, we vow to serve with Michael the Archangel, the Defender of the Faith, and the hosts of the Lord to defend the souls of all mankind against the deceptions and divisions of the laggards and the fallen ones and the entire luciferian rebellion.

X. FREE WILL, ANTICHRIST, ARMAGEDDON

We recognize, in the words of Jesus, that "in a universe of absolute good will and perfection, it must be recognized that the freedom to choose, known as free will, has permitted mankind to depart from the perfection of God and to act as a creator in his own domain." We recognize that by the misguided use of free will, many souls have elected to follow the path of the denial of the Real Self as God and, through pride, rebellion, ego ambition, and selfishness, have taken the way of Antichrist and united, albeit unwittingly, with the forces of the dragon, the beast, the false prophet, and the great whore abroad in the world. Thus, having placed themselves outside the circumference of God's awareness of all that is real, these souls, by their denial of the Christ and the Buddha, may, as an alternative to the ascension, pass through the second death as the result of the final judgment before the Court of the Sacred Fire and the Four and Twenty Elders.

Therefore in defense of the freedom, the light, the individuality, and the victory of all souls, we do accept the calling given to the body of God on earth to challenge every form of evil, the energy veil, or maya—personal and impersonal, embodied or disembodied. And we accept our responsibility as sons and daughters of God to pursue the calling of the Christed ones to expand the flame of life, truth, and love in the hearts of all mankind.

We understand that because of the presence in the universe of these fallen ones, influencing and being influenced by the Liar and his lie, there is now going on within the soul of a cosmos and within the universe the Battle of Armageddon betwixt the forces of light and darkness. We acknowledge the supremacy of the light and of the Christed ones in the Battle of Armageddon and pledge our lives and our flames—heart, head, and hand—to the drawing of souls into the flame of God-reality, the I AM Presence, and the true teachings of Jesus the Christ, Gautama the Buddha, and the entire Spirit of the Great White Brotherhood. Therefore our ultimate dedication is to individual self-mastery and the ascension in the light for ourselves and for every man, woman, and child upon the planet.

XI. SELFLESSNESS, SACRIFICE, SURRENDER

We accept the path of selflessness, the sacrifice of the lesser self, and the surrender of all aspects of the human consciousness to the Divine Self as the goal of the path we have chosen as we serve step by step, measure by measure, to replace every aspect of mortality with immortality, every aspect of the corruptible nature with the Incorruptible One, every aspect of the human consciousness with the divine.

XII. LAW OF THE TITHE

Understanding the law of the tithe to be the law of the abundant life, understanding Jesus' admonishment on giving freely as we have freely received, understanding the mission of the Christed ones in the words of Jesus "I am come that they might have life, and that they might have it more abundantly," we do therefore pledge our tithe in support of the Church Universal and Triumphant as one-tenth of our supply.

Notes: *The Church Universal and Triumphant's summary clearly distinguishes its position from other "I AM" groups. While its teachings have consistently departed from traditional Christianity, the church has retained the strongest attachment to Christian symbols of the several "I AM" organizations.*

* * *

THE DECLARATION OF FAITH (SANCTUARY OF THE MASTER'S PRESENCE)

I believe in God, The Mighty "I AM", God Presence within all life, and in the Holy Christ Self, through which the Will of God manifests in the world of Form.

I believe in the Eternal Three-fold Power of the Holy Spirit, which is the Divine Essence of all Being.

I believe in the Universal Brotherhood of man, and in the fellowship and communion of the Great White Brotherhood and Hierarchy of Heaven, with man.

I believe in the forgiveness of all transgressions against the Law of Life, through love; the purification of the human soul through the conscious recognition and use of the Sacred Fire; the ascension into Christ Perfection through the mastery of substance and energy in thought, feeling and desire, and I believe in Life Everlasting through the Light of God that never fails to produce perfection when called into action through Divine Love.

Miscellaneous Theosophical Groups

THE CREED [CHRISTIAN COMMUNITY (ANTHROPOSOPHICAL SOCIETY)]

An Almighty Being of God, spiritual-physical, is the Foundation of existence, of the heavens and the earth, Who goes before His creatures like a Father.

Christ, through whom men attain the re-animation of the dying earth existence, is to this divine Being as the Son, born in eternity.

In Jesus the Christ entered as man into the earthly world. The birth of Jesus upon earth is a working of the Holy Spirit, Who, that He might spiritually heal the sickness of sin upon the bodily nature of mankind, prepared the Son of Mary to be the vehicle of the Christ.

The Christ Jesus suffered under Pontius Pilate, the death of the Cross and was lowered into the grave of the earth.

In death he became the Helper of the souls of the dead who had lost their divine nature.

Then He overcame death, after three days.

Since that time He is the Lord of the heavenly forces upon earth and lives the Fulfiller of the deeds of the Father, the Ground of the World.

He will in time unite for the advancement of the world with those whom through their bearing He can wrest from the death of matter.

Through Him can the Healing Spirit Work.

Communities whose members feel the Christ within them may feel themselves united in a Church to which all men who are aware of the health-bringing power of the Christ.

They may hope for the Overcoming of the sickness of sin, for the continuance of man's being and for the preservation of their life, destined for eternity.

Notes: *The Creed is taken from the liturgy of the community, the Act of the Consecration of Man. It is recited by the priest(ess) after the Gospel lesson is read. Before reciting it, the officiant takes off his/her stole, signifying that the words are spoken in a non-priestly capacity, thus allowing freedom to those in the congregation unprepared to accept the statement. While this creed follows the format of the Apostles' Creed, its content consistently departs from that of the older creed in numerous, if often subtle, ways. The Creed deals with the physicality of God, uses the abstract phrase "the Christ," and ignores the concept of "resurrection of the body" while addressing the escape from the "death of matter."*

Chapter 7

Magick Family

Ritual Magick

THE AQUARIAN MANIFESTO [AQUARIAN ANTI-DEFAMATION LEAGUE (AMERICAN GNOSTIC CHURCH)]

All Sentient Beings have the Right to worship Who, What, Where, When, Why and How they wish, provided that they do not violate the similar Rights of others. All Sentient Beings have, as well, the Right (some would say Duty) to develop their Talents mental, physical, psychic and others to the highest degree possible; subject as always to the equal Rights of others. It is in this complex interplay of Rights that the Children of the Aquarian Age may be distinguished from their ancestors of previous Ages.

According to Astrological Tradition, the term "Aquarian Age" implies a time in which there is increased concern with the ways in which the individual can live by his or her own lights, while guaranteeing the same Freedom to all others. All those, therefore, who work for the greater Evolution of Consciousness and Freedom may be justly called "Aquarians," regardless of the day or year of their actual birth.

Aquarians—Neo-Pagan, Neo Christian, Agnostic or of any Faith—are by definition tolerant of ALL Pro-Life Beliefs and Organizations. They do not proclaim the existence of any One True Right-And-Only Way, but rather that every Sentient Being must find her or his own Path.

We will NOT, however, in the name of Tolerance or any other Ideal allow ourselves to be persecuted or exterminated by Anti Life individuals or organizations, whether political or religious.

As Aquarians we do NOT, in our religious services, magical rituals, psychic activities or in our private lives, engage in the commission or encouragement of Felony-Crimes With Victims, (as defined by Civil Law and modern Sociological Research). We do NOT, therefore, engage in Ritual Murder, Rape, Maiming, Torture of Animals, Grand Larceny, or other Heinous Crimes, and we will no longer quietly accept accusations that we do so.

Neither do Aquarians use their Talents whether we call them "psychic," "magical," "spiritual," "paranormal," or whatever—to achieve ends or through means that, if done physically would constitute such Felony-Crimes With Victims. Accusations in this area will not go uncountered either.

We know full well that the New Witchburners are seeking to once again light the Stakes of Persecution with the Fires of Bigotry and Hate. Equally well do we know that, despite our innumerable differences with one another, the Time has come for us to stand Together against the forces of Fear and Oppression. The very survival of ourselves, our children and our planet depend upon the outcome of our present struggles.

The Aquarian Anti-Defamation League will exist for the purpose of defending Aquarian Individuals and Ideals from those Witchburners who would destroy them. We shall attempt to use whatever means exist to preserve, protect and defend our Religious, Civil, Economic, and Human Rights, as well as our Reputations, from ALL those who would slander, libel, defame, suppress or otherwise persecute us for our Beliefs.

We shall no longer Allow self righteous followers of Anti Life Beliefs to prevent us from the free exercise of our Human and Constitutional Rights. We shall no longer allow anyone with impunity to publically accuse us of being "Satanists," "Devil Worshippers," "Charlatans," "Lunatics" or any other loaded terms of Slander and Libel designed to denigrate, defame or prevent us from the peaceful and legal spreading of our Beliefs. We shall no longer hesitate to bring Civil and/or Criminal charges against our would be Inquisitors whenever possible, no matter how wealthy or powerful they may be.

Aquarians Together—Witches, Warlocks, and Wizards, Psychics, Priests and Parapsychologists, Mystics, Mediums and Magicians, Astrologers, Diviners and Occultists of both Sexes and all Races, many Faiths and Traditions, Ages and Nationalities, hereby agree upon our Battle Cry as we declare War upon those who would persecute us!

NEVER AGAIN THE BURNING!!

Notes: *Written by P. E. Isaac Bonewits and issued in 1973 for the short-lived Aquarian Anti-Defamation League, the*

THE AQUARIAN MANIFESTO [AQUARIAN ANTI-
DEFAMATION LEAGUE (AMERICAN GNOSTIC
CHURCH)] (continued)

Aquarian Manifesto has been seen as a civil rights declaration for Pagans and ceremonial magicians in general. At least one group, the American Gnostic Church, has adopted it as part of its official teachings.

*   *   *

STATEMENT BY THE ORDER OF THELEMA

THE ORDER OF THELEMA is a small group of occultists basing its practices upon THE BOOK OF THE LAW as revealed to the Master Therion. We came to an acceptance of this book through a personal encounter with the divine forces which gave rise to the authorship of it. We believe that we are being directed by the agents of the Goddess Nuit; and that we are among Her Chosen.

We believe that on an ultimate or noumenal level, all reality is a Unity: Thus we are Pantheistic on the level of mystical attainment. However, on the phenomenal level of reality, we find that Godhead has refracted Itself into multi-aspect Deity: Thus we are Polytheistic on the Magickal level of attainment. We have chosen to accept the God and Goddess forms of ancient Egypt as the most adequate pattern of the interrelated functions of Godhead.

Among our immediate activities are studies in practical Magick, techniques of Yoga (Hatha and Kundalini), and metaphysics. Some of our members have been long-time practitioners of Wicca-Craft; and as a result, we partake of the celebration of Life and Nature.

We believe that for too long, groups following the various paths of wisdom and power have been in conflict over minor points of doctrine (tragic because all doctrines eventually resolve themselves into one), or petty jealousies. Our real enemy is and always has been ignorance and superstition. We are syncretic in our beliefs, and we try to absorb the wisdom that is freely given by others; and we freely offer what insights we might have.

Notes: *This statement defines the use of Egyptian mythical symbols by the Order of Thelema, which understands reality on both a mystical and magical level. "Thelema" is the Greek word for "will." Master Therion is one of the magical names assumed by Aleister Crowley.*

*   *   *

LIBER LXXVII (ORDO TEMPLI ORIENTIS)

Oz: "the law of the strong: this is our law and the joy of the world."—*AL.II.21*

"Do what thou wilt shall be the whole of the law."—*AL.I.40.*

"thou hast no right but to do thy will. Do that, and no other shall say nay."—*AL.I.42-3.*

"Every man and every woman is a star."—*AL.I.3.*

There is no god but man.

1. Man has the right to live by his own law—
   to live in the way that he wills to do:
   to work as he will:
   to play as he will:
   to rest as he will:
   to die when and how he will.

2. Man has the right to eat what he will:
   to drink what he will:
   to dwell where he will:
   to move as he will on the face of the earth.

3. Man has the right to think what he will:
   to speak what he will:
   to write what he will:
   to draw, paint, carve, etch, mould, build as he will.
   to dress as he will:

4. Man has the right to love as he will:—
   "take your fill and will of love as ye will,
   when, where, and with whom ye will."—*AL.I.51.*

5. Man has the right to kill those who would thwart these rights.

"the slaves shall serve."—*AL.II.58.*

"Love is the law, love under will."—*AL.I.57.*

Notes: *Each member of the Ordo Templi Orientis (O.T.O.), at one point in his/her career in the order, is responsible for the publication and distribution of multiple copies of Liber LXXVII (also known as Liber Oz), which states the basic principles of the thelemic world view. It is used by all branches of the O.T.O. as well as other groups that rely heavily upon the writing of Aleister Crowley. The text of Liber Oz consists of quotations taken from* The Book of the Law, *also known as Liber AL, the bible of the O.T.O.*

*   *   *

THE CONFESSION FROM THE GNOSTIC MASS OF THE ORDO TEMPLI ORIENTIS

I believe in one secret and ineffable LORD; and in one Star in the Company of Stars of whose fire we are created, and to which we shall return; and in one Father of Life, Mystery of Mystery, in His name CHAOS, the sole viceregent of the Sun upon the Earth; and in one Air the nourisher of all that breathes.

And I believe in one Earth, the Mother of us all, and in one Womb wherein all men are begotten, and wherein they shall rest, Mystery of Mystery, in Her name BABALON.

And I believe in the Serpent and the Lion, Mystery of Mystery, in His name BAPHOMET.

And I believe in one Gnostic and Catholic Church of Light, Life, Love and Liberty, the Word of whose Law is THELEMA.

And I believe in the communion of Saints.

And, forasmuch as meat and drink are transmuted in us daily into spiritual substance, I believe in the Miracle of the Mass.

And I confess one Baptism of Wisdom, whereby we accomplish the Miracle of Incarnation.

And I confess my life one, individual, and eternal that was, and is, and is to come.

Notes: *Where possible, members of the Ordo Templi Orientis (O.T.O.) gather weekly for the Gnostic Mass, a magical ritual based upon the Roman Catholic mass, but completely rewritten to embody the symbolism of thelemic magick. The confession is difficult to decipher apart from some understanding of the thelemic world view and the unique meaning given some ancient symbols. The cryptic language of the confession revolves around sex magick.*

*　　*　　*

Witchcraft and Neo-Paganism

PRINCIPLES OF WICCAN BELIEF (AMERICAN COUNCIL OF WITCHES)

1. We practice Rites to attune ourselves with the natural rhythm of life forces marked by the Phases of the Moon and the Seasonal Quarters and Cross Quarters.

2. We recognize that our intelligence gives us a unique responsibility toward our environment. We seek to live in harmony with Nature, in ecological balance offering fulfillment to life and consciousness with an evolutionary concept.

3. We acknowledge a depth of power far greater than is apparent to the average person. Because it is far greater than ordinary, it is sometimes called "supernatural," but we see it as lying within that which is naturally potential to all.

4. We conceive the Creative Power in the Universe as manifesting through polarity—as masculine and feminine—and that this same Creative Power lives in all people, and functions through the interaction of the masculine and feminine. We value neither above the other, knowing each to be supportive of the other. We value Sex as pleasure, as the symbol and embodiment of life, and as one of the sources of energies used in magical practice and religious worship.

5. We recognize both outer worlds and inner or psychological worlds—sometimes known as the Spiritual World, the collective Unconscious, the Inner Planes, etc.—and we see the interaction of these two dimensions as the basis for paranormal phenomena and magical exercises. We neglect neither dimension for the other, seeing both as necessary for our fulfillment.

6. We do not recognize any authoritarian hierarchy, but do honor those who teach, respect those who share their greater knowledge and wisdom, and acknowledge those who have courageously given of themselves in leadership.

7. We see religion, magick, and wisdom-in-living as being united in the way one views the world and lives within it—a world-view and philosophy-of-life, which we identify as Witchcraft, the Wiccan way.

8. Calling oneself a "Witch" does not make a witch—but neither does heredity itself, or the collecting of titles, degrees, and initiations. A Witch seeks to control the forces within him/herself that make life possible in order to live wisely and well without harm to others, and in harmony with Nature.

9. We acknowledge that it is the affirmation and fulfillment of life, in a continuation of evolution and development of consciousness, that gives meaning to the Universe we know, and to our personal role in it.

10. Our only animosity toward Christianity, or toward any other religion or philosophy-of-life, is to the extent that its institutions have claimed to be "the only way" and have sought to deny freedom to others and to suppress other ways of religious practice and belief.

11. As American Witches, we are not threatened by debates on the history of the Craft, the origins of various terms, the legitimacy of various aspects of different traditions. We are concerned with the present, and our future.

12. We do not accept the concept of "absolute evil," nor do we worship any entity known as "Satan" or "the devil" as defined by the Christian tradition. We do not seek power through the suffering of others, nor do we accept the concept that personal benefit can be only derived by denial to another.

13. We acknowledge that we seek within Nature for that which is contributory to our health and well-being.

Notes: *In the early 1970s some witches attempted to organize a national fellowship based on a conciliar model. During the American Council of Witches' brief existence, it adopted a statement which has been the main artifact surviving the organization. The statement is still occasionally used.*

The Principles acknowledge the basic masculine-feminine polarity in the universe, the pleasurableness of sex, magical power as natural and creative, and a oneness with nature. The Principles deny any relationship to Satanism and attempt to mediate the arguments concerning the various Wiccan "traditions."

*　　*　　*

WHAT IS A NEO-PAGAN? (AQUARIAN TABERNACLE CHURCH)

The term "pagan" comes from the Latin "paganus," which simply meant "country dweller." Today, most people who define themselves as Pagans use the word as a general term for "native and natural religions, usually polytheistic, and their members."

In simple terms Paganism is a positive, natural-based religion, preaching brotherly love and harmony with all life-forms. Its origins are found in early human development of religion; animistic deities gradually being refined to become a main God or Goddess of All Nature. This God or Goddess—bearing different names at different times and in different places—can be compared to the

WHAT IS A NEO-PAGAN? (AQUARIAN TABERNACLE CHURCH) (continued)

Jesus and Mary figures of Christianity. Paganism is *not* anti-Christian; it is simply *pre*-Christian.

Most Pagans (of various persuasions) seem to agree that their similarities are often of more importance than their specific doctrinal distinctions or ethnic focuses. Some of these common beliefs may include:

1. *The idea that divinity is immanent (internal) as well as transcendent (external).* This is often phrased as "Thou art God" and "Thou art Goddess."

2. *The belief that divinity is just as likely to manifest itself as female.* This has resulted in a large number of women being attracted to the faiths and joining the clergy.

3. *A belief in a multiplicity of "gods" and "goddesses,"* whether as individual deities or as facets of one or a few archetypes. This leads to multi-valued logic systems and increased tolerance towards other religions.

4. *A respect and love for nature as divine in Her own right.* This makes ecological awareness and activity a religious duty.

5. *A distaste for monolithic religious organizations and a distrust of would-be messiahs and gurus.* This makes Pagans hard to organize, even "for their own good," and leads to constant schisming, mutation and growth in the movements.

6. *The firm conviction that human beings were meant to lead lives filled with joy, love, pleasure and humor.* The traditional western concepts of sin, guilt and divine retribution are seen as sad misunderstandings of natural growth experiences.

7. *A simple set of ethics and morality based on the avoidance of actual harm to other people* (and some extend this to some or all living beings and the planet as a whole).

8. *The knowledge that with proper training and intent, human minds and hearts are fully capable of performing all the magic and miracles they are ever likely to need,* through the use of natural psychic powers.

9. *A belief in the importance of celebrating the solar, lunar and other cycles of our lives.* This has led to the investigation and revival of many ancient customs and the invention of some new ones.

10. *A minimum amount of dogma and a maximum amount of eclecticism.* Pagans are reluctant to accept any idea without personally investigating it, and are willing to use any concept they find useful, regardless of its origins.

11. *A strong faith in the ability of people to solve their current problems on all levels, public and private.* This leads to . . .

12. *A strong commitment to personal and universal growth, evolution and balance.* Pagans are expected to be making continuous efforts in these directions.

13. *A belief that one can progress far towards achieving such growth, evolution and balance through the carefully planned alteration of one's "normal" state of consciousness,* using both ancient and modern methods of aiding concentration, meditation, reprogramming and ecstacy.

14. *The knowledge that human interdependence implies community cooperation.* Pagans are encouraged to use their talents to actually help each other as well as the community at large.

15. *An awareness that if they are to achieve any of their goals, they must practice what they preach.* This leads to a concern with making one's lifestyle consistent with one's proclaimed beliefs.

Notes: *This statement, not a creed in any formal sense, is one of several documents attempting to summarize not only the perspective of the Aquarian Tabernacle Church, but also that of Neo-Paganism in general. This statement is the product of a community that has tolerated a wide variety of belief while retaining some sense of a commonly held core of belief in such concepts as the divine nature of individuals, polytheism, the astrological cycles, and the joyful life.*

*   *   *

A VIKING MANIFESTO [ASATRU FREE ASSEMBLY (VIKING BROTHERHOOD)]

The Viking Brotherhood is a body dedicated to preserving, promoting, and practicing the Norse religion as it was epitomized during the Viking Age, and to furthering the moral and ethical values of courage, individualism, and independence which characterized the Viking way of life.

We believe in the existence of several gods and goddesses, the chief of whom is Odin, the father of the gods and the god of war, poetry, and magic. Thor is also a warrior, but his aspect is more that of the toiler or worker. Balder represents the gentle and refined in Norse culture, Freyr is the god of growth and fertility, and Loki is a mischievous and traitorous god who often runs afoul of the other gods. The goddess Friggs is Odin's wife, Freye is the female counterpart of Freyr, Hels watches over the dead in Hel, and there are other lesser deities.

We believe that those who lead a life in accordance with the precepts of Norse Paganism and who die the death of a hero in battle will be received into Valhalla, the Hall of the Slain. Here they will make wassail and fight until the great last battle, Ragnerok. Those who do not die a worthy death will go down to Hel, a gloomy and cheerless place.

We believe in the existence of other supernatural entities besides our gods, to include Valkyries, the "Choosers of the Slain," female beings who bear the body of the fallen hero to Valhalla.

Because of our set of values we do not "worship" our gods in the usual sense of the word. We do not bend our knee even to Odin, or petition him, or otherwise deny our individuality and personal sovereignty. The gods are for us intelligent personifications of the forces of the Universe and examples for those who follow the Viking Way, not masters or superentities into which one becomes absorbed.

We see a cosmos in conflict - a Universe in which collectivism in its many forms, from communism to fascism to Christianity and a myriad others, threatens to destroy forever the individuality which we Vikings cherish so much. It is our historical role to oppose as best we can this trend toward collectivism in whatever guise it may appear.

We believe in heroism, which to us means not only courage and strength but also a sense of what is honorable and worthy of a hero.

We believe in nature not because it is fashionable to do so or because we are nature mystics, but because our spiritual forebearers were wild and untamed men who were educated in wild and untamed places - the tumultous seas and the forbidding forests. The wilderness has traditionally been the refuge of free men.

Finally, we affirm that the Viking Way is open to all regardless of their race or the country of their origin, for it is the mind and the heart which identify one as a Viking, not any superficial factor.

Notes: *This is one of a series of manifestos produced by Pagan groups in the 1970s. The Viking Brotherhood, now known as the Asatru Free Assembly, published its statement of Norse Paganism in 1972.*

*   *   *

MANIFESTO (ATLANTION WICCA)

HISTORY OF ATLANTION WICCA: Atlantion Wicca is based on teachings and dedicated to the memory of Elizabeth Sawyer, the Witch of Edmonton. For her part in the Craft she was hanged at Tyburn, England, on Thursday, April 19, 1621. The reason for her execution was that she by the use of diabolical help and out of malice did Witch to death one Agnes Ratcleife, a neighbor of hers. These were the charges brought down on her by the courts with no mention given to the help she gave the local farmers with their crops, the numerous babies she delivered, and the fevers she lowered when many were drawn to death's doors by the filth they were forced to live in during the seventeenth century. We however remember the babies, the crops, and the fevers, and we try to teach others to do the same.

REGULATIONS OF ATLANTION WICCA: Atlantion Wicca has as its rule book a "Book of Shadows" consisting of almost two hundred laws, many of which cannot be found in existing books. Rituals for conducting the various Sabbats, Esbats, New Moon and Full Moon Ceremonies together with the various rituals for Opening and Closing the Circle, Initiations, etc.

GENERAL VIEWS OF ATLANTION WICCA: We of Atlantion Wicca believe that nothing should be done to reflect a bad image of the Craft, for all of us have been reincarnated and we realize all too well what can happen when the Christians decide to raise up in force to squelch the Pagans. It is with this thought in mind that we forbid the use of drugs, sacrificing of any kind, orgies, public nudity while representing the sect, and in general any other type of behavior that might reflect an adverse reaction to the sect.

GOALS OF ATLANTION WICCA: Our goal is to set up in the Central New York area several working covens based on the tradition handed down to us by our ancestors. We wish to work with the serious student of the Craft and help him or her to find the right path to our Beloved Lady. We encourage inquiries, write editorials for local newspapers, and we are trying to present to the public what we feel is the true image of the Craft. We are trying to wash the ideas out of people's minds put there by movies like Rosemary's Baby and Simon King of the Witches, and by news stories like those written on the Charles Manson case. We are trying to prevent another Inquisition brought on by ignorance of the masses. We are trying to obtain freedom of religion laws for those of the Craft so that we may all be free to worship how, when, and where we want. We are trying to make contact with other members of the Craft, and other Pagan groups through joining groups like the Themis Council, and by having our names listed in various newsletters directed toward Craft and Pagan groups.

Notes: *This short-lived Wiccan group published its statement in 1972.*

*   *   *

THE FIREBEAR MANIFESTO (BROTHERS OF THE EARTH)

The feminist covens have achieved an incredible depth of experience these past years. They have described a vision of people drawn together to celebrate the life and life-images around them in themselves, their groups, their worlds, and the Cosmos. Women working and playing together to find new levels in power and awareness of self, and with others. They redefine the robotic roles which they have been handed as to who they are and how they must be. They meet in the nude or clothed, they worship the Goddess and Nature, their work is personal and political; they discover and revel in the celebration of womanspiritflesh.

I am the being called Firebear.

I seek the birthing place of the New Man, so that I may join him again to throw off the false shackles of civilization. To feel the natural beast joyously howl from inside— to greet the dawn as Osiris, consort to Her,—to live in the cities and towns, but with the wiliness and wisdom of Coyote, the Trickster—to respect the WoodGod Pan, to call upon the SwiftHealer Hermes, to marvel at the ArtistOracle Apollo, and to worship the grandeur of GrandFather Sky.

I have visions.

I am in a dark wood. Around a low fire I sit with other men like myself. We are dressed or not, but in some way adorned to reflect our powers and true ways. We have all journeyed together, and journey still, away from the vampiric influences of staid culture and conventional mind-sets. We realize, like our shaman brothers, that we must see the world as new each day. We realize that there

THE FIREBEAR MANIFESTO (BROTHERS OF THE
EARTH) (continued)

are worlds we ignore, yet that does not mean they are
beyond our reach.

In this circle we discover and channel the eternal power of
mensynergy. It comes first from finding out how we make
ourselves smaller and smaller, day by day. We are brought
up to yield to authority, yet it keeps us short of our own
authenticity. We have power over our bodies and minds
that we have never realized and step-by-step we can learn
to heal ourselves. We build armor around ourselves and
other men, making them alien to us instead of embracing
them as one flesh with us.

"Man is not a body only. The heart, the spirit, is man. And
this spirit is an entire star, out of which he is built. If,
therefore, a man is perfect in his heart, nothing in the
whole light of Nature is hidden from him . . . The first
step in the operation of these sciences is this: to beget the
spirit from the inner firmament by means of the imagination."—Paracelsus (16th c. hermetic)

How do we develop our power-from-within?

We gather in a circle, arms around bodies, and gather our
auras of light to heal. We visualize ourselves and our loved
ones and those in need as filled with the power that can be
man's, our wills united. We invoke the powers of the deep
forest, the red lion, the piercing moon.

We gather in the comfort of our castles and discuss the
power and vision of our true dreams: the dreams that we
yearn for during the days, and the dreams that come
unbidden to us in the nights. We gather in the fields to
play, to feel the exhilaration and dance of fun and
movement and energy awaken in and between our men-
flesh. We feel the natural joy of cooperative and supportive
activity with our kind. Our collective body learns from the
individuals within it. No one shall have power over
another, even in games of competition, because we play to
play, and to be together; not to beat an enemy, for there is
no enemy except the chains we place on ourselves from
within.

We gather to work on our anger, too. We are not good, we
are not bad, we simply are, and to ignore the dark and
inner parts that brood inside or that simmer below the
surface is to whip the beast until it turns on us and rends
us. So we tell our tales, every man jack of us, so that the
importance of the beasts can be seen, and the power
transformed and turned back into its natural place.

We gather to learn how to use the strength that Nature-
Spirit gave us. We learn to harness ourselves and our arts
in a spirit of experimentation and care, so that we can
bring our power-from-within to bear naturally—not with
fear and violence, but with strength, should we need to
nurture and defend. And we will build a community to
empower ourselves and those we love.

We gather to learn that we haven't really seen the world
but only our illusion of it, and that we have a place and a
reason to be here. "Man is an organ in the body of the
universe." (the Hermetic tradition)

And most of all, *we gather in a spirit of awareness and
knowledge and celebration of the spirit-that-moves-in-all-
things, and the joy of our hearts and flesh in this world, and
the harmony of it all.* We tell our stories and write our
rituals and bring the full power of pageantry, theatre, play,
and healing to create magick that will be with us within
our circle and throughout our mundane lives.

"Now again we see that all is unbegun. The only danger is
not going far enough. If we go deep enough, we reach
common life, the shared experiences of man, the world of
possibility. If we do not go deep enough, if we live and
write half-way, there are obscurity, vulgarity, the slang of
fashion, and several kinds of death."—Muriel Rukeyser

Notes: *This unofficial statement was printed in the periodical of the Brothers of the Earth, a Neo-Pagan group
celebrating men's mysteries. It is a positive response to the
feminist aspect of Neo-Paganism, and while unofficial, it
summarizes the most common perspectives and opinions
expressed by those affiliated with the Brothers of the Earth.*

*   *   *

MAJOR BELIEFS OF CELTIC WICCA (CHURCH AND SCHOOL OF WICCA)

1. God is the overseeing intelligence that created the
universe and the side.

2. The ultimate aim of each individual is to reach the
sphere of God.

    To reach the sphere of God, all evil must be removed
from the soul or spirit. Basic training in good and
evil is received on earth and continues in the side.
The lowest level in the side, 'guides,' are learning to
give unselfishly of their time and effort to help those
on earth. When each level is adequately mastered,
the soul or spirit progresses. Several complete life-
times in any given level may be required to master it.
Long discussions can be heard in coven meetings on
the number of levels of progression on earth and in
the side. The number generally accepted is ten levels
on each side of the invisible barrier. Progression on
earth is divided into ten steps, called in Celtic Wicca
levels ten through one.

3. As on earth, so in the side.

    There is a similarity in the two sides of the invisible
barrier. The side is organized in a rational way.
Rather than one being who attends to every detail on
earth, there is a realistic delegation of God's responsibility and authority through the ten levels. It
should be recognized that the directions from on
high are imperfectly transmitted through the levels
in the side; you must temper your messages from the
side by the use of your own intelligence.

4. Hell is within the mind of man.

    Wicca does not believe in a hell to which souls are
assigned when they've been naughty on earth. Hell is
here on earth. It is inside you. The frustration of
being unable to get or to do something, the temptation to take the easy road that will harm someone,
and the fears of having your errors catch up with

you: these things cause regret, and when they are allowed to rule the life, this regret becomes hell with sleepless nights and mind-torturing dreams.

5. Good is external.

It consists in helping the less fortunate with love, understanding, and consideration. One of the basics of Wicca is helping: first within the coven and then, with the coven's agreement, outside. This help is not the giving of conscience money to the less fortunate. It is the help which a person, animal, or plant needs to develop naturally and to become in tune with its place in the scheme of natural development. When you give money, you develop dependence. When you give help, you develop character.

6. Evil in the soul must be eliminated for progression to the higher levels.

Wicca is not an organization of social workers; but, in common with other philosophies, it does require its followers to conscientiously help in diminishing evil. First you must set your house in order by refusing to perpetrate evil acts. In Wicca you take only your own conscience into account. When you knowingly defraud someone of his rights, your own conscience is troubled and you have added spots of soil on your soul. The only way to expurgate these spots is to make restitution to the one who was defrauded. As you develop, you perceive that acts which in yesteryear seem irreproachable turn reproachable and then evil. This remembrance of past acts and your changed opinion of them is the surest sign of your development.

7. Reincarnation is for those who have not progressed far enough on earth.

We have noted before that progression is by learning and selflessness. A spirit is rewarded for its learning by progressing to the next level; conversely it is returned to the previous level when its learning is incomplete.

8. All must live in harmony with nature.

Until the time when we all live on chemicals, you will rely on nature to supply the the majority of your needs. All living things have a soul, from the minutest bacteria to man. These souls can feel, and they respond to the stimulus of their environment.

9. The development and care of the earthplane shell is a sacred duty.

The earthplane shell, your body, should be kept in the best possible physical shape because most illnesses slow or even reverse soul development. The God of Wicca loves all. Your earthplane shell is the most perfectly developed of all the shells on earth and is a manifestation of God's love. Your body is not to be ritually deformed by circumcision or tattooing or silicone injections, and is to be kept naked or minimally bound up on all possible occasions. The Greeks were the last nation to practice Wicca tenets with regard to the beauty of the body. Naked Olympian athletes, their tanned bodies perfected, trained, and glistening, must have been a wonderful sight. When the soul becomes a spirit, the body literally becomes a shell. It can be burnt or used to the best advantage of those left on earth.

10. Power is available from the human mind and from the spirits.

These two sorts of power are different and must be used correctly and with understanding.

a. Mind or raised power is obtained by the concentration of as many persons as possible on the one thought that will result in the desired goal. Wicca believe that thoughts have power. Experimenters at Duke University have photographed thoughts. It is also a fact that by careful concentration pendulums can be made to swing or the roll of the dice altered.

b. Spirit power is called down to help Wicca in tasks that are beyond the capability of thought power. The main area where the spirit is used is in prediction. This requires that the mind be made blank so that the spirits can communicate.

11. Good begets good; evil begets evil.

There is a reaction to all positive and negative thoughts and deeds. The world is gradually admitting that positive thinking gets good results. Many corporations led by hard-headed businessmen are giving their executives courses in positive thinking. This is of course a manifestation of raised power, affecting the minds of others telepathically. Wicca have known and used these effects for thousands of years. It has been found that when the power is used for self-gain a terrible toll is exacted because the evil use draws evil to the practitioner.

12. The development level of souls and spirits is presently degrading.

The constant pleas of the old Wicca for fertility have been answered. The over-population of the world proceeds apace, and with this overpopulation more and more souls are called from the side. These souls are taken from the less developed spirits of the higher primates; consequently we are seeing a lowering of the development level throughout the system.

SUMMARY

Celtic Wicca believes in:

1. An overseeing God who delegates authority throughout the universe.

2. The development cycle wherein the souls of elemental living things are developed upward through man and thence through the side to the sphere of God. Reincarnation is a result of incomplete development.

3. The rationality of the system. Everything is basically simple and not run by magic.

4. Hell does not exist except as it is envisioned within ourselves.

5. Good is giving help. Evil must be diminished. Good begets good and evil begets evil.

MAJOR BELIEFS OF CELTIC WICCA (CHURCH AND SCHOOL OF WICCA) (continued)

6. Each must live in harmony with those above and below himself on the scale (both on the earthplane and in the side).

7. There are two sorts of power: spirit and thought. Each has its respective uses. Wicca uses both.

8. The present system is degrading. We must help it to improve.

Notes: *This statement, which draws heavily on nineteenth-century ritual magic, has been published in a number of sources by one of the larger Wiccan organizations. The Church and School of Wicca believes in a form of reincarnation for those who have not yet progressed to a suitable condition to advance to higher things. The group is unique among Wiccan groups for its silence on the Mother deity.*

*   *   *

DOGMA AND DOCTRINE (CHURCH OF SEVEN ARROWS)

DOGMA

1. Each Being is, as a Spirit, a Living Medicine Wheel of Infinite Beauty, Capability, and Power; and Each is a Mirror of Every Other, Including Creator.

   Source(s): Directly stated in the Mythos, though one might also develop a similar Idea from looking at the Basic Principles and Operational Laws of Magical Technology in conjunction with an Idea that Before the Beginning, Creator was the Only ISness.

2. A Being (Spirit) Cannot be Destroyed, though its Condition can be Changed, even into such a Condition that It may Attempt to Not-Exist, or to seem to Not-Exist, or be Led to Think it is Not-Existing or is Capable of Not-Existing.

   Sources(s): Basically derived from the Mythos-statement of Each Being's Likeness (Reflection) of Creator, taken in conjunction with Creator's Apparent Omnipotence and Eternalness, though the results of the Past-Life Researches at Church Of Seven Arrows give strong support to the Dogma-position.

3. The Universe exists in a state of Patterned Change, with Defined Realms of Authorities and Responsibilities for Each of the Beings Therein.

   Source(s): Derived from the Mythos-descriptions of the Creations of the Realms and Contents, the Creations of Earth's Species-forms, and of Grandmother's Assignment of a Specific Function to Human-Species, though direct Observation of Earth's Ecology (Life-System) would give rise to a similar Idea, as do the Past-Life Researches at Church Of Seven Arrows.

4. Though the Right of any Being to Exist be Fully Established by Its Existing, this does Not Automatically Establish the Acceptability or "Rightness" of a Particular Manifest or Form Chosen by that Being for a Particular Time or Place.

   Source(s): Derived from the Mythos-descriptions of the Creations and Assignments of Position or Function, plus the History-records of Errors-of-Manifest and the Resulting World-Changes or Cleansings, and further supported by the results of the Past-Life Researches at Church Of Seven Arrows.

5. Bodies, of Whatever Nature, be but Masks Housing the Spirit(s) Within.

   Source(s): Directly from the Mythos-statement that Everything in the Universe has Spirit, and supported by the results of Shamanic entries into, and observations of, the Internal Operations of the Sub-Atomic, Atomic, Molecular, Continental, and Planetary-scale Realms.

6. The Basic Purpose of Humanity be to Lead the Beings of Earth in Harmonious Song to the Ear of Creator.

   Source(s): Directly stated in the Mythos-account of the Creation of Human-species.

7. There is No Single Path of Religious or Spiritual Practice that be Proper for Every Person or Being or Place.

   Source(s): Derived from the Mythos-descriptions of a Variety of Realms, Authorities, and Responsibilities, and given support by the Past-Life Researches at Church Of Seven Arrows, plus Shamanic Explorations into the various Realms of the Cosmogony.

8. As Above, so Below.— which is to say that the Basic Principles and Mechanics of the Universe are the Same for the Material as for the Spiritual, even though They may Manifest Differently in the Material than They Manifest in the Spiritual.

   Source(s): Derived from the Mythos-Idea of Singleness of Purpose and Direction in the Creation, plus the Mythos-statement of the "Reflection"-Nature of Beings, though Evidential Support arises from the Experiential Workability of the Idea when it is Applied as a Basic Principle in Magical, Mystical, and Religious Technologies.

In Summary, a Seeker deciding to become Fully Initiate in the Path of Church Of Seven Arrows will be Required to have a "Working Knowledge" of the Mythos and Cosmogony used by Church Of Seven Arrows as given in earlier chapters, *Plus* being Required to have Examined the Dogmas given above using the Procedures given earlier in this chapter, *And* Found Them Acceptable as Truths by which to Live as an Initiate Practitioner of the Way of the Church Of Seven Arrows.

DOCTRINE

1. Remember Always that Your Basic Purpose be to Live in Growth and Happiness that Your Life may Sound Harmonious in the Ear of Creator.

   Commentary: To the extent that an Individual Focusses On, and Progresses Toward, such Personal Goal, the Mythos-Described "Human Problems" will be Remedied and Fulfillment of the Mythos-Given Purpose for Humankind will be Furthered.

2. Know and Live in Accord With Natural Law, being Ever Mindful to Keep Nature's Balances, both Within and Without Yourself.

Commentary: Doing Thusly will Minimize the chances of Ill-Health and other causes for Unhappiness and Internal Disharmonies, Plus "Leading" (by Example!) Other Beings to do Likewise, thus Contributing toward Fulfillment of Humankind's Function and Purpose within Earth's Ecology.

3. Study the Sciences, both Ancient and Modern, Learning their Proper Uses in Benefitting both Yourself and Others.

Commentary: By such Means, the Mythos-Described "Ignorances" of the Human Spirit can be Remedied on an Individual Level, the Individual thereby Enabled to Understand and Carry Out more Effectively her/his Basic Function and Purpose.

4. Know and Be Yourself; You Have a Right to Be Here and Follow Your Own Path so long as you Hinder None Other in Their Doing Likewise.

Commentary: This Self-Knowing, in combination with the Carrying Out of #2 above, will Greatly Promote Your Carrying Out of #1; and the "Non-Interference" Policy regarding Others allows Them the "space" to do Likewise with Their Lives, thus Promoting Fulfillment of the General (Humankind and Others') Functions and Purposes as given per the Mythos.

5. Know and Understand the Powers and Guardians, Using their Aid and Worshipping as You will, Letting Others do Likewise, even though You May Not Understand Their Ways.

Commentary: The "Know and Understand . . . " is part of Remedying the Mythos-Described "Ignorance" of the Human Spirit; the "Using their Aid" is a means of Further Gaining Understanding (to the same End); and the "Letting Others . . . " of course Promotes Harmony AND the Others' Development as They may (as Individuals in Their Own Right) Require.

6. Make No Self-Destructive Agreements, and Let No Other Use You for Their Self-Destruction.

Commentary: NOT to be Equated with Physical-Body Loss or Destruction!!! Self-Destruction, insofar as it Requires Restriction of Awareness, Understanding, and/or Ability-Usage when Considered Relative Spirits, is Clearly Contrary to Fulfillment of Humankind's Function and Purpose in Creator's-Nephew's-Grandmother's Designs as Described in the Mythos.

7. Do Not Cage any Human or Other Free Being.

Commentary: "Cage" Relative Spirits relates to the Forcible Prohibiting or Inhibiting of Growth in Awareness, Understanding, and/or Ability-Development, something Clearly Contrary to the Mythos-Given "Leadership"-Adjuration. (Suppressed Beings do Not Make Joyous and/or Harmonious Song!!!)

8. Take No Life Except for Food or Self-Preservation— and That Only with Proper Respect and Consideration.

Commentary: Given the Observable "Food-Chain" Physical Hierarchy, the Killing of Bodies seems part of Grandmother's Design if issues of Food are involved; however, in view of Spiritual Considerations (such as "Everything has Spirit."), there are matters of Acknowledgement and Communications in Being-to-Being Relationships to be Handled.

And given the Rights and Authorities and so forth Considerations as they relate to Interferences ("NON-Authorized" per Mythos, etc.!) and Suppressions, the Protection of one's Rights May Sometimes Require the Discorporation of some Other Being by way of "Instruction"; however, even so, the matters of Acknowledgement and Communications in Being-to-Being Relationships need to be Handled.

9. Love Whom You Will so long as Your Agreed-Upon Obligations to Home and Community be Fulfilled.

Commentary: This is Specific Application of Doctrines 1, 4, 6, and 7 to some of the Situations and Problems of Human Interactions arising in the Cultural Situation we face in Modern America (and in any other Culture that "sets about" to "standardize" the Spirits of its Inhabitants!).

10. Never Use the Ancient Sciences of Magic and Religion to Harm Others lest Like or Greater Harm Befall You – Except that in Cases of Direct and Mortal Threat which You Did Nothing to Provoke, You May Use Any Means Available in Self-Defense.

11. Use the Ancient Sciences of Magic and Religion when Needful, but Never for Purposes of Show, Pride, or Vainglory.

12. Set No Material Price nor Tribute for Your Use of the Ancient Sciences of Magic and Religion for the Benefit of Others.

Notes: *The complete belief system of the Church of Seven Arrows is found in volume two of its publication,* Shaman's Notes. *It consists of a lengthy statement of the church's underlying Mythos and Cosmology as well as the Dogma and Doctrine. Dogma is defined as those unalterable basic ideas and/or beliefs individuals must hold if they are on a spiritual path. If they reject the dogma, they are, in fact, not on that path. Doctrine, on the other hand, are statements of "work-a-day" applications of the dogma. Doctrine is subject to change, but only in line with the dogma. Reproduced here are the Dogma, complete with explanatory statements, and the Doctrine.*

* * *

DELPHIAN MANIFESTO (DELPHIC COVEN)

OUR FAITH:

As Wicca Traditionals, we are Celtic in that we take our muse from the Cauldron of Kerridwen, and will at length become as the radiant browed Taliesin. We have a Horned God and a Moon Goddess. We visualize the Horned One as a Big Horn Sheep, or a stag with a tremendous horn spread, white as snow and brazen shod, Fleet of foot, wild and untamed in a primeval forest, He is also Lord of the Sun, as well as Saturnian shadows. The giver of wisdom

DELPHIAN MANIFESTO (DELPHIC COVEN) (continued)

and dispenser of judgements. We associate Him with pine trees and cones, Juniper, Sage, Indian Paint Brush, wild sun flowers and all pungent spices.

Our Lady of the Moon and also the sea is associated with white cats, horses, rabbits and all Taurian creatures. Also with various trees and flowers: aspen, plum, apple, wild roses and Shooting Star. Sweet smelling herbs are Her domain. She is the Foam Born Spirit that moves upon the surface of the waters, the rippling laughter of a creek, the Eternal Mother.

We also have Greco-Egyptian leanings, with a strong affinity for the ancient shrine of Apollo in Delphi, Apollo being a God of the arts. A coven totem is the Owl of Athena, patroness of wisdom. We feel a calling to the temples of the Egyptian Mysteries as well. There is an emphasis on Bast, the Cat Goddess, and Hathor, the horned Cow Goddess, and Thoth, the Ibis headed God of wisdom. Also Isis, the Mother Goddess, and the Great Cat Ra who destroyed the dragon of darkness. The cat is another coven totem.

PHILOSOPHY:

Can be summed in the words of Diogenes Laertius— ". . . for a man (or woman) living amid immortal gods, is in no respect like a mortal being." The dragon of darkness is the great fetter of ignorance which we must overcome through educational enlightenment, communication, and involvement with others who are like minded.

We believe that physical death is by no means the end of life, but the opening of another more beautiful chapter when one has completed his or her earthly incarnations and fulfilled his or her Karmic responsibilities.

WAY OF LIFE:

We believe that our great unfoldment lies in freedom of expression . . . the arts in all forms. This leads to freedom of thought, imagination, and then to freedom of spirit. Members of our coven may have any style or design they wish for robes, any fabric, any color, as long as it is a solid color. The same goes for Craft tools. Whenever possible we encourage members to make with their own hands the necessary items, and to embellish them as they desire. Development of psychic ability follows this freedom. This involves card reading, precognitive dreams, astrology, visions and mediumistic development. Candles and incenses are used to promote the proper state of mind, much as the hypnotic vapors of the chasm aided the trance condition of the Delphic Pythoness. Ritual baths are required, as it was in bygone days when seekers who wished to enter the Delphic Temple were required first to bathe in the Sacred Spring of Castalia. Since the cosmic Life-Force is manifest in all living things, these also are sacred. The Earth is a living breathing thing to be reverenced and looked after, as are all the lesser creatures. Therefore, we must do our part to preserve it from ecological destruction. Our magics are those of the Earth. Blessed Be.

Notes: *This statement was issued in 1972.*

MANIFESTO OF THE GEORGIANS (GEORGIAN CHURCH)

The aims and purposes of the Georgians shall be:

1. To worship the Gods of the Old Religion.
2. To aid the members to progress and improve themselves mentally, physically, and spiritually.
3. To work Magick for the benefit of members and any others who may seek our aid for right purposes.
4. To aid others in learning the Craft who truly desire the knowledge of the Craft for proper reasons.
5. To combat the untruths, and to spread the truth about the Craft to those outside the Craft.
6. To work for peace, harmony, and unity among the various branches of the Craft.
7. To work for a better understanding of, and a better relationship between Man and Nature.

Notes: *This church, named for George Patterson, its founder, published its manifesto in 1973.*

*   *   *

THE BLESSING PRAYER, DECLARATION OF FAITH OF THE BRITISH TRADITIONS, AND THE ORDAINS (NEW WICCAN CHURCH)

THE BLESSING PRAYER

In the name of Dryghtyn,
(Dryghtyn is old Anglo-Saxon for "Great Lord")

The Ancient Providence
(The one who provided for all creation. "Providence" means "Fate" or "Fortune.")

which was from the beginning,
(the Dryghtyn has always existed, every thing else, even the Gods, came after it)

and is for all eternity,
(the Dryghtyn will never cease to exist)

male and female
(the Dryghtyn is bisexual and can create by itself)

the original source of all things
(the Dryghtyn divided itself into the Goddess and the God and they, in turn, created everything else)

All knowing
(the Dryghtyn knows everything - the Goddess knows half of everything and the God knows the other half)

all pervading
(the Dryghtyn is every where, all the time)

all powerful
(the Dryghtyn possesses all the power in the universe; it can do absolutely anything)

Changeless

(this is a great mystery, for, even though the Dryghtyn divided itself it neither gains nor loses any in any way, thus it remains forever a unity and complete)

Eternal
(perhaps the Goddess and the God will recombine some day - we do not know - but the Dryghtyn will always exist)

The Dryghtyn is the one creator that all great world religions worship. The Jews call it Elohim (later replaced by the lesser YHWH); the Moslems call it Allah; the Chinese call it the Tao; the Egyptians called it Ptah; the Sioux call it Wakan Tonka ("Great Spirit"); the Sikh call it Akal ("True Name"); the Hindu call it Brahma; and the ancient Germans called it the Drichtin. The Italian Witches (the Strega) believe the creator was female to begin with and divided off a portion of herself and changed it into the God. Some English Witches have adopted this idea from "Aradia, Gospel of the Witches," a Strega book, but it is not the original English belief. Keltic mythology has numerous different Gods and creation stories, so it is impossible to state a single Theology for the Keltic Witches. Christians believe in the three parts of the Creator (Father, Son and Holy Spirit), but do not believe in the Creator itself. Wicca believe in the Creator and its two parts. Wicca are therefore monotheists, and Christians are not.

The Lady of the Moon
(The Goddess)

The Lord of Death and Resurrection
(The God)

The Mighty Ones of the Four quarters, the Kings of the Elements
(the Lords of the Watchtowers)

The Mighty Dead
(Those who have evolved to the point that they no longer incarnate, such as Merlyn, and Apollonius of Tyana.)

DECLARATION OF FAITH OF THE BRITISH TRADITIONS

We, the undersigned, being Witches of various British Traditions, in recognition of our common origin and similarity of religious practice, do ordain and declare these articles to strengthen our religion, emphasize our uniformity of belief, and to demonstrate to the people and governments of this planet our serious dedication to the worship of the Gods. Witchcraft is composed of numerous traditions, but it is ONE religion. Therefore, we do declare:

Article I. That we are Wicca and our religion is Witchcraft.

Article II. That we give due worship to the Gods, and obey their will.

Article III. That we worship both the Goddess of the Moon and her consort, the God of Death and Resurrection.

Article IV. That the Art is the secret of the Gods and may only be used in earnest and never for show or vain glory.

Article V. That we will never do anything to disgrace the Gods, the Mighty Ones, the religion or its members.

Article VI. That we will never do anything which will bring us into unfavorable contact with the Law of the Land, or any of our persecutors.

Article VII. That a Wicca (Witch) is a proper person who has been validly initiated within a Magic Circle by a Witch of the opposite sex who has the authority to perform the initiation.

Article VIII. That the power may only be passed from woman to man and man to woman, and that a man shall never initiate a man and a woman shall never initiate a woman.

Article IX. That we will ever keep secret and never reveal: the secrets of the religion; the identity, rank or residence of any Wicca without their expressed permission; the location of any secret meeting place of the Wicca; the identity of any person attending such a meeting be they Wicca or not; the secret writings of the Craft or the methods of working magic.

Article X. That we will celebrate our Mysteries in secret and never permit a cowan (non-witch) to observe or participate in our secret ceremonies, rituals or rites.

Article XI. That we will never use magic to kill or injure anyone except in self defense.

Article XII. That we will never use magic to take revenge against anyone.

Article XIII. That we will never curse anyone.

Article XIV. That we will never kill or injure any living thing as a sacrifice or offering to the Gods. This prohibition does not include pricking the finger as demanded at initiation.

Article XV. That we do not believe in the divinity of Jesus Christ and that we do not mock or parody Christianity.

Article XVI. That we do not believe in the existence of Satan or the devil nor do we worship him.

All this we do declare by the Gods and our past lives and our hope of future ones to come.

So mote it be.

THE ORDAINS

May the blessings of the Goddess and the God be on all who keep these laws which are ordained and the curses of both the God and the Goddess be upon all who break them.

So be it ordained: The law was made and ordained of old. The Law was made for the Wicca to advise and help them in their need. The Wicca shall give due worship to the Gods and obey their will, which they ordain, for it was made for the good of the Wicca as the worship of Wicca is good for the Gods, for the Gods ever love the Wicca. As a

THE BLESSING PRAYER, DECLARATION OF FAITH OF THE BRITISH TRADITIONS, AND THE ORDAINS (NEW WICCAN CHURCH) (continued)

man loveth a woman, so the Gods love man. And it is necessary that the circle which is the temple of the Gods should be duly cast and purified, that it may be a fit place for the Gods to enter. And the Wicca shall be properly prepared and purified to enter into the presence of the Gods. With love and worship in their hearts, they shall raise the power from their bodies to give power to the Gods, as has been taught of old. For in this way only may man have communion with the Gods, for the Gods cannot help man without the help of man.

Let each High Priestess govern her coven with justice and love, with the help of the High Priest and the Elders, always heeding the advice of the messenger of the Gods if he comes.

And the High Priestess shall rule her coven as the representative of the Goddess, and the High Priest shall support her as the representative of the God. And the High Priestess shall choose whom she will, be he of sufficient rank, to be her High Priest. For, as the God himself kissed her feet in the fivefold salute, laying his power at the feet of the Goddess because of her youth and beauty, her sweetness and kindness, her wisdom and justice, and her generosity. So he resigned all his power to her. But the High Priestess should ever mind that all power comes from him, it is only lent, to be used wisely and justly. And the greatest virtue of a High Priestess be that she recognize that youth is necessary to the representative of the Goddess, so will she gracefully retire in favor of a younger woman should the coven so decide in council. For a true High Priestess realizes that gracefully surrendering the place of pride is one of the greatest virtues, and that thereby will she return to that place of pride in another life, with greater power and beauty.

She will heed all complaints of all brothers and strive to settle all differences among them. So be it ordained. If there be any quarrel or dispute among the Brethren, the High Priestess shall straight away convene the Elders and inquire into the matter and they shall hear both sides, first alone, then together, and they shall decide justly no favoring one side on the other. But it must ever be recognized that there will always be people who will ever strive to force others to do as they will. Such as these are not necessarily evil and they oft have good ideas and such ideas should be talked over in council. But if they will not agree with their Brothers or if they say I will not work under this High Priestess. To those who must ever be chief there is one answer. Avoid the coven or seek another one, or make a coven of your own, taking with you those who will go. Ever recognizing there are people who can never agree to work under others but at the same time, there are some people who cannot rule justly. To those who cannot, justly the answer be those who cannot bear your rule will leave with out you. For none may come to meeting with those whom they are at variance. So if either cannot agree, get hence, for the craft must ever survive. It has ever been the Law of the Brethren to avoid disputes. Any of the third may claim to found a new coven because they live over a

league from the Covenstead or are about to do so. Any one living within the covendom and wishing to form a new coven shall tell the Elders of their intention and on the instant avoid their dwelling and remove to the new covendom. Members of the old coven may join the new one when it is formed, but if they do, they must utterly avoid the Old Coven. The Elders of the old and new covens should meet in peace and brotherly love to decide the new boundaries. Those of the craft who live outside both covendoms may join either coven but not both. All may, if the Elders agree, meet for the great festivals if it be truly in peace and brotherly love. But splitting the coven oft means strife, so for this reason these laws were made of old and may the curse of the Gods be on any who disregard them.

In the old day when witches extended far, we were free and worshipped in the great temples. But in these unhappy times we must celebrate our sacred mysteries in secret! So be it ordained, that none but the Wicca may see our mysteries, for our enemies are many and torture loosens the tongue of man. So be it ordained that no coven shall know where the next coven bide, or who its members be, save only the priest and priestess and messenger. And there shall be no communication between them, save by the messenger of the Gods. And only if it be safe may the covens meet in some safe place for the great festivals, and while there, none shall say whence they have come, nor give their true names. To this end that any be tortured, in their agony they may not tell what they do not know.

So be it ordained, that no one shall tell any one not of the craft, who be of the Wicca, nor give any names or where they bide, or in any way tell anything which can betray any of us to our foes. Nor may he tell where the Covendom be, or the Covenstead, or where the meetings be. And if any break these laws, even under torture, the curse of the Gods shall be upon them, that they may never be reborn on earth but remain where they belong, in the hell of the Christians.

If any speak of the craft, say "Speak not to me of such, it frightens me, it is evil luck to speak of it." For this reason, they have their spies everywhere. These speak as if they were well affected to us, as if they would come to our meetings, saying, "My mother used to worship the Old Ones. I would I could go myself." To such as these, ever deny all knowledge. But to others, say, it is foolish to talk of witches flying through the air. To do so they must be light as thistledown. And men say witches be blear eyed, old crones, so what pleasure can there be at a meeting such as folks. And say, "Many wise men say there be no such creatures." Ever make it a jest.

It is not forbidden to say as Christians do, "There be witchcraft in the land," because our oppressors of old make it hereby not to believe in witchcraft and so a crime to deny it which thereby puts you under suspicion. But ever you say, I know not of it here. Perchance there may be, but far off, I know not where. But ever speak of them as old crones, consorting with the devil and riding through the air. And ever say, "But how may they ride through the air if they are not light as thistledown."

But the curse of the Gods be upon any who cast suspicion on any of the brotherhood, or who speaks of any real meeting place where any abide.

Ever remember that you are the hidden children of the Gods, so never do aught to disgrace them. Never boast, never threaten, never say you wish ill to anyone. So be it ordained: In the olden days we could use the Art against any who ill treated the Brotherhood. But in these evil days, we must not do so for our enemies have devised a burning pit of everlasting fire into which they say their god casts all the people who worship him, except the very few who are released by their priests spells and masses. And this be chiefly by giving monies and rich gifts to receive his favor for their god is ever in need of money. But as the Gods need our aid to make fertile man and crops, so the god of the Christians is ever in need of man's help to search out and destroy us. Their priests ever tell them that any who help us are damned to this hell forever, so men be mad with the terror of it. But they make men believe that they may escape this hell if they give us over to the tormentors so for this reason all be forever saying, thinking, "If I catch one of the Wicca, I shall escape the fiery pit." So for this reason, we have our hidels and men search long and not finding any, say, "There be none, or if there are, they are in a far country." But when one of our oppressors dies, or even is sick, ever is the cry, "This is witches malice," and the hunt is up again and even though they slay ten of their own to one of ours, still they care not, for they have countless thousands, while we are few indeed. So be it ordained that none shall use the art in any way to do ill to any, however much they injure us. Harm none, and now times many believe we exist not. So be it ordained that this law shall ever continue to help us in our plight. No one however great an injury or injustice they receive, may use the art in any way to do ill or harm to any. But they may after consult with all, use the art to restrain the Christians from harming us or taxing others, but only to permit or constrain them. To this end men will say, "Such a one is a mighty searcher out and persecutor of old women whom they deem to be witches, and none has done him skith, so it is proof they cannot or more truly there are none." For all know full well that many folk have died because someone had a grudge against them, or were persecuted because they had money or goods to seize, or because they had none to bribe the searchers. And many have died because they were scolding old women. So much that men now say that only old women are witches. And this is to our advantage and turns suspicion away from us. In England and Scotland it is now many a year since a witch has died the death. But any misuse of the power might raise the persecution again. So never break this law, however much you are tempted and never consent to it being broken in the least. If you know it is being broken, you must work strongly against it. And any High Priestess who consents to its breach must immediately be deposed for it is the blood of the Brethren they endanger. No good, if it is safe and only if it is safe, and keep strictly to the old law.

So be it ordained: Keep a book in your own hand of write. Let brethren copy what they will, but never let this book out of your hand and never keep the writings of another, for if it be found in their hand of write, they will be taken and tortured. Each shall guard his own writings and destroy them whenever danger threatens. Learn as much as you may by heart and when danger is past rewrite your book. For this reason, if any die, destroy their book if they have not been able to, for, if it be found, it is clear proof against them, for our oppressors know that you may not be a witch alone, so all their kin and friends be in danger of arrest. Therefore destroy everything not necessary. If your book is found on you, it is clear proof against you. The same with the working tools. Let them be as ordinary things that many have in their houses. Let the pentacles be of wax that they may be melted or broken at once. Have no sword lest your rank allows you one. Have no names or signs or anything. Write the names and signs in ink before consecrating them and wash it off immediately after. Do not bigrave them lest they cause discovery; let the colors of the hilts tell which is which.

If you are arrested you may be tortured. Keep all thought of the craft from your mind. Say you had bad dreams, that a devil caused you to write this without your knowledge. Think to yourself, "I know nothing, I remember nothing, I have forgotten it all." Drive this into your mind. If the torture be too great to bear say, "I will confess, I cannot bear this torment, what do you want me to say, tell me and I will say it." If they try to make you tell of the Brotherhood, do not. But if they try to make you speak of the impossible, such as flying through the air, consorting with the devil, sacrificing children or eating mens flesh, say I had bad dreams, I was not myself, I was crazed. Not all magistrates are bad, if there be an excuse they may show mercy. If you have confessed to aught, deny it afterwards. Say you babbled under torture, you know not what you said. If you are condemned, fear not. The Brotherhood is powerful, they will help you to escape if you are steadfast. But if you betray aught, there is no hope in this life or that to come. If you go steadfast to the pyre, drugs will reach you, you will feel naught. You but go to the ecstasy of the Goddess.

If the craft have any appendage, let all guard it and help to keep it clear and good for the craft. And let all justly guard all monies of the craft. And if any brother truly wrought it, it is right they have their pay, if it be just, and this be not taking money for the art, but for good and honest work.

And ever the Christians say, "the laborer is worthy of his hire," but if any brother work willingly for the good of the craft, without pay, it is to their greater honor. Never accept money for the use of the art, for money ever smeareth the taker. It is sorcerers and conjurors and priests of the Christians who ever accept money for the use of their arts. And they sell dwale, and evil love spells and pardons, to let men escape from their sins. Be not as these. If you accept no money, you will be free from temptation to use the art for evil causes. All may use the art for their advantage or for the advantage of the craft only if it harm none. But ever let the coven debate this at length. Only if all are satisfied and none are harmed, may the Art be used. If it is not possible to achieve your ends one way, perchance the aim may be achieved by acting in a different way so as to harm none. May the curse of the Gods be upon any who break this law. So be it ordained. It is

THE BLESSING PRAYER, DECLARATION OF FAITH OF THE BRITISH TRADITIONS, AND THE ORDAINS (NEW WICCAN CHURCH) (continued)

judged lawful if any of the craft need a house or land and none will sell, to incline the owner's mind so as to be willing to sell, providing it harms him not in any way and the full price is paid without haggling. Never bargain or cheapen anything while you live by the Art.

So be it ordained. Let the Craft keep books with the names of all herbs which are good, and all cures, so all may learn. But keep another book with all the Bales (poisons) and spices (aphrodisiacs) and let only the Elders and other trustworthy people have this knowledge.

So be it ordained. Remember the Art is the secret of the Gods and only may be used in earnest and never for show or vain glory. Magicians and Christians may taunt us [and] say, "You have no power. Do magic before our eyes, then only will we believe," seeking to cause us to betray our Art before them. Heed them not. For the Art is Holy and may only be used in need. And the curse of the Gods be upon any who break this law.

It is ever the way with women and men also that they ever seek new love, nor should we reprove them for this, But it may be found a disadvantage to the Craft, as many a time it has happened that a High Priest or High Priestess impelled by love has departed with their love, that is they have left the coven. Now if a High Priestess wishes to resign, she may do so in full coven, and the resignation is valid. But if they should run off without resigning, who may know if they may not return in a few months? So the law is, if a High Priestess leaves her Coven, she be taken back and all be as before. Meanwhile, if she has a deputy, that deputy shall act as High Priestess for as long as the High Priestess is away. If she returns not at the end of a year and a day, then shall the coven elect a new High Priestess. Unless there is good reason to the contrary, the person who has done the work shall reap the benefit of the reward, maiden and deputy of the High Priestess.

It is the old law and the most important of all laws that no one may do anything which will endanger any of the craft, or bring them into contact with the law of the land or any persecutors.

In any dispute between the brethren, no one may invoke any laws but those of the craft, or any tribunal but that of the Priestess, Priest, and Elders.

So be it ordained. Order and discipline must be kept. The High Priestess or the High Priest may and should punish all faults. To this end, all of the craft must receive correction willingly. All, properly prepared, the culprit kneeling shall be told his fault and his sentence pronounced. Punishment shall be the scourge, followed by something amusing. The culprit must acknowledge the justice of the punishment by kissing the hand of the Priestess on receiving sentence and again thanking for punishment received.

Notes: *The beliefs of the New Wiccan Church, a West Coast Wiccan fellowship of covens, are found in three documents. The first, The Blessing Prayer, reproduced here with a church-produced commentary following each phrase, is*

considered equivalent to the Apostles' Creed for the Christian Church. The Declaration of Faith, written in the early 1970s, summarizes the beliefs of the New Wiccan Church and other covens who trace their origins to the British Gardnerian tradition. The declaration was "distilled" from the last and most lengthy document, The Ordains. The three documents emphasize a polytheistic belief with central worship directed to the Goddess and her consort, the God; the necessary role of both men and women in ritual duties; and the proper use of magical power.*

* * *

BASIC PRINCIPLES [TEMPLE OF THE GODDESS WITHIN (MATILDA JOSLYN GAGE COVEN)]

AMONG OUR BASIC PRINCIPLES ARE:

1. We believe in the primary importance of a distinctly feminist perspective in our religion and our goals for a better world.

2. We believe in worshipping the Goddess as the primary Deity and as an expression of the life-force of the universe; we believe the male principle is a "complementary" but not superior force.

3. We believe that all members of the Matilda Joslyn Gage Coven should be like-minded; we believe that coven members should share a unity of purpose and agreement about goals, so that coven members can work together easily and happily.

4. We believe our coven must be experimental and eclectic, finding a tradition of Feminist Wicce among the varieties of Wicca (Wicce) that exist and flourish.

5. We believe in the necessity of taking public action, as a coven and as individuals, as relates to our feminist goals.

6. We believe in the necessity of taking private actions consistent with our feminist goals.

7. We believe that feminist men can enter into coven ceremonies, subject to the consensus of coven members.

8. We believe the Matilda Joslyn Gage Coven is a teaching coven; we believe that new members may join us at the Equinoxes and Solstices, and that continuing members are learning more about feminist spirituality.

9. We believe that we as witches are seeking wisdom.

10. We believe that Wicce is a religion of love.

11. We believe that the power we achieve must be used towards the betterment and care of this entire planet.

12. We believe that we must work with Nature.

Notes: *Within the larger Wiccan/Neo-Pagan community, feminist Wicce (Witchcraft) forms a significant part. The Matilda Joslyn Gage Coven of Sacramento, California, was an early feminist coven formed in the summer of 1977. It has since disbanded but some of its impulse flowed into the Temple of the Goddess Within, now located in Oakland, California. While promoting a feminist perspective, the* *coven was not anti-male and recognized the male aspect of the deity.*

*   *   *

Satanism

THE 9 SATANIC STATEMENTS (CHURCH OF SATAN)

1. Satan represents indulgence, instead of abstinence!

2. Satan represents vital existence, instead of spiritual pipe dreams!

3. Satan represents undefiled wisdom, instead of hypocritical self-deceit!

4. Satan represents kindness to those who deserve it, instead of love wasted on ingrates!

5. Satan represents vengeance, instead of turning the other cheek!

6. Satan represents responsibility to the responsible, instead of concern for psychic vampires!

7. Satan represents man as just another animal, sometimes better, more often worse than those that walk on all fours, who because of his "divine spiritual and intellectual development" has become the most vicious animal of all!

8. Satan represents all of the so-called sins, as they all lead to physical or mental gratification!

9. Satan has been the best friend the church has ever had, as he has kept it in business all these years!

The record speaks for itself — SATAN RULES THE EARTH!

REGIE SATANAS!   HAIL SATAN!

Notes: *These nine statements, which summarize the basic stance of Satanists toward the world, were written by Anton LaVey, founder of the Church of Satan. They have been accepted by other Satanic groups, especially those composed of former members of the Church of Satan. Widely circulated as a basic manifesto, The 9 Satanic Statements opened LaVey's first book,* The Satanic Bible.

Chapter 8

Middle Eastern Family

Main Line Judaism

THE THIRTEEN PRINCIPLES OF THE FAITH (RABBI MOSES MAIMONIDES)

1. I believe with perfect faith that the Creator, blessed be his name, is the Author and Guide of everything that has been created, and that he alone has made, does make, and will make all things.

2. I believe with perfect faith that the Creator, blessed be his name, is a Unity, and that there is no unity in any manner like unto his, and that he alone is our God, who was, is, and will be.

3. I believe with perfect faith that the Creator, blessed be his name, is not a body, and that he is free from all the accidents of matter, and that he has not any form whatsoever.

4. I believe with perfect faith that the Creator, blessed be his name, is the first and the last.

5. I believe with perfect faith that to the Creator, blessed be his name, and to him alone, it is right to pray, and that it is not right to pray to any being besides him.

6. I believe with perfect faith that all the words of the prophets are true.

7. I believe with perfect faith that the prophecy of Moses our teacher, peace be unto him, was true, and that he was the chief of the prophets, both of those that preceded and of those that followed him.

8. I believe with perfect faith that the whole Law, now in our possession, is the same that was given to Moses our teacher, peace be unto him.

9. I believe with perfect faith that this Law will not be changed, and that there will never be any other law from the Creator, blessed be his name.

10. I believe with perfect faith that the Creator, blessed be his name, knows every deed of the children of men, and all their thoughts, as it is said, It is he that fashioneth the hearts of them all, that giveth heed to all their deeds.

11. I believe with perfect faith that the Creator, blessed be his name, rewards those that keep his commandments, and punishes those that transgress them.

12. I believe with perfect faith in the coming of the Messiah, and, though he tarry, I will wait daily for his coming.

13. I believe with perfect faith that there will be a resurrection of the dead at the time when it shall please the Creator, blessed be his name, and exalted be the remembrance of him for ever and ever.

For thy salvation I hope, O Lord! I hope, O Lord, for thy salvation! O Lord, for thy salvation I hope!

For thy salvation I hope, O Lord! I hope, O Lord, for thy salvation! O Lord, for thy salvation I hope!

Notes: *Judaism is generally viewed as a religion of deed rather than creed. While there are numerous writings concerning Judaism, only rarely have there been attempts to summarize the faith in a creed-like statement. One interesting attempt to assemble a set of such credos from a variety of individual Jews (though collected in the cause of Reconstructionism) can be found in Ira Eisenstein's Varieties of Jewish Belief (New York: Reconstructionist Press, 1966). Of course, the Shema provides a basic statement of the Jewish perspective in the midst of a Pagan world: "Hear O Israel, the Lord is our God, the Lord is One." That sentence (which has slightly variant renderings in English) is taken from the Scripture, Deuteronomy 6:4. Beyond the Shema, only one statement has received wide acknowledgement as a perceptive synopsis of Jewish belief—the twelfth-century "creed" of Rabbi Moses Maimonides.*

The Thirteen Principles of the Faith is the single most acceptable summary of the common beliefs of religious Jews. Maimonides was a twelfth-century rabbi residing in Egypt who is remembered for his codification of Jewish law. The text reproduced here is from an Orthodox Jewish morning prayer liturgy. It is noteworthy that in the early nineteenth century, when South Carolina Jews issued a statement of their Reform position, they revised Maimonides' creed.

THE FUNDAMENTAL BELIEFS OF JUDAISM (GERMAN RABBINICAL ASSOCIATION, 1897)

1) Judaism teaches the unity of the human race. We all have one Father, one God has created us.

2) Judaism commands: "Love thy neighbor as thyself," and declares this command of all-embracing love to be the fundamental principle of Jewish religion. It therefore forbids every sort of animosity, envy, malevolence, or unkindness towards any one of whatsoever race, nationality, or religion. It demands justice and righteousness and forbids injustice, improbity, fraud, taking unfair advantage of the need, the heedlessness, and the inexperience of a fellow-man, as well as usury, and the usurious employment of the powers of a fellow-man.

3) Judaism demands consideration for the life, health, powers, and possessions of one's neighbor. It therefore forbids injuring a fellow-man by force, or cunning, or in any other iniquitous manner depriving him of his property, or leaving him helplessly exposed to unlawful attacks.

4) Judaism commands holding a fellow-man's honor as sacred as one's own. It therefore forbids degrading him by evil reports. vexing him with ridicule, or mortifying him.

5) Judaism commands respect for the religious conviction of others. It therefore forbids aspersion or disrespectful treatment of the religious customs and symbols of other religions.

6) Judaism commands the practice of charity towards all, clothing the naked, feeding the hungry, nursing the sick, comforting those that mourn. It therefore forbids limiting our care to ourselves and our families, and withholding sympathy when our neighbors suffer.

7) Judaism commands respect for labor; each in his place shall take part by means of physical or mental labor, in the work of the community, and strive for the blessings of life by busy, creative activity. It therefore demands the cultivation, development, and active employment of all our powers and capabilities. On the other hand, it forbids inactive enjoyment of life and idleness confident of support by others.

8) Judaism commands absolute truthfulness: our yea shall be yea, our nay, nay. It therefore forbids distortion of truth, deceit, hypocrisy, double dealing and dissimulation.

9) Judaism commands walking humbly with God and in modesty among men. It therefore forbids self-conceit, arrogance, pride, presumptuousness, boasting and disparagement of the merits of others.

10) Judaism demands peaceableness, placability, mildness, benevolence. It therefore commands the return of good for evil, to suffer rather than inflict injury. It therefore forbids taking revenge, nursing hatred, bearing a grudge, abandoning even an adversary in his helplessness.

11) Judaism commands chastity and sanctity of marriage. It therefore forbids dissoluteness, license, and relaxation of family ties.

12) Judaism commands the conscientious observance of the laws of the state, respect for obedience to the government. It therefore forbids rebellion against governmental ordinances and evasion of the law.

13) Judaism commands the promotion of the welfare of one's fellow-men, the service of individuals and communities in accordance with one's ability. It therefore forbids slothful indifference to the common weal and selfish exclusion from the societies instituted for charitable purposes and for the betterment of mankind.

14) Judaism commands that its adherents shall love the state, and willingly sacrifice property and life for its honor, welfare and liberty.

15) Judaism commands sanctification of the name of God through acts and it bids us exert ourselves to hasten the time in which men shall be united in the love of God and the love of one another.

Notes: *In 1897, the leaders of the several branches of German Judaism adopted a statement. Typical of the manner in which many approach Judaism (as a religion in which deed is more important than belief), the statement emphasizes the commandments of Judaism while limiting theological considerations to the affirmation of one Creator God.*

* * *

A STATEMENT OF JEWISH DOCTRINE FROM *RELIGIOUS BODIES IN AMERICA* (1936)

The Jewish religion is a way of life and has no formulated creed, or articles of faith, the acceptance of which brings redemption or salvation to the believer, or divergence from which involves separation from the Jewish congregation. On the other hand, it has certain teachings, sometimes called doctrines or dogmas, which have been at all times considered obligatory on the adherents of the Jewish religion.

The unity of God.—The fundamental doctrine of the Jewish religion is that God is One. At all times the religion of the Jew vigorously protested against any infringement of this dogma of pure monotheism, whether by the dualism of the East or by the Trinitarianism of the West. It never permitted the attributes of justice and of love to divide the Godhead into different powers or personalities. God is a Spirit without limitations of form, eternal, noncorporeal, unique, omniscient, omnipotent, and one. "Hear, O Israel: The Lord our God, the Lord is One" is the declaration of faith which the Jew pronounces daily and breathes it even in his hour of death. God is the Creator of the world. He is also the preserver of the world, its ruler, and the arbiter of its destiny. He was God from the very beginning, and the worship of other gods is a rebellion against the universal God beside whom there is no other. "Look unto Me, and be ye saved, all the ends of the earth; for I am God and there is none else." (Isaiah, xlv, 22). He is the God of righteousness, mercy, love, and holiness; the ideal of moral perfection. God is "our Father, our Redeemer for everlasting" (Isaiah, lxiii, 16); He is not remote from mortal man in his need, but He is rather, as Jewish sages have put it "near, nearer than any other help or sympathy can be," who "appears to each according to his capacity or temporary need." A Jew cannot compromise with idolatry or polytheism; indeed he is enjoined to give his life rather than to renounce the purity of his religion.

The world and man.—The world is a cosmic unit and it is good. The Holy One created and sustains the earth and the heaven, light and darkness, life and death; and the world is ruled by everlasting wisdom and kindness. There is no cosmic force for evil, no principle of evil in creation. There is no inherent impurity in the flesh or in matter, and man is not subject to Satan. There is no original sin; sin is the erring from the right path. The crown and the acme of God's creation is man. He is capable of perfection without the aid of an extraneous being, and, being born free, is able to choose between good and evil, and is endowed with intelligence; "God created man in His own image" and made him "but little lower than the angels." From one man did all the races of the earth descend, and thus they constitute one family. This doctrine of the unity of the human family is a corollary of the doctrine of the unity of God. The One God is in direct relation with man, all men, there being no mediator between God and man, and all men may attain to immortality through following the good life; for immortality, the Jewish religion teaches, is the reward of human righteousness. There is in this respect no distinction between its own adherents and those of other faiths. As one ancient teacher exclaims: "I call heaven and earth to witness that whether it be Jew or gentile, man or woman, manservant or maidservant, according to their acts does the divine spirit rest upon them."

The future of mankind and Israel.—The perfection of humanity through the unfolding of the divine powers in man is the aim of history. There is to be a divine kingdom of truth and righteousness on this earth. Daily the Jew concludes his prayers by declaring his hope to behold speedily the time when God, in the glory of His might, will be manifested, and the abominations will be removed from the earth and idolatry utterly cut off, and He will perfect the world as the kingdom of the Almighty, and all flesh will call upon His name. This kingdom is the hope of mankind and the goal toward which it is striving. Whether or not this universal kingdom of God will be preceded by the day of God or by a universal judgment when "all that work wickedness shall be stubble," Jewish religion teaches the coming on this earth of a social order of human perfection and bliss, of peace without end, when none shall hurt or destroy, and when the earth shall be full of the knowledge of the Lord (Isaiah chapters ix, xi); this is the Messianic era.

Israel is a unique people that shall never cease (Jeremiah xxxi, 36). It is not claimed that this people is better than others or that it possesses a special share of the divine love; but it is affirmed, and the Jew daily declares this faith in his prayers, that God has brought them near to His great name, to give thanks unto Him, and to proclaim His unity. In this sense Israel is called a "kingdom of priests and a holy nation" (Exodus xix, 6), selected or assigned by God for His special purpose. Because of this duty they are taken to task more severely than others: "You only have I known of all the families of the earth, therefore I will visit upon you all your iniquities" (Amos iii, 2). It is a widespread Jewish interpretation that the Servant of the Lord described in Isaiah refers not to an individual but to the Jewish people as a group. Israel is God's witness (Isaiah xli–xliii), testifying to His existence and His unity. The duty of Israel, its imperishability and restoration (Deuteronomy xxx, 1-4) and the blessed future that awaits mankind, are doctrines of the Jewish religion.

The Law.—The belief in the unity of God, in the future hope of the world, and in the other doctrines is of no value unless one lives in accordance with the requirements of the beliefs. The emphasis is not on belief, but on righteous conduct. What is required is service of the Lord, a just system of human conduct in accordance with statutes and ordinances, "which if a man do, he shall live by them." The duty of man, created in the image of God, is to order his life entirely in accordance with the will of God, and only by so doing can he attain perfection and fulfill his destiny. And what does God desire of man? That was definitely conveyed to him. Already the first man, Adam, had received divine revelation for his conduct and for that of his descendants; others followed, until Moses received the full revelation, all the commandments and the statutes and the ordinances, which should govern the life of man and lead him to moral and religious perfection. This revelation, as contained in the Five Books of Moses, constitutes the Law of Moses, the Law, the Torah, the Written Law, and it must be understood in the light of Jewish tradition, the Oral Law. This Torah of divine origin, which will not be changed, is the foundation of the Jewish faith; and that the Jew must order his life in accordance with the Torah has always been a basic principle of the Jewish religion. To fear God and to keep His commandments is the whole duty of man.

The Torah, written and oral, preeminently emphasizes the principle of justice; other principles stressed are purity and truth, optimism and hope, joy and thanksgiving, holiness and the love of God. Righteousness and compassionate love are demanded for the fatherless, the widow, the oppressed, the stranger, and even the criminal; charity is *zedakah*, justice to the needy; and compassion is required even for the dumb animal. Further, a man's life must be permeated by purity of heart and built on truth. For, "the seal of the Holy One is truth" and "upon truth rests the world." Hope and optimism are other requirements, and hope is but rarely deferred to the world to come, but a man must rather wait for the moral and spiritual advancement of mankind in this world. At times this world is declared to be "like a vestibule in which one prepares for the palace," nevertheless, "one hour devoted to repentance and good deeds in this world is more valuable than the entire life of the world to come." A man should "rejoice before the Lord" and gratefully enjoy his gifts and fill other hearts with joy and thanksgiving: asceticism is discouraged. The whole life of man is holy, for the "Lord our God is holy," and man's life should be motivated by the love of God. Twice daily a Jew recites the *Shema'*, a

A STATEMENT OF JEWISH DOCTRINE FROM *RELIGIOUS BODIES IN AMERICA* (1936) (continued)

declaration which contains the words "Thou shalt love the Lord thy God with all thy heart and with all thy soul and with all thy might." It implies the purest motives for action, specifically serving the Lord, not from fear but rather out of love and for the sake of God and the glorification of His name; the doing of good, not in view of any reward, but for its own sake: and the love of man and the most unselfish devotion and the willing surrender of one's life itself whenever the cause of God demands.

Other fundamental teachings of the law, written and oral, are freedom of will and human responsibility, divine providence, retribution, resurrection of the dead, the power of repentance and of prayer. Man is free, the choice between good and evil having been left to him as a participant of God's spirit; man is responsible for his own actions. In close relation with the doctrine of divine providence stands that of retribution—that God rewards the righteous and punishes transgressors. The doctrine of the soul's immortality and of a future life in which retribution shall take place is plainly set forth in the Talmud, and the belief in the resurrection of the dead is closely connected with the doctrines of immortality and of retribution in the hereafter. Emphasis is laid on the power of repentance to avert from man the evil which threatens and to procure for him God's grace, and on the efficacy of the prayer "of all that call upon Him in truth." There is no need for any mediator when one prays to God, "for the Lord is nigh unto all them that call upon Him." He hears great and small alike.

The Torah emphasizes the need of study and education. It imposes a duty upon every father to instruct his children and upon the community to provide for the general instruction of old and young. The law sanctifies labor and makes the teaching of a trade whereby one may earn his living a duty upon the father and upon the communal authorities. Each man is enjoined to build a home and to contribute to the welfare of human society; celibacy, except under rare circumstances, is unlawful. Systematic care of the poor is a duty of a community. Love of one's country and loyalty to his government is enjoined upon every Jew, and he is solemnly adjured to seek the peace of his country and to pray for the welfare of its government.

Side by side with these universal principles of conduct the Torah surrounds the Jewish people with numerous laws and rites. Some laws, also called testimonies, have been given to make Israel testify to God's miraculous guidance, such as the festive seasons of the year; others, called signs, are tokens of the covenant between God and Israel, such as circumcision and the Sabbath; and still others, also called statutes, are divine marks of distinction—special means to preserve Israel and its group life. The covenant at Sinai made Israel a society "of priests and a holy nation" and laws were given to them designed to preserve the priestly character of the nation. Some of these appeal to the human reason while others do not, but even those which human intelligence is unable to grasp, are, through belief in their divine origin, vouchsafed the same high religious importance. Judaism is bound up with the Jewish people. "Ye

shall be holy unto Me: for I the Lord am holy, and have set you apart from the peoples, that ye should be Mine" (Leviticus xx. 26). These particularistic religious obligations of the Torah, written and oral, enabled the small Jewish people to resist the disintegrating forces of the idolatry and error which surrounded them, and encouraged the Jews to live by the principle, ascribed by the early rabbis to Abraham, "let all the world stand on the one side, I side with God and shall win in the end." The laws gave the Jews the strength to withstand the persecutions of the nations and the vicissitudes of time, and to fight for the truth amidst a hostile world. The Jewish religion knows of no sacraments, in the sense of rites by which a person is brought in bodily relationship to God; but the whole life of the Jew, even his commonest acts, are invested with religious obligations and meanings, and they are regarded as a sign of merit; as the rabbis have put it, "The Holy One, blessed be He, was pleased to bestow merit upon Israel and therefore heaped upon them laws and commandments." A pious man is "eager in the pursuit of religious obligations" and they fill the life of the Jew with a higher joy.

The Jewish religion in its relation to other faiths.—The Jewish religion enjoins upon its adherents the application of one law for Jew and members of other faiths, home-born or stranger; "Ye shall have one manner of law, as well for the stranger as for the home-born" (Numbers xxiv, 22). The harsh expressions found sometimes in ancient Jewish lore, concerning the heathen and the laws against him, are directed against the moral depravity ascribed to the heathen because of his unchastity and violence; he is always under grave suspicion of immoral conduct. The Jewish religion recognizes two classes of proselytes—"a proselyte of the gate" is one who abandons idolatry and accepts instead the seven Noachian laws of humanity, while "a proselyte of righteousness" is one who submits to the Abrahamic rite and becomes a full member of the House of Israel. No distinction whatever is drawn between a born Jew and a proselyte of righteousness. In former centuries, the Jews carried on an extensive proselytizing propaganda; later the world conditions prevented it. But whether as a result of that interference or not, proselytizing activities have since been neglected. In the fullness of time, however, the prophetic promises of the universal recognition of God will be fulfilled, and as the Jew expresses it in his prayers on New Year's Day, "God will reign in His glory over the whole universe and all the living shall say, the Lord, God of Israel, is King, and His kingdom ruleth over all."

Notes: *This statement was prepared for the United States Bureau of the Census for its 1936 (and last) edition of* Religious Bodies in America *by Dr. H. S. Linfield of the Jewish Statistical Bureau. It varied in no substantial manner from the statement appearing in the 1926 edition; it can thus be construed as representing the concensus of opinion of the major branches of American Judaism prior to World War II. It avoids mention of those issues that most differentiate Reform, Orthodox, and Conservative Jewish congregations. The statement mentions the "restoration" of Israel in passing, and ends with an affirmative paragraph on proselytization. It was written shortly before the Reform* *congregations adopted a new statement, the Columbus Platform.*

*   *   *

FROM THE *CONSTITUTION* [UNITED SYNAGOGUE OF AMERICA (1916) (CONSERVATIVE JUDAISM)]

The objects of said corporation shall be: The advancement of the cause of Judaism in America and the maintenance of Jewish tradition in its historical continuity; to assert and establish loyalty to the Torah and its historical exposition; to further the observance of the Sabbath and the Dietary Laws: to preserve in the service the reference to Israel's past and the hopes for Israel's restoration; to maintain the traditional character of the liturgy, with Hebrew as the language of prayer; to foster Jewish religious life in the home, as expressed in traditional observances; to encourage the establishment of Jewish religious schools, in the curricula of which the study of the Hebrew language and literature shall be given a prominent place, both as the key to the true understanding of Judaism, and as a bond holding together the scattered communities of Israel throughout the world. It shall be the aim of the United Synagogue of America, while not endorsing the innovations introduced by any of its constituent bodies, to embrace all elements essentially loyal to traditional Judaism and in sympathy with the purposes outlined above.

Notes: *In their constitution, Conservative Jewish leaders stated their objectives in such a manner as to distinguish them from both the Reform and Orthodox communities.*

*   *   *

PREAMBLE TO THE CONSTITUTION [WORLD COUNCIL OF SYNAGOGUES (1959) (CONSERVATIVE JUDAISM)]

Moved by an abiding faith in God, a deep love for His Torah, and a profound concern for the future of Judaism, the Jewish people, and all mankind, and

Keenly conscious of the responsibility which has fallen upon our generation, having experienced the nadir of disaster and having witnessed the miracle of deliverance, to preserve, enrich and transmit to coming generations our precious legacy of faith, learning, piety and wisdom and the ideals of universal peace, justice, and brotherhood, and

Desirous of strengthening Jewish life throughout the world, without impairing the essential, traditional autonomy of every Jewish community.

We, the representatives of like-minded congregations from different climes and continents, do hereby establish the World Council of Synagogues for the following purposes:

To foster the Jewish tradition in its historic continuity;

To promote the study of Torah and the observance of mitzvot;

To advocate the centrality and preeminence of the synagogue in the life of the Jewish people;

To further the study of the Hebrew language as the repository of our sacred literature and our accumulated spiritual and cultural heritage, and as the most potent cultural bond among Jews throughout the world;

To deepen our dedication to the prophetic ideal of creating in the land of our fathers a Jewish community which shall pattern its life by the ideals and teachings of the Torah, and which shall seek to be "a light unto the nations"; and,

To relate the ideals and practices of Judaism to contemporary life and thought to the end that mankind's spiritual and ethical aspirations may be enhanced and God's Kingdom may be established on this earth.

Notes: *The World Council of Synagogues, a worldwide organization of Conservative Jews in which American Jews play an important role, provided a recent statement of the unique Conservative Jewish traditional perspective.*

*   *   *

PRINCIPLES ADOPTED BY THE ORTHODOX JEWISH CONGREGATIONAL UNION OF AMERICA (1898) (ORTHODOX JUDAISM)

This Conference of delegates from Jewish congregations in the United States and the Dominion of Canada is convened to advance the interests of positive Biblical Rabbinical and Historical Judaism.

We are assembled not as a synod, and, therefore, we have no legislative authority to amend religious questions, but as a representative body, which by organization and cooperation will endeavor to advance the interests of Judaism in America.

We favor the convening of a Jewish Synod specifically authorized by congregations to meet, to be composed of men who must be certified Rabbis, and

a.   Elders in official position (cf. Numbers XI:16);

b.   Men of wisdom and understanding, and known amongst us (cf. Deut. I:13);

c.   Able men, God-fearing men, men of truth, hating profit (cf. Exodus XVIII:21).

We believe in the Divine revelation of the Bible, and we declare that the prophets in no way discountenanced ceremonial duty, but only condemned the personal life of those who observed ceremonial law, but disregarded the moral. Ceremonial law is not optative; it is obligatory.

We affirm our adherence to the acknowledged codes of our Rabbis and the thirteen principles of Maimonides.

We believe that in our dispersion we are to be united with our brethren of alien faith in all that devolves upon men as citizens; but that religiously in rites, ceremonies, ideals and doctrines, we are separate, and must remain separate in accordance with the Divine declaration: 'I have separated you from the nations to be Mine.' (Lev. XX:26.)

And further, to prevent misunderstanding concerning Judaism, we reaffirm our belief in the coming of a personal

**PRINCIPLES ADOPTED BY THE ORTHODOX JEWISH
CONGREGATIONAL UNION OF AMERICA (1898)
(ORTHODOX JUDAISM) (continued)**

Messiah and we protest against the admission of proselytes into the fold of Judaism without *millah* (circumcision) and *tebilah* (immersion).

We protest against intermarriage between Jew and Gentile; we protest against the idea that we are merely a religious sect, and maintain that we are a nation, though temporarily without a national home, and

Furthermore, that the restoration to Zion is the legitimate aspiration of scattered Israel, in no way conflicting with our loyalty to the land in which we dwell or may dwell at any time.

Notes: *In July 1898 delegates from approximately 100 Orthodox congregations met in New York City to form the Orthodox Jewish Congregational Union of America, now known as the Union of Orthodox Jewish Congregations, the largest of the Orthodox Jewish bodies in America. During the meeting, a set of principles representative of the Orthodox position, as opposed to the recently published Reform Pittsburgh Platform, was adopted, though the delegates understood clearly the limitations of any statement they might issue. The statement remains a strong assertion of the traditional Orthodox perspective.*

* * *

**CRITERIA OF JEWISH LOYALTY [JEWISH
RECONSTRUCTIONIST FOUNDATION
(RECONSTRUCTIONIST JUDAISM)]**

1) We want Judaism to help us overcome temptation, doubt and discouragement.

2) We want Judaism to imbue us with a sense of responsibility for the righteous use of the blessings wherewith God endowed us.

3) We want the Jew so to be trusted that his yea will be taken as yea and his nay as nay.

4) We want to learn how to utilize our leisure to best advantage physically, intellectually and spiritually.

5) We want the Jewish home to live up to its traditional standards of virtue and piety.

6) We want the Jewish upbringing of our children to further their moral and spiritual growth, and to enable them to accept with joy their heritage as Jews.

7) We want the synagogue to enable us to worship God in sincerity and in truth.

8) We want our religious traditions to be interpreted in terms of understandable experience and to be made relevant to our present day needs.

9) We want to participate in the upbuilding of Eretz Yisrael as a means to the renaissance of the Jewish spirit.

10) We want Judaism to find rich, manifold and ever new expression in philosophy, in letters and in the arts.

11) We want all forms of Jewish organization to make for spiritual purpose and ethical endeavor.

12) We want the unity of Israel throughout the world to be fostered through mutual help in time of need and through cooperation in the furtherance of Judaism at all times.

13) We want Judaism to function as a potent influence for justice, freedom and peace in the life of men and nations.

Notes: *This Reconstructionist Jewish statement functions in a manner somewhat analogous to articles of faith. Following theorist Mordecai Kaplan's idea of Judaism as a religious civilization, the Reconstructionist Sabbath Prayer Book asserts: "In view of the changed conditions in Jewish life, the criterion of loyalty to Judaism can no longer be the acceptance of a creed, but the experience of the need to have one's life enriched by the Jewish heritage."*

* * *

**ARTICLES OF FAITH [THE REFORM SOCIETY
OF ISRAELITES (1825) (REFORM JUDAISM)]**

1. I believe with a perfect faith, that God Almighty (blessed be His name!) is the Creator and Governor of all Creation; and that He alone has made, does make and will make all things.

2. I believe with a perfect faith that the Creator (blessed be His name!) is only one unity; to which there is no resemblance and that He alone has been, is and will be God.

3. I believe with a perfect faith that the Creator (blessed be His name!) is not corporeal; nor to be comprehended by any understanding capable of comprehending only what is corporeal; and that there is nothing like Him in the universe.

4. I believe with a perfect faith that the Creator (blessed be His name!) is the only true object of adoration, and that no other being whatsoever ought to be worshipped.

5. I believe with a perfect faith that the soul of man is breathed into him by God and is therefore immortal.

6. I believe with a perfect faith that the Creator (blessed be His name!) knows all things, and that He will reward those who observe His commands, and punish those who transgress them.

7. I believe with a perfect faith that the laws of God, as delivered by Moses in the Ten Commandments, are the only true foundation of piety toward the Almighty, and of morality among men.

8. I believe with a perfect faith, that morality is essentially connected with religion, and that good faith toward all mankind, is among the most acceptable offerings to the Deity.

9. I believe with a perfect faith, that the love of God is the highest duty of his creatures, and that the pure and upright heart is the chosen temple of Jehovah.

10. I believe with a perfect faith that the Creator (blessed be His name!) is the only true Redeemer of all His children, and that He will spread the worship of His name over the whole earth.

Notes: *Among the earliest documents of American Reform Judaism is the 1825 statement issued by the Reform party associated with the synagogue in Charleston, South Carolina. The articles are based upon the traditional creed-like formulation of Jewish belief written by Maimonides, now adapted to the new Reform concerns.*

* * *

PITTSBURGH PLATFORM [CENTRAL CONFERENCE OF AMERICAN RABBIS (1885) (REFORM JUDAISM)]

First—We recognize in every religion an attempt to grasp the Infinite, and in every mode, source, or book or revelation held sacred in any religious system, the consciousness of the indwelling of God in man. We hold that Judaism presents the highest conception of the God idea as taught in our holy Scriptures and developed and spiritualized by the Jewish teachers, in accordance with the moral and philosophical progress of their respective ages. We maintain that Judaism preserved and defended, midst continual struggles and trials and under enforced isolation, this God idea as the central religious truth for the human race.

Second—We recognize in the Bible the record of the consecration of the Jewish people to its mission as priest of the one God, and value it as the most potent instrument of religious and moral instruction. We hold that the modern discoveries of scientific researches in the domains of nature and history are not antagonistic to the doctrines of Judaism, the Bible reflecting the primitive ideas of its own age, and at times clothing its conception of Divine Providence and justice, dealing with man in miraculous narratives.

Third—We recognize in the Mosaic legislation a system of training the Jewish people for its mission during its national life in Palestine, and to-day we accept as binding only the moral laws, and maintain only such ceremonies as elevate and sanctify our lives, but reject all such as are not adapted to the views and habits of modern civilization.

Fourth—We hold that all such Mosaic and rabbinical laws as regulate diet, priestly purity, and dress, originated in ages and under the influence of ideas altogether foreign to our present mental and spiritual state. They fail to impress the modern Jew with a spirit of priestly holiness: their observance in our days is apt rather to obstruct than to further modern spiritual elevation.

Fifth—We recognize, in the modern era of universal culture of heart and intellect, the approaching of the realization of Israel's great Messianic hope for the establishment of the kingdom of truth, justice, and peace among all men. We consider ourselves no longer a nation, but a religious community, and therefore expect neither a return to Palestine, nor a sacrificial worship under the sons of Aaron, nor the restoration of any of the laws concerning the Jewish state.

Sixth—We recognize in Judaism a progressive religion, ever striving to be in accord with the postulates of reason. We are convinced of the utmost necessity of preserving the historical identity with our great past. Christianity and Islam being daughter religions of Judaism, we appreciate their providential mission to aid in the spreading of monotheistic and moral truth. We acknowledge that the spirit of broad humanity of our age is our ally in the fulfillment of our mission, and therefore, we extend the hand of fellowship to all who operate with us in the establishment of the reign of truth and righteousness among men.

Seventh—We reassert the doctrine of Judaism, that the soul of man is immortal, grounding this belief on the divine nature of the human spirit, which forever finds bliss in righteousness and misery in wickedness. We reject as ideas not rooted in Judaism the beliefs both in bodily resurrection and in Gehenna and Eden (Hell and Paradise) as abodes for everlasting punishment or reward.

Eighth—In full accordance with the spirit of Mosaic legislation, which strives to regulate the relation between rich and poor, we deem it our duty to participate in the great task of modern times, to solve on the basis of justice and righteousness, the problems presented by the contrasts and evils of the present organization of society.

Notes: *The debates over Reform Judaism led to the formation of a rabbinical association, the Central Conference of American Rabbis, in 1889. In 1885, a group of prominent Reform rabbis, led by Issac M. Wise, drew up and adopted the Pittsburgh Platform and in 1889 presented it to the Central Conference. Though never officially adopted by the Conference, the document was generally assumed to be a statement of the Conference's position.*

The Platform affirms some of Reform Judaism's most controversial ideas such as the abandonment of many of the laws of the Mosaic code and hope for a Messianic kingdom among all people. It is reflective of the early non-Zionist position of the Reform movement, declaring a loss of expectation of any return to Palestine by the Jewish people. This position was reversed in the Columbus Platform of 1937.

* * *

COLUMBUS PLATFORM [CENTRAL CONFERENCE OF AMERICAN RABBIS (1937) (REFORM JUDAISM)]

1. JUDAISM AND ITS FOUNDATIONS

1. NATURE OF JUDAISM. Judaism is the historical religious experience of the Jewish people. Though growing out of Jewish life, its message is universal, aiming at the union and perfection of mankind under the sovereignty of God. Reform Judaism recognizes the principle of progressive development in religion and consciously applies this principle to spiritual as well as to cultural and social life.

Judaism welcomes all truth, whether written in the pages of Scripture or deciphered from the records of nature. The new discoveries of science, while replacing the older scientific views underlying our sacred literature, do not conflict with the essential spirit of religion as manifested in the consecration of man's will, heart and mind to the service of God and of humanity.

2. GOD. The heart of Judaism and its chief contribution to religion is the doctrine of the One, living God, Who rules the world through law and love. In Him all existence has its creative source and mankind its ideal of conduct. Though transcending time and space, He is the indwelling Presence of the world. We worship Him as the Lord of the Universe and as our merciful Father.

3. MAN. Judaism affirms that man is created in the Divine image. His spirit is immortal. He is an active co-worker with God. As a child of God, he is endowed with moral freedom and is charged with the responsibility of overcoming evil and striving after ideal ends.

4. TORAH. God reveals Himself not only in the majesty, beauty and orderliness of nature, but also in the vision and moral striving of the human spirit. Revelation is a continuous process, confined to no one group and to no one age. Yet the people of Israel, through its prophets and sages, achieved unique insight in the realm of religious truth. The Torah, both written and oral, enshrines Israel's ever-growing consciousness of God and of the moral law. It preserves the historical precedents, sanctions and norms of Jewish life, and seeks to mold it in the patterns of goodness and of holiness. Being products of historical processes, certain of its laws have lost their binding force with the passing of the conditions that called them forth. But as a depository of permanent spiritual ideals, the Torah remains the dynamic source of the life of Israel. Each age has the obligation to adapt the teaching of the Torah to its needs in consonance with the genius of Judaism.

5. ISRAEL. Judaism is the soul of which Israel is the body. Living in all parts of the world, Israel has been held together by the ties of a common history, and above all, by the heritage of faith. Though we recognize in the group-loyalty of Jews who have become estranged from our religious tradition a bond which still unites them with us, we maintain that it is by its religion and for its religion that the Jewish people have lived. The non-Jew who accepts our faith is welcome as a full member of the Jewish community.

In all lands where our people live, they assume and seek to share loyally the full duties and responsibilities of citizenship and to create seats of Jewish knowledge and religion. In the rehabilitation of Palestine, the land hallowed by memories and hopes,

we behold the promise of renewed life for many of our brethren. We affirm the obligation of all Jewry to aid in its upbuilding as a Jewish homeland by endeavoring to make it not only a haven of refuge for the oppressed but also a center of Jewish culture and spiritual life.

Throughout the ages it has been Israel's mission to witness to the Divine in the face of every form of paganism and materialism. We regard it as our historic task to cooperate with all men in the establishment of the kingdom of God, of universal brotherhood, justice, truth and peace on earth. This is our Messianic Goal.

II. ETHICS

6. ETHICS AND RELIGION. In Judaism religion and morality blend into an indissoluble unity. Seeking God means to strive after holiness, righteousness and goodness. The love of God is incomplete without the love of one's fellowmen. Judaism emphasizes the kinship of the human race, the sanctity and worth of human life and personality and the right of the individual to freedom and to the pursuit of his chosen vocation. Justice to all, irrespective of race, sect or class is the inalienable right and the inescapable obligation of all. The state and organized government exist in order to further these ends.

7. SOCIAL JUSTICE. Judaism seeks the attainment of a just society by the application of its teachings to the economic order, to industry and commerce, and to national and international affairs. It aims at the elimination of man-made misery and suffering, poverty and degradation, of tyranny and slavery, of social inequality and prejudice, of ill-will and strife. It advocates the promotion of harmonious relations between warring classes on the basis of equity and justice, and the creation of conditions under which human personality may flourish. It pleads for the safeguarding of childhood against exploitation. It champions the cause of all who work and of their right to an adequate standard of living, as prior to the rights of property. Judaism emphasizes the duty of charity, and strives for a social order which will protect men against disabilities of old age, sickness and unemployment.

8. PEACE. Judaism, from the days of the prophets, has proclaimed to mankind the ideal of universal peace. The spiritual and physical disarmament of all nations has been one of its essential teachings. It abhors all violence and relies upon moral education, love and sympathy to secure human progress. It regards justice as the foundation of the well-being of nations and the condition of enduring peace. It urges organized international action for disarmament, collective security and world peace.

III. RELIGIOUS PRACTICE

9. THE RELIGIOUS LIFE. Jewish life is marked by consecration to these ideas of Judaism. It calls for faithful participation in the life of the Jewish community as it finds expression in home, synagogue

and school and in all other agencies that enrich Jewish life and promote its welfare.

The Home has been and must continue to be a stronghold of Jewish life hallowed by the spirit of love and reverence, by moral discipline and religious observance and worship.

The Synagogue is the oldest and most democratic institution in Jewish life. It is the prime communal agency by which Judaism is fostered and preserved. It links the Jews of each community and unites them with all Israel.

The perpetuation of Judaism as a living force depends upon religious knowledge and upon the education of each new generation in our rich cultural and spiritual heritage.

Prayer is the voice of religion, the language of faith and aspiration. It directs man's heart and mind Godward, voices the needs and hopes of the community and reaches out after goals which invest life with supreme value. To deepen the spiritual life of our people, we must cultivate the traditional habit of communion with God through prayer in both home and synagogue.

Judaism as a way of life requires, in addition to its moral and spiritual demands, the preservation of the Sabbath, festivals and Holy Days, the retention and development of such customs, symbols and ceremonies as possess inspirational value, the cultivation of distinctive forms of religious art and music and the use of Hebrew, together with the vernacular, in our worship and instruction.

These timeless aims and ideals of our faith we present to a confused and troubled world. We call upon our fellow Jews to rededicate themselves to them and, in harmony with all men, hopefully and courageously to continue Israel's eternal quest after God and His kingdom.

Notes: *The Columbus Platform replaced the earlier Pittsburgh Platform (1885), the prime positional statement of Reform Judaism. Among the most important changes in this new document, Zionism (the return of Jews to Palestine) was affirmed. The Platform also welcomed non-Jews to accept the Jewish faith.*

*   *   *

Black Judaism

THE TWELVE PRINCIPLES OF THE DOCTRINES OF ISRAEL WITH SCRIPTURAL PROOF [COMMANDMENT KEEPERS CONGREGATION OF THE LIVING GOD (BLACK JEWS)]

Principle No. 1. *The New Creation.*—Gen. 1:1, 5; Ez. 14:6; Isa. 28:11, 12; Ez. 36:26, 28; Ez. 14:26, 31; Jer. 31:31; Joel 2:28-39; Mal. 1:2

Principle No. 2. *The Observance of All the Laws of God, Given to Us Through Moses Our Teacher.*—Gen. 2:1, 3; Ex. 31:18, 32, 15, 16; Deut. 29:29; Isa. 58:13, 14; Dan. 7:25; Ez. 8:16; Num. 15:32, 33; Psalm 1:1, 4; Ez. 46:1

Principle No. 3. *Divine Healing.*—Ex. 23:25; Ex. 15:26; Psalm 103:1, 3; Isa. 53:4, 5; Psalm 41:2, 4; Jer. 8:22; 2 Chron. 30:20; Psalm 107:20; Hos. 7:1

Principle No. 4. *The Administration of Feet Washing and All the Rites of the Passover.*—Gen. 18:3; Gen. 19:2; 43:24; 34:32

Principle No. 5. *Tithes and Offerings; the Early Duty of the People of God.*—Gen. 14:18, 20; 28:20, 22; Lev. 27:30, 32; Mal. 3:8, 12; Neh. 10:37, 39; Deut. 14:21; Hag. 1:1, 6

Principle No. 6. *The Eating of Koshered Foods According to Israel's Law.*—Lev. 11:1, 12; Deut. 14:2, 3; Isa. 65:4-5; 66:17

Principle No. 7. *Everlasting Life.*—Gen. 5:24; 2 Kings 2:11; Hos. 13:13, 14; Psalm 49:6, 9; 118:17; Prov. 7:1, 3, 23; 6:23

Principle No. 8. *Absolute Holiness According to the Law of God.*—Gen. 17:1; Exod. 3:5; Deut. 14:2; Ex. 19:6; Lev. 10:10; 20:7; Psalm 86:2; Isaiah 6:3; 35:8

Principle No. 9. *The Resurrection of the Dead (Black Israel).*—Hos. 13:13, 14; Ezra 37:11, 12; Job 14:5-14, 15; 19:26; Isaiah 35:10; Ezek. 37

Principle No. 10. *The Restoration of Israel.*—Isa. 1:26; Jer. 30:17, 18; 27:22; Joel 2:25; Isa. 11:10, 11, 12; Jer. 31:31, 34

Principle No. 11. *The Coming of the Messiah.*—Deut. 18:15, 18, 19; Mal. 3:1; Isa. 41:2, 3, 4; Isa. 9:6, 7

Principle No. 12. *The Theocratic Age.*—Gen. 49:9-10; Isa. 11:1; 5:9-10

Notes: *These principles were "codified" by Rabbi Arthur Wentworth Matthew, the founder of the Commandment Keepers, a black Jewish synagogue in New York City.*

*   *   *

BLACK CHRISTIAN NATIONALIST CREED (PAN AFRICAN ORTHODOX CHRISTIAN CHURCH)

I Believe, that human society stands under the judgement of one God, revealed to all and known by many names. His creative power is visible in the mysteries of the universe, in the revolutionary Holy Spirit which will not long permit men to endure injustice nor to wear the shackles of bondage, in the rage of the powerless when they struggle to be free, and in the violence and conflict which even now threaten to level the hills and the mountains.

I Believe that Jesus, the Black Messiah, was a revolutionary leader, sent by God to rebuild the Black Nation Israel and to liberate Black People from powerlessness and from the oppression, brutality, and exploitation of the white gentile world.

I Believe that the revolutionary spirit of God, embodied in the Black Messiah, is born anew in each generation and that Black Christian Nationalists constitute the living remnant of God's Chosen People in this day, and are

141

BLACK CHRISTIAN NATIONALIST CREED (PAN AFRICAN ORTHODOX CHRISTIAN CHURCH) (continued)

charged by him with responsibility for the Liberation of Black People.

I Believe that both my survival and my salvation depend upon my willingness to reject INDIVIDUALISM and so I commit my life to the Liberation Struggle of Black People and accept the values, ethics, morals and program of the Black Nation, defined by that struggle, and taught by the Pan-African Orthodox Christian Church.

Notes: *The Pan African Orthodox Christian Church is a Christian church with a creedal statement very much in line with the nationalism of Black Judaism, which has always had an ambivalent relationship to traditional Christianity.*

* * *

Miscellaneous Jewish Groups

I BELIEVE (RABBI JOSEPH H. GELBERMAN, LITTLE SYNAGOGUE)

1. I believe that most of my beliefs are not necessarily in harmony with the truth, as I believe with P.P. Quimby, that man is made up of beliefs and truths.

2. I believe that there is an eleventh commandment which states: *Thou shalt have purpose.*

3. I believe that my purpose in life is to be *totally alive,* i.e., to express the basic principles inherent in the five letters of the word *alive:* to be Aware, to be Loving, to be Intuitive, to be Victorious, to be Enthusiastic about every nuance of life.

4. I believe in the separation of Rabbi and Synagogue. Like the Talmudic Rabbis we should never have an employer-employee relationship with any congregation.

5. I believe that there is a special purpose for my life: twice I have been miraculously saved.

6. I believe that whatever I am, I have chosen to be that way.

7. I believe that the purpose of my life is to grow in four ways simultaneously: physically, emotionally, intellectually and spiritually.

8. I believe that my Karma in life is to be Jewish i.e. to be a joyous Jew.

9. I believe in reincarnation, who I was and who I shall be are already combined in that which I am now.

10. I believe in the partnership with God as the mystery of Creation. It is I and God that can and will finish the creation.

11. I believe in the joy of life though I'm not always happy. *Joy* and *Happiness* are two different concepts. Joy is inner centered, happiness is outer centered.

12. I believe in the importance of tradition, therefore, my basic philosophy of life is: *Never instead, always in addition.*

13. I believe that my aim in life is not to become a saint, certainly not a sinner, but a sage. I'm not a machine, ergo, not programmed, but respond spontaneously to each situation as it happens with wisdom and justice.

14. I believe that the Kabbalah wisdom is an integral part of Torah and my religion and therefore it is to be shared with all who are willing to pursue it.

15. I believe that I am responsible for the actions of my life and therefore, as a responsible person, can transmute my erroneous ways to the will of God.

16. I believe that there is a part of God's soul in me which I call Neshamah which yearns to be Godlike and thus try to overcome doubt, discouragement and temptation.

17. I believe that it is important for me to express daily my gratitude to my parents who imbued in me the love of Torah — wisdom, a sense of responsibility and a sense of virtue and piety.

18. I believe in the concept of Kitov — that life is basically good and therefore I am to search for the joy and goodness in life.

19. I believe that being created in the image of God means that I am meant to express my Godlikeness in terms of loving all my fellow beings regardless of race, creed or nationality.

20. I believe that:

    I am the reality of things that seem

    I am the waking who am called the dream

    I am the utmost height there is to climb

    I am stability, all else will pass

    I am eternity encircling time

    Kill me, none may, conquer me, nothing can

    I am God's soul fused in the heart of man

21. Finally, I believe in Interfaith as a means to reach out to my fellow beings and tell them: *Please trust me, hold my hand and let's walk together to the mountain of the Lord and listen to His words addressed to each one of us: 'You are all my beloved children and I love all of you.'*

Notes: *Rabbi Joseph H. Gelberman of the Little Synagogue has attempted to build a Judaism that draws upon Hassidic, New Thought, and New Age traditions and is open to non-Jewish religion. In the opening paragraph of this personal statement, he refers to Phineas Parkhurst Quimby, the New England mental healer often cited as the founder of New Thought.*

* * *

AFFIRMATIONS FOR HUMANISTIC JEWS (SHERWIN T. WINE, SOCIETY FOR HUMANISTIC JUDAISM)

Humanistic Jews want to bring their beliefs and their behavior together and to find their integrity. They are eager to affirm:

That they are disciples of the Secular Revolution.

That the Secular Revolution was good for the Jews.

That reason is the best method for the discovery of truth.

That morality derives from human needs and is the defense of human dignity.

That the universe is indifferent to the desires and aspirations of human beings.

That people must ultimately rely on people.

That Jewish history is a testimony to the absence of God and the necessity of human self-esteem.

That Jewish identity is valuable because it connects them to that history.

That Jewish personality flows from that history — and not from official texts that seek to describe it.

That Jewish identity serves individual dignity — and not the reverse.

That the Jewish people is an international family that has its center in Israel and its roots in the Diaspora.

That the humanistic Gentile has a positive role to play in the life of the Jewish people.

Notes: *These affirmations were written by Rabbi Sherwin T. Wine, head of the Humanistic congregation in suburban Detroit, Michigan. Although not an official document, the statement expresses the secular religiosity of the Society for Humanistic Judaism.*

*   *   *

FUNDAMENTALS (SOCIETY OF JEWISH SCIENCE)

1. The Jewish faith is the only faith we acknowledge. Jewish Science is the application of the Jewish Faith to the practices of life.

2. We believe wholeheartedly in the efficacy of prayer. We believe that no prayer, when properly offered, goes unanswered.

3. We shall endeavor every day of our lives to keep serene; to check all tendencies to violence and anger; to keep calm even in the face of unpleasant and discouraging circumstances.

4. We shall strive to be cheerful every day of our lives. The Talmud says that the Divine Presence departs from one who is in gloom. It is God's design that man should find joy and cheer in his existence on this earth.

5. We shall seek to cultivate an attitude of love and good-will towards everyone. We shall make no room in our heart for hatred or bitterness. The world was created on a plan of divine love, and to admit thoughts of hatred or malice is to violate the plan of God.

6. We shall cultivate a disposition to contentment, envying no one, and praising God for the good he has already bestowed upon us. Contentment is the greatest friend of happiness; envy, its greatest enemy.

7. We shall make conscious effort to banish worry and fear from our lives. We regard these two as the greatest enemies of mankind and give them no place in our consciousness.

8. We shall trust in God's goodness in every circumstance of our life.

9. We believe that death is an elevation to eternal life, and not a cessation of existence.

10. We believe that God is the Source of Health and the Restorer of Health.

11. In these fundamentals, we, in Jewish Science, profess our wholehearted belief in the efficacy of prayer; we acknowledge the duty of keeping serene and cheerful, of cherishing good-will and contentment, of banishing worry and fear; we declare our trust in God's goodness and love; we profess our assurance of immortality because we have faith in God's loving-kindness and the everlastingness of His creations.

Notes: *Rabbi Joshua Lichtenstein attempted to build a metaphysical Judaism that would function in the Jewish community much as Christian Science did in the larger context of American society. In his basic textbook, he outlined a declaration of the ideals by which Jewish Scientists (metaphysicians) were to govern their lives day by day.*

Islam

THE FUNDAMENTAL ARTICLES OF FAITH IN ISLAM [HAMMUDAH ABD AL-ATI (SUNNI ISLAM)]

A faithful Muslim believes in the following principal articles of faith:

1. He believes in One God, Supreme and Eternal, Infinite and Mighty, Merciful and Compassionate, Creator and Provider. This belief, in order to be effective, requires complete trust and hope in God, submission to His Will and reliance on His aid. It secures man's dignity and saves him from fear and despair, from wrong and confusion. The reader is invited to see the meaning of Islam as explained above.

2. He believes in all the messengers of God without any discrimination between them. Every known nation had a warner or messenger from God. These messengers were great teachers of the good and true champions of the right. They were chosen by God to teach mankind and deliver His Divine message. They were sent at different times of history and every known nation had one messenger or more. During certain periods two or more messengers were sent by God at the same time to the same nation. The Holy Qur'an mentions the names of twenty-five of them, and a Muslim believes in them all and accepts them as authorized messengers of God. They were, with the exception of Muhammad, known as "national" or local messengers. But their message, their religion, was basically the same and was called ISLAM; because it came from One and the Same Source, namely, God, to serve one and the same purpose, and

that is to guide humanity to the Straight Path of God. All the messengers with no exception whatsoever were mortals, human beings, endowed with Divine revelations and appointed by God to perform certain tasks. Among them Muhammad stands as the Last Messenger and the crowning glory of the foundation of prophethood. This is not an arbitrary attitude, nor is it just a convenient belief. Like all the other Islamic beliefs, it is an authentic and logical truth. Also, it may be useful to mention here the names of some of the great messengers like Noah and Abraham, Ishmael and Moses, Jesus and Muhammad, may the peace and blessings of God be upon them all. The Qur'an says:

"Say you: 'We believe in God, and the revelation given to us, and to Abraham, Ishmael, Isaac, Jacob and the Tribes; and that which was given to Moses and Jesus, and that which was given to all prophets from their Lord. We make no difference between one and another of them, and we bow to God (in Islam).'" (Qur'an 2:136, cf. 3:84; 4:163-165; 6:84-87)

3. A true Muslim believes, as a result of article number two, in all the scriptures and revelations of God. They were the guiding light which the messengers received to show their respective peoples the Right Path of God. In the Qur'an a special reference is made to the books of Abraham, Moses, David and Jesus. But long before the revelation of the Qur'an to Muhammad some of those books and revelations had been lost or interpolated, some neglected or concealed. The only authentic and complete book of God in existence today is the Qur'an. In principle a Muslim believes in the previous books and revelations. But where are their complete and original versions? They could be still at the bottom of the Dead Sea, and there may be more Scrolls to be discovered. Or perhaps more information about them will become available when the Christian and Jewish archaeologists reveal to the public the complete original findings of their continued excavations in the Holy Land. For a Muslim, there is no problem of that kind. The Qur'an is in his hand complete and authentic. Nothing of it is missing and no more of it is expected. Its authenticity is beyond doubt, and no serious scholar or thinker has ventured to question its genuineness. The Qur'an was made so by God Who revealed it and made it incumbent upon Himself to protect it against interpolation and corruption of all kinds. Thus it is given to the Muslims as the standard or criterion by which all the other books are judged. So whatever agrees with the Qur'an is accepted as Divine truth, and whatever differs from the Qur'an is either rejected or suspended. God says: "Verily We have, without doubt, sent down the Qur'an; and We will assuredly guard it (from corruption). (Qur'an 15:9; Cf. 2:75-79; 5:13-14 and 41. See also references in (2) above.)

4. A true Muslim believes in the angels of God. They are purely spiritual and splendid beings whose nature requires no food or drink nor sleep. They have no physical desires of any kind or material needs, but spend their days and nights in the service of God. There are many of them, and each one is charged with a certain duty. If we cannot see the angels with our naked eyes, it does not necessarily deny their actual existence. There are many things in the world that are invisible to the eye or inaccessible to the senses, yet we do believe in their existence. There are places we have never seen and things like gas and ether that we could not see with our naked eyes, smell or touch or taste or hear; yet we do acknowledge their existence. Belief in the angels originates from the Islamic principle that knowledge and truth are not entirely confined to the sensory knowledge or sensory perception alone. (Qur'an 16:49-50; 21:19-20. See also references in (2) above.)

5. A true Muslim believes in the Last Day of Judgement. This world will come to an end some day, and the dead will rise to stand for their final and fair trial. Everything we do in this world, every intention we have, every move we make, every thought we entertain, and every word we say, all are counted and kept in accurate records. On the Day of Judgement they will be brought up. People with good records will be generously rewarded and warmly welcomed to the Heaven of God, and those with bad records will be severely punished and cast into Hell. The real nature of Heaven and Hell and the exact description of them are known to God only. There are descriptions of Heaven and Hell in the Qur'an and the Traditions of Muhammad but they should not be taken literally. In Heaven, said Muhammad, there are things which no eye has ever seen, no ear has ever heard, and no mind has ever conceived. However, the Muslim believes that there definitely will be compensation and reward for the good deeds, and punishment for the evil ones. That is the Day of Justice and final settlement of all accounts.

If some people think that they are shrewd enough and can get away with their wrong doings, just as they sometimes escape the penalty of the mundane laws, they are wrong, they will not be able to do so on the Day of Judgement. They will be caught right on the spot defenceless, without any lawyer or counsel to stand in their behalf. All their deeds are visible to God and counted by His agents. Also, if some pious people do good deeds to please God and seem to get no appreciation or acknowledgement in this temporary world, they will eventually receive full compensation and be widely acknowledged on That Day. Absolute Justice will be done to all.

Belief in the Day of Judgement is the final relieving answer to many complicated problems of our world. There are people who commit sins, neglect God and indulge in immoral activities, yet they seem to be "superficially" successful in business and prosperous in life. And there are virtuous and God-minded people, yet they seem to be getting less rewards for their sincere efforts and more suffering in the present world. This is puzzling and incompatible with the Justice of God. If the guilty people can escape the mundane law unharmed and, on top of that, be more prosperous, what is, then, left for the virtuous people? What will promote the cause of morality and goodness? There must be some way to reward goodness and arrest evil. If this is not done here on this earth—and we know it is not done regularly or immediately—it has to be done some day, and that is the Day of Judgement. This is not to condone injustice or tolerate mischief in this world, but is to warn the deviants from the Right Path and remind them that the Justice of God shall run its full course sooner or later. (See, for example, the previous references of the Qur'an.)

6. A true Muslim believes in the timeless knowledge of God and in His power to plan and execute His plans. God is not indifferent to this world nor is He neutral to it. His knowledge and power are in action at all times to keep order in His vast domain and maintain full command over His creation. He is Wise and Loving, and whatever He does must have a good motive and a meaningful purpose. If this is established in our minds, we should accept with good Faith all that He does, although we may fail to understand it fully, or even think it is bad. We should have strong Faith in Him and accept whatever He does because our knowledge is limited and our thinking is based on individual or personal considerations, whereas His knowledge is limitless and He plans on a universal basis.

This does not in any way make man fatalist or predestinarian. It simply draws the demarcation line between what is God's concern and what is man's responsibility. Because we are by nature finite and limited, we have a finite and limited degree of power and freedom. We cannot do everything, and He graciously holds us responsible only for the things we do. The things which we cannot do, or things which He Himself does, are not in the realm of our responsibility. He is Just and has given us limited power to match our finite nature and limited responsibility. On the other hand, the timeless knowledge and power of God to execute His plans do not prevent us from making our own plans in our own limited sphere of power. On the contrary, He exhorts us to think, to plan and to make sound choices, but if things do not happen the way we wanted or planned them, we should not lose Faith or surrender ourselves to mental strains and shattering worries. We should try again and again, and if the results are not satisfactory, then we know that we have tried our best and cannot be held responsible for the results, because what is beyond our capacity and responsibility is the affair of God alone. Muslims call this article of Faith the belief in "Qudaa" and "Qadar", which simply means, in other words, that the Timeless Knowledge of God anticipates events, and that events take place according to the exact

Knowledge of God. (Qur'an, for example, 18:29; 41:46; 53:33-62; 54:49; 65:3; 76:30-31.)

7. A true Muslim believes that God's creation is meaningful and that life has a sublime purpose beyond the physical needs and material activities of man. The purpose of life is to worship God. This does not simply mean that we have to spend our entire lives in constant seclusion and absolute meditation. To worship God is to know Him; to love Him; to obey His commandments; to enforce His law in every aspect of life; to serve His cause by doing the right and shunning the evil; and to be just to Him, to ourselves, and to our fellow human beings. To worship God is to "live" life not to run away from it. In brief, to worship God is to imbue ourselves with His Supreme Attributes. This is by no means a simple statement, nor is it an over-simplification of the matter. It is most comprehensive and conclusive. So if life has a purpose and if man is created to serve that purpose, then he cannot escape the responsibility. He cannot deny his existence or ignore the vital role he has to play. When God charges him with any responsibility, He provides him with all the required assistance. He endows him with intelligence and power to choose his course of conduct. Man, thus, is strongly recommended by God to exert his utmost to fully serve the purpose of his existence. Should he fail to do that, or misuse his life or neglect his duties, he shall be responsible to God for his wrong deeds. (See, for example, the Qur'an 51:56-58.)

8. A true Muslim believes that man enjoys an especially high-ranking status in the hierarchy of all the known creatures. He occupies this distinguished position because he alone is gifted with rational faculties and spiritual aspirations as well as powers of action. But the more his rank excels, the more his responsibility grows. He occupies the position of God's viceroy on earth. The person who is appointed by God to be His active agent, must necessarily have some power and authority, and be, at least potentially, endowed with honour and integrity. And this is the status of man in Islam; not a condemned race from birth to death, but a dignified being potentially capable of good and noble achievements. The fact that God chose His messengers from the human race shows that man is trustworthy and capable, and that he can acquire immense treasures of goodness. (Qur'an 2:30-34; 6:165; 7:11; 17:70-72 and 90-95.)

9. A true Muslim believes that every person is born "Muslim." This means that the very course of birth takes place in accordance with the Will of God, in realization of His plans and in submission to His Commands. It also means that every person is endowed with spiritual potentialities and intellectual inclinations that can make him a good Muslim, if he has the right access to Islam and is left to develop his innate nature. Many people can readily accept Islam if it is properly presented to them, because it is the Divine formula for those who want to satisfy their moral and spiritual needs as well as their natural aspirations and want to lead a constructive and

sound life whether personal or social, national or international; whether spiritual or socio-economic. This is so because Islam is the universal religion of God, the Maker of human nature, Who knows what is best for human nature. (Qur'an 30:30; 64:1-3; 82:6-8.)

10. A true Muslim believes that every person is born free from sin and good, like a blank book. When the person reaches the age of maturity he becomes accountable for his deeds and intentions, if his development is normal and if he is sane. Man is not only free from sin until he commits sin, but he is also free to do things according to his plans on his own responsibility. This dual freedom: freedom from sin and freedom to do effective things, clears the Muslim's conscience from the heavy pressure of Inherited Sin. It relieves his soul and mind from the unnecessary strains of the Doctrine of Original Sin.

This Islamic concept of freedom is based upon the principle of God's justice and the individual's direct responsibility to God. Each person must bear his own burden and be responsible for his own actions, because no one can expiate for another's sin. Thus, a Muslim believes that if Adam had committed the First Sin, it was his own responsibility to expiate for that sin. To assume that God was unable to forgive Adam and had to make somebody else expiate for his sin, or to assume that Adam did not pray for pardon or prayed for it but it was not granted, would be extremely illogical and contrary to God's mercy and justice as well as to His attribute of forgiveness and power to forgive. To assume the said hypothesis, would be an audacious defiance of common sense and flagrant violation of the very concept of God. (See the reference in article 9 above, and Qur'an 41:46; 45:15; 53:31-42; 74:38.)

On this rational basis as well as on the authority of the Qur'an a Muslim believes that Adam realized what he had committed and prayed to God for pardon, like any other sensible sinner would. It is also on the same basis, a Muslim believes, that God the Forgiving and Merciful granted Adam pardon. (Qur'an 2:35-37; 20:117-122.) Hence, a Muslim cannot possibly accept the doctrine that Adam with the whole human race had been condemned and unforgiven until Jesus came to expiate for their sins. Consequently, a Muslim cannot entrtain the romantic story of Jesus' death on the cross just to do away with all human sins once and for all.

Here the reader must be cautioned against any wrong conclusions. A Muslim does not believe in the crucifixion of Jesus by his enemies because the basis of this doctrine of crucifixion is contrary to Divine mercy and justice as much as it is to human logic and dignity. Such a disbelief in the doctrine does not in any way devaluate the Muslim's reverence for Jesus, or degrade the high status of Jesus in Islam, or even shake the Muslim's belief in Jesus as a distinguished prophet of God. On the contrary, by rejecting this doctrine the Muslim accepts Jesus but only with more esteem and higher respect, and looks upon his original message as an essential part of Islam. So let it be stated, again, that to be a Muslim a person must accept and respect all the prophets of God without any discrimination. The general status of Jesus in Islam will be further discussed in a later chapter.

11. A true Muslim believes that man must work out his salvation through the guidance of God. This means that in order to attain salvation a person must combine Faith and action, belief and practice. Faith without action is as insufficient as action without Faith. In other words, no one can attain salvation until his Faith in God becomes dynamic in his life and his beliefs are translated into reality. This is in complete harmony with the other Islamic articles of Faith. It shows that God does not accept lip service, and that no true believer can be indifferent as far as the practical requirements of Faith are concerned. It also shows that no one can act on behalf of another or intercede between him and God. (See, for example, the Qur'an 10:9-10; 18:30; 103:1-3.)

12. A true Muslim believes that God does not hold any person responsible until He has shown him the Right Way. This is why God has sent many messengers and revelations, and made it clear that there would be no punishment before issuing a guidance and sounding the alarm. So, a person who has never come across any Divine revelations or messenger, or a person who is insane is not held responsible to God for failing to obey the Divine instructions. Such a person will be responsible only for not doing what his sound common sense tells him to be good and right. But the person who knowingly and intentionally violates the Law of God or deviates from His Right Path will be punished for his wrong deeds. (Qur'an 4:165; 5:16 & 21; 17:15.)

This point is very important for every Muslim. There are many people in the world who have not heard of Islam and have no way of knowing about it. Such people may be honest and may become good Muslims, if they find their way to Islam. If they do not know and have no way of knowing, they will not be responsible for failing to be Muslims. Instead, the Muslims who can present Islam to such people will be the ones responsible for failing to invite them to Islam and show them what Islam is. This calls upon every Muslim throughout the globe not only to preach Islam in words but to live according to it and let others see it in action and practice. (See, for example, the Qur'an 3:104; 16:125.)

13. A true Muslim believes that in human nature, which God created, there is more good than evil, and the probability of successful reform is greater than the probability of hopeless failure. This belief is derived from the fact that God has tasked man with certain assignments and sent messengers with revelations for his guidance. If man were by nature a hopeless case, impossible to reform, and without expectation of any

good from him, how could God with His absolute wisdom assign him responsibilities and invite him to do or shun certain things? How could God do that, if it were all in vain? The fact that God cares for man and takes a stand in his interest proves that man is neither helpless nor hopeless, but is more appreciative of and inclined to good than otherwise. Surely with sound Faith in God and due confidence in man miracles can be worked out, even in our own times. To understand this properly, one has to carefully study the relevant passages in the Qur'an and reflect on their meanings.

14. A true Muslim believes that Faith is not complete when it is followed blindly or accepted unquestioningly unless the professor of such a faith is fully satisfied. If Faith is to inspire action, and if Faith and action are to lead to salvation, then Faith must be founded on unshakeable convictions without any deception or compulsion. In other words, the person who calls himself a Muslim because of his family traditions, or accepts Islam out of fear or under coercion or blind imitation is not a complete Muslim in the sight of God. A Muslim must build his Faith on well-grounded convictions beyond any reasonable doubt and above uncertainty. If he is not certain about his Faith, he is invited by God to search in the open book of Nature, to use his reasoning powers, and to reflect on the teachings of the Qur'an. He must search for the indisputable truth until he finds it, and he will certainly find it, if he is capable and serious enough. (See, for example, the Qur'an 2:170; 43:22-24.)

This is why Islam demands sound convictions and opposes blind imitation. Every person who is duly qualified as a genuine and earnest thinker is enjoined by Islam to employ his faculties to the fullest extent. But if a person is unqualified or uncertain of himself, he should pursue his thinking only as far as his limits can take him. It will be quite in order for such a person to rely only on the authentic sources of religion, which are sufficient in themselves, without applying to them any critical questioning of which he is incapable. The point is that no one can call himself a true Muslim unless his Faith is based on strong convictions and his mind is clear from doubts. Because Islam is complete only when it is based on strong convictions and freedom of choice, it cannot be forced upon anybody, for God will not accept this forced faith. Nor will He consider it a true Islam if it does not develop from within or originate from free and sound convictions. And because Islam insures freedom of belief many non-Muslim groups lived and still live in the Islamic countries enjoying full freedom of belief and conscience. Muslims take this attitude because Islam forbids compulsion in religion. It is the light which must radiate from within, because in Islam no one can make up another's mind. This does not exempt the parents from responsibility for their children. Nor does it condone their being indifferent to the spiritual welfare of their

dependents. In fact, they should do everything possible to help theirs build a strong inspiring faith.

To establish Faith on sound grounds, there are various parallel avenues. There is the Spiritual approach which is based mainly on the Qur'an and the Traditions of Muhammad. There is also the rational approach which eventually leads to Faith in the Supreme Being. This is not to say that the Spiritual approach lacks sound rationality. Nor is the rational approach deprived of inspiring spirituality. Both approaches, in fact, overlap one another and may well become in a state of lively interaction. Now if a person is sufficiently equipped with sound rational qualities, he may resort to the rational approach or to the Spiritual approach or to both, and may be confident that his conclusion will be right. But if a person is incapable of profound inquiry or is uncertain of his reasoning powers, he may confine himself to the Spiritual approach and be contented with the knowledge he can derive from the authentic sources of religion. The point is that whether one uses the Spiritual approach or the rational technique or both, one will in the end come to Faith in God. All these avenues are equally important and accepted by Islam, and, when properly channelled, lead to the same end, namely, Faith in the Supreme Being.

15. A true Muslim believes that the Qur'an is the word of God revealed to Muhammad through the agency of the Angel Gabriel. The Qur'an was revealed from God piece by piece on various occasions to answer certain questions, solve certain problems, settle certain disputes, and to be man's best guide to the truth of God and eternal happiness. Every letter in the Qur'an is the word of God, and every sound in it is the true echo of God's voice. The Qur'an is the First and most authentic Source of Islam. It was revealed in Arabic. It is still and will remain in its original and complete Arabic version, because God has made it His concern to preserve the Qur'an, to make it always the best guide for man, and to safeguard it against corruption. (See, for example, the Qur'an 4:82; 15:9; 17:9; 41:41-44; 42:7, 52-53.)

In testimony to God's conservation, the Qur'an is the only Scripture in human history that has been preserved in its complete and original version without the slightest change in style or even punctuations. The history of recording the Qur'an, compiling its chapters and conserving its text is beyond any doubt not only in the minds of Muslims but also in the minds of honest and serious scholars. This is a historical fact which no scholar from any faith—who respects his knowledge and integrity—has ever questioned. As a matter of fact, it is Muhammad's standing miracle that if all mankind were to work together they could not produce the like of one Qur'anic chapter. (Qur'an 2:22-24; 11:13-14; 17:88-89.)

16. A true Muslim believes in a clear distinction between the Qur'an and the Traditions of Muhammad. The Qur'an is the word of God whereas the Traditions of

THE FUNDAMENTAL ARTICLES OF FAITH IN ISLAM [HAMMUDAH ABD AL-ATI (SUNNI ISLAM)] (continued)

Muhammad are the practical interpretations of the Qur'an. The role of Muhammad was to convey the Qur'an as he received it, to interpret it, and to practise it fully. His interpretations and practises produced what is known as the Traditions of Muhammad. They are considered the Second Source of Islam and must be in complete harmony with the First Source, namely, the Qur'an, which is the Standard and the Criterion. If there be any contradiction or inconsistency between any of the Traditions and the Qur'an, the Muslim adheres to the Qur'an alone and regards everything else as open to question because no genuine Tradition of Muhammad can ever disagree with the Qur'an or be opposed to it.

REMARKS

In this discussion of the cardinal articles of Faith in Islam, I have deliberately differed from the Traditional view on the subject. I did not confine them to five or six articles. Instead, I tried to include as many Principles as was possible. But it should be pointed out here that all the articles of Faith mentioned above are based upon and derived from the teachings of the Qur'an and the Traditions of Muhammad. I could have quoted more verses from the Qur'an and many parts of the Traditions to show the foundation of these articles of Faith. This was not done because of the limitations of space. However, the Qur'an and the Traditions of Muhammad are available references for any detailed study.

I have also kept to a minimum the use of Western terminology and technical language like predestination, fatalism, free will and so on. This was done deliberately because I wanted to avoid confusion and technicalities. Most of the technical terms used in religion among non-Arabic speaking people lead to misunderstanding, when applied to Islam, and give wrong impressions. I realize that I could not serve the purpose of this work if foreign religious terms were adopted and applied to Islam. If I were to use the alien religious terminology here, I would have had to add many qualifications and comments to clarify the picture of Islam. This also would have required much more space which I could not possibly afford under the circumstances. So, I tried to explain things in ordinary simple language, and this same course will be followed in the remainder of the book.

Notes: *Like Judaism, Islam has not produced creedal statements in any profusion. Translated from the Arabic, Islam's basic creedal statement is as follows: "There is no God but Allah. Muhammad is His Messenger." There are also five beliefs commonly presented as Articles of Faith in North American Islamic literature. For Sunni Muslims, these are: 1) Belief in the Unity of God; 2) Belief in God's Angels; 3) Belief in Books of God; 4) Belief in God's Prophets; 5) Belief in Life after Death. These articles have been expanded upon in the Fundamental Articles of Faith in Islam. This statement of Islamic belief written by Hammudah Abd Al-Ati, director of the Canadian Islamic Center in Edmonton, Alberta, was included in his book*

Islam in Focus. The book is popular among North American Sunni Muslims and has been reprinted on several occasions. In the remarks at the end of the Articles, the author explains his method in producing them.

*　　*　　*

ARTICLES OF FAITH [SAIYADUL ULAMA (SHI'A ISLAM)]

ARTICLES OF FAITH

The fundamental principles of Islam are five:

1. *Tauhid* i.e. Belief in the Unity of God.
2. *'Adl* i.e. Belief in Divine Justice.
3. *Nubuwat* i.e. Belief in the Apostles of God.
4. *Imamat* i.e. Belief in the viceregents of the Prophet.
5. *Ma'ad* i.e. Belief in the Day of Judgement.

Let us take one by one in regular sequence. Tauhid comes first. This is the foundation stone of religion. It draws attention towards God Who is the Creator and the Central Figure for the entire humanity. God is the Creator. Man is His creation. This leads to the idea that all men are equal by right of birth, and answerable to their Creator for their acts. They cannot freely indulge in their passions and work at cross-purposes. By virtue of this faith the entire humanity is strung into one thread. Differences of race, country, caste and colour are shed. All being subject to the same Power should act in conformity and have common religious outlook. The Creator is Omnipotent and Omnipresent. Minutest movements of man cannot escape His notice; man should therefore beware of neglecting His laws and should not be elated at his unobserved misdeed. Certainly it is noted by Him Who alone has the power to reward and to punish. He is the Sole Master. His pleasure should be the chief concern of man and he should dread to incur His displeasure. He is the Mightiest. Man should not be awed by the might of any earthly soul. God alone can help man achieve his object—no task, however difficult should therefore be deemed unsurmountable. He alone is the Prop of the weak. One should not despair of one's weakness. This faith leads to the conception of a vast human brotherhood every unit of which should be imbued with the feeling of unity and equality among them and should jointly and individually march towards the common goal for all, set by Him and should strictly observe religious tenets and always pray for His aid in joint or individual undertakings. People of such faith will have self-respect enough not to humble themselves before any material power and confidence enough never to despair. These are the qualities that become great people for their march onward.

DIVINE JUSTICE ('ADL)

It is part and parcel of the faith in the Unity of God. God's acts are all just and good. There can be no shadow of evil in His acts. Every act of His is full of wisdom and foresight. The justness of His actions demands justice from man in his acts. He has made man master of his acts. This is a gift from Him to man. Man should utilize this gift with the utmost propriety. The opposite of justice is tyranny. Tyrants override God's Law and God has condemned them.

The faith in the justness of God's actions cements the foundations of the mutual rights of the members of the vast human brotherhood stated above. None of the members of that society would look down upon the others. They would know that differences of positions in this world are ephemeral and that in the eye of God all are equal. He will reward and punish the rich and the poor alike for their good and bad deeds—Wealth or poverty of man in this world would not weigh with Him in meeting out justice. This faith creates in man the feeling of performing his duties justly and to weigh his deeds.

God does not countenance extremes. Moderation is perfection. Belief in Divine Justice teaches moderation to man. Those who do not overstep the limits of moderation can rightly be called just and they are Muslims in the true sense of the word.

THE INSTITUTION OF PROPHETS (NUBUWAT)

Belief in the prophets is the third essential of Islam. A Prophet is the vice-regent of God on earth. He communicates God's commands to man. No one has a right to question those commands or criticise a Prophet's decisions. A prophet is the best model of all that is good in character and standard. Human weaknesses like partiality, selfishness, egotism and hankering after position are to a great extent mastered by His true adherents and in this lies the secret of the well being of humanity. He is infallible.

IMAMAT

A prophet like any man is mortal. If after the demise of a prophet man is left without a guide the evils a man is prone to will raise their heads again. All the order that the Prophet had brought about will be disrupted. Appointment of Imams checks this disruption. Man knows that after the death of a prophet there is a central figure to help him stick to the right path. An Imam is a model of perfection himself and well versed in Divine Law. Like a prophet is also infallible. Loyalty to the Imam is as essential as loyalty to the Prophet. He alone becomes the central figure after the death of the Prophet.

There comes a time, like the present, when access to the Imam is an impossibility. The recognised scholars who have mastered the teachings of the Prophet and Imams, the successors of the Prophet, are then to be approached and the instructions and orders given by them according to the Qur'an and Sunnat to be strictly followed. The order set up in pursuance of such instructions will be the Islamic order.

The arrangement stated above is sufficient proof that Islam admits the necessity of a central figure. The status, however, of this central figure is not ethical but Divine. His sway will be on the hearts of his followers who will always hold God to be the real Sovereign and the worldly formed kingdom to be nothing.

Of course loyalty to the earthly ruler cannot be avoided. Necessities for the protection of life, property and for maintenance of peace demand it. But this ruler can neither be Eternal nor Divine.

Islam lays down no foundation for material rule. It makes arrangements for the perfection of man and shapes people who may be counted model men under the guidance of the Prophet, his nominated successors and scholars of religion.

RESURRECTION

Having made all arrangements for the guidance of man reward to those who obey the guides and punishment to those who disobey is the demand of God's justice; otherwise there can be no difference between the pious and the impious. The Day fixed for this is called the Day of Judgment.

The above essentials show that they are so well-connected links of Divine arrangement that if any of them is suppressed the entire edifice will tumble down.

The aim of all the essentials is to recognise the absolute Sovereignty of God and not to humble our selves by paying homage to any material power.

Notes: *There are five Articles of Faith commonly presented in North American Islamic literature. For the Shi'a Muslim, these are: 1) Belief in the Unity of God; 2) Belief in Divine Justice; 3) Belief in the Apostles of God; 4) Belief in the Vice-regents of the Prophet; 5) Belief in the Day of Judgment. These articles have been expanded upon by Saiyadul Ulama in his pamphlet* What Is Islam?, *which has circulated particularly among Indian- and Pakistani-American Shi'a Muslims. The prime point of difference between Sunni and Shi'a is over the doctrine of the imans, or vice-regents, of the Prophet.*

* * *

Sufism

PURPOSE (PROSPEROS)

A. "To bear witness in an age of material greatness to the primacy of the spiritual; to interpret the importance of spiritual dimensions in practical affairs and common concerns, and to spell out what free man can do to act effectively in the present world crisis."

B. "To give man a new identity (actually show him how to recognize his only true identity) and to develop and channel this concept beyond his presently cognized equipment and resources."

C. "To foster and develop spiritually-motivated action in social and civil life."

Notes: *Prosperos is one of several groups that found inspiration in the work of Georgei Gurdjieff, the mystical teacher who brought his own brand of Sufism to the West in the early twentieth century.*

THE OBJECTS OF THE SUFI ORDER AND SUFI THOUGHTS (SUFI ORDER)

THE OBJECTS OF THE SUFI ORDER

1. To realize and spread the knowledge of unity, the religion of love and wisdom, so that the bias of faiths and beliefs may of itself fall away, the human heart may overflow with love, and all hatred caused by distinctions and differences may be rooted out:

2. To discover the light and power latent in man, the secret of all religion, the power of mysticism, and the essence of philosophy, without interfering with customs or belief.

3. To help bring the world's two opposite poles, East and West, closer together by the interchange of thought and ideals, that the Universal Brotherhood may form of itself, and man may see with man beyond the narrow national and racial boundaries.

SUFI THOUGHTS

1. There is one God, the Eternal, the Only Being; none else exists save He.

2. There is one Master, the Guiding Spirit of all souls, who constantly leads His followers towards the light.

3. There is one Holy Book, the sacred manuscript of nature, the only scripture which can enlighten the reader.

4. There is one Religion, the unswerving progress in the right direction toward the ideal, which fulfils the life's purpose of every soul.

5. There is one Law, the Law of Reciprocity, which can be observed by a selfless conscience together with a sense of awakened justice.

6. There is one Brotherhood, the human Brotherhood, which unites the children of earth indiscriminately in the Fatherhood of God.

7. There is one Moral Principle, the love which springs forth from self-denial, and blooms in deeds of beneficence.

8. There is one Object of Praise, the beauty which uplifts the heart of its worshipper through all aspects from the seen to the unseen.

9. There is one Truth, the true knowledge of our being within and without, which is the essence of all wisdom.

10. There is one Path, the annihilation of the false ego in the real, which raises the mortal to immortality and in which resides all perfection.

Notes: *Most of the mystically-oriented Sufi groups operating in the United States are small, function on a very informal level, and do not publish statements. Through its brief declarations, the Sufi Order attempts to state in words the order's ideal of oneness, which is captured most fully in the individual's spiritual life.*

Black Islam

OUR BELIEFS (AHMADIYYA ANJUMAN ISHAAT ISLAM, LAHORE, INC.)

(1) That there is no God but Allah and Muhammad is His Messenger.

(2) After the Holy Prophet (peace be upon him), Allah has completely barred the appearance of a prophet, old or new.

(3) After the Holy Prophet, Gabriel can never descend and bring Prophetic Revelation *(Wahy Nubuwwah)* to any person.

(4) If Gabriel were to descend with one word of Prophetic Revelation *(Wahy Nubuwwah)* on any person, it would contradict the two complementary verses:

"This day have I perfected your Religion for you" (5:5); "He is the Messenger of Allah and the Last of the prophets."

(5) The Holy Prophet also said: "I am Muhammad and I am Ahmad and I am *al-'Aqib* (the one who comes last) after whom there can be no prophet." (Al-Bukhari: Kitab al-Manaqib)

(6) In the light of the above Islamic fundamentals, the Holy Founder of the Ahmadiyya Movement never claimed to be a *Nabi,* but the God-Ordained Mujaddid ("The Promised Messiah") of the 14th Islamic Century, having been expressly raised to re-establish the predominance of Islam in the world.

(7) He named his followers 'Ahmadi' after the Holy Prophet's *Jamali* (beatific) name 'Ahmad'.

(8) He proclaimed that no verse of the Holy Qur'-an has been abrogated nor shall ever be abrogated.

(9) All the Companions of the Holy Prophet and the Imams are venerable.

(10) It is spiritually conducive to our Faith to accept the revivalist Islamic missions of *all Mujaddids (Renovators).*

(11) *Any one who declares his faith in the* Kalimah (Muslim formula of faith—*la ilaha ilallahu Muhammadur Rasulullah)* is a Muslim.

Notes: *This creed clearly distinguishes (in articles 5 and 6) the Ahmadiyya Anjuman Ishaat, Lahore, from the Ahmadiyya Movement of Islam, the other group following the teachings of Mizra Ghulam Ahmad. The Ahmadiyya Anjuman Ishaat, Lahore, does not recognize Ahmad as a prophet (and hence equal to Muhammad), but merely as a "mujaddid," (literally, a "restorer of Islam"), a promised messiah, one of several figures who have appeared to revive Islam when it was at a low point in its development.*

BELIEFS OF THE AHMADIYYA MOVEMENT OF ISLAM

(1) We believe that God exists and to assert His existence is to assert a most important truth.

(2) We believe that God is ONE, without an equal in heaven or in earth. Everything else is His creation, dependent upon Him and His subsistence. He is without son or daughter or father or mother or wife or brother. He is one and unique.

(3) We believe that God is Holy, free from all imperfections and possessed of all perfections. There is no imperfection which may be found in Him and no perfection which may not be found in Him. His power and knowledge are unlimited. He encompasses everything and there is nothing which encompasses Him. He is the First, the Last, the Manifest, the Hidden, the Creator, the Master. He is the Loving, the Enduring. His actions are willed, not constrained or determined. He rules today as He ever ruled before. His attributes are eternal.

(4) We believe that angels are a part of God's creation. As the Quran has it, angels do what they are bidden to do. They have been created in His wisdom to carry out certain duties. Their existence is real and references to them in the Holy Book are not metaphorical. They depend on God as do all men and all other creatures.

(5) We believe that God speaks to His chosen Servants and reveals to them His Purpose. Revelation comes in words. Man lives by revelation and through it comes to have contact with God. The words in which revelation comes are unique in their power and wisdom. Their wisdom may not be revealed at once. A mine may be exhausted but not the wisdom of revelation. Revelation brings us divine ordinances, laws, and exhortations. It also brings us knowledge of the unseen and of important spiritual truths. It conveys to us the approval of God as well as His disapproval and displeasure, His love as well as His warnings. God communicates with man through revelation. The communications vary with circumstances and with the recipients. Of all divine communications the most perfect, the most complete, the most comprehensive is the Holy Quran. The Holy Quran is to last for ever. It cannot be superseded by any future revelation.

(6) We also believe that when darkness prevails in the world and man sinks deep in sin and evil, it becomes difficult for him to rise again without the help of God. Then out of His mercy and beneficence God chooses one of His own loving, loyal servants, charges him with the duty to lead and guide other men. As the Quran says, not a people but have had a warner sent to them (35:25). God has sent Messengers to every people. Through them God has revealed His Will and His Purpose. Those who turn away from them ruin themselves, those who turn to them earn the love and pleasure of God.

(7) We also believe that divine messengers belong to different spiritual ranks and contribute in different degrees to the fulfilment of the ultimate Divine Design. The greatest of all messengers is the Holy Prophet MUHAMMAD (on whom the peace and the blessings of God). He is the chief of all men, messenger to them all. The revelation he received was addressed to all mankind. The whole of this earth was a mosque for him. Time came when his message spread to lands and climes beyond Arabia. People forsook gods of their own conception and began to believe in the ONE and only God that the Holy Prophet Muhammad taught them to believe. The coming of the Holy Prophet marked an unparalleled spiritual revolution. Justice began to reign instead of injustice, kindness instead of cruelty. If Moses and Jesus had existed in the time of the Holy Prophet Muhammad they would have had to believe in him and to follow him.

(8) We also believe that God hears our prayers and helps us out of difficulties. He is a living God, His living character being evident in all things at all times. God continues His benevolent interest in His servants and His creatures. When they need His help He turns to them with His help. If they forget Him, He reminds them of Himself and of His concern for them. "I am near indeed; I answer the prayer of every supplicant when he supplicates to Me. Let them, therefore, harken unto Me and believe in Me, so that they may go aright." (2:187).

(9) We also believe that from time to time God determines and designs the course of events in special ways. Events of this world are not determined entirely by unchanging laws called the Laws of Nature. For, besides these ordinary laws there are special laws through which God manifests Himself. It is these special laws which bring to us evidence of the Will, the Power and Love of God. Too many there are who deny this. They would believe in nothing besides the laws of nature. Yet laws of nature are not all the laws we have. Laws of nature are themselves governed by the wider Laws of God. Through these laws, God helps His chosen servants. Through them He destroys His enemies. Moses could not have triumphed over a cruel and mighty enemy, but for the special laws of God. The Holy Prophet Muhammad could not have triumphed over Arabs determined to put an end to him and his mission except for the laws of God, which worked on his side. In everything that he encountered, God helped the Holy Prophet. At last with 10,000 followers he re-entered the valley of Mecca out of which 10 years before he had to flee for his life. Laws of nature cannot account for these events.

(10) We also believe that death is not the end of everything. Man survives death. He has to account for what he does in this life, in life hereafter. The Power of God guarantees human survival.

(11) We believe, that unless forgiven out of His infinite Mercy, unbelievers go to Hell. The object of Hell is

BELIEFS OF THE AHMADIYYA MOVEMENT OF ISLAM (continued)

not to give pain to the inmates but only to reform them. In Hell unbelievers and enemies of God spend their days in wail and woe and continue so until the Mercy of God encompasses the evil-doers and their evil. Truly did the Holy Prophet say, "A time will come when Hell will be emptied of all sinners." (Tafsir-ul-Maalam-ut-tanzil).

(12) Similarly we believe that those who believe in God and the Prophets, the angels and the books, who accept the guidance which comes from God, and walk in humility and abjure excesses of all kinds, will all go to a place called Heaven. Peace and pleasure will reign here and God will be present to all. Low desires will disappear. Men will have attained ever-lasting life and become an image of their Creator.

Notes: *This statement emphasizes the beliefs the Ahmadiyya hold that are identical to those of orthodox Islam. The statement does not cover those beliefs that have led to the denunciation of the Ahmadiyya Movement of Islam by the majority of Muslims, primarily the elevation of founder Hazrat Mirza Ghulam Ahmad to the status of a Prophet. The beliefs enunciated by Ahmad are also affirmed by the Ahmadiyya Anjuman Ishaat Islam, Lahore, Inc., the other branch of the Ahmadiyya movement.*

* * *

THE MUSLIM PROGRAM [AMERICAN MUSLIM MISSION (NATION OF ISLAM)]

WHAT THE MUSLIMS BELIEVE

1. WE BELIEVE in the One God Whose proper Name is Allah.

2. WE BELIEVE in the Holy Qur-an and in the Scriptures of all the Prophets of God.

3. WE BELIEVE in the truth of the Bible but we believe that it has been tampered with and must be reinterpreted so that mankind will not be snared by the falsehoods that have added to it.

4. WE BELIEVE in Allah's Prophets and the Scriptures they brought to the people.

5. WE BELIEVE in the resurrection of the dead—not in physical resurrection—but in mental resurrection. We believe that the so-called Negroes are most in need of mental resurrection: therefore, they will be resurrected first.

Furthermore, we believe we are the people of God's choice, as it has been written, that God would choose the rejected and the despised. We can find no other persons fitting this description in these last days more than the so-called Negroes in America. We believe in the resurrection of the righteous.

6. WE BELIEVE in the judgment; we believe this first judgment will take place as God revealed, in America . . .

7. WE BELIEVE this is the time in history for the separation of the so-called Negroes and the so-called

white Americans. We believe the black man should be freed in name as well as in fact. By this we mean that he should be freed from the names imposed upon him by his former slave masters. Names which identified him as being the slave master's slave. We believe that if we are free indeed, we should go in our own people's names—the black peoples of the earth.

8. WE BELIEVE in justice for all, whether in God or not; we believe as others, that we are due equal justice as human beings. We believe in equality—as a nation—of equals. We do not believe that we are equal with our slave masters in the status of "freed slaves."

We recognize and respect American citizens as independent peoples and we respect their laws which govern this nation.

9. WE BELIEVE that the offer of integration is hypocritical and is made by those who are trying to deceive the black peoples into believing that their 400-year-old enemies of freedom, justice and equality are, all of a sudden, their "friends." Furthermore, we believe that such deception is intended to prevent black people from realizing that the time in history has arrived for the separation from the whites of this nation.

If the white people are truthful about their professed frienship toward the so-called Negro, they can prove it by dividing up America with their slaves.

We do not believe that America will ever be able to furnish enough jobs for her own millions of unemployed, in addition to jobs for the 20,000,000 black people as well.

10. WE BELIEVE that we who declared ourselves to be righteous Muslims, should not participate in wars which take the lives of humans. We do not believe this nation should force us to take part in such wars, for we have nothing to gain from it unless America agrees to give us the necessary territory wherein we may have something to fight for.

11. WE BELIEVE our women should be respected and protected as the women of other nationalities are respected and protected.

12. WE BELIEVE that Allah (God) appeared in the Person of Master W. Fard Muhammad, July, 1930; the long-awaited "Messiah" of the Christians and the "Mahdi" of the Muslims.

We believe further and lastly that Allah is God and besides HIM there is no God and He will bring about a universal government of peace wherein we all can live in peace together.

WHAT THE MUSLIMS WANT

This is the question asked most frequently by both the whites and the blacks. The answers to this question I shall state as simply as possible.

1. We want freedom. We want a full and complete freedom.

2. We want justice. Equal justice under the law. We want justice applied equally to all, regardless of creed or class or color.

3. We want equality of opportunity. We want equal membership in society with the best in civilized society.

4. We want our people in America whose parents or grandparents were descendants from slaves, to be allowed to establish a separate state or territory of their own—either on this continent or elsewhere. We believe that our former slave masters are obligated to provide such land and that the area must be fertile and minerally rich. We believe that our former slave masters are obligated to maintain and supply our needs in this separate territory for the next 20 to 25 years—until we are able to produce and supply our own needs.

   Since we cannot get along with them in peace and equality, after giving them 400 years of our sweat and blood and receiving in return some of the worst treatment human beings have ever experienced, we believe our contributions to this land and the suffering forced upon us by white America, justifies our demand for complete separation in a state or territory of our own.

5. We want freedom for all Believers of Islam now held in federal prisons. We want freedom for all black men and women now under death sentence in innumerable prisons in the North as well as the South.

   We want every black man and woman to have the freedom to accept or reject being separated from the slave master's children and establish a land of their own.

   We know that the above plan for the solution of the black and white conflict is the best and only answer to the problem between two people.

6. We want an immediate end to the police brutality and mob attacks against the so-called Negro throughout the United States.

   We believe that the Federal government should intercede to see that black men and women tried in white courts receive justice in accordance with the laws of the land—or allow us to build a new nation for ourselves, dedicated to justice, freedom and liberty.

7. As long as we are not allowed to establish a state or territory of our own, we demand not only equal justice under the laws of the United States, but equal employment opportunities—NOW!

   We do not believe that after 400 years of free or nearly free labor, sweat and blood, which has helped America become rich and powerful, that so many thousands of black people should have to subsist on relief,. charity or live in poor houses.

8. We want the government of the United States to exempt our people from ALL taxation as long as we are deprived of equal justice under the laws of the land.

9. We want equal education—but separate schools up to 16 for boys and 18 for girls on the condition that the girls be sent to women's colleges and universities. We want all black children educated, taught and trained by their own teachers.

   Under such schooling system we believe we will make a better nation of people. The United States government should provide, free, all necessary text books and equipment, schools and college buildings. The Muslim teachers shall be left free to teach and train their people in the way of righteousness, decency and self respect.

10. We believe that intermarriage or race mixing should be prohibited. We want the religion of Islam taught without hinderance or suppression.

    These are some of the things that we, the Muslims, want for our people in North America.

Notes: *The Muslim Program, divided into two segments, What the Muslims Believe and What the Muslim Wants, details the assumptions upon which the Nation of Islam was built in the 1960s. In the 1970s, The Muslim Program was largely abandoned by the American Muslim Mission as it moved toward orthodox Sunni Muslim belief. However, the Program remains central to the several Nation of Islam factions such as the one led by Louis Farrakhan. The crucial element in the Program, which separates the Nation of Islam from orthodox Islam, is item 12 concerning the appearance of Allah as Master W. Fard Muhammad.*

*   *   *

Zoroastrianism

THE MAZDAZNAN CONFESSION (MAZDAZNAN MOVEMENT)

I am a Mazdaznan who worships but one God, who is in me and I am in Him.

I recognize all things throughout time and space with their diverse causations to be the result of Infinite thought.

I acknowledge all things in matter to be the means to an end and not the end of the Intelligence of God. I realize matter to be the result of the operations of God's intelligence through substance co-existent with intelligence through Infinite Thought.

I see in the countenance of man the male creative principle of God the Father, and in the woman I recognize the pro-creative female principle of God the Mother, and in the child I realize the perpetuative principle of destiny as Our Savior through life, and add that these three images of God constitute the one Holy Family, reproduced and multiplied into the greater Family of God and the Congregation of Gods with its endless chain of associations.

I confess all the painful in matter to be the result of obstinacy on the part of substance through its processes of creations and evolutions, declining to yield to the peaceful operations of intelligence, thus introducing repulsion and impelling resistance.

I hold that all misunderstanding through the processes of creation and evolution is to be eliminated through the application of the higher intelligence, and that for this reason man must take up his work where the Spirit of God left to our care.

I join the sentiments of our Blessed Mother as expressed through the ideal of Ainyahita, that *I am here upon this earth to reclaim the earth, to turn the deserts into a paradise, a paradise most suitable unto God and His associates to dwell therein.*

I declare with Our Father of the pure faith through the *reality* of His Holy One, Zarathushtra, to stand for *Good Thought, Good Word, Good Deed.*

I agree with the saving power of the sonship of God through the incarnation of Christ in his command, *Love thy neighbor as thyself.*

I confide in the power of God. I shall set aside the useless and hold to the good. By the direction of perfect wisdom I shall choose the better part.

I deny the bonds of ancestral relation through sickness, sin and sorrow and sever myself from the pre-natal influence of inherited tendencies, and herewith annul association with evil, error and illusion.

I shall no longer recall to my mind my offenses nor the offenses of forefathers, but exercise all the attributes and endowments of my birthright which come to me through the blessings of *Mazda*, without measure and abundantly, that I may thus verify the words of God, *I shall remember their sins no more*, and continue to bear in mind, *What man soweth that he shall reap!*

I shall follow the *still small voice* in all its directions as coming from the realm of God, that by right living I may always demonstrate the full Truth through the health of the body and most ably perform my duty in a spirit of obedience—prove the power of mind through reason, logic, consideration, discrimination and deduction—have assurance of soul communion, comfort in spirit and the joys of life everlasting.

I shall conduct my life in a way that the knife shall never need be resorted to and herbal medicines never need to pass my lips, but in their stead holy spells through the formulas of invocations and prayers exemplify the perfect life in God on earth.

I shall ever laud creation and through the objects thereof worship the Lord God Mazda, and in all things of Nature, whether great or small the creature, behold the face of my Creator.

With mine eyes lifted beyond the mountain tops and my heart fixed by the burning fire of love I shall daily join in harmonious accord the prayer of the faithful worshipers— the prayer thrice spoken distinctly and with the presence of mind fixed upon the meaning of every word—the prayer that heals the body and assures tranquility to the mind— the prayer that gives solace to the soul and whispers to the spirit, *Peace,*—the prayer breathed in tuneful measure with fervor, zeal and the spirit of assurance, *on one single expiration.*

May Mazda be rejoiced and His Associates continue to be victorious. May obstinacy in this home be destroyed through the Virtue of Obedience, discord by Peace, avarice by Generosity, vanity by Wisdom, false witness by Truthfulness, that the Immortals may long bless it with maintenance and friendly help.—Never the splendor of Prosperity or Progeny be distinguished, that we may shine with purity and see Thee face to face, O Mazda, attaining attributes leading unto worlds without end. May peace come to one and all, and may there be given to this country purity, dominion, profit, majesty and splendor. This is my wish. Be it so.

Notes: *The oldest of the American Zoroastrian groups, the Mazdaznan Movement, has issued a confession.*

*   *   *

Bahaism

SUMMARY OF BAHA'I TEACHINGS OF THE BAHA'I WORLD FAITH

1. The oneness of mankind.

2. Independent investigation of truth.

3. The foundation of all religions is one.

4. Religion must be the cause of unity.

5. Religion must be in accord with science and reason.

6. Equality between men and women.

7. Prejudice of all kinds must be forgotten.

8. Universal peace.

9. Universal education.

10. Spiritual solution of the economic problem.

11. A universal language.

12. An international tribunal.

Notes: *The Baha'i World Faith accepts the writings of Baha'u'llah and Abdu'l-Baha as sacred texts. While the Bahais have no creed, they have frequently attempted to summarize the teachings. In one such summary circulated by the Bahais and reproduced here, twelve principles are listed. This list should not be taken as exhaustive. Other lists with varying numbers of items have also been circulated.*

Chapter 9

Eastern Family

Hinduism

THE SUPREME COMMAND (ANANDA MARGA YOGA SOCIETY)

He who performs Sadhana twice a day regularly, the thought of Paramapurusa will certainly arise in his mind at the time of death, his liberation is a sure guarantee—therefore every Ananda Margii will have to perform Sadhana twice a day invariably—verily is this the command of the Lord. Without Yama and Niyama, Sadhana is an impossibility; hence the Lord's command is also to follow Yama and Niyama. Disobedience to this command is nothing but to throw oneself into the tortures of animal life for crores of years. That no one should undergo torments such as this, that he might be enabled to enjoy the eternal blessedness under the loving shelter of the Lord, it is the bounden-duty of every Ananda Margii to endeavour to bring all to the path of bliss. Verily is this a part and parcel of Sadhana to lead others along the path of righteousness.

—Shrii Shrii A'nandanu'rti

Notes: *This statement comes from an aggressively missionary Hindu organization as a guiding document for all members.*

*　　*　　*

A SHORT STATEMENT OF THE PHILOSOPHY OF KRISHNA CONSCIOUSNESS (INTERNATIONAL SOCIETY OF KRISHNA CONSCIOUSNESS)

1. By cultivating a bona fide spiritual science, we can be free from anxiety and achieve pure, unending, blissful consciousness in this lifetime.

2. We are not our bodies but eternal spirit souls, parts and parcels of God (Krsna).

3. Krsna is the eternal, all-knowing, omnipresent, all-powerful, and all-attractive Personality of Godhead, the sustaining energy of the entire cosmic creation, and the seed-giving father of all living beings.

4. The Absolute Truth is present in all the world's great scriptures, particularly the ancient Vedic literatures, whose *Bhagavad-gita* records God's actual words.

5. We should learn the Vedic knowledge from a genuine spiritual master—one who has no selfish motives and whose mind is firmly fixed on Krsna.

6. Before we eat, we should offer to the Lord the food that sustains us. Then Krsna becomes the offering and purifies us.

7. We should offer to Krsna all that we do and do nothing for our own sense gratification.

8. The recommended way to achieve mature love of God in this age of Kali (quarrel) is to chant the Lord's holy names. For most people it is easiest to chant the Hare Krsna *mantra.*

   Hare Krsna, Hare Krsna, Krsna Krsna, Hare Hare Hare Rama, Hare Rama, Rama Rama, Hare Hare.

Notes: *Members of the International Society of Krisha Consciousness (ISKCON), the Hare Krishna movement, are believers in a personal deity to which they give daily devotion. The repetition of the Hare Krishna mantra is an important daily duty of disciples. The statement of philosophy has been published in every issue of the society's major periodical,* Back to Godhead, *for many years.*

*　　*　　*

AIMS AND TENETS (YOGODA SAT-SANGA MOVEMENT) AND AIMS AND IDEALS (SELF-REALIZATION FELLOWSHIP)

AIMS AND TENETS

1. Universal all-round education, and establishment of educational institutions for the development of man's physical, mental and spiritual natures.

2. Contacting Cosmic Consciousness—the ever-new, ever-existing, ever-conscious Bliss-God—through the scientific technique of concentration and meditation taught by the Masters of all ages.

3. Attaining bodily health through the "Yogoda" technique of recharging the body-battery from inner life-energy.

4. Intelligently maintaining the physical body on unadulterated foods, including a large percentage of raw fruits, vegetables and nuts.

5. Physical, mental and spiritual healing.

6. Establishing, by a scientific system of realization, the absolute basic harmony and oneness of Christianity, Hindu Yoga teachings, and all true religions.

7. Serving all mankind as one's larger Self.

8. Demonstrating the superiority of mind over body, and of soul over mind.

9. Fighting the Satan of Ignorance—man's common enemy.

10. Establishing a spiritual unity between all nations.

11. Overcoming evil by good; overcoming sorrow by joy; overcoming cruelty by kindness.

12. Realization of the purpose of life as being the evolution from human consciousness into divine consciousness, through individual struggle.

13. Realization of the truth that human life is given to man to afford him opportunity to manifest his inner divine qualities, and not for physical pleasure nor selfish gratifications.

14. Furthering the cultural and spiritual understanding between East and West, and the constructive exchange of the distinctive features of their civilizations.

15. Uniting science and religion through study and practical realization of the unity of their underlying principles.

AIMS AND IDEALS

To disseminate among the nations a knowledge of definite scientific techniques for attaining direct personal experience of God.

To teach that the purpose of life is the evolution, through self-effort, of man's limited mortal consciousness into God Consciousness; and to this end to establish Self-Realization Fellowship temples for God-communion throughout the world, and to encourage the establishment of individual temples of God in the homes and in the hearts of men.

To reveal the complete harmony and basic oneness of original Christianity as taught by Jesus Christ and original Yoga as taught by Bhagavan Krishna; and to show that these principles of truth are the common scientific foundation of all true religions.

To point out the one divine highway to which all paths of true religious beliefs eventually lead: the highway of daily, scientific, devotional meditation on God.

To liberate man from his threefold suffering: physical disease, mental inharmonies, and spiritual ignorance.

To encourage "plain living and high thinking"; and to spread a spirit of brotherhood among all peoples by teaching the eternal basis of their unity: kinship with God.

To demonstrate the superiority of mind over body, of soul over mind.

To overcome evil by good, sorrow by joy, cruelty by kindness, ignorance by wisdom.

To unite science and religion through realization of the unity of their underlying principles.

To advocate cultural and spiritual understanding between East and West and the exchange of their finest distinctive features.

To serve mankind as one's larger Self.

Notes: *Shortly after Paramahansa Yogananda arrived in the United States in the 1920s, he circulated a statement concerning the organization he had founded, then called the Yogoda Sat-Sanga. In more recent years, that statement has undergone revision and emerged as the Aims and Ideals of the organization under its current name, the Self-Realization Fellowship. The older statement makes several references to the "kriya yoga" system taught by Yogananda, a "scientific system of realization." These references have been deleted from the more recent statement.*

* * *

THE ETERNAL TRUTHS (SELF-REVELATION CHURCH OF ABSOLUTE MONISM)

I AM AN ABSOLUTE MONIST. I BELIEVE:

"Truth is one; men call it by various names."

"God, Brahman, is Consciousness-Existence-Bliss Absolute."

"Everything is the manifestation of God, the divine Reality."

"The soul of man is of identical nature with the God of the universe."

"Realize thyself."

"By the realization of one's own self, the absolute Self is realized."

"God is the light of the heavens and the earth."

"He who realizes God becomes one with God."

"I am that I am."

"I and my Father are one."

"I am Brahman, the absolute Self."

Notes: *A Westernized branch of the Vedanta movement, the Self-Revelation Church of Absolute Monism has attempted to render the basic affirmation of the Vedanta philosophy in a set of brief statements.*

* * *

MEMBERSHIP STATEMENT OF SRI RAM ASHRAMA

All members should study and manifest the following five resolutions:

1. The will to neither kill nor injure.

2. The will always to speak the truth and to act truthfully.

3. The will always to remain honest and not to pilfer.

4. The will to direct all bodily and mental energies toward reality.

5. The resolution not to take gifts or seek rewards with the idea of piling them up for personal gain.

All members should study and follow these eight steps or principles:

1. Yama - firm determination to lead life in the light of truth.

2. Niyama - firm activity of mind and body to lead life toward truth by way of these five methods:

   a) Cleanliness of body and mind.

   b) Contentment.

   c) Critical examination of senses.

   d) Study of physics, metaphysics, and psychology.

   e) Realization of the oneness of individual existence with universal existence; complete self-surrender.

3. Asana - physical, biological, chemical, and bio-chemical exercising for the purpose of refining mind and body to study Truth.

4. Pranayama - the control of enerty or prana.

5. Pratyahara - displacement of psychic energy from the lower regions and its sublimation to higher purposes.

6. Dharana - fixation of attention on a particular object or idea with the aim of steadying the mind and making it absolutely fit and pliant.

7. Dhyana - continuous meditation and focusing of attention on that particular object or idea.

8. Samadhi - transformation of all attention into that particular object.

Three other principles to be followed by all members on the Path:

1. To be devoted and dedicated to the practice of Vichara as taught by Sri Bhagavan Ramana Maharshi.

2. Non-violence, or Ahimsa—to abstain from causing pain at any time, in any way, however small in mind, word or body, to any living thing, including oneself, is non-violence. All other abstinences and observances lead up to it and have to be brought into action before full non-violence can be attained. It is said that they exist only for the sake of non-violence, and further, that without non-violence, their practice is fruitless.

3. Truth or Satya—According to testimony of the inner faculties and senses, to show things as they are with the aim of doing good in friendly words and without deceit is Truth.

Notes: *In its constitution, the Sri Ram Ashrama has a lengthy statement in the section on membership which delineates basic concepts and teachings. In essence, this statement presents the ashrama's consensus on matters of belief and practice. The various items are part of the common teachings of yogic philosophy.*

* * *

PLEDGE AND DASASHRAM DISCIPLINES (TEMPLE OF COSMIC RELIGION)

PLEDGE

On this day we take the pledge that we dedicate our lives for Universal peace, to bridge the east and west and to bring understanding among people through the message of love and wisdom of all sages and saints.

"We live as one family with Prem (Love Divine) in the name of God Who is our Father". Let this be the meditation for the whole world. If every one meditates on this thought, God will certainly bless His children with happiness and peace.

Let the whole world have one ideal which the great sages of the Himalayas taught and that is, "Sarve Jananam sukhino bhavanthu", let all people be happy. Let there be peace in the world, peace above and peace within. Om Shantih Shantih Shantih

We work for this, day and night through:

1. Establishing Dasashram branches all over the world to teach the message of the sages and saints of east and west.

2. Through installing the Image of the Lord of Love (Panduranga) as the symbol of the holy east.

3. We initiate people for spiritual training in eternal religion (Sanatana Dharma) to serve God and saints through humanity.

4. Our ideas of peace extends not only to humanity but to all animals, the plant kingdom and the whole creation of God.

   (1) Bhuta-daya (compassion) to all creatures

   (2) Kshama (forgiveness)

   (3) Dharma (Divine Law)

   (4) Prema (Love Divine)

   (5) Satya (truth)

   (6) Jnana (wisdom)

   (7) Seva (service)

   (8) Shanti (peace)

These are the eight "Daivi Sampat" or divine attributes which makes man perfect. This comes through the realization of God or God-realization will come by developing these divine qualities.

   Shoucha (inner and outer purity)

   Shraddha (unflinching faith in God and Guru)

   Sadhana (spiritual discipline)

These three make man eligible for Grace of God and the Grace of God brings love and peace ineffble which is the be-all and end-all of our existence.

The technique to reach this state is NAMA (chanting of the name divine) and PREMA (yoga of Love divine) which includes Hatha yoga, Raja yoga, Dhyana yoga, Bhakti yoga and Karma yoga or the yoga of knowledge, the yoga of mediation, the yoga of devotion and the yoga of selfless service, yoga for health and purification of Nadis and yoga of psychological self-discipline.

God bless all with His supreme love.

Om and Prem, Sant Keshavadas

DASASHRAM DISCIPLINES

1. We belong to Sanatana Vedic Hindu Dharma.

2. We have faith in the Vedas, Vedanta or Upanishads Brahmasutras, Bhagavad Gifa, Mahabharata, Ramayana; Eighteen Puranas, Manusmruti and all spiritual literature that is not against the Sanatana Vedic Scriptures.

3. We believe Mother India to be the Karma-Bhumi; Ganges water to be most Holy Water; Cow is to be worshipped as the mother and non-killing of any animal consciously, as our Great Dharma. We believe Mother as God, Father as God, Guru as God and Guest as God and we strive to realise God in everything and Everywhere.

4. We consider Gayatri as the greatest of all Mantras and "OM" as our symbol of God.

5. We believe in worshipping God through images and rituals, but always with the knowledge to realise God in us and in everything.

6. Sanatana Dharma is the Eternal and Ancient wisdom of God and this is a Way of Life Divine.

7. As an outer symbol of our inner conviction we wear:

   (a) "OM" symbol

   (b) White clothes (Sattwa Guna)

   (c) Tulsi or Rudrakshi beads &

   (d) Nam or Holy mark and Vibhuti the holy ashes.

8. We believe in Brahma, Vishnu and Siva as the three aspects of ONE GOD and We worship all Gods described in our Scriptures as the manifestation of one God.

9. We believe in the Doctrine of Incarnation of God and the Doctrine of Reincarnation of man.

10. We believe Gnana, Karma and Bhakti-Yogas to be the greatest of all the yogas, the others being the practical preparatory Yoga which lead towards the three major yogas. We call the integration of the three major yogas as "Prema Yoga" and practise it.

"Love born of wisdom practised in selfless service could solve all problems of Humanity."

Notes: *Embedded in these two guiding documents for the members of the Temple of Cosmic Religion are the basic beliefs espoused by the temple and its leader, Sant Keshavadas.*

WHAT DO WE BELIEVE? (TEMPLE OF KRIYA YOGA)

1. There is only one ultimate law, and that law is God.

2. There is only one spirit, and that spirit is God.

3. There is only one love, and that love is God.

4. The universe is meaningful and you have your rightful place in it.

5. Illumination and fulfillment are possible in this lifetime.

Notes: *This brief statement presents several affirmations that undergird the extensive teaching program of the Temple of Kriya Yoga.*

* * *

UNIVERSAL UNDERSTANDING (YASODHARA ASHRAM SOCIETY)

God is universal, yet man has followed many paths in seeking him. Outwardly these ways of search differ, owing to their various traditions and to the separate historical and cultural circumstances in which each has arisen. At its finest, each religion is suited to answer the spiritual, emotional and psychological needs of the particular people or group among whom it has developed.

In the past, unfortunately, these inevitable differences between creeds have become hardened and exaggerated by man-made laws and doctrines, so that the various religious movements have helped to divide men rather than to unite them.

Yet underlying all religions there are certain universal and ethical concepts; all religions advocate—as fundamental principles—truth, love, selflessness, and moderation. They are also alike in making use of certain essential spiritual practices, such as prayer, chanting and meditation.

Now, in an age when the spiritual and physical perils of mankind loom larger than ever before, and ignorance has gained its maximum destructive power, it is necessary that religion should unite rather than divide, and that the ideal of brotherhood in spiritual understanding should at last be put into practice. This can come about only when the unwisdom of religious exclusiveness is recognized, and the adherents of all creeds are willing to cultivate spiritual companionship in freedom and universal tolerance.

Yasodhara Ashram aims to provide a setting in which people — no matter what their religious affiliation, or lack of affiliation — who are conscious of this pressing need for spiritual unity, may come together in the search for universal principles and unifying practices; and yet remain free in their personal search for spiritual enlightenment.

Notes: *This statement gives expression to a popular Hindu notion about the universal essence of religion.*

Sikhism

INITIATION INSTRUCTIONS FOR THE RUHANI SATSANG

Before the living Master (an adept in the science of the Sound Current or Word), gives Initation, he wishes that every prospective initiate abide by the following instructions:

I. To cultivate and develop the five cardinal virtues which constitute the bedrock of spirituality. These are:

1. *Ahimsa* or Non-injury to all living creatures, and more so to fellow beings, by thoughts, words and deeds—the injunction in this behalf being: "Injure not a human heart for it is the seat of God." We must have respect for others' feelings and tolerance for others' opinions.

2. *Satayam* or Truthfulness: As God is Truth, we must practice Truth in all our dealings. If Truth resides in every heart, it must manifest itself in life and action. "Be true to thyself and it must follow as night the day, thou canst not be false to any man." We must therefore avoid falsehood at all costs. It includes, besides downright lies, hypocrisy and dishonesty, *suppresso veri* (suppression of truth), and *suggestio falsi* (suggestions of false ideas).

3. *Brahmcharya* or life of Chastity: It includes continence in thoughts, words and deeds. We must not cast covetous eyes on others nor entertain impure thoughts within, for "Chastity is life and sexuality is death." If we want to tread the Path of Life Eternal, we must be chaste and clean both within and without.

4. *Prem* or love for all living creatures and more so for all human beings. Let there be hatred for none. The entire manifestation is the handiwork of God and must therefore be loved and respected. "He who does not know love, cannot know God."

5. *Nishkam Seva* or Selfless Service to all living creatures in sorrow and distress. If one limb of the body is in torture, the other limbs can have no rest.

    "Service before self" should therefore be our motto in life.

II. To practice these three purities - in Diet, Livelihood and Conduct.

1. *Ahar* or Diet. What we eat goes to constitute the body and the mind. "Sound mind in a sound body" is a well known aphorism. We can neither have one nor the other with unwholesome diet. A strictly vegetarian diet consisting of vegetables and fruits, both fresh and dried, cereals, dairy products like milk, cream, butter, cheese, yogurt, etc., is essential for all aspirants for Truth. We must, therefore avoid meat, meat juices, fish, fowl, eggs both fertile and unfertile, or anything containing any of these ingredients in any form or in any degree. Every action has a reaction and flesh eating involves contracting fresh Karmas and thus helps to keep the inexorable Karmic wheel in motion for we have to reap what we sow. We cannot have roses if we sow thistles.

    The above prohibitions apply equally to all kinds of Alcohlic drinks, intoxicants, opiates and narcotic drugs, as they tend to dull our consciousness and make one morbid.

    "The body is the temple of living God" and it must, therefore, be kept scrupulously clean.

    Any prospective candidate for initiation should therefore try vegetarian for at least three to six months, to ensure that he or she can adhere to it, when put on the Path.

2. *Vibar* or Livelihood: Closely associated with diet, are the means of livelihood. There are no shortcuts in spirituality. The end here does not justify the means, as it may be construed to do so, anywhere else. The ignoble means to earn one's living, do contaminate one's diet, the very source of life itself. So an honest living by the sweat of one's brow is essential in this line. The life plant has therefore to be nurtured with pure water, to make it sound and healthy, a fit instrument for the efflorescence of spirituality.

3. *Achar* or Conduct. The above remarks apply equally to one's conduct in life. Every thought, every word and every deed, good or bad, leaves an indelible imprint on the mind and has to be accounted for. Hence the necessity for right thoughts, right aspirations and right conduct, all of which constitute the hedge around the tender sapling of spirituality. The details in this behalf have been dealt with under the five virtues discussed above.

III. *Satsang* or Association with Truth: The guidance of the Living Master is of supreme importance. A Master is a Master indeed, a Master in all three phases of life: A Guru or Master on the physical plane, sharing our joys and sorrows, guiding affectionately each one of us in our wordly affairs, and above all imparting spiritual instructions: a Guru Dev or Radiant Form of the Master on Astral and Causal regions helping the spirit in meditation at each place and Sat Guru or Master of Truth or Truth itself in the Beyond.

The importance of attending Satsangs or spiritual gatherings can not be over emphasised. Theory always preceeds practice. It is but necessary to understand clearly the teaching of the Master in all their bearings, before starting spiritual practice. The Master is the be-all and end-all on the spiritual path. He, however, does not ask for blind faith, though experimental faith is necessary for the purpose, to start with. He emphatically expresses: "Believe not the words of the Master, unless you see the Reality

INITIATION INSTRUCTIONS FOR THE RUHANI
SATSANG (continued)

yourself" or at least have some experience of it yourself.

IV. Spirituality: It is a path of love, discipline and self control. After the initial spiritual experience given at the time of Initiation, the rest depends on relentless regular practice as enjoined by the Master. Daily practice with loving faith, in all sincerity and humility, is the cornerstone round which each disciple must turn, so as to make progress on the Path. Love for the Master means implicit obedience to His commandments.

V. To Eschew All Symbolism and Rituals: The observance of religious practices, rites and rituals, keeping fasts and vigils, going on pilgrimages, etc., and doing breathing exercises are the elementary steps only which go to create in you a desire for turning to or meeting God. You have made best use of them when you are put on the way back to God, which is the science of the Word or the Sound Current and is one for all humanity. A devotee of this science need not indulge in the elementary steps. In short, all acts involving physical labor belong to the realm of the physical world while we have to rise above the body and bodily consciousness to get contact with the primal manifestations of the Godhead: Light and Sound. You cannot pray God with hands. "God is Spirit and can only be worshiped in spirit."

VI. Record of Conduct and Progress: Every seeker after God is enjoined to maintain a strictly impartial record of his daily conduct, so as to find out his weaknesses and try to weed them out one by one; to note his/her progress on the Path and the various difficulties and shortcomings in the way. The diary so maintained is to be sent to the Master every four months for further guidance. For this purpose regular forms are available and can be obtained from the nearest center.

VII. Application for Initiation: Every true aspirant for spiritual science, who can adhere to the above, after preliminary abstinence in diet for about three to six months, can put in an application on the form prescribed for the purpose, giving his brief life sketch, age, marital status and the like along with a copy of his or her photograph. All applications for Initiation are to be forwarded to the nearest representative of the Master for His approval, and instructions in Initiation are given only after the Master authorizes them. The place and time of Initiation are communicated in each case by the representative.

VIII. Ruhani Satsang or Path of the Masters: The science of the living Masters is the most ancient and the most perfect science the world has ever seen. It is the most natural and the easiest to follow, and can be followed by men of all ages. Married life, avocation, caste and creed, social and religious beliefs, poverty or illiteracy, etc., are no bars. It is an inner science of the soul and consists in contacting the soul with the Oversoul, with the help and guidance of the spiritual adept, well versed in the theory and the practice of *Para Vidya* or the Science of the Beyond and capable of granting some first-hand spiritual experience at the very first sitting. Nothing is to be taken on trust or make-believe. Miracles, spiritual healings, psychic phenomena, fortunetelling, akashic records and worldly desires are all to be left aside, for these are positive hindrances on the Path. The entire energy is to be conserved for internal progress.

Seek ye first the Kingdom of God, and all things shall be added unto you.

This is the highest Truth that has been taught from hoary antiquity by sages and seers since the day of creation. It is unalterable and shall remain so. God, Godway and Godman can never suffer any change and shall ever remain eternal.

Notes: *The single representative statement from among Sikh groups derives from one of the "Sant Mat" organizations which, because they retain a living guru, are not considered true Sikhs by the more orthodox. Since the death of Kirpal Singh, founder and leader of Ruhani Satsang, three organizations have claimed to be led by his successor—the Kirpal Light Satsang, the Sant Bani Ashram, and the Sawan Kirpal Ruhani Mission. Each offers the same instructions to new initiates.*

* * *

Buddhism

SUMMARY OF BUDDHA'S DHARMA (DWIGHT GODDARD)

INTRODUCTION

The Buddha's Dharma ought not to be considered as a system of philosophic or intellectual thought, much less as a system of ethical idealism. Strictly speaking, even less is it a religion based upon authority. It is simply a way of life which Buddha called the Eightfold Noble Path and the Middle Way, and which he said would lead him who followed it to emancipation of body, to enlightenment of mind, to tranquillity of spirit, to highest Samadhi. That is, it is a system of mind-control leading to highest perfect cognition. He did not make it up—it is the record of his own experience under the Bodhitree, when he himself attained Enlightenment.

The summary is introduced by what is known as the Twelve Nirdanas, or the Chain of Simultaneous Dependent Originations *(paticca-samutpada)*. Then he taught the Four Noble Truths upon which he based the Eightfold Noble Path. These are all briefly summarized.

THE TWELVE NIRDANAS

1. Because of Ignorance *(avidya)* the principle of individuation as discriminated from Enlightenment which is the principle of unity and sameness the primal unity becomes divided into thinking, thinker and discriminated thoughts by reason of which there appear the "formations" of karma.

2. Because of these "forms" *(samsara)*, the principle of consciousness emerges.

3. Because of the principle of consciousness *(vijnana)*, mentality and body emerge.

4. Because of mentality and body *(nama-rupa)*, the six sense minds and organs appear.

5. Because of the six sense minds and organs *(shadayatana)*, sensations and perceptions arise.

6. Because of sensations and perceptions *(spasha)*, feelings and discriminations arise.

7. Because of feelings and sensations *(vedana)*, thirst and craving arise.

8. Because of thirst and craving *(trishna)*, grasping and clinging appear.

9. Because of grasping and clinging *(upadana)*, conception takes place.

10. Because of conception *(bhava)*, the continuing process of existence goes on.

11. Because of the continuing process of existence *(jeti)*, growth, sickness, old age, decay and death take place.

12. Because of sickness, old age and death *(jana-marana)*, "sorrow, lamentation, pain, grief and despair arise. Thus arises the whole mass of suffering." In all this

> "No doer of the deeds is found,
> No one who ever reaps their fruit.
> Empty phenomena are there.
> Thus does the world roll on.
> No god, no Brahma, can be found,
> No maker of this wheel of life.
> Empty phenomena are there,
> Dependent upon conditions all."

THE FOUR NOBLE TRUTHS

1. The universality of suffering.

2. The cause of suffering rooted in desire.

3. By ending desire, suffering comes to an end.

4. The way to end desire and hence to end suffering, is to follow the Eightfold Noble Path.

THE EIGHTFOLD NOBLE PATH

1. RIGHT IDEAS: The Twelve Nirdanas and the Four Noble Truths. Not only should one understand them but he should make them the basis of all his thinking and understanding of life, he should make them the basis for a life of patient and humble acceptance and submission.

2. RIGHT RESOLUTION: He should make it the purpose of his life to follow the Noble Path. In loyalty to this purpose he should be willing to give up anything that is contrary to it, or which hinders his progress. He should be willing to pay any cost of comfort, or self denial, or effort, in order to attain its goal. He should not do this for any selfish motive but that he might devote the merit of its attainment to all

animate life. And finally he should make his great Vow *(Pranadana)* not to enter Nirvana until all others may enter with him.

3. RIGHT SPEECH: Speech is the connecting link between thought and action; words often obscure the Truth within one's own mind, and often give a false impression to those that hear them. It is important therefore, that one should restrain his speech. It should always be characterized by wisdom and kindness. Undue loudness, over emphasis, and excitement should be avoided. Speech should not be prompted by prejudice, fear, anger, nor infatuation, nor self-interest. Careless, idle and flippant words should be avoided. All invidious distinctions, and discriminations, and dogmatic assertions and negations, should be avoided. Words that are liable to cause hard feelings, such as repeating scandal, mean or angry words, words that deceive or cause misunderstandings, or that tend to arouse passion and lust, should never be uttered. In general speech should be limited to asking and answering necessary questions, and because speech is so easily conditioned by crowd psychology, all formal speech before groups, audiences and crowds should be avoided.

4. RIGHT BEHAVIOR. Besides behaving according to the general rules of propriety, one should be especially careful to keep the Five Precepts:—Not to kill but to practice kindness and harmlessness toward all animate life. Not to steal or covet what does not belong to one, but to practice charity and going without things oneself. Not to commit adultery but to practice purity of mind and sexual self-control. Not to lie but to practice honesty and sincerity in thought, word and deed. Not to partake of alcoholic drinks or drugs, or anything that weakens one's mind-control, but to practice abstinence and self-control.

The reason that Buddha made keeping the Precepts so important was not so much for ethical reasons as for its bearing on mind development and its goal of the attainment of highest cognition and enlightenment. One can not progress toward this high goal if he is living a wicked or self-indulgent life. Even the keeping of the Precepts is only a beginning, for as disciples advance on the Path and undertake the homeless life, there are five other Precepts that must also be observed, namely: Not to use ointments or condiments and not to eat between meals. Not to wear jewelry or expensive clothes, but to practice humility. Not to sleep on soft beds but to resist all tendency to sloth and sleepiness. Not to attend entertainments, dances, concerts or to take part in games of chance; keeping the mind at all times under strict control. Not to have anything to do with money or precious things, but to practice poverty.

5. RIGHT VOCATION. One must not engage in any business or profession that involves cruelty or injustice to either men or animals. His life must be free from acquisitiveness, deceit or dishonesty. He must have nothing to do with war, gambling,

prostitution. It must be a life of service rather than a life of profit and indulgence. For those who wish to devote their entire attention to attaining enlightenment it must be a Homeless Life, free from all dependence or responsibility for property, family life or society.

The ideal life, therefore, for one who has resolved to follow the Noble Path is the Homeless Life. But before one is willing and able to do this, he should come as near to it as possible while living the ordinary life of a householder. Being engaged in the family, social and economical life of the world, he will often find it difficult to do much more than keep the Precepts, but as he advances on the Path he can at least in part observe the other precepts, and as fast as it becomes possible, he can separate from his family and business, and undertake to live more simply and abstemiously and devote more time to his devotional practices. If there is any personal or family property it should gradually be disposed of, so that being free from family and property responsibilities, he may more exclusively undertake the Homeless Life.

In cutting himself off from all relations and responsibilities with the household and worldly life, the Homeless Brother does so with the single purpose of devoting himself to the attainment of enlightenment and Buddhahood, not for selfish reasons but that he may share his attainment and merit with whoever may need his instruction or help. In making his decision to follow the Homeless Life he does so in perfect faith that the Lay Brothers and other Homeless Brothers will take good care of him.

Some may think that this homeless, mendicant life might have been possible and rewarding under the primitive and simple conditions of patriarchical life, but that it would be impossible and foolish and futile under the more complex conditions of our modern, acquisitive, comfort-seeking, excitement-loving conditions, founded as they are upon scientific materialism and enforced by conventions, laws, courts and police. If we count one's comfort and convenience important, it probably is. But are they of first importance? Is not enlightenment, the ending of suffering, the attainment of peace, of far more importance? If they are then any discipline, any deprivation, any inconvenience, any suffering even, is fully warranted. It would be different if there was any easier method known, but Buddha, who was perfectly enlightened, presented it as the only possible Path. Is it not for us who are seeking enlightenment and peace of mind, and who are following Buddha, to have faith in his Noble Path and give it a fair trial? It is noticeable, however, that doubt as to its reasonableness and possibility is not voiced by those who have tried it but by those whose habits and comforts would be curtailed and interfered with.

The Buddha's Dharma is too deep and inclusive to be translated into writing and even less to be completely understood and fully realized by the study of the Scriptures alone. It must be carried out into practice, systematically, earnestly, persistently. The source of all truth is within one's own mind and heart, by the practice of Dhyana, it issues forth in unutterable treasures of compassion and wisdom.

But more significant than that, it is by means of dhyana practised by free minds in undisturbed solitude that the deeper realizations of Truth issue forth spontaneously in unseen spiritual ways to implant intimations and seeds of faith and hope in the minds of others. Thus one, who in the midst of the world's unrest, craving and suffering, has found wisdom and peace, radiates from his being a serenity and compassion and wisdom that emancipates and enlightens others. He is already a Buddha. Being one with Buddha in the blissful peace of Samadhi, he will be radiating compassion and wisdom toward this Saha world of suffering and drawing in to his peace the world's woe. He has learned the secret of the Dharma breathing—going forth, drawing in—in eternal rhythm.

6. RIGHT EFFORT. As one advances along the Path, he needs something more than ethical Precepts to guide and activate his progress, namely, he needs spiritual ideals. To meet this need, the Dharma presents Six Paramitas: (1) Dana Paramita. One should cherish a spirit of unselfish charity and good will that will prompt him to the giving of material gifts for the relief of need and suffering, being especially thoughtful of the needs of the Homeless Brothers, and always remembering that the greatest gift is the gift of the Dharma. (2) Sila Paramita. This same spirit of good-will towards others, the clearing sense of his oneness with all sentient beings, will first prompt him to greater sincerity and fidelity in keeping the Precepts himself for their sakes. Next it will lead him to ignore and forget his own comfort and convenience in offering wherever needed the more intangible gifts of compassion and sympathy and personal service. (3) Kshanti Paramita. This Paramita of humility and patience will help him to bear without complaint, the acts of others without fear or malice or anger. It will help him to bear the common ills of life, the difficulties of the Path and the burden of his karma. It will keep him free from both elation or discouragement as he meets the extremes of success or failure, and will help him to always maintain an equitable spirit of serenity and peacefulness. (4) Virya Paramita. This Paramita of zeal and perseverance will keep one from becoming indolent, careless and changeable. This Paramita is not intended so much to prompt one to outward acts of charity and propaganda as it is wholly concerned with these inner states of mind that affect one's control of mind and attainment of highest cognition and unceasing compassion. The results of behavior are not all outward and apparent; they also affect one's inner habits and dispositions and are surely

registered in one's karma. One does not truly attain until he becomes earnest and faithful in both outward behavior and inner states of mind. Therefore, one should be earnest and persevering and faithful in cherishing right ideas, right purposes, right effort, right devotional practices, right vows. (5) Dhyana Paramita. This Paramita of tranquility prompts one to practice one-pointedness of mind. One should always keep his mind concentrated on the task in hand, undistracted by thoughts of policy, or its relation to one's selfish advantage or comfort. It will often prompt one to a course far different from the old competitive, acquisitive, exciting habits of the worldly life. One must often disregard personal comfort and advantage in an effort to be truly sympathetic and charitable. But so long as one acts from motives of sympathy and kindness the mind will be undisturbed by consequences, and so long as one has no desires, he will be undisturbed by conditions. So long as the mind is free from greed, anger, fear and egoism, it rests in peace. The mind should be trained, therefore, to be concentrated on spiritual ends. (6) Prajna Paramita. This Paramita prompts one to be yielding to the suggestions of wisdom. Thus far we have been considering aspects of spiritual behavior that are more or less under the control of one's own mind, but now in this Wisdom Paramita, we should cease from all self-direction of will and effort and, remaining tranquil in spirit, should yield ourselves in effortless ways, a free channel for the flow of mingled wisdom and compassion.

7. RIGHT MINDFULNESS. This stage of the Noble Path is the culmination of the intellective process and the connecting link with the intuitive process. The goal to be reached is the establishment of a habit of looking at things truthfully, at their meaning and significance rather than at their discriminated appearances, and relations. This is quite different and an advance from the instinctive reactions of the will-to-live, to enjoy, to propagate. It is also quite different and a further advance beyond the habit of considering things by their differences and relations. The senses can give one sensations and perceptions which the lower mind unites and names and discriminates, but they have little value in truth. Things seem real but they are not, they seem good and bad, big and little, right and wrong, but they are not. They often seem necessary but they are not. This consciously discriminated stream of appearances is only food for the higher intellectual mind to digest and assimilate, which by doing enables one to cognize more truthfully the realness or falsity of these first impressions. But the conclusions of the intellectual mind are not final for it can only arrive at a knowledge of relations among things which we think are true. If one is to gain an immediate awareness of Truth, he must transcend the intellectual mind, also. To make the highest and best use of the intellectual mind, however, it is necessary to first practice "recollective mindfulness," which is the Seventh Stage of the Noble Path.

The Seventh Stage is usually translated, Mindfulness. It consists in recollecting and mediating upon the conclusions of the intellectual mind, seeking to understand their true meaning and significance.

8. RIGHT DHYANA. The Eighth Stage of the Noble Path is called in Sanskrit, Dhyana. It is a difficult word to translate into English because of its unfamiliar content of meaning. The nearest term is "concentration of mind" although in Pali this stage is named, "rapture." There are, thus, two aspects to it: the first is its active aspect of concentration, the second is a passive aspect of realization, or rapture. Having tranquillized the mind by the practice of the Seventh Stage of Mindfulness, to practice the Eighth Stage of Dhyana, one should sit quietly with empty and tranquil mind, but with attentive and concentrated mind, keeping the mind fixed on its pure essence. If attention wavers and vagrant thoughts arise, one should humbly and patiently regulate the mind anew, again and again, stopping all thinking, realizing Truth itself.

In doing this breathing plays an important part. Right breathing consists in breathing gently, deliberately, evenly. Think of it as filling the whole body to the top of the head, then gently pressing it downward to the abdomen, let it quietly pass away. Ordinarily we think of its course as being in a straight line, up and down, but it is better to think of it as a circle or loop always moving in one direction—upward to the head, downward to the abdomen, upward to the head and so on. Then forgetting the breathing, think of this circle moving more and more slowly and growing smaller and smaller until it comes to rest at a point between the eyes, the "wisdom eye" of the ancient, between the pineal and pituitary glands of the moderns. Hold the attention there, realizing its perfect balance and emptiness and silence.

At first it may be advisable to hold some simple thought conception in mind, such as counting the out-going breaths, or repeating Buddha's name, or some "koan" puzzle that can only be solved intuitively. But *avoid thinking about them*, keeping the mind fixed on its pure essence. In the primitive days of Buddhism, masters encouraged their disciples to keep in mind the abhorrent and painful aspects of the body, and the empty and transitory nature of all component things; but in later times and Western lands, not liking to think of disgusting and negative things, we more often go to the other extreme and think of the beautiful, noble and rewarding things of life, of wisdom and compassion and purity and solitude and joy and peace. But the right way is to avoid both extremes, keeping the mind fixed on its pure essence, unperturbed by any differentiations whatever.

In the course of this discipline, various psychic effects appear—colors, sounds, visions, raptures, etc., and beginners are apt to become elated or discouraged by them, and to measure their success or failure by their appearing or not appearing. But this is all wrong. All these transitory psychic experiences should be ignored and forgotten; they are only milestones on the path and will be left behind as we move upward toward emancipation and enlightenment and perfect equanimity. The goal is not some entrancing rapture, or indescribable vision; it is highest perfect Wisdom and a great heart of Compassion and blissful Peace. Then ceasing all thought, realize its unceasing calm and silence.

THE FOUR JNANAS, OR HOLY STATES

1. COMPASSION. As the mind progresses towards Enlightenment, it becomes aware of clearing insight and sensitiveness as to the essential unity of all animate life, and there awakens within him a great heart of compassion and sympathy drawing all animate life together, harmonizing differences, unifying all dualisms.

2. JOY. With the disappearing of all sense of difference between self and others and all dualisms, the heart becomes filled with a great rapture of gladness and joy.

3. PEACE. Gradually as the difference between suffering and happiness fades away, this feeling of gladness and joy is transmuted into perfect tranquillity and peacefulness.

4. EQUANIMITY. Gradually even the conception of difference and likeness vanishes and all notions of even joy and peace drop out of sight, and the mind abides in the blissful peace of perfect Equanimity.

THE TEN BODHISATTVA STAGES

For a long time the above Four Holy States engrossed the attention of the Pali Scriptures and Southern Buddhists, but gradually there appeared among Northern Buddhists and in the Sanskrit Scriptures a new vision of the goal of the Buddha's Noble Path. The enjoyment of the Four Raptures for one's self to their culmination in Nirvana, seemed less worthy and satisfying, and meditation on the deeper implications of the Buddha's Dharma, led the great Mahayana Masters to the vision of the Ten Stages of Bodhisattvahood.

1. *Premudita*. Based upon the perfect practice of the Dana Paramita, the Bodhisattva enters the stage of gladness and Joy.

2. *Vimala*. Based upon the Sila Paramita, the Bodhisattva enters upon the perfect practice of purity wherein there is neither joy nor the absence of joy but the mind abides in perfect Peace.

3. *Prabhakari*. Based upon the perfect practice of the Kshanti Paramita, the Bodhisattva enters upon the stage of self-luminous humility in which there is absent even the conception of joy or peace—the stage of perfect Equanimity, of effortless, self-shining patience.

4. *Archismati*. Based upon the perfect practice of the Virya Paramita, the Bodhisattva enters upon the stage wherein there is conviction and purpose and zeal and determination and perseverance. It is the stage of unceasing, in-drawing, effortless "Energy."

5. *Sudurgaya*. Based upon the perfect practice of the Dhyana Paramita, the Bodhisattva enters upon the overcoming stage of self-mastery and the attainment of tranquillity that is based upon unshakable confidence.

6. *Abhimukhi*. Based upon the perfect practice of the Prajna Paramita, the Bodhisattva enters upon the realization stage of Samadhi. While still being in touch with the passions and discriminations of the Saha world, he turns his mind inward by his faculty of intuitive insight to the realization of the intrinsic emptiness and silence of the mind's pure essence.

7. *Durangama*. The Bodhisattva, having attained highest Samadhi, leaves behind all remembrance of discriminations and wholly abiding in the Mind's Pure Essence, he attains within his mind a "turning about" from which he never again recedes. It is the stage of "far-going."

8. *Acala*. This is the "immovable stage," in which the Bodhisattva attains the Samapatti graces and transcendental powers. Having attained a clear understanding of all inner and outer conditions, his mind accepting things as they are, he neither desires to return to the world or to enter Nirvana. He has no desire or purpose except to live a pure life of *anutpatika-dharma-kshanti-gocaya*—a life of patient submissive acceptance.

9. *Sadhumati*. This is the state of perfect identity with *anuttara-samyak-sambodhi*—highest perfect Wisdom. In this state the Bodhisattva has passed beyond all thought of individuation, or discrimination, or integration; he has passed beyond all dualisms, all incompleteness, and is abiding in perfect balance and equanimity realizing the blissful peace of unceasing Samadhi. But still he retains in mind a memory of the world's ignorance and suffering, unreal as it is in fact, but untainted and undisturbed by it, his mind overflowing with compassion, he goes forth in wisdom and love for its emancipation and enlightenment.

10. *Dharmamaga*. In this highest state, the Bodhisattva becomes wholly identified with the Great Truth Cloud and, like a cloud saturated with Truth and Compassion, he becomes Tathagata, his life perfectly integrated with the lives of all, and goes forth to sprinkle the rain of the Good Law by which the seed of enlightenment takes root in the minds of all sentient beings and in the long last brings them to Buddhahood.

NIRVANA

In the more primitive type of Buddhism as still held in Ceylon and Burma, the end of the Path is the attainment of Arhatship and, when life passes, to Nirvana. What then is Nirvana? The root meaning of the word is the extinguishment of a fire when the fuel is all consumed. That is, in Southern Buddhism, when the fires of earthly passion die down, and the disciple becomes an Arhat, free from all desire, and life passes, he is said to have attained Nirvana, or Parinirvana. In Northern Buddhism, Nirvana has a more philosophic meaning: it means the state where not only the fires of earthly passion have died down and earthly life has passed, but all karmaic desire for individual life is extinguished and the disciple has passed into the unitive life of Buddhahood.

The term *pratyakabuddha*, as used by both schools, means a disciple or an arhat who is selfishly desiring Nirvana for his own satisfaction. Such a disciple, according to the Mahayana school has ceased to follow the Path at the seventh stage of Bodhisattvahood and "passes to his nirvana." But after a Bodhisattva attains the eighth stage there is, thereafter, "no more recension," and he goes on to the attainment of highest perfect Wisdom which constrains him, instead of passing to Nirvana, to return to the Saha world of Ignorance and suffering for its liberation and enlightenment. Hence the saying in the Lankavatara Sutra: "For Buddhas there is no Nirvana."

The question may be asked, how, in this world of ignorance, suffering and death, we are to recognize these "returning" Buddhas and Tathagatas? Please recall that Bodhisattvas as they attain the ninth and tenth stages of Bodhisattvahood lose all individuation as human personalities to become identified with Buddhahood in the Great Truth Cloud, and as "formless" Tathagatas attain boundless potentiality and command of skillful means and transcendental powers of self-mastery and efficiency, and as the integrating principle of Buddhahood, are able to take any form they think best, or to be present wherever there is need to support and to draw all sentient beings to enlightenment and Buddhahood. By our practice of Dhyana, as we attain moments of intuitive Samadhi, we integrate our lives with this ever present Buddha-nature, and when we attain highest perfect Samadhi, we become one with all the Buddhas, enjoying their blissful peace, and becoming able ourselves to return to this Saha-world of suffering for its emancipation and enlightenment.

American and European Buddhists, before they can commonly attain Enlightenment and Buddhahood, will need their own method for practicing the Eighth Stage of the Noble Path, but such a Right Method can not be formulated until the Buddha that is taking form within our own minds, comes. Some among us must first attain the Seventh and Eighth of the Bodhisattva Stages and himself have experienced the Durangama Samadhi of "Far-going" and the Acala Samadhi of "No-recension" before he will be worthy of being employed as a skillful device and convenient means for formulating such a Right Method for practicing the Eighth Stage of the Noble Path. "When He comes, we shall be like Him, for we shall see Him as He is." "Even so come, Lord Maitreya!"

Notes: *Dwight Goddard was a prominent early twentieth-century American Buddhist convert. He prepared a massive compilation of Buddhist texts for an English-speaking audience in* A Buddhist Bible *(1932, 1938). At the end of the volume he compiled a variety of brief statements. Together, these statements outline the Buddhist path and are used by almost all branches of Buddhism. That section of the book is reproduced here along with Goddard's introduction and commentary on the eightfold path (about which different Buddhists have the most marked disagreement).*

* * *

Theravada Buddhism

THE NATURE AND PURPOSE (NEO-DHARMA)

The world view of Neo-Dharma can be summarized into four major concepts:

1. The universe is regulated by impartial and unchanging laws.
2. Knowledge of these laws is acquired by insight and by unprejudiced reasoning in the light of one's experiences—not by faith in scriptures or mystical revelations.
3. Moral law, like physical law, is inherent in the workings of nature. Greed, hatred and egotism result in proportionate amounts of unhappiness for one who is responsible for such motivations.
4. This three-dimensional realm of space, time and matter is not the only level of existence. The concrete world of sense perception is a reality, but it is not the only possible dimension of reality.

Since human actions are nearly always the results of their preceding mental conditions, good and evil are best defined as being states of mind rather than types of behavior. Therefore, Neo-Dharma advocates maturation and improvement of one's personality by means of five practices:

1. Development of wisdom and understanding—that is, progressive development of one's intellectual faculties for the sake of better understanding life.
2. Development of insight into one's own personality and awareness of one's conscious and subconscious motivations.
3. Purification of the mind—that is, removal of greed, hatred, fear, egotism, lethargy, etc.
4. Discipline of the mind and body.
5. Cultivation of four states of mind—friendship, kindness, compassion and equanimity.

The beliefs and practices of Neo-Dharma are closer to those of Theravada Buddhism than to any other religious or philosophical institution, and it is from the original teachings of Buddha that the above principles have been derived. "Dharma" is the name for the teaching or gospel

THE NATURE AND PURPOSE (NEO-DHARMA) (continued)

of Buddha, and Neo-Dharma is in agreement with the basic teachings of the Dharma.

Notes: *Founded in 1960, Neo-Dharma is possibly the oldest Theravada Buddhist group in America. This statement attempts to interpret its teachings without recourse to the special vocabulary of Buddhism, which has become more familiar to the public since the early 1960s when this statement was composed.*

* * *

Japanese Buddhism

PROFESSION OF FAITH (BUDDHIST CHURCHES OF AMERICA)

I. We affirm our faith in Amida Buddha, whose infinite light of wisdom and compassion shines on all corners of the universe.

II. We feel deeply that our hearts are dark with ignorance and passions, that even our good acts are tainted with the poison of selfishness and that by ourselves we are incapable of true goodness.

III. We are firmly determined to seek the spirit of Amida's Primal Vow which embraces all and forsakes none, which frees us from the world of impermanence and assures our birth into the Pure Land.

IV. We rely wholeheartedly on Amida's grace and, renouncing all good works contrived by self-power, we depend for our enlightenment on faith in Other Power.

V. We rejoice that this grace is accorded freely and equally to us as well as all other living beings, and this joy pervades our every thought and act.

VI. We recite NAMU AMIDA BUTSU in gratitude for the great Compassionate Vow.

VII. We regard all things with profound thankfulness, and whether suffering or happiness comes to us, we are content in the realization that Amida's grace is always with us.

VIII. We search within ourselves by the light of Amida's Compassion and find that we have drowned in the ocean of selfish desires, that we have lost our way in the pursuit of power and gain. Though we have entered the company of the faithful, we are pained that true joy does not brighten our hearts.

IX. We treasure the Dharma and long to hear it again and again until we are fired with zeal to practice it. We strive to avoid the sinners' way and to model our conduct on that of virtuous people. We desire the company of good friends who follow the same Way, and we wish to be good friends to all who need us. We are resolved to persevere unceasingly in the aspiration for enlightenment and in gratitude for Amida's grace.

X. We resolve to do our daily tasks with the same whole-hearted reverence as if they were religious duties. We devote ourselves to being good members of our families, good workers in our jobs, and good citizens of our country. In this we seek no reward and simply act as our gratitude prompts us.

XI. The power of NAMU AMIDA BUTSU clears the path before us, gives us courage, frees us from evil influences, and brings countless good influences to bless us. It casts the light of infinite love and insight onto the road of our life.

Notes: *Only one Buddhist group has attempted to render its teachings into a creed-like formula. The Buddhist Churches of America is the largest Buddhist organization in North America. Its Profession describes its form of Pure Land Buddhism from Japan.*

* * *

THREE PRINCIPLES (GEDATSU CHURCH OF AMERICA)

We shall observe the teachings of Gedatsu Kongo and pledge utmost effort to live the life of Gedatsu.

We shall endeavour in every way to return appreciation and gratitude for all.

We shall rely upon the Law of Karma and firmly establish peace of mind in our daily lives as it stands.

Notes: *This creed-like statement, the Three Principles, is found in the ritual book of the Gedatsu Church and repeated weekly by members during worship.*

* * *

GOLDEN CHAIN AFFIRMATION, PLEDGE, AND CREED (JODO MISSION)

GOLDEN CHAIN

I am a link in Lord Buddha's golden chain of love that stretches around the world. I must keep my link bright and strong.

I will try to be kind and gentle to every living thing, and protect all who are weaker than myself.

I will try to think pure and beautiful thoughts, to say pure and beautiful words, and to do pure and beautiful deeds, knowing that on what I do now depends my happiness or misery.

May every link in Lord Buddha's golden chain of love become bright and strong, and may we all attain Perfect Peace.

PLEDGE

To the Buddha who promised to be present in His Teaching, We pledge our loyalty and devotion. We dedicate our thoughts, words and deeds to his Service and to the Way of life He laid down for us. We resolve to follow his Example and to have reverence for our religion, respect for our parents and teachers, and love for all forms of life.

THE CREED

We thank the Lord Buddha for showing to us the Way of Freedom.

We will endeavor to walk in His Noble Path every day of our lives.

Notes: *Common to many Japanese Buddhist groups are three brief documents that affirm basic Buddhist beliefs. Rendered into English by the several Japanese-American organizations, the Golden Chain Affirmation, Pledge, and Creed appear in hymnals and ritual books with minor variations in wording. The text reproduced here comes from that used by the Jodo Mission, but it can also be found in the material of such other groups as the Buddhist Churches in America and the Soto [Zen] Mission. These three items are repeated by Japanese Buddhists much as the Apostles' Creed or Nicene Creed are repeated by Christians. In the text of the Golden Chain Affirmation, Nichiren Buddhists add a threefold repetition of their mantra, "Namu Myoho Renge Kyo." The Shingon Mission alters the text of the Creed and terms it The Promise.*

*   *   *

THE PROMISE (SHINGON MISSION)

We thank the Lord Buddha and the Saviour Kobo-daishi for showing us the Way of finding peace. We will endeavor to walk in the Noble Path They showed us, everyday of our lives.

Namu Sakyamuni Butsu

Namu Daishi Henjo Kongo

Notes: *The text of what is termed The Creed by other Japanese Buddhist groups is called The Promise in the songbook of the Shingon Buddhists. It varies significantly from the standard text used by other Japanese Buddhists in its addition of a reference to Shingon Buddhism's founder, Kobo-daishi, who is ranked with Buddha.*

*   *   *

Chinese Buddhism

THE ORDER OF THE UNIVERSE AND THE TWELVE THEOREMS OF THE UNIQUE PRINCIPLE (EAST WEST FOUNDATION)

THE ORDER OF THE UNIVERSE

1. That which has a face has a back. (Negation of the law of identity and contradiction in space.)
2. That which has a beginning has an end. (Negation of the above in time.)
3. There is nothing identical in the universe. (Negation of the law of identity.)
4. The bigger the face, the bigger the back. (Negation of the law of the exclusive middle.)

5. All antagonisms are complementary, for example, beginning-end, front-back, justice-injustice, freedom-slavery, happiness-unhappiness, rise-fall, expansion-contraction, love-hate. (Negation of formal logic.)
6. All antagonisms can be classified in two categories—Yin and Yang—and they are complementary. (Foundation of universal dialectic logic.)
7. Yin and Yang are the two arms of Infinity, Absolute Oneness, God, or the Infinite pure expansion.

TWELVE THEOREMS OF THE UNIQUE PRINCIPLE

1. Yin and Yang are the two poles of the infinite pure expansion.
2. Yin and Yang are produced infinitely, continuously, and forever from the infinite pure expansion itself.
3. Yin is centrifugal; Yang is centripetal. Yin, centrifugal, produces expansion, lightness, cold, etc. Yang, centripetal, produces constriction, weight, heat, light, etc.
4. Yin attracts Yang; Yang attracts Yin.
5. All things and phenomena are composed of Yin and Yang in different proportions.
6. All things and phenomena are constantly changing their Yin and Yang components. Everything is restless.
7. There is nothing completely Yin or completely Yang. All is relative.
8. There is nothing neuter. There is always Yin or Yang in excess.
9. Affinity or force of attraction between things is proportional to the difference of Yin and Yang in them.
10. Yin expels Yin; Yang expels Yang. Expulsion or attraction between two things Yin or Yang is in inverse proportion to the difference of their Yin or Yang force.
11. Yin produces Yang; Yang produces Yin in the extremity.
12. Everything is Yang at its center and Yin at its periphery (surface).

Notes: *These two sets of statements summarize the basic teachings of Michio Kushi, founder of the East West Foundation. The principles, drawn from Chinese philosophy, also form the basis for the natural medical system, macrobiotics, which Kushi advocates.*

*   *   *

Tibetan Buddhism

FUNDAMENTAL PRINCIPLES (PANSOPHIC INSTITUTE)

1) The philosophic dualism so deeply ingrained in the mind of Man (responsible for Man's original mental

FUNDAMENTAL PRINCIPLES (PANSOPHIC
INSTITUTE) (continued)

development) is today seen to be only an illusion.
There are no absolutes of good and evil, or any other
dichotomies.

2) However, Man possesses inherent qualities of honesty, justice and courage. Without needing to fear
awesome Deities, it is possible to apply these
qualities to the basic ethical code without hypocrisy,
thereby ceasing to cause harm to oneself or other
beings.

3) It is only reasonable to strive to live according to
these values, and to desire such conduct from others.
But to discipline the self it is necessary to defeat
greed, anger and sloth, Man's three main enemies to
progress.

4) Life is a process of evolution, both of physical form
and of individual spirit or consciousness. By the
defeat of greed, anger and sloth, and the cultivation
of honesty, justice and courage, the evolution of
Mankind as a whole and of the individual is
hastened.

5) If the emotions are mastered and one's mind is made
calm, efforts can be directed toward the increase of
awareness. This results in an expanded understanding of life and one's relationship to the cosmos and
the all-pervading Divine Consciousness which en-
souls it.

6) These principles represent the Path from the
darkness of spiritual ignorance to the state of
Enlightenment (Illumination). They are symbolized
as a reality through the lives of humanity's great
spiritual Masters. Each individual can develop the
innate divinity in his or her own nature.

7) Such development brings FREEDOM from karma
or fate, the results of previous thoughts, desires and
actions. If one who is so freed then chooses to work
for the similar freedom of others, the evolution of
Mankind (and through Man all life) is hastened. This
is the Bodhisattva or Savior Ideal: the dedication to
assist in the eventual Enlightenment of all beings.

Notes: *The principles of the Pansophic Institute attempt to
state the basics of Tibetan Buddhism without resorting to
the technical Tibetan terminology commonly employed by
followers.*

*　　*　　*

Shinto and the Japanese New Religions

DAILY TEACHING (KONKO KYO)

1. On this day, pray with a sincere heart. The divine
favor depends on your own heart.

2. Remember the universe is your eternal home.

3. Have faith. To have faith is to keep Kami in your
heart.

4. Since man is the master of all things, let his faith be
in harmony with the way of the universe.

5. Food is bestowed as a blessing for the life of man.

6. Instead of worrying, have faith in Kami.

7. Pray for health. Make your body strong, for it is the
basis of all things.

8. With a grateful heart, receive your food.

9. Suffering is a divine favor in disguise.

10. To have faith is to live fully day to day.

11. All men are brothers as children of Kami.

12. A peaceful home is rooted in faith.

13. The birth of a child derives not from your own
strength, but from the blessing of Kami.

14. As you love your own children, understand Kami's
love for you.

15. Do not give yourself over to selfish desires.

16. Overeating and overdrinking is the cause of hunger.

17. Pray first and then seek treatment for your illness;
then, you will receive the divine favor.

18. You need not practice religious austerities, just
pursue your occupation diligently.

19. Faith is not simply listening to words of instructions;
let it be an expression from the heart.

20. Treat every man with respect. If you treat any man
lightly, you will not receive the divine favor.

21. A heart of love is the heart of Kami.

22. Now hear the sound of the opening of the universe
and be awakened.

23. Training in faith is as gradual as the progress of your
studies.

24. Maintain your faith even under favorable conditions.

25. Open your spiritual eyes without depending on your
physical eyes.

26. Your lifetime is a training period of faith.

27. You should not break the bond with Kami. Kami
will keep the bond with you.

28. Enrich your faith. You must have faith now and
always.

29. You should do whatever you do with sincerity.

30. Faith is like a sacred fire. Hand it down from
generation to generation, without losing it.

31. Without faith, the world would be dark.

*　　*　　*

KYO JI (FUNDAMENTAL TEACHINGS)
(MAHIKARI OF AMERICA)

1. The three spiritual worlds, the Divine, the Astral,
and the present (Physical) worlds, are not subjects
pertaining to ideology and philosophy.

They, in reality exist and are closely connected as air
is to life. They are infinite and omnipresent sources

of spiritual energy and of the emanation of Divine Light.

Hence, they are above religion, beyond the influence of races or religious dominations made by human intelligence. They are determined by the Divine Law which is the arrangement for eternal flourishing of the universe and are full of wonder.

Motosu Hajimari Kamu, the Creator, is the source of Power which unites and administers all for the eternal flourishing of His creatures. He is the master of mankind, all spirits and materials.

He is the source of Spiritual Wisdom, and manifests as the Cosmic Will, Light, and Absolute Power to shine upon the universe.

Moses, Buddha, Jesus, Confusis, and Mencius were the holy messengers of God, Su no Kami. There are no religious denominations in the Divine World.

2. It is the great destiny for mankind to build a holy century of Divine (heavenly) Civilization that is to come by complying with His great love and the Divine understanding of truth. This is the supreme order for mankind.

Regardless of religious denominations, all man should practice what is written in this book at all times, as this is the origin of the "practice of truth".

This righteous way of devotion to Su no Kami is not intended for Mahikari Bunmei Kyodan only, but for all human beings. This is *SU-KYO* (to respect the original Divine Teachings).

3. All seemingly truthful and pseudo-teachings have come to an end as well as salvation by a weak, white, passive light. Now the time has come to perceive quietly and directly, the true light of God and to master the Divine Light.

Experience this for yourself because it is the first appearance of the Divine Law prophesied by Buddha and Jesus.

This is the history of mankind and the sublime moment of religious renaissance. Present teachings are old and deteriorating or they are disguised or provisional.

The dawning of the Spiritual Civilization has come . . . a true, new civilization for the restoration of theocracy and the achievement of the Divine Administration.

This will be the final opportunity for the door of heaven to open up for mankind.

This is an era for SUMEI GODO (unification of the five great religious) and YOSUKA (to transmit the power of Su no Kami). It is time for us to become evangelists for the Divine teaching.

4. The earth is originally one; the world is one; the origin of mankind is one; the root of all religious is one.

Become heralds for the coming civilization of
MI RO KU, ME SHI A
5   6   7,   3   4   5
the Cross (+ = Kami, God) civilization and SANJUJI (triple cross) civilization.

Grow as a child of God and become a *TANE BITO* (seed person) for the coming Holy Century. Practice MAHIKARI NO WAZA and cultivate your soul. This is the secret Art to overcome religious divisions. Elevate your soul and master *SEIHO* (Divine Theory) obediently.

Become an instrument for the Divine Administration and be His disciples. This will be the most fruitful epoch for mankind.

5. The time for mankind to trifle with ideological existence of God is over. Time of meaningless prayers are over. It is time for mankind to realize the pragmatism of *SU KYO* (to respect the original Divine Teachings) in their daily living.

These prayers are the foundation for all religions. God allows all human beings to participate in His Plan through prayer, practicing and performing Mahikari no waza.

This is a marvelous method to revive the essence of all teachings and religions of the world. It is possible to actualize perfect health; free from disease and poverty and to enjoy harmonious love and peace. All mankind will be profoundly moved after witnessing such miracles.

It is man's responsibility, a supreme duty to God, to create a world where each and every man may enjoy true happiness.

*   *   *

GOREIGEN (DIVINE MAXIM) (SHINREIKYO)

The path to God as taught by Shinreikyo is nothing else but the universal law which applies to the three existences of past, present and future.

All that takes place in the universe is based on this unique principle. True happiness and lasting prosperity become a reality to those who abide by this law, while the fate of all earthly things is ultimate destruction if this rigid law is resisted. Disaster brought by disease and calamity is no exception. Therefore, the divine teachings of Shinreikyo are the only teachings that every living person should pursue. All that is asked of its followers is to practise the teachings of Shinreikyo with deep faith.

Chapter 10

Unclassified Christian Churches

BASIS OF FELLOWSHIP (CHRISTIAN CATHOLIC CHURCH)

FIRST — That we recognize the infallible inspiration and sufficiency of the Holy Scriptures as the rule of faith and practice.

SECOND — That we recognize that no persons can be members of the Church who have not repented of their sins and have not trusted in Christ for Salvation.

THIRD — That such persons must also be able to make a good profession, and declare that they do know, in their own hearts, that they have truly repented, and are truly trusting Christ, and have the witness, in a measure, of the Holy Spirit.

FOURTH — That all other questions of every kind shall be held to be matters of opinion and not matters that are essential to Church unity.

Notes: *The Christian Catholic Church is best known for the emphasis upon spiritual healing practiced by its founder, John Alexander Dowie. This brief statement is reflective of the ecumenical spirit of the church.*

*   *   *

DOCTRINE (CHRISTIAN UNION)

Seven cardinal principles are considered essential to the organization.

I.   The Oneness of the Church of Christ.

II.   Christ the Only Head.

III. The Bible the Only Rule of Faith and Practice.

IV.   Good Fruits the Only Condition of Fellowship.

V.   Christian Union Without Controversy.

VI.   Each Local Church Governs Itself.

VII. Partisan Political Preaching Discountenanced.

In addition to these principles the position taken by The Christian Union on the fundamental doctrines of the Word of God is as follows:

1.   The Bible is infallible, the inspired and authoritative Word of God.

2.   There is one God, eternally existent in three persons—Father, Son, and Holy Spirit.

3.   We believe in: the Deity of Christ, His conception by the Holy Spirit and His virgin birth; His sinless life, miracles, and vicarious and atoning death; His bodily resurrection and ascension to the right hand of the Father; His personal return in power and glory.

4.   Salvation is wholly of grace but conditioned upon repentance toward God and faith toward Jesus Christ. Regeneration and justification follow the meeting of these conditions.

5.   The Holy Spirit indwells believers, gives power for service and holy living, guides into truth, produces the fruits of Christian character; and carries on toward perfection the sanctification of believers.

6.   We believe in the resurrection to immortality of the bodies of believers at the return of the Lord Jesus which shall be changed so they shall be literal, spiritual, and immortal bodies like unto Christ's own glorious body.

7.   We believe that man was created by God and not by any accidental or spontaneous, or self propagated occurrence, action, method, or process. As a result of his fall, death passed upon all men and sin entered into the world. Therefore condemnation rests upon each person who has reached the age and development with which comes accountability before God, and he is lost forever, except he be born again.

8.   The church of Christ is composed of all Spirit regenerated believers.

Thus it can be seen that The Christian Union is committed to a conservative and fundamental interpretation of the Christian Faith.

Notes: *The Christian Union has as its main objectives: 1) the promotion of fellowship among God's people; 2) the proclamation of the gospel at home and abroad; and 3) the declaration of the "whole Council of God" for the edification of believers. In keeping with these goals, the doctrinal principles are held to a summary of the fundamentals. Emphasis is placed on Christianity as a life to be lived.*

OUR MESSAGE [FAMILY OF LOVE (CHILDREN OF GOD)]

I. OUR SAMPLE PROVES OUR SERMON

1. WE ARE HERE TO PREACH NOT A 50% OR A 70%, BUT A TOTAL, 100% LIVING FOR GOD: Living in a totally new society, loving one another and having the truth. Our message will go over the whole world. They have heard from the church that Jesus saves, but they don't want any part of churchianity. But they will hear about Jesus from you because you will be living it.

2. YOU WILL BE A LIVING EXAMPLE OF THE TRUTH. You are preaching it in the greatest way of preaching—by living it! Jesus' last prayer for His disciples was that "they may be one . . . that the world may believe . . . and know that Thou (God) hath sent Me." In other words, Jesus was saying that this unity with each other and God is the sample that will prove to the world the reality of His Message.

3. IT'S TRUE WHEN IT COMES TO THE FINAL SHOWDOWN THAT ONLY THE MIRACLE-WORKING POWER OF THE HOLY SPIRIT of God Himself can really do the job of winning their hearts but they must see Him doing it through us first of all! They must see this miracle-working power at work in our lives, as a genuine living sample and proof that the sermon can happen!

4. JESUS NOT ONLY PREACHED HIS MESSAGE, BUT HE LIVED IT! He was not only the Living Word, the Sermon, but He was also the Living Work, the Sample. For He said He had not only "spoken unto them", but He also had "done the works that none other man did."

5. HOWEVER, DON'T PUT THE CART BEFORE THE HORSE, THE SAMPLE BEFORE THE SERMON: remember, the words are the cause and the kids and Colonies are the effect!

6. COLONY LIVING IS NOT OUR MAIN MESSAGE. It's just a sample that proves the words.

7. WITNESSING HIS WONDER-WORKING WORDS TO THE WORLD IS OUR MAIN TASK, and our main motive should be to obey God and get the message out. But remember, the sample sells the sales talk. You are product and proof that it works! So, "Let your light so shine before men that they may see your good works, and glorify your Father which is in heaven."

II. OUR MESSAGE OF LOVE AND DISCIPLESHIP

8. OUR MESSAGE OF LOVE IS TAKEN FROM OUR REVOLUTIONARY HAND-BOOK, THE BIBLE, and is simply that "God so loved the world that He gave His only begotten Son (Jesus), that whosoever believeth in Him should not perish but have everlasting life."

9. "FOR ALL HAVE SINNED and come short of the glory of God." "There is none righteous, no, not one." "All we like sheep have gone astray, and the Lord hath laid on Him the iniquity of us all."

10. "THE WAGES OF SIN IS DEATH, BUT THE GIFT OF GOD IS ETERNAL LIFE through Jesus Christ our Lord." "Not by works of righteousness which we have done, but according to His mercy He saved us."

11. "FOR BY GRACE ARE YE SAVED, THROUGH FAITH, and that not of yourselves; it is the gift of God: not of works, lest any man should boast." "If we confess our sins, He is faithful and just to forgive us." "Believe on the Lord Jesus Christ, and thou shalt be saved."

12. "YE SHALL RECEIVE POWER after that the Holy Ghost is come upon you, and ye shall be witnesses unto Me."

13. WE ALSO BELIEVE THAT ALL THOSE WHO WISH TO BE JESUS' DISCIPLES SHOULD: "Go . . . into all the world and preach the Gospel to every creature!" "Go out into the highways and hedges and compel them to come in!" "Sell all that thou hast and give to the poor . . . and come follow Me!"

14. "HE THAT FORSAKETH NOT ALL THAT HE HATH, CANNOT BE MY DISCIPLE." "Seek ye first the Kingdom of God and His righteousness and all these things shall be added unto you." "Warn the wicked of his wicked way to save his life."

15. "ALL THAT BELIEVED WERE TOGETHER AND HAD ALL THINGS COMMON." "And they continued steadfastly in the Apostles' doctrine and fellowship, and in breaking of bread, and prayers." "And daily in the temple and in every house, they ceased not to teach and preach Jesus Christ."

16. SO THERE'S NOTHING NEW ABOUT OUR MESSAGE—GOD'S MESSAGE THROUGH US! IT'S THE SAME MESSAGE JESUS PREACHED, the same message His disciples preached; but they not only preached it—they also lived it, just like we're doing. That's the difference! The scribes and pharisees were preaching it, but they weren't practising it.

17. THAT'S THE DIFFERENCE BETWEEN THE CHURCHES AND US! Jesus said to the common people, "The scribes and pharisees (the church leaders) sit in Moses' seat: All therefore they bid you observe, that observe and do, but do not ye after their works: for they say and do not." And that goes for today's churches too!

III. OUR MESSAGE OF DOOM AND JUDGMENT AGAINST THIS WORLD'S SYSTEMS

18. IN EVERY AGE GOD HAD HIS LAST PROPHET who gave them God's last words. Today they are being given it through us, before God gives it to them.

19. THE MESSAGE OF JEREMIAH, the Prophet of Doom, was revealed to us in December of 1961,

when I was very ill, and God said this was to be our message from now on—the Doomsday, End-Time Warning Message. We are to become as a red flashing warning light to the World, a sombre warning of serious danger ahead.

20. AS WITH JEREMIAH, GOD HAS "SET THEE OVER THE NATIONS and over the kingdoms to root out, and to pull down, and to destroy and to throw down their idols with the spiritual weapons of God's Word) and to build and to plant (God's spiritual kingdom in the hearts of men)."

21. "AND I (GOD) WILL UTTER MY JUDGMENTS AGAINST THEM (through you) touching all their wickedness who have forsaken Me and have burned incense unto other gods and worshipped the works of their own hands." "But if they will not obey (our warnings), I will utterly pluck up and destroy that nation, saith the Lord!"

22. GOD HAS ALSO CALLED US, EVEN AS HE DID THE PROPHET EZEKIEL, TO BE WATCHMEN unto the House of Israel, those who were supposed to be His Church; therefore we're to hear His Words and give them warning from the Lord.

23. AS HE TOLD EZEKIEL, GOD HAS TOLD US: "Son of man, I have made thee a watchman unto the House of Israel: therefore hear the word at My mouth and give them warning from Me. When I say unto the wicked, Thou shalt surely die; and thou givest him not warning, nor speakest to warn the wicked from his wicked way, to save his life; the same wicked man shall die in his iniquity; but his blood will I require at thine hand. Yet if thou warn the wicked, and he turn not from his wickedness, nor from his wicked way, he shall die in his iniquity; but thou hast delivered thy soul."

24. OUR MAIN WITNESS (WHICH INCLUDES BOTH OUR WAY OF LIFE AND OUR SERMON) IS THAT WE ARE AGAINST THE SYSTEM; that is 95% of our witness. It is a damning witness against them. By the System, I'm not talking about the legal laws—I'm talking about the damnable Satanic principles of which the damned System is built, its laws of selfishness and do your own thing and keep on living just as you did, refusing any change.

IV. A TWO-FOLD MESSAGE

25. OUR MESSAGE IS TO "FEAR GOD AND GIVE GLORY TO HIM; for the hour of His Judgment is come: and worship Him that made Heaven, and earth, and the sea, and the fountains of waters."

26. IN OTHER WORDS, WE TELL PEOPLE TO FOLLOW GOD OR RECEIVE HIS JUDGMENTS. So in a way our message is two-fold: against the rebellious System and for God's Sheep.

27. OUR MAJOR JOB IS TO STAND UP AS GOD'S STRONGEST WITNESSES before both the Church and the whole world and to explain to them what's happening and to lead and encourage and feed God's Children to the very End!

28. WE'RE THE MIGHTY ARMY OF CHRISTIAN SOLDIERS FIGHTING A RELENTLESS WAR FOR THE TRUTH AND LOVE OF GOD, AGAINST THE CONFUSION OF BABYLON— the anti-God, anti-Christ Systems of this world, whether Godless educations, Christless religions, vicious economics, or the hellish wars of the traditions, boundaries and prejudices of selfish, greedy and Godless man.

V. WHY WE PREACH REVOLUTION, NOT REFORMATION

29. IT IS IMPOSSIBLE, AS JESUS SAID, TO REFORM THE OLD, FOR THEY WILL NOT ACCEPT IT and in the attempt the bottle will be broken and the contents lost.

30. THE OLD RELIGIOUS AND ECONOMIC SYSTEMS CANNOT BE PATCHED UP, for they are tattered, threadbare, and rotten and must be cast upon the fires of His Judgment that He may create "a new Heaven and a new earth" in which "old things are passed away and all things are become new."

31. SO IT IS ALWAYS NECESSARY TO ROOT OUT, PULL DOWN, DESTROY and throw down the old in order to build and to plant the new; there just isn't room for both.

32. THERE IS NO SUCH THING AS THE PEACEFUL COEXISTENCE OF GOOD AND EVIL! I came not to bring peace, but a sword! One or the other has to conquer. One or the other has to be destroyed that the other might live. Ye cannot serve God and Mammon. "Ye cannot serve two masters."

33. YE CANNOT BELONG TO BOTH THE SYSTEM AND THE REVOLUTION, the forces of reaction and the forces of change! It's impossible: as Jesus said, you'll either hate the one, and love the other, or hold to the one and despise the other. You'll either stay in the System or drop out. There's no such thing as hanging somewhere in between, suspended between Heaven and Hell in some kind of compromiser's limbo!

34. YOU'VE GOTTA DROP OUT IF YOU'RE GONNA LIVE, or else you'll die with the old, and the worn out System will collapse on top of you!

35. HOWEVER, WE ARE NOT TALKING ABOUT PHYSICAL, VIOLENT REVOLUTION that doesn't do anything but a lot of damage, and that doesn't change the hearts of the System one tiny little bit, but just creates another System where things are just as bad, if not worse.

36. WE'RE TALKING ABOUT A SPIRITUALLY VIOLENT REVOLUTION that absolutely rends your heart right out completely and gives you a new Spirit, the Holy Ghost of God! "A new heart also will I give you, and a new spirit will I put within you."

OUR MESSAGE [FAMILY OF LOVE (CHILDREN OF GOD)] (continued)

37. WHEN JESUS WENT SAYING, "REPENT, for the Kingdom of heaven is at hand". He was saying "Revolt, revolute, have a Revolution!"

38. THE BIBLICAL WORD "REPENT" COMES FROM THE GREEK WORD "METANOIA", which means a complete change of mind or a total turning around and going in the opposite direction or to "revolute"—so repentance is a revolution. It means to change your direction—change everything.

39. CHANGE YOUR WAY OF LIVING—not just your so-called heart, but your whole life and the way you live and the way you work! That's a Revolution!

40. THAT'S WHAT JESUS PREACHED! And that's the kind of Revolution we've got! For, "the Kingdom of Heaven suffereth violence, and the violent take it by force."

VI. DELIVERING THE MESSAGE

41. THE TRUTH FEEDS SOME AND CHOKES OTHERS. To some we're like a lion; to others, like a lamb. To the wolves we're as lions; to the sheep we're as lambs. There are times to roar and times to bleat. Just please, pray God you'll know the difference!

42. HIS WORD NEVER CHANGES, Christ doesn't change, but God keeps moving every day.

43. IT MAY BE THE SAME MESSAGE, BUT IT IS VARIED EVERY DAY TO SUIT THE NEED and adapt to the situation. As Paul himself conceded, we must become all things to all men in order that we might win some.

44. THEREFORE, THERE ARE CERTAINLY DIFFERENCES IN APPROACHES—To the Roman as a Roman, to the Jew as a Jew, to the Greek as a Greek, and to the Japanese as a Japanese. It's a matter of communication in order to make our message understandable and our witness comprehensible and our lives interpretable in the' terms, language and even gestures that they understand.

45. BUT LIKE THE MESSAGE OF EVERY TRUE PROPHET OF GOD, THE TRUTH OFTEN HURTS, and no matter how lovingly you present it, some people may resent it bitterly and blame you for what God said! So use lots of love and wisdom. Be very cautious and try not to take one side or the other—we're on God's side!

46. SOME OF THESE LETTERS ARE HIGHLY CONTROVERSIAL. But they have to get out; people have to know the truth, and we have to obey the Lord! But you don't have to convince them. Leave the decision to them.

VII. REACTION TO OUR MESSAGE

47. A. ENEMIES: FOR A WHILE WE WILL BE BIG NEWS AND GET PATTED ON THE BACK FOR OUR GOOD WORK converting the radicals and dopers, but soon they will realise what a threat we are to their children and to their System. We are a kind of Communist that their kids have not been conditioned against—Christian Communists!

48. THEY CAN TELL THEIR KIDS THAT WE ARE WRONG and evil and a Marxist Communist front, but their kids will know better.

49. THE COMMUNISTS TODAY SAY "JESUS WAS A VIOLENT REVOLUTIONARY." This is the ammunition that the leaders of Moloch (education) and Baal (church) will use against us to link us with the violent, physical revolutionaries and turn their followers, the common people, against us; and eventually their leaders will pull a Mt 12:14: "Then the Pharisees went out and held a council against him, how they might destroy him".

50. BUT ALL THOSE THAT DO LIFT EVEN A FINGER AGAINST ONE OF THE HAIRS OF THY HEADS SHALL PERISH. So ridiculous are those nincompoops who fight God's Children.

51. B. VAST MAJORITY (silent majority): The thousands to whom He had preached, had healed, and fed were seldom to be counted on for loyalty or faithfulness or genuine discipleship.

52. THE VAST MAJORITY COULDN'T CARE LESS; they're not even interested, except when you attract their attention momentarily, as Jesus did with His miracles.

53. THE VAST MAJORITY ARE ALWAYS WRONG, that is, in the world at large! And they can usually easily be swayed by a very wicked minority of enemies, as the religious leaders did when they persuaded the crowds that Jesus, Who fed and healed them, should be crucified. They'll do it to us someday too, and, in a measure, already have upon occasion.

54. C. SHEEP: DURING JESUS' 3 1/2 YEARS OF PUBLIC MINISTRY THE NUMBER OF TRUE DISCIPLES OR GENUINE FOLLOWERS WAS FEW—about 12 to 70, to be exact. The true followers, the true disciples, willing to forsake all, truly follow His teaching and truly obey His Words will always be the infinitesimal minority. "Because straight is the gate and narrow is the way which leadeth unto Life and few there be that find it."

55. VERY FEW MEN ARE SO IDEALISTIC AS TO BE WILLING TO GIVE UP THEIR OWN SINS IN ORDER TO PLEASE GOD that they might try to save their fellowman! —Only a few! God help us to find those few!

56. A PROPHECY: FOR THEY CRY UNTO ME AND CALL UPON ME IN THEIR DISTRESS AND THEIR HUNGER, for they are as sheep having no shepherd and they are scattered abroad throughout all the earth.

57. THEREFORE, I HAVE GIVEN THEM A SHEPHERD that shall guide them into the fold of the True Shepherd.

58. MY VOICE SHALL THEY HEED THROUGH MY SERVANT DAVID! For My sheep hear My

Voice and know My Voice, and they follow Me, and the Voice of the stranger they will not follow.

Notes: *Originally issued in 1975, this document summarizes the message, without mention of the more controversial teachings, of this early Jesus People group. Emphasis is placed upon the apocalyptic aspect of the message, with little hope being offered for the world and a call for revolution. Scriptural references and cross references to other writings of the Children of God have been deleted.*

* * *

THE AFFIRMATIONS (FREE CHURCH OF BERKELEY)

God is not dead.

God is bread.

The bread is rising.

Bread means revolution.

God means revolution.

Murder is no revolution.

Revolution is love.

Win with love.

The radical Jesus is winning.

The world is coming to a beginning.

The whole world is watching.

Organize for a new world.

Wash off your brother's blood.

Burn out the mark of the Beast.

Join the freedom meal.

Plant the people's park.

The asphalt church is marching.

The guerrilla church is recruiting.

The people's church is striking.

The submarine church is surfacing.

The war is over.

The war is over.

The war is over.

The Liberated Zone is at hand.

Notes: *The Free Church of Berkeley was an expression of the radical Protestant Christianity of the 1960s. It developed its own liturgy, one part of which was the Freedom Meal, the church's equivalent to the Lord's Supper. The Affirmations is taken from that liturgy and serves as a poetic summary of the church's activist stance.*

* * *

ARTICLES OF FAITH (MOUNT ZION SANCTUARY)

I. THE SCRIPTURES.

We believe the Holy Bible contains the divine revelation of the eternal GOD; that it is the expression of His will to man; written by holy men of old, divinely moved and inspired by the Holy Spirit; and is the divinely appointed standard and guide to our faith and practice. II. Peter 1:20-21; II. Tim. 3:15-17; Rom. 16:25-27; Psa. 119:105.

II. THE TRUE GOD.

We believe there is one God—eternal, immortal, invisible, omniscient, omnipotent and omnipresent: the Supreme and Omnipotent Creator and Ruler of the universe. Gen. 1 and 2; Psa. 90:2; I. Tim. 1:17; Eph. 4:6.

III. THE LORD JESUS CHRIST.

We believe that Jesus is the Christ, the son of the living God; that He was in the beginning with God; that all things were created by Him, and without Him was not anything made that was made. John 1:1-14; Heb. 1:1-3; Luke 3:22; Matt. 16:15-16; John 17:1, 20-26.

IV. INCARNATION AND VIRGIN BIRTH.

We believe that Christ, the Son, was in the beginning with God, the Father, and became, by voluntary consent party to the marvelous plan of redemption, conceived by the determinate counsel and foreknowledge of God before the world was; and that the child, Jesus, immaculately conceived of the Holy Spirit and born of the Virgin Mary, was the physical body thus prepared for the incarnation of the Christ, the Son of the living God, manifested in the flesh, that He might destroy the works of the devil, and do the will of God on the earth, in executing the plan of redemption for fallen man. Isa. 9:6; Luke 1:26-38; Heb. 10:5-7; I. John 3:8.

V. THE HOLY SPIRIT.

We believe that the Holy Spirit, the Comforter, proceeding from God, the Father, is the executive power of God, by which the Church is born again, taught, instructed, inspired, energized and empowered for its God-given ministry; and that every believer is commanded to be filled therewith. John 14:15-18; 15:26; 16:7-11; 3:3-8; Eph. 5:18; Acts 1:8; Luke 24:49; Acts 2:1-4.

VI. THE FALL OF MAN.

We believe man was created holy, and in his holy estate enjoyed the personal presence and fellowship of his Creator with unspeakable Edenic happiness; but by willful and voluntary transgression, he fell from his Edenic bliss, and under just condemnation was banished therefrom, to suffer the death of separation from God, and become a bond-slave to Satan, without defense or excuse. Gen. 3:1-24; Rom. 5:12-19; I. Cor. 15:21-22.

VII. THE ATONEMENT.

We believe in the sacrificial death and vicarious atonement of the Lord Jesus Christ, for man's sin; that "He was wounded for our transgressions, He was bruised for our iniquities: the chastisement of our peace was upon Him; and with His stripes we are healed;" that, "being justified freely by His blood, we are saved from wrath through Him." Rom. 5:9; Isa. 53:5; John 3:14-17; I. Peter 2:24; 3:18; Heb. 9:28.

VIII. THE RESURRECTION AND ASCENSION

We believe in the triumphant bodily resurrection of Jesus Christ, and His glorious ascension with the same body, glorified, into heaven, to the right hand of the Majesty on high, where He ever lives as our High Priest, making intercession for us. Matt. 28:1-6; Luke 24:36-48; Heb. 7:22-28; Acts 1:9-11; Eph. 4:8-10.

IX. JUSTIFICATION.

We believe Jesus Christ was delivered for our offenses, and raised for our justification; that being justified by faith in His death and resurrection, we have peace with God through our Lord Jesus Christ; by Whom we have now received the atonement. Rom. 4:25; 5:1-9.

X. SANCTIFICATION AND HOLINESS.

We believe it is the privilege of every believer to be sanctified wholly, spirit, soul and body; that we are sanctified only in the proportion that we live and obey the Word of God; that we are sanctified and made holy as we obey the Truth, "Thy Word is Truth." We are commanded to be holy as He is holy; for "without holiness no man shall see the Lord." I. Thess. 5:23; John 17:17-19; Lev. 20:7; Matt. 5:48; Heb. 12:14.

XI. DIVINE HEALING.

We believe divine healing is a part of the atonement, and is a Gospel privilege, which has never been withdrawn from the believing Church. Isa. 53:6; Matt. 8:17; Heb. 13:8; Matt. 28:18-20.

XII. WATER BAPTISM.

We believe that immersion, which symbolizes death, burial and resurrection of the believer, is the only Scriptural mode of water baptism; demonstrated by the baptised of our Lord Jesus Christ — being baptised in this manner; leaving us an example that we should follow in His steps. Rom. 6:3-5; Matt. 3:13-17: I. Peter 2:21.

XIII. THE SABBATH DAY.

We believe the Seventh Day is still the sabbath of the Lord our God; that He has never changed, nor authorized anyone else to change His holy day from the Seventh to any other day. We find no authority anywhere in the Scriptures for the first day observance, nor any evidence of the first day resurrection, upon which the erroneous claim for the first day Sabbath observance is based. Psa. 89:34; Deut. 4:2; Prov. 30:6; Rev. 22:14, 18, 19.

XIV. SECOND COMING.

We believe the second coming of our Lord Jesus is very near; that it will be personal, literal, pre-millennial; that He is coming to reign on the earth; and that the saints will reign with Him a thousand years; and of the increase of His government and peace there will be no end. Acts 1:9-11; James 5:7-8; Rev. 1:7; Isa. 9:6-7; Rev. 20:4; 5:10.

XV. THE CHRISTIAN CHURCH.

We believe the Christian Church, built upon the foundation of the Apostles and Prophets, and Jesus Christ the Chief Cornerstone, is a body of born again believers, who follow Christ, as their perfect example in all things; and His teachings as their infallible guide; and are as thoroughly detached and separate from the world as was He! walking in holiness of life and character; that its work and ministry is supported financially, on the Bible plan of tithes and freewill offerings. Num. 18:20-21; Mal. 3:8-12.

XVI. PLEDGE TO FEDERAL GOVERNMENT.

We believe that the Constitution of the United States is largely, if not entirely, an inspired document; and we pledge our loyalty to the Constitutional Government of the U.S.A., and to non-combatant service in time of war. Rom. 13:1-10; Ex. 20:13.

* * *

Homosexually Oriented Churches

DECLARATION OF FAITH, THE PROCLAMATION OF FAITH, AND THE MANIFESTO [COMMUNITY OF THE LOVE OF CHRIST (EVANGELICAL CATHOLIC)]

DECLARATION OF FAITH

We believe in God, Creator of all, of the heavens and of the earth, Who goes before creation as our common Parent, calling us to Choose Life!—and to God's deeds we testify:

God calls the worlds into being, creates persons in God's own image and sets before us the Way of Life.

God seeks in holy love to liberate all people from sin and alienation.

Christ, through Whom humanity attains New Life, is the Word of God spoken in eternity: Whom in the alone-born of God, Jesus of Nazareth, has come to us as our Messiah and Liberator, entering our humanity by the conception of the Holy Spirit in the virgin Mary, and sharing our common lot conquered sin and reconciles the world to God. Jesus suffered the death of the cross.

After three days, Christ Jesus rose from the dead.

Jesus bestows upon us the Holy Spirit, regenerating and sanctifying persons, creating and renewing Community in the love of Christ: binding in covenant faithful people of all ages, sexes, races and tongues.

The Holy Spirit of God, sent through Jesus, calls us into the Church-Community to accept the cost and joy of discipleship: to be Jesus' friends in the service of the people; to preach the Gospel to all peoples in the world; to bring the Good News to the poor; to proclaim liberty to the captives, new vision to the unseeing, freedom to those in bondage, liberation to the oppressed, the time of the Lord to all; to share in Jesus' Baptism and eat at Jesus' Table until Christ comes again; to join in Jesus' suffering and victory.

The Bible is the divinely inspired Word of God, spoken by the Holy Spirit through prophets and apostles; interpreted by the Holy Spirit given to women and men in the Church-Community of Jesus: and is our guide in faith and discipline as the pointer to the inward Word of God, the Light which enlightens every person who comes into the world.

Jesus promises to all who have faith liberation from the bondage of sin and oppression, fullness of grace and strength for the struggle for justice and peace through the Spirit; Jesus' own Presence in our midst in trial and rejoicing, and eternal life in God's Kingdom, the liberated Community which has no end. Amen.

THE PROCLAMATION OF FAITH

Praising and offering thanks, truly we proclaim:

The One God, Sovereign and Eternal, Who Creates, Redeems and Sustains all, is the Foundation of the heavens and the earth and all that dwell therein, Who calls us to Choose Life. God is One: and Faith and Charity are joined eternally. Therefore, to the deeds of God we testify:

God calls the worlds into being, creates us in the divine image and likeness, and sets before us the Way of Life, seeking in Holy Love to liberate all people from alienation, sin and hatred.

In Jesus of Nazareth, the Eternal Word of God has come to us and shared our common lot, as foretold by the Prophets: in the fulness of time entering our humanity by the Work of the Holy Spirit Who, that God might spiritually heal the separation of sin, prepared the Son of Mary to be the vehicle of the Word, so that Jesus Christ is fully human and fully Divine, both natures maintained in perfect union so that there is One Christ, our Sovereign Saviour, Who overcame sin, sickness and death, and reconciled the earth to God. In the days of Pontius Pilate, Jesus Christ suffered the death of the Cross and was buried; and after three days, by the Power of God, overcame death.

Christ bestows upon us the Paraclete, the Spirit of Light, of Truth and of Love. In Jesus Christ all glory is given to the One Eternal God through the Holy Spirit; Who unites, for the advancement of humanity and the earth in the Reign of God, with those who through Faith are wrested from the principalities and powers, the rule of evil in the world: binding in covenant the Mystical Body of Christ, the blessed company of all faithful people even from the foundation of the world.

Through Holy Spirit, the Wisdom of God, Jesus Christ calls us to accept the cost and joy of discipleship in the journey from darkness to the Light: to share in Christ's Baptism and eat at Christ's Table.

Christ promises to all who bear Faith liberation from the bondage of sin and fulness of grace; the Presence of the Holy Spirit through trial and rejoicing; and eternal life in the Community of Love, the New Jerusalem, the Reign and Dominion of God which has no end and in the Light of which we walk. Amen.

MANIFESTO

The People's Church Collective is a community within the revolutionary Movement which relates to the radical tradition of Jesus, the Prophets & the Church of Liberation: an ecumenical voluntary association for the spiritual renewal, consecration and transformation of Humanity & the World. The Work to which we are called is the Celebration of Life! the maximal actualization of the creative potential of the Whole Person and of all Life, the realization of ultimate personal freedom and personal responsibility in Community in harmonious relationship with one another.

As Jesus our Brother & Liberator said: "I Am come that they might have Life and have it more abundantly." (John 10:10). We are called upon to bring the Life More Abundant to all and thus to realize the Universal Free Community of Sister/Brotherhood in the Creative Life.

Explore in action, in the Service of the People, in the Movement for Liberation: and you come face to face with the God of the Universe, the Power behind nature, history and freedom. Explore, in contemplation, the inner life: and you find the God of the human heart, the Beingness beyond space and time. God is there in the midst of the world and in the inner person: and God is One.

Has not the Community of Love—the Kingdom of God— been promised to the poor & lowly, and was not the Liberator of the world a Carpenter & a Convict?

We come together to restore the apostolic revolution of transforming Love meaningfully for contemporary Humanity; to Serve the People and do the Work of the renewed Christ-Teaching in our Age for the spiritual realization & actualization of All—both now and in generations yet unborn—; to fulfill the need of our Age for Jesuene Discipleship (a free & revolutionary Christianity: "Yes, a Christian revolutionary. And not a revolutionary who happens to be a Christian or in spite of being a Christian, but revolutionary because Christian."—Eric Gill) bearing witness, in a time of technological greatness to the primacy of the Creative Spirit; to unify the learning of the Age with Christ and the Christ with the learning of the Age and thus to bring about the beautiful non-violent free Community of Love.

Members of the P.C.C. covenant with the Community in the words of the ancient initiate's vow: "I have beheld a Spark of the Divine Humanity. That Spark, the Christ within, must be nurtured, as the flickering ember is shielded from the driving rain, even at the cost of my life."

The real Church, the Church of Liberation, has no self-interest but Humanity & the World. It claims to be Universal, and therefore it is set over against each and every society in which it finds itself as an international conspiracy for the Life More Abundant, in accord with Jesus Charter given to it: "to bring the Good News to the poor: to proclaim liberty to the captives, new vision to the unseeing, freedom to those in bondage, liberation to the oppressed, the Time of Liberation to All." (Luke 4:18-19)

Jesus our Brother is Christ and Liberator, who died, who rose, who comes again in the ever-present Now! The Cross must be raised again at the center of the People's struggle for a transformed world, and not merely on the steeple of the church. Jesus was not crucified in a cathedral between two candles, but on a cross between two political prisoners (mis-translated "thief" by theologians); at the town garbage-heap, at a cross-roads so cosmopolitan that they had to write his title in Hebrew & Latin & Greek: at the kind of place where cynics talk smut & thieves curse & soldiers gamble. That is where Jesus died, and that is what Jesus died about: and that is where the church ought to be & what the church ought to be about—the bringing into being a transformed world, the beautiful non-violent free Community of sister/brotherhood in the Creative Life. Walk down the streets of the city and take a moment out

DECLARATION OF FAITH, THE PROCLAMATION OF
FAITH, AND THE MANIFESTO [COMMUNITY OF THE
LOVE OF CHRIST (EVANGELICAL CATHOLIC)] (continued)

to talk to adolescent runaways, youth without homes, street-people, students; to the aged, largely discarded by an affluent society; to Women & Gay males oppressed by the bureaucratic structures & ideology of a patriarchal sexist society; to Black, Amer-Indian & Third World people oppressed by the institutions & ideology of a racist society; to Workers thrown out of work & on the dole due to technological advance used for profit rather than for humane ends & the internal contradictions of a capitalist society in its death-throes; to war-resisters, peacemakers & radicals who rightly feel the institutional church has betrayed the revolutionary Gospel: look at the parallel oppression of Gay people, ethnic minorities & political dissenters in state-socialist nations: and know in your gut the alienation of a world-wide cross-section of the People.

It is precisely in this time & place that we are called by the Spirit to participate in the revolutionary life-style of Love & Service of the People taught by Jesus our Brother & Liberator.

Even in the present hostile environment, as much as possible, we are called to live, in a concrete way, those changes we wish to see in Humanity & a new society. This means we must work for inward transformation while developing the Way of Life of the new society: "forming the structure of the new society within the shell of the old" (IWW).

This is the work of the universal androgynous Community of sister/brotherhood in the Creative Life, an already existing Principle of Truth in Christ on the spiritual/archetypal level and one to be brought into external manifestation through the revolutionary struggle of the People in the Creative Spirit. Humanity begins where the State ends. You cannot serve God & Mammon, Christ & the State. Let Humanity begin!

Serve the People and thus serve Christ who is known inwardly—personally/outwardly in the People collectively:

"Now who so despised and lost, but what shall be my
  Saviour?
Is there one yet sick and suffering in the whole world? or
  deformed, condemned, degraded?
Thither hastening, I am at rest—for this one can absolve
  me.
O, I am greedy of love—all, all are beautiful to me!
You are my deliverers every one—from death, from sin,
  from evil—
I float, I dissolve in you!
O bars of self, you cannot shut me now.
O frailest child, O blackest criminal,
Whoe'er you are I never can repay you—though the world
  despise you, you are glorious to me;
For you have saved me from myself,
You delivered me when I was in prison—
I passed through you into heaven,
You were my Christ to me."—Edward Carpenter

"In the secret quarters, in the underground, in Greenwich Village, Saint Germain, among the campus students planning sit-ins and freedom rides, in the hidden quarters of Africa, wherever change is initiated, in the midst of changes, in the march to the sea, in the picket lines in front of embassies, the worth of the world is proclaimed. In the invisible lofts where the anarchists and pacifists defy money and the structures of society, where the lies are being examined and reversed, lies which are the allies of death, in these places is the poetry which is the language of God." (from a 1962 P.C.C. brochure: quotation from Judith Malina & Julian Beck)

The only effective Work of the Gospel today is to be found in a Community serving the People with that "poetry which is the language of God," a Community of non-violent revolutionary Love & Action, affirming that the revolution is New Life for all Humanity and taking up the claims of the Good News for this age, claims which have been largely abandoned by the institutional church since its sell-out to the State in the IVth century c.e.

Jesus Teaching calls us to comfort the afflicted and afflict the comfortable: but in the ages of its sell-out to the State, the institutional church has been more concerned with comforting the comfortable & so has added to the affliction of the already oppressed. In Nazi Germany the institutional church sold out & went under. Its identity was not with the oppressed but with the oppressor. Then an alternative Community, a "Confessing Church" stood up & made its witness in its own blood. Is it possible that such a time will come to us? Is it possible that now is that time?

Looking at the world-crisis today, the People's Church Collective responds: Yes! "Now is the time of choice! Now is the day of liberation!" (2 Cor. 6:2) Therefore, we come together to do the Work of Jesus' revolution—a truly humanistic revolution— in our time, proclaiming the Creative Spirit in transforming Love and Serving the People (vide. Matt. 25:31-46; Acts 2:44-6)

Faith divorced from a revolutionary commitment to social liberation is a mockery! (*vide.* James 2:1-26) The determination of the Movemental Church, of which the P.C.C. is only one manifestation, is to be those people of a new order who live by the values and revolutionary priority of Jesus and the Community of Liberating Love which is motivated by the Creative Spirit, even in the midst of the hostility and oppression of the State. We wish to serve the People by proclaiming the Good News of Liberation in the Christ, by articulating the ethical demands of discipleship, by working for peace, freedom and human dignity for all, and by serving in day-to-day needs as they arise and as we are able.

Notes: *Over the years the Community of the Love of Christ (Evangelical Catholic) has issued various statements that embody the Church's belief as it relates both to the historical Christian tradition and to contemporary social issues. All of the statements have been written and/or edited to eliminate sexist (non-inclusive) language. Distinctive emphases of the community are seen in the inclusion of phrases such as "the image of God in all persons," "liberation," "the beautiful* *non-violent free community of sister/brotherhood,"* and *"the radical tradition of Jesus."*

* * *

PREAMBLE TO THE CONSTITUTION (GAY ATHEISTS LEAGUE OF AMERICA)

Because Atheism recognizes the supremacy of *reason,* and bases its ethics on the experience of living, independent of any arbitrary authority, creed, dogma or ritual; and

Because the primary source of hostility against Lesbians and Gay males has been organized religion, resulting in:

—an irrational hatred and suppression of same-sex affectional and sexual preferences, which, when unfettered by dogma, are natural, beautiful and healthy expressions of love, which should be encouraged rather than discouraged; and

—the harassment and incarceration by governments of Lesbians and Gay males; and

—denial to Lesbians and Gay males of the right to equal access to government programs, which they are compelled to support; and

—discrimination against Lesbians and Gay males in jobs, housing, and public accommodations; and

Because, in spite of religion's longstanding practice of suppressing same-sex affectional and sexual preference, many Lesbians and Gay males, reluctant to interpret the world rationally, have felt compelled by the pervasive and irrational forces of religion to form their own religious groups, loosely based upon the established religious organizations, but which change the religious dogma so that ancient myths and teachings, which are clearly anti-Lesbian and anti-Gay male, are ignored, while the remainder of the myths and teachings are adhered to:

We hereby adopt this constitution of the GAY ATHEISTS LEAGUE OF AMERICA with the following purposes:

(1) To provide a forum where Lesbian and Gay male Atheists can meet, and can exchange and disseminate ideas;

(2) To counterbalance the predominance, within the Lesbian and Gay male movement, of religiously-oriented organizations;

(3) To work toward the complete separation of church and state, and, in particular, to oppose the influence of religious conditioning, and the tax-free institutions which support such conditioning, on legislators, judges, and law enforcement agents when they pass, interpret and enforce the laws that affect the lives of Lesbians and Gay males;

(4) To promote a positive image of Lesbians and Gay males, and of the virtues of Atheism as a philosophical stance of freedom from the mind-control of religion, a stance that holds that women and men can be ethical without the influence and intervention of superstition.

Notes: *Frequently reprinted, this statement presents the league's rationale.*

* * *

DOCTRINE, SACRAMENTS, RITES (METROPOLITAN COMMUNITY CHURCH)

DOCTRINE: Christianity is the revelation of God in Jesus Christ and is the religion set forth in the Scriptures. Jesus Christ is foretold in the Old Testament, presented in the New Testament, and proclaimed by the Christian Church in every age and in every land.

Founded in the interest of offering a church home to all who confess and believe, the Universal Fellowship of Metropolitan Community Churches moves in the mainstream of Christianity.

Our faith is based upon the principles outlined in the historic creeds: Apostles and Nicene.

We believe:

1. In one triune God, omnipotent, omnipresent and omniscient, of one substance and of three persons: God - our Parent-Creator; Jesus Christ the only begotten son of God, God in flesh, human; and the Holy Spirit - God as our Sustainer.

2. That the Bible is the divinely inspired Word of God, showing forth God to every person through the law and the prophets, and finally, completely and ultimately on earth in the being of Jesus Christ.

3. That Jesus . . . the Christ . . . historically recorded as living some 2,000 years before this writing is God incarnate, of human birth, fully God and fully human, and that by being one with God, Jesus has demonstrated once and forever that all people are likewise Children of God, being spiritually made in God's image.

4. That the Holy Spirit is God making known God's love and interest to all people. The Holy Spirit is God, available to and working through all who are willing to place their welfare in God's keeping.

5. Every person is justified by Grace to God through faith in Jesus Christ.

6. We are saved from loneliness, despair and degradation through God's gift of grace, as was declared by our Saviour. Such grace is not earned, but is a pure gift from a God of pure love. We further commend the community of the faithful to a life of prayer; to seek genuine forgiveness for unkind, thoughtless and unloving acts; and to a committed life of Christian service.

7. The Church serves to bring all people to God through Christ. To this end, it shall arrange for regular services of worship, prayer, interpretation of the Scriptures, and edification through the teaching and preaching of the Word.

179

DOCTRINE, SACRAMENTS, RITES (METROPOLITAN COMMUNITY CHURCH) (continued)

SACRAMENTS: THIS CHURCH EMBRACES TWO HOLY SACRAMENTS:

1. BAPTISM by water and the Spirit, as recorded in the Scriptures, shall be a sign of the dedication of each life to God and God's service. Through the words and acts of this sacrament, the recipient is identified as God's own Child.

2. HOLY COMMUNION is the partaking of blessed bread and fruit of the vine in accordance with the words of Jesus, our Sovereign: "This is my body . . . this is my blood." (Matthew 26:26-28). All who believe, confess and repent and seek God's love through Christ, after examining their consciences, may freely participate in the communal meal, signifying their desire to be received into community with Jesus Christ, to be saved by Jesus Christ's sacrifice, to participate in Jesus Christ's resurrection, and to commit their lives anew to the service of Jesus Christ.

RITES: The Rites of the Church as performed by its duly authorized ministers shall consist of the following:

1. The RITE OF ORDINATION is the setting apart of duly qualified persons for the professional ministry of this church. It is evidenced by the laying on of hands by authorized ordained clergy, pursuant to these By-Laws.

2. The RITE OF ATTAINING MEMBERSHIP IN THE CHURCH, Mission or Study Group, shall be conducted by the pastor, interim pastor or worship coordinator before a local congregation at any regular worship service. After completing classes for instruction in the beliefs and doctrines of the church, a baptized Christian may become a member in good standing of the local church group through a letter of transfer from a recognized Christian body or through affirmation of faith.

3. The RITE OF HOLY UNION and the RITE OF HOLY MATRIMONY are the spiritual joining of two persons in a manner fitting and proper by a duly authorized clergy of the Church. After both persons have been counseled and apprised of their responsibilities one towards the other, this rite of conferring God's blessing may be performed.

4. The RITE OF FUNERAL OR MEMORIAL SERVICE is to be fittingly conducted by the ministers of the Church for the deceased.

5. The RITE OF LAYING ON OF HANDS or prayer for the healing of the sick in mind, body or spirit is to be conducted by the ministers of the Church, at their discretion, upon request.

6. The RITE OF BLESSING may be conducted by the ministers of the Church for persons, things and relationships, when deemed appropriate by the minister. This includes the dedication of a church building to the glory of God.

Notes: *This document is taken from Article II of the church's constitution.*

*   *   *

SIX PRECEPTS (TAYU FELLOWSHIP)

1) I will Confront Ignorance, Seek Understanding, Love Innocence.

2) I will accept nothing for which I am not willing and able to pay.

3) I will create the most fulfilling existence of which I am capable.

4) I will harm nothing in Creation without its consent.

5) I will love Myself, I will love Others also.

6) I will Satisfy Needs, Surrender Desires, Expect Surprises.

Notes: *According to the Tayu Fellowship, members live by these six precepts.*

Chapter 11

Unclassified Religious Groups

SUMMARY OF DOCTRINES (CHURCH OF THE NEW SONG)

1. The DOCTRINE OF FREEDOM OF RELIGION to develop and enjoy peacefully the faith of the people on Earth and *spaceforth,* whether they be in prison or out personally (see Mizan 304.54-63).

2. The DOCTRINE OF THE CLARITY to help make their faith more clear and in harmony with nature, and thus *inverse* the process of pollution which the population of the Earth has committed against the environment of this planet (see Mizan 102.04-05).

3. The DOCTRINE OF THE DEMOCRATIZATION OF SCRIPTURES to *guide themselves* closer to the truth among all the religions in the world (see Mizan 108.75 and 400.29 and 201.02-05 and 304.11).

4. The DOCTRINE OF THE INFIXUS combining both the Doctrine of the Clarity and the Democratization of Scriptures to accomplish the *inversal* of pollution more readily and improve world relations synergetically (see Mizan 102.04-05 and 108.75 and 400.29 and 304.11 and 201.02-05).

5. The DOCTRINE OF HEALTHESIS which is that everybody on Earth is at least entitled to (1) something to eat, (2) somewhere to sleep, (3) somebody to love, and (4) something to wear including the Sacrament of Ascorbation (at least 500 to 1000 milligrams of Vitamin C per day with any other supplements for health and depollution as prescribed through *The Complete Book of Vitamins* published by Rodale Press, Emmaus, Pennsylvania, United States of America, 1977) to *genetically* aid the difficult process of thinking less split-mindedly and more synergetically, since lack of ascorbate in humanity has been one of the causes of the split-mindedness on Earth thus far, because, unlike other animals on this planet, the human body does not yet manufacture its own ascorbation within, so it must be taken to eat from external sources. Remember, your body is your home; don't junk it up (see Mizan 107.81 and 401.96-97).

6. The DOCTRINE OF SYNERGY OF SPEECH to say what is on your mind and *develop* freedom of honesty, rather than remain all pent-up with it or frustrated by it (see Mizan 108.11-15 and 102.06).

7. The DOCTRINE OF SEMINARS to meet in groups and deal with their problems by connecting up their ideas with reality through the *resocializing process of faith exchanging and synergetical considerations* toward an Apocalyptic future as promised in scripture (see Mizan 304.64-97).

8. The DOCTRINE OF ACOLIGHTS to help free themselves of past errors and immutual circumstances by candidly selecting an acolight partner and working together justly with him or her, instead of having to sneak around or circumvent procedures for good companionship or the consensual validating experience necessary *to form a more perfect union* in harmony with nature (see Mizan 403.97 and 401.31 and 106.26 and 401.52).

9. The DOCTRINE OF LOVEPARTNERSHIP which can be developed into *synergetical marriage* or Sacred Unity for people who fall in love with each other and want to become each other's spouse in terms of law as mizanically outlined (see Mizan 400.93-94 and 106.21).

10. The DOCTRINE OF BIOMENTOLOGY to study *how* two or more things can work together more justly (that is, synergetically) and to share this research for truth in relations with others both personally and professionally (see Mizan 108.61 and 403.65-66 and 304.87).

11. The DOCTRINE OF FREEDOM OF RESOCIALIZATION including the Apocalyptic Unifactions to give people a *new start* and biomentally develop *synergetical relations* between Adam and Eve today as a daily resocial experience of applied mizanic law (see Mizan 400.83-88 and 402.57-60 and 102.01 and 105.14-15 and 107.40).

12. The DOCTRINE OF JUSTICE BY SYNERGY BETWEEN FACTS AND LAW for the healing of the nations worldwide eventually and the historical enjoyment of Gridarian Democracy to *coordinate*

our energies and glorify our species in space and
time, hopefully contacting other worlds as a United
World Ourselves (see Mizan 401.01-99 and 304.88-
89).

*   *   *

THE 21 PRECEPTS (PERFECT LIBERTY
KYODAN)

1. Life is art.
2. Man's life is a succession of self-expressions.
3. Man is a manifestation of God.
4. Man suffers if he fails to express himself.
5. Man loses his true self when swayed by feelings and
    emotion.
6. Man's true self is revealed when his ego is effaced.
7. All things exist in mutual relationship to one
    another.
8. Live radiantly as the sun.
9. All men are equal.
10. Strive for creating mutual happiness.
11. Have true faith in God.
12. There is a way (function) peculiar to every "name"
    (existence).
13. There is a way for men, and there is another for
    women.
14. All is for world peace.
15. All is a mirror.
16. All things progress and develop.
17. Comprehend what is most essential.
18. At every moment man stands at the crossroads of
    good and evil.
19. Act when your intuition dictates.
20. Live in perfect unity of mind and matter.
21. Live in Perfect Liberty.

Creed/Organization Name and Keyword Index

Creed names are indicated by italic type, while organizations and religious traditions appear in regular type. Page numbers are preceded by their volume numbers (roman numerals); boldface references indicate entries found in this volume.

A

Aaronic Order **III, 21**

(Abrahamic Faith); Church of God General Conference II, 256

Abridgement of Doctrine (International Liberal Catholic Church) **III, 111**

Abstracts of Principles [Banner Herald (Progressive)] II, 177

Abundant Living Christian Fellowship (Kingsport, Tennessee) II, 50

Account of Our Religion, Doctrine and Faith (Hutterite Brethren) **III, 38**

An Act of Gnosis (Ecclesia Gnostica) **III, 110**

Addition to the Twenty-nine Important Bible Truths [Church of God (World Headquarters)] II, 13

Additions to the Twenty-five Articles of Religion (African Methodist Episcopal Church) I, 277

Additions to the Twenty-five Articles of Religion (African Methodist Episcopal Zion Church) I, 278

Additions to the Twenty-five Articles of Religion (Asbury Bible Churches) I, 266

Additions to the Twenty-five Articles of Religion (Christian Methodist Episcopal Church) I, 278

Additions to the Twenty-five Articles of Religion (Congregational Methodist Church) I, 270

Additions to the Twenty-five Articles of Religion (Evangelical Methodist Church) I, 270

Additions to the Twenty-five Articles of Religion (Evangelical Methodist Church of America) I, 270

Additions to the Twenty-five Articles of Religion (Southern Methodist Church) I, 273

Advent Christian Church II, 255, 257

Advent Christian Church; Primitive II, 257

Adventist; Church of God II, 263

Adventist Church; Seventh-Day II, 258

Adventist Reform Movement; Seventh-Day II, 262

Adventist; Seventh-Day II, 258

Adventist; Sunday II, 255

Aetherius Society **III, 98**

Affirmation of Faith [Ashland Theological Seminary-Brethren Church (Ashland, Ohio)] II, 107

An Affirmation of Our Faith (Baptist General Conference) II, 185

The Affirmation of St. Louis (1976) I, 26

Affirmations (Church of the Awakening) **III, 100**

Affirmations for Humanistic Jews (Sherwin T. Wine, Society for Humanistic Judaism) **III, 142**

The Affirmations (Free Church of Berkeley) **III, 175**

Affirmations of the Ethical Movement (American Ethical Union); Statement of Principles and **III, 2**

African Methodist Episcopal Church I, 263, 277

African Methodist Episcopal Zion Church I, 263, 278

African Orthodox Christian Church; Pan **III, 141**

African Orthodox Church I, 35, 37

African Union First Colored Methodist Protestant Church I, 263

African Universal Church II, 71

Ageless Wisdom; International Church of **III, 89**

Agnostics; Society of Evangelical **III, 14**

Agreed Upon Beliefs of the Green River (Kentucky) Association of United Baptists II, 191

Ahmadiyya Anjuman Ishaat Islam, Lahore, Inc. **III, 150**

Ahmadiyya Movement of Islam **III, 150, 151**

Aims and Ideals (Self-Realization Fellowship); Aims and Tenets (Yogoda Sat-Sanga Movement) **III, 155**

Aims and Tenets (Yogoda Sat-Sanga Movement) and Aims and Ideals (Self-Realization Fellowship) **III, 155**

(Alabama); Assembly of Yahvah II, 282

Alexander's Creed (Church of Jesus Christ in Solemn Assembly) **III, 23**

Alice Bailey Groups **III, 109**

Allegheny Wesleyan Methodist Connection I, 310

Allen); The New Thought Religion and Philosophy (Abel L. **III, 50**

Alpha and Omega Christian Church and Bible School II, 81

Altrurian Society **III, 52**

Amana Church Society **III, 35**

Amber/Crystal Light Bearers (Sisters of Amber) **III, 97**

Amended Christadelphians II, 193

American Atheists, Inc. **III, 1**

American Baptist Association II, 153, 158

American Baptist Churches in the U.S.A. II, 162

American Catholic Church **III, 109**

American Catholic Church, Archdiocese of New York I, 36

American Church; Neo- **III, 100**

American Council of Christian Churches II, 236

183

Articles of Faith [The Reform Society of Israelites (1825) (Reform Judaism)] **III, 138**
Articles of Faith (Union Association of Regular Baptist Churches) II, 169
Articles of Faith (United Holy Church of America) II, 78
Articles of Faith (United Pentecostal Church) II, 67
Articles of Faith (Wesleyan Tabernacle Association) I, 320
Articles of Our Faith (International Church of Ageless Wisdom) **III, 89**
Articles of Religion (American Rescue Workers) I, 284
Articles of Religion (Bible Missionary Church) I, 323
Articles of Religion (Evangelical Congregational Church) I, 279
Articles of Religion [Free Methodist Church (1974)] I, 295
Articles of Religion [Free Methodist Church (Prior to 1974)] I, 293
Articles of Religion (Fundamental Methodist Church) I, 271
Articles of Religion (Pentecostal Church of Zion) II, 46
Articles of Religion (Reformed Episcopal Church); Declaration of Principles and I, 29
Articles of Religion (Wesleyan Church) I, 305
Articles of Religion [Wesleyan Methodist Church (1968)] I, 308
Asatru Free Assembly (Viking Brotherhood) **III, 120**
Asbury Bible Churches I, 266
(Ashland, Ohio); Brethren Church II, 116
Ashland Theological Seminary-Brethren Church (Ashland, Ohio) II, 107
Ashram Society; Yasodhara **III, 158**
Ashrama; Sri Ram **III, 156**
Assemblies of God II, 78, 84
Assemblies of God; General Council of the II, 27, 34, 36, 43
Assemblies of God International; Independent II, 36
Assemblies of the Called Out Ones of Yah II, 282
Assemblies of the Lord Jesus Christ II, 53, 71
Assemblies of the World; Pentecostal II, 63, 67, 71
Assemblies of Yahweh II, 284
Assemblies of Yahweh (Michigan) II, 285
Assembly of Yahvah (Alabama) II, 282
Assembly of Yahvah (Oregon) II, 282
Associate Reformed Presbyterian Church I, 230
Associated Brotherhood of Christians II, 56
Associated Church of God II, 269
Associated Churches of Christ (Holiness) I, 321
Associated Churches of God II, 263, 281
Association of Free Lutheran Congregations I, 145
Association of Fundamental Gospel Churches II, 107
Association of Independent Methodists I, 267
Association of Religious Science Churches; International **III, 60**
Association of Seventh Day Pentecostal Assemblies II, 81
Assyrian Church of the East I, 38
Athanasius (Symbolum Quicunque); The Creed of I, 2
Atheists, Inc.; American **III, 1**
Atheists League of America; Gay **III, 179**
Atlantion Wicca **III, 121**
The Augsburg Confession (1530) I, 39
Authentic Lutheranism; Federation for I, 147
Awakening; Church of the **III, 100**
Awareness; Organization of **III, 96**

B

Baha'i World Faith **III, 154**
Bahaism **III, 154**
Bailey Groups; Alice **III, 109**
Banner Herald (Progressive) II, 177
Baptist Association; American II, 153, 158
Baptist Association; Minnesota II, 164
Baptist Association of America; Conservative II, 159, 162
Baptist Bible Fellowship II, 154
Baptist Brethren; Old German II, 116
Baptist; Calvinist Missionary II, 153
Baptist Church; General Conference of the Evangelical II, 19
Baptist Church of Canada; Covenanted II, 178
Baptist Church of the Pentecostal Faith; Free Will II, 15, 190
Baptist Church; Pentecostal Free Will II, 27
Baptist Churches; General Association of Regular II, 153, 162
Baptist Churches in the U.S.A.; American II, 162
Baptist Churches; New Testament Association of Independent II, 167
Baptist Churches; Union Association of Regular II, 169
Baptist Conference; North American II, 169
Baptist Convention; Black II, 153
Baptist Convention; Minnesota II, 167
Baptist Convention; National II, 153
Baptist Convention; National Primitive II, 181
Baptist Convention; Northern II, 162
Baptist Convention of America; National II, 153
Baptist Convention of Ontario and Quebec II, 157
Baptist Convention; Southern II, 153, 169, 173
Baptist Faith and Message (1963) (Southern Baptist Convention) II, 173
Baptist Faith and Message (1925) (Southern Baptist Convention) II, 169
Baptist Fellowship; Fundamental II, 161, 162
Baptist Fellowship; Southwide II, 177
Baptist; General II, 185
Baptist General Conference II, 185
Baptist General Conference; Seventh-Day II, 192
Baptist Missionary Association II, 157
Baptist; Primitive II, 177
Baptist; Seventh-Day II, 192
Baptists; Duck River and Kindred Associations of II, 160
Baptists; General Association of General II, 186
Baptists; Green River (Kentucky) Association of United II, 191
Baptists; National Association of Free-Will II, 19, 187, 191
Basic Beliefs (Aaronic Order) **III, 21**
Basic Beliefs (Rocky Mountain Yearly Meeting) II, 145
Basic Principles [Temple of the Goddess Within (Matilda Joslyn Gage Coven)] **III, 130**
Basic Principles (Universal Church of the Master) **III, 94**
Basic Tenets of the Truth of Life Movement, Summary of Teachings, and the Seven Promulgations of Light (Seicho-No-Ie) **III, 56**
Basic Tenets of Theologia 21 [Church of the Trinity (Invisible Ministry)] **III, 53**
Basis of Fellowship (Christian Catholic Church) **III, 171**

C

Evangelical Methodist Church I, 263, 270
Evangelical Methodist Church of America I, 263, 270
Evangelical Orthodox (Catholic) Church I, 13
Evangelical United Brethren I, 279, 313
Evangelical Wesleyan Church I, 295
Evangelicalism; Fundamentalism/ II, 235
Evangelicals; National Association of II, 108, 119, 121, 144, 146, 235
Evangelism Crusades; International II, 83
Evangelistic Association; California II, 30
Evangelistic Association, Church of God II, 266

F

Faith and Doctrine (Church of Jesus Christ Restored) **III, 27**
Faith and Doctrine (Independent Fundamental Churches of America) II, 244
Faith and Doctrine (Ohio Bible Church) II, 247
Faith; Church of God by II, 82
Faith Churches; International Convention of II, 50
Faith; Defenders of the II, 80
Faith (Free Will Baptist Church of the Pentecostal Faith) II, 15
The Faith of Free-Will Baptists (National Association of Free-Will Baptists) II, 187
Faith of God; Foundation **III, 103**
The Faith of the Church Outlined (Church of the Living God, the Pillar and Ground of Truth) II, 76
Faithists; Universal Brotherhood of **III, 98**
Family of Love (Children of God) **III, 172**
Federation for Authentic Lutheranism I, 147
Federation of St. Thomas Christian Churches **III, 110**
Fellowship); Church of the Living God (Christian Workers for II, 73
Fellowship of Grace Brethren Churches II, 114
Fellowship of the Inner Light **III, 96**
Filioque Controversy, 1875; Old Catholic Agreement on the I, 7
Final Judgment; Church of the **III, 105**
Fire-Baptized Church; Pentecostal II, 78
Fire-Baptized Holiness Church II, 23, 26, 27, 78
Fire-Baptized Holiness Church of God of the Americas II, 78
Fire-Baptized Holiness Church; Pentecostal II, 15
The Firebear Manifesto (Brothers of the Earth) **III, 121**
First Born; Church of the **III, 24**
First Born; General Assembly and Church of the II, 35
First Colored Methodist Protestant Church; African Union I, 263
First Congregational Methodist Church of America I, 270
First Congregational Methodist Church of the U.S.A. I, 263
First Principles (House of Prayer for All People) II, 303
Five Years Meeting II, 135
Flying Saucer Groups **III, 98**
Forked Deer Association (Regular) II, 179
The Formula of Concord (1580) I, 69
Foundation Faith of God **III, 103**
Foursquare Gospel; International Church of the II, 36, 304
The Fourteen Theses of the Old Catholic Union Conference, Bonn, Germany, 1874 I, 6
Free Church Association; Norwegian-Danish I, 258

Free Church; Evangelical II, 243
Free Church of America; Evangelical I, 257
Free Church of Berkeley **III, 175**
Free Lutheran Congregations; Association of I, 145
Free Methodist Church I, 283, 293, 295
Free; Miscellaneous European II, 147
Free Will Baptist Church of the Pentecostal Faith II, 15, 190
Free Will Baptist Church; Pentecostal II, 27
Free-Will Baptists; National Association of II, 19, 187, 191
Friends Alliance; Evangelical II, 118, 121, 144, 146
Friends Church, Eastern Division; Evangelical II, 119
Friends Church, Eastern Region; Evangelical II, 119
(Friends) Quakers II, 118
Friends United Meeting-Western Yearly Meeting II, 127
Friends United Meeting-Western Yearly Meeting (1881) II, 121
From the Constitution [United Synagogue of America (1916) (Conservative Judaism)] **III, 137**
Full Gospel Church in Christ **III, 44**
Full Gospel Minister Association II, 83
Fundamental Articles of Faith (General Council of the Churches of God) II, 277
The Fundamental Articles of Faith in Islam [Hammudah Abd Al-Ati (Sunni Islam)] **III, 143**
Fundamental Baptist Fellowship II, 161, 162
Fundamental Beliefs (Associated Churches of God) II, 263
Fundamental Beliefs (Church of God Evangelistic Association) II, 266
The Fundamental Beliefs of Judaism (German Rabbinical Association, 1897) **III, 134**
Fundamental Beliefs (Seventh-Day Adventist Church) II, 258
Fundamental Churches of America; Independent II, 241, 244, 247
The Fundamental Doctrine of the Church (Church of God by Faith) II, 82
Fundamental Fellowship II, 160, 161
Fundamental Gospel Churches; Association of II, 107
Fundamental Methodist Church I, 271
Fundamental Principles (Christian Assembly) **III, 52**
Fundamental Principles (Pansophic Institute) **III, 167**
Fundamental Principles (Schwenkfelder Church) II, 147
Fundamentalism/Evangelicalism II, 235
Fundamentals (Society of Jewish Science) **III, 143**

G

Gay Atheists League of America **III, 179**
Gedatsu Church of America **III, 166**
Gelberman, Little Synagogue); I Believe (Rabbi Joseph H. **III, 142**
General Assembly and Church of the First Born II, 35
General Association of General Baptists II, 186
General Association of Regular Baptist Churches II, 153, 162
General Baptist II, 185
General Baptists; General Association of II, 186
General Church of the New Jerusalem **III, 85**
General Conference Mennonite Church II, 106
General Conference of the Church of God II, 274

H

I

T